THE SCARLET THREAD

TRACING GOD'S INCREDIBLE PLAN

MARTHA McCALLUM
&
KEITH McCALLUM

Published by Xenos Publishing
A Ministry of Xenos Christian Fellowship
1340 Community Park Drive
Columbus, OH 43229
1-800-698-7884
www.xenos.org
Printed in the United States of America.
ISBN 1-59067-009-4

We dedicate this book to Scot McCallum, our much-loved son and brother, who dynamically lived out, and taught so many others about the saving Grace in God's Incredible Plan. Through an untimely accident, Scot went to be with his Lord while serving as a missionary in Eastern Europe, leaving behind his wife Amy and daughters, Kate and Kelly.

We miss Scot's engaging personality, his infectious laugh, his insightful Bible teachings, and so much more. But we do not grieve without hope:

> "God will bring back with Jesus all the Christians who have died… we will meet the Lord in the air and remain with Him forever."
> *I Thessalonians 4:14, 17b* (NLT)

ACKNOWLEDGEMENTS

In the early presentations of *God's Incredible Plan,* we called it "A Pictorial Panorama of the Bible." My good friend and co-author Jane Hamblin painted beautiful oil paintings depicting God's Kingdom versus the Counterfeit Kingdom from Eternity Past to Eternity Future. We were invited into local churches and home Bible studies for 12-week presentations, which included much of the material in this book.

In recent years, my son Scot had written "Grounding Group Bible Studies," incorporating *God's Incredible Plan.* We were starting to rewrite the book when Scot's fatal accident occurred. Following Scot's death, my son Keith undertook this project, using his biblical knowledge and considerable journalistic and computer expertise. I am so appreciative of the many months he dedicated to the research and writing of this book while serving as Pastor of Xenos Christian Fellowship in Cleveland, Ohio. I also thank my husband John for his typing, e-mailing, and patience, as Keith and I worked and reworked the manuscript long distance.

We decided to change the title from *God's Incredible Plan* to *The Scarlet Thread* because The Scarlet Thread of Redemption is a traditional title used for God's Redemptive Plan: His plan of buying us out of our slavery to sin and eternal death. Tracing this "Thread" through the Bible discloses the "Mystery" of God's Love, revealed supremely in the sacrifice of Christ on the Cross for our sins: "He (Christ) having offered one sacrifice for sins for all time." *Hebrews 10:12a*

We want to acknowledge the insightful teaching and writing of my son, Dennis McCallum, about "God's Wisdom in a Mystery, the Hidden Wisdom." (1 Corinthians 2:7), which we quote extensively. Dennis is one of the Lead Pastors at Xenos Christian Fellowship (www.xenos.org). We are also indebted to many authors, whose books are listed in the Bibliography on page 313.

Finally, Keith and I want to thank Xenos Christian Fellowship in Columbus, Ohio, for publishing *The Scarlet Thread.* Our sincere gratitude goes to Jay Reilly, Laura Avers and Chris Kavinsky, who faithfully laid out, edited, and gave oversight to final drafts and details of each chapter. And to Eric Barker, Suzanne Fox and Catherine Gilbert for their work on the early drafts of our text. The encouragement of the many Xenos "sojourners" who came into a personal relationship with Christ through *God's Incredible Plan* has been so motivating. It is our earnest prayer that the Holy Spirit will use *The Scarlet Thread* to bring many more into the Kingdom of God.

Martha McCallum (March 2005)

It was a daunting project at first—not because the scope is so vast, although it is—but because it meant working closely with Martha, my mother. There were numerous forewarnings from those familiar with her firm resolve, together with those knowing my eccentricities. Yet it was a harmonious partnership and a rare, perhaps last, opportunity to collaborate. He is a God of peace.

I grew up in the early '60s watching the Panorama evolve. Really, it was an ancient work, handed down by my grandmother to her little girl in the intricate artwork of Clarence Larkin[A] from the late 19th Century. I added my own artwork of Jacob's ladder in Sunday school for Mom's 20th Century version of it. I was dragged along as she taught the Panorama at churches and small neighborhood Bible studies, and I witnessed the electric effect on people as their eyes were opened to the vastness of God's Incredible Plan.

From her obscure efforts and flimsy, cardboard Panorama, it could be said without exaggeration, that a movement was sparked in Columbus that flourished into Xenos Christian Fellowship with all its ministries and rippling effects on the lives of tens of thousands. I have seen with my own eyes that God's Incredible Plan is not a theory. It is a practical, consequential kingdom, formed by God's hand inside people across the globe who all, "have loved His appearing."

After my brother's heartbreaking death in 2003, the work regained a new urgency, because the brevity of life here is so near and foolishly unexpected. I wanted to finish the book before Martha also died; she is 83.

So many others were equally driven by this vision and supported the effort by their unselfish love, working in the background, and wading through the early drafts. Among these were Greg, Mark, Rick, Levi, Joe, Alex, Joel, Ted, Terry, Rich and many others who bore the brunt of my absence in planting new churches in northeastern Ohio.

Most notably, my loving wife Darlene was always beside Martha and me, adding her deep spiritual insight and sweet temperament. Now, my own children—Sean, Kyle and Connor—are watching and participating like I did at their age, equally enthralled with the joy of witnessing the spread of God's Kingdom in the hearts of those who seek the Almighty God, the King of Kings.

This book was never about money or fame—the message should never be profaned this way. Instead, it is about offering people like these, along with the next generation, a glimpse of God's work among the human race. May others continue it, and may this meager effort help them along.

Keith McCallum (April 2005)

(A) Clarence Larkin. *Dispensational Truth.* Enlarged and Revised ed. Philadelphia, PA: Rev. Clarence Larkin Est, 1918. Reprint, 36th.

CONTENTS

A BOOK FOR BUSY PEOPLE

Recognizing that today's reading audience is accustomed to a more fast-paced content, we offer some conveniences that hopefully will make this book more absorbing.

Our primary goal is to make the Old and New Testaments of the Bible accessible to the reader. Quotation Blocks directly from the Bible are used extensively throughout the book, in the hope of launching the reader into a direct study of the Bible itself. We wish to demonstrate God's Word is relevant, interesting and surprisingly understandable.

We employ a technique called Assertions, designed to challenge the reader to interact critically with the evidence of the surrounding text. God is the creator of analytical thought, and the Bible offers answers for rational minds, which the Assertions help demonstrate.

Whenever God's Word is examined, people grow excited and begin asking more questions than a single book can possibly answer. Some readers are genuinely blocked by these questions or interests, so we provide brief Sidebars to grapple with some of the more common issues.

 At the end of each chapter, we offer Further Consideration, also to address critical issues. Except where noted, all Scripture citations are taken from the New Living Translation.

We are targeting a wide audience. For those unfamiliar with the Bible, we coin simple phrases to embody recurrent themes. For new Bible students, we hope to provide a solid footing in the Bible and familiarity with related issues, such as history. For Bible teachers or inquisitive minds, the End Notes offer useful details.

Yet, there must be a sense of priority with so much available material. So we trust our readers will grapple with the central theme, which is quite simply, God's Incredible Plan.

INTRODUCTION

Going far back, before the violent birth of our Universe and before the relentless, forward march of time, far beyond the grasp of human imagination—back into the realm of Eternity Past, eons of time without atoms, electrons, or photons…ages without starlight—there we find space is not empty. There is radiance, a vastness "Full of Light from the Lord." In this Eternity Past is God Himself, "the Creator of all light, and He shines forever without change," the "Eternal Father" without cause and without end, personal and cognizant of the Incredible Plan soon to be unleashed—all "before the foundations of the earth."

His name is Yahweh. He already knew all about you, your choices and potential choices, the purpose you will build for yourself or might build, the creativity and contributions you might withhold or bring into His Incredible Plan for the Universe.

To the Creator God you are significant; your potential is boundless. "For we are God's masterpiece," His word says. He not only knows us, but even more, "Long ago, even before He made the world, God loved us." He created us with kind intentions, "in order that in the coming ages He might show the incomparable riches of His grace, expressed in his kindness to us in Christ Jesus." In His mind, you were a magnificent creation.

How amazing it is: the same God who formed the grandeur of this Universe also prepared a wondrous and satisfying opportunity for you, lasting into Eternity Future—if you want it.

It is true; God invites you to enter into a personal relationship with Him. Even more, He invites you to become an active participant in His Incredible Plan. "For we are God's co-workers" and "fellow-heirs with Him," His word says. This is His invitation: "Come…inherit the kingdom prepared for you from the foundation of the world."

God made it possible for you to rise above the tiny world of timed, sequential events and see it all from His eternal point of view. It means you can discover eternal life for yourself. It is rather like watching the parade of human history from a helicopter, above and outside time. From His vantage, we capture the drama of God's plan rippling across time, revealed in stages. Other spiritual beings also watch these events unfold with rapt attention:

"It is all so wonderful that even the angels are eagerly watching these things happen." *1 Peter 1:12b*

The problem is we find it hard to believe God is interested in us as individuals. For this reason, He came as a simple human being to reveal His purpose in a way we can understand: "My purpose is to give life in all its fullness," He said. "I have told you this so that you will be filled with my joy. Yes, your joy will overflow!"

He waits patiently for our response: to continue or not with this Incredible Plan.

KINGDOMS IN CONFLICT

BEHIND TIME

"To you it has been granted to know the mysteries of the kingdom of God…"
Luke 8:10 (NASB)

A CONVERSATIONAL GOD

ℙ **How absurd it would be if God left us to stumble through history without Revelation!**

What kind of God creates individuals with intelligence and curiosity only to abandon them with unanswered questions? What honorable king abandons his throne and leaves his people struggling in chaos? No worthy parent abandons a child—how then is it possible for the Creator to create and then retreat behind cold indifference?

To the contrary, God has spoken; He did not withdraw. He laid a foundation for an enduring Kingdom, enlarged it over time, revealed it with clarity, and then at great personal expense He invited us to participate. This is what God's timeless Revelation is all about.

ℙ **It is equally absurd to presume that God cannot preserve Revelation intact and clearly presented.**

GOD IS Although this book begins with the assumption that God exists, we offer some consideration of the question in the Further Consideration sections of the book. In the final analysis, an objective thinker will admit that denial of God's existence is a faith position—that is, a religious position. An abundance of reasonable evidence for His existence is available. That "God is only a great imaginative experience," as D.H. Lawrence[1] claimed, is not a scientific fact.

The question of God's existence cannot be trivialized, especially if God is self-revealing as this book demonstrates. His self-revelation calls for a response: will you invest even minimal time to consider the issue? The potential reward is monumental: to discover the personal God who is at hand, and offers purpose for our lives!

Only an incompetent God cannot protect His Revelation from distortion, fully intact over time. Why provide Revelation if it degenerates into a tangled collection of superstition and myth as some imagine?

God did preserve His Revelation throughout the centuries, and archeology can verify it today.[A] Popularly known as The Bible, this Revelation claims it is "The Word of God," the only book known to make such a bold assertion while still offering verifiable proof: that God Himself has spoken.

∽ **Only a limited and short-sighted God would confine His Revelation to a single culture or elite class.**

The Bible is a highly diversified book, written over the course of some 1,500 years in 66 books by scores of different authors, from Kings to mere fishermen. It originated from the broad spectrum of humanity, and addresses the vast sweep of human needs—still, it touches our most individual concerns.

Despite its diverse background, the Bible is a surprisingly unified story about God's love for humanity. Unlike other revered writings, the Bible is not a collection of observations. It tells a single story from beginning to end. Engulfing the expanse of time, it unveils a spectacular struggle of violence and betrayal against God—even while He offers peace, restored fellowship and love.

This is what God's Incredible Plan is all about: God revealing Himself and His plan to satisfy man's restless drive for significance, answering our most troubling questions.

Consider this...
It is difficult to explain how so many different authors writing across such a lengthy time span could possibly orchestrate such a unified story – unless God Himself directed it.

From the outset, the Bible confronts us with an active God, personal and interacting with His created beings. Yahweh is His name.[B]

∽ **God Is Involved!**

Although God is infinitely sovereign, how remarkable it is to discover He is not aloof or indifferent to the human condition. He is above and outside of creation, yet intimately involved with it, and out of love He exposes Himself to the same violence and suffering. He knows you in detail, to the extent that "the very hairs of your head are numbered."[2] He did not leave us to grope in the dark alone.

(A) See Further Consideration at the end of this chapter for archeological and other important proofs.

(B) Yahweh means literally, "I Am."

KEEP LOOKING DOWN!

Among the billions of heavenly bodies in the universe, it is thrilling to discover that God chose Planet Earth as the epicenter of His Kingdom Plan. There may be other worlds and places, but only on Planet Earth has God established His Eternal Throne and will finally eliminate the obscenity of injustice and suffering.[3]

⌒ God has a plan for the Universe that affects everyone.

Here the fractured universe is at war with itself—a violent rebellion in progress—and here God heals it. The Bible proclaims this from cover to cover, and God is moving history toward an inescapable conclusion:

> I heard a loud shout from the throne, saying, "Look, *the home of God is now among his people!* He will live with them, and they will be his people. God himself will be with them." *Revelation 21:3*

This is the essence of God's kind intention for creation: a desire to indwell and fellowship with His created beings. "God is love," the Bible declares,[4] and His Kingdom is held together by loving, viable relationships. We were created with a deep longing for such a kingdom.

To understand God's plan for Planet Earth, we must go back to the beginning—even before the beginning. It is overwhelming to grasp that shadowy, veiled continuum we call Eternity Past—where the genius of God's Incredible Plan begins with events before and behind time itself. Yet, God reveals it to us. It is so vital to consider God's point of view in order to discover the significance of creation.

Consider this...

Real purpose comes from God, not our brief activities. The details of our lives overwhelm us so easily; they leave some people with an unnecessary sense of hopelessness, and others with a false sense of confidence.

God offers a concrete view of reality that transcends fleeting events:

> This confidence is like a strong and trustworthy anchor for our souls. It leads us through the curtain of heaven into God's inner sanctuary. *Hebrews 6:19*

His expansive viewpoint enables us to "Keep Looking Down" on this brief interlude between Eternity Past and Eternity Future. Our 70-plus years here are only long enough to make a few significant decisions—and then God continues on with His Eternal Plan. If we Keep Looking Down we can grasp the vast and coherent viewpoint of God:

> We are asking that you may see things, as it were, from His point of view, by being given spiritual insight and understanding. *Colossians 1:9*

THE CREATION OF ANGELS

Somewhere in Eternity Past, even before the material universe existed, God created a teeming civilization of creatures called angels,[C] vast populations of luminous individuals appearing all at once.[5] What a spectacular sight it must have been when the starless, empty universe burst alive with these luminescent creatures!

At Christmas, angels are portrayed as darling, innocent creatures flying about the heavens, singing melodically. The truth is quite different.

The Bible depicts them as ingenious, powerful and well-organized beings[6] working together to execute God's will,[7] with different ranks of authority and dignity: a sophisticated society. There are archangels, cherubim, "world rulers" and simply "rulers." They form "dominions" ruled by "thrones."[8] Their numbers are "myriads upon myriads," meaning literally an uncountable population, a host of beings.[9] The universe is teeming with angelic life and societies.

Their appearance is at once exquisite and yet overpowering. A human instinctively falls down, weak-kneed, and desires to worship.[10] They are ancient and immortal beings, with experience and knowledge surpassing the most powerful human minds in history.[11] Yet, like humans they are intensely relational, with the full range of emotions: joy, sadness and even rage.

FREE WILL
∂ **God implanted the core of His image into angels: the capacity for self-determination.**

His title is el-Shaddai[12]—the Sovereign and Almighty God—and He gave angels this ability to make Sovereign Choices, called Free Will. The Bible calls angels "Sons of God"[13] because they bear His image, and it might be said that God established "miniature gods," God unleashed a potent force in Free Will, because it opened the possibility of dominions outside of God's authority.

With Free Will, the angelic hosts forged a vigorous society of talented individuals who still managed to live together harmoniously, so atypical of gifted minds, it seems. Their culture was atypical: no police or coercion was necessary. Their

---

HOW MANY ANGELS ARE THERE? In the middle ages, it is said that theologians called Scholastics debated how many angels can dance on the head of a pin, a useless and speculative debate. Yet, the Bible does give sobering insight into their numbers.

In Revelation 5:11 it says God is surrounded by "myriads of myriads" of angels, a Jewish idiom meaning "uncountable number." In Matthew 18:10 Christ says there are at least enough angels for every child on the face of the earth.

How many angels are there? One thing we can say: an incredibly large population!

(C) "Angel" means literally "messenger," which gives insight into the essential role these creatures play in God's plan.

cooperation was founded on a shared love with God and for each other—a network of love relationships binding it together.

Although they worked within God's Kingdom, they were not beasts of burden. They were participants with God, singing with delight as God created the universe, sharing the awe of His artistry, shouting with amazement as He set galaxies in motion. How long this joyous society continued is unknown, because it belongs in the realm outside of time, in Eternity Past.

What an incredible society God created! What boundless potential for creativity and advancement in this new civilization—all within the context of cooperative and even warm-hearted relationships! It was more than a society; perhaps we should call it a vast family, the Family of God without the alienation or petty divisions in human families today.

✍ What brings us now into a world scarred by warfare and death?

Violent rebellion ripped apart the fabric of Eternity Past, the Bible says, and the broken world that emerged is only a short parenthesis. God will build His Kingdom. Other kingdoms and dominions may exist momentarily, yet time as we know it will cease to exist some day. Despite current events, God's Eternal Plan actually determines the flow of history, not kings or guns or money.

Something exciting is at hand: the beginning and also the final destination of all history—God's Kingdom—is in motion and gaining momentum. God gave us Revelation so we can latch onto this movement, here and now. He pleads for careful consideration:

> Never forget how close you were to the Kingdom of God. *Luke 10:11b (Living)*

FURTHER CONSIDERATION

THE PROBLEM OF REVELATION

Any claim about God should answer a critical question: what is the source of this revelation about God? This is the most vital question to ask. Nobody accepts a personal check without proper identification, so why would anyone accept revelation about God without inquiring about its source? Claims about God carry far greater implications than a bounced check.

Known as the Problem of Revelation, the issue faces anyone who makes conclusions about God, even concluding Revelation is impossible, as some think.

HOW TO SIFT THROUGH ALL THE REVELATIONS 'FROM GOD'?

People are surprised to discover that among the sacred texts of the world, only the Bible presents itself as *Revelation* directly from God, and offers objective proof. The preponderance of sacred literatures—especially pantheistic[D] religions from the East like Hinduism, Buddhism and all their descendants found in recent Western religions[14]—all these trace their source to human intuition.[15] Not surprisingly, these speculative writings are uncertain and often conflicting opinions and experiences impossible to reconcile. Although these sacred texts are exceedingly diverse, they share a common problem: there is no evidence, no supporting proof behind these speculations. "Theory itself, as theory, is regarded as being supremely worthy."[16]

It is no exaggeration that sacred writings typically require a basic presumption of belief without evidence, a view known as fideism:

> I believe because it is absurd; it is certain because it is impossible![17]

Of the remaining literatures actually claiming divine revelation, the Bible alone offers objective and verifiable proof substantially different from the subjective evidence offered by writings like Qu'ran.[18] This is significant, because if God spoke,

---

(D) Pantheism "is a doctrine which identifies God with the universe, or regards the universe as a manifestation of God." [The New Oxford Dictionary of English, © 1998].

intending for us to listen, we need evidence to distinguish His Word from human speculation. An atheist puts it well:

> If God exists, there will be evidence of this; signs will emerge which point to such a conclusion. *B. C. Johnson, The Atheist Debater's Handbook.*[19]

IS THERE ANY WAY TO PROVE A 'SCRIPTURE'?

The Bible welcomes an honest, skeptical challenge, a distinguishing characteristic from all other literatures:

> In the variety and fullness of the evidence on which it rests, the text of the New Testament stands absolutely and unapproachably alone among ancient prose writings. *F.J.A. Hort, Cambridge Professor of Greek.*[20]

The Bible is firmly rooted in history, a record of God's activities in human time and space. Archeologists and historians are continuously corroborating its trustworthiness in matters of fact—despite exhaustive skeptical accusations—so we can have confidence when it touches on spiritual matters.

The life and physical resurrection of Jesus Christ is one such point of substantiation, an event "as well authenticated as anything in antiquity."[21] Repeatedly, challenges brought against the Bible's historicity led skeptical historians and archeologists to conclude the Bible is a remarkable source of reliable history. Repeatedly, "memories enshrined only in the Bible were restored to their proper places in ancient history by the studies of archeologists."[22]

God offers still more: verifiable, fulfilled prophecy. So unlike the vague and incomprehensible so-called 'predictions' from mystics like Nostradamus,[23] biblical prophecies are clear and verifiable. The Bible stands alone among other sacred writings in this regard. The numbers are mind-boggling: almost 27 percent of its content is devoted to 737 prophesied events, adding up to 8,352 verses. Amazingly, about 600 different prophetic events are fulfilled already—more than enough to place this book in a class by itself.[24] Only authentic, supernatural Revelation could possibly foresee a clear future, and the God of the Bible throws down the gauntlet on this point:

> Let them bring forth and declare to us what is going to take place...
> Or announce to us what is coming. *Isaiah 41:21-22*

No other scripture rises to the challenge of verification like the Bible. During the course of this book, many such prophecies will be detailed, the origins of which are difficult to explain without a supernatural source.

ARE NOT ALL SCRIPTURES EQUALLY TRUE?

It is unreasonable to hold that all scriptures are equally true when their claims about God arise from such radically different sources. Some scriptures are steeped in gross error and contradiction. Greek myth, for example, holds that the sun is actually a chariot drawn by horses; Egyptian myth holds that the clouds originate when "the god Aspu masturbates and his semen issues in clouds."[25] To any reasonable thinker, these views of God are not equally true with all other views of God. "Once we begin to admit that some religious teachings are false, we have to wonder where the line should be drawn. Should only those 'worst' religions be rejected, such as those promoting human sacrifice or cannibalism? ...why would we reject some but not others?"[26]

In reality, nobody can function in a world where all things are equally true:

> All religions, plainly and simply, cannot be true. Some beliefs are false, and we know them to be false...In the real life struggles between right and wrong, justice and injustice, life and death, we all realize that truth does matter. *Ravi Zacharius.*[27]

WHO REALLY KNOWS WHAT THE ORIGINAL BIBLE CONTAINED?

Since the Bible is so ancient, with some books more than 3,000 years old, many wonder what the original writings actually contained back then. Fortunately, modern archeology answers this question with strong confidence, as one eminent archeologist summarizes:

> Both the authenticity and the general integrity of the books of the New Testament may be regarded as finally established.[28]

> In contrast to the total number of over 5,000 New Testament manuscripts known today, other religious and historical books of the ancient world pale in significance... Livy's History of Rome has only 20 manuscripts, and Caesar's Gallic Wars is known from a mere 9 or 10 manuscripts.[29]

For the Old Testament, the earliest manuscript available dated to the 10th Century, and there was much speculation about its relationship to the originals. However, the debate was effectively silenced when the Dead Sea Scrolls (DSS) were discovered, closing that 1,000-year gap. Most of the Old Testament (OT) manuscripts were dated from 250 to 100 B.C., and, "The significance of the DSS for textual studies is unquestioned...Early results in general confirm the accuracy of the existing Hebrew text."[30] Amazingly, "it is reasonably correct to say that there is at least 95 percent agreement between the various biblical texts found near the Dead Sea and the OT we have had all along. Most of the variations are minor, and none of the doctrines have been put in jeopardy."[31]

With so many ancient texts available we can identify copyist errors and insertions, and isolate where and when such changes began appearing. It is widely acknowledged, even by secular scholars, that today's Bible accurately transmits the original texts. "The interval then between the dates of original composition and the earliest extant evidence becomes so small as to be in fact negligible."[32]

A CHALLENGE TO INVESTIGATE!

Many resources cited in the bibliography offer a convincing treatment of the evidence for the Bible's authority.[33] The small investment of time required to consider the evidence will yield exciting results with potentially life-changing rewards.

THE SON OF THE DAWN

An unfamiliar principle invades creation...

> ✑ **At the apex of God's angelic creation stands a most magnificent and breathtaking creature named Lucifer.**

"Son of the Dawn" is his name, or Lucifer, which captures the essence of his radiant beauty.[1]

In a rare glimpse into Eternity Past, we find Lucifer elevated to the highest position in creation—standing beside God Himself, guarding the very throne of God.[2] Anyone approaching God approached Lucifer first.

LUCIFER THE BEAUTIFUL

This was also the most gifted and superb of all the angelic creation, a tribute to God's creative power. Even God said:

> You were the perfection of wisdom and beauty. *Ezekiel 28:12*

The passage describes a creature of dazzling beauty. Lucifer's towering majesty evokes an urge to fall down and worship him "as an angel of light" according to the Bible.[3] What a stark contrast to the popular myths depicting Lucifer as a beastly, medieval gargoyle!

A modern naiveté assumes that anything spiritual must be good.[4] The Bible says, however, charismatic and potent spirits exist with disguised evil intentions. Humans are no match for such creatures.

THE HEART OF REBELLION

✑ **This magnificent creature threw all his gifting and power into a wholesale rebellion that splintered the universe.**

At some point in Eternity Past, this highest and most powerful angel ignited a rebellion against God. Standing beside God's throne, watching the glory and worship directed toward God, the Son of the Dawn grew envious and brooding, finally reaching a simple but fatal decision: he too should receive worship.

It was an obscene thought never before conceived within creation. How long he hesitated, contemplating the harrowing implications, we do not know. When the decision was made, it erupted in violent threats:

> I will ascend to heaven and rule the angels! I will take the highest throne! I will make myself like the Most High! *Isaiah 14:13* (LB), and *Isaiah 14:14* (NASB)

That was it, stark and resolute: Lucifer would submit to nobody! He threw aside the Eternal Plan and will of his Creator, and launched into the uncharted territory of rebellion against God, improvising as he went. The die was cast, and the universe was unalterably changed.

Made in God's image, endowed with powerful talents and a capacity for self-rule, he was highly adept at launching this unprecedented course: rebellion against Almighty God.

This was no subtle refinement of God's creation, and it spawned a great metamorphosis, from beautiful Lucifer into "Satan": the Adversary. God describes the creature that emerged:

> You were blameless in all you did from the day you were created until the day evil was found in you. Your great wealth filled you with violence... Your heart was filled with pride because of all your beauty. You corrupted your wisdom for the sake of your splendor. *Ezekiel 28:15-17*

At the core of this emerging rebellion was pride inflated beyond reality: "Your heart was filled with pride," it says. Like Pandora's Box, once conceived, Pride flourishes with self-seeking momentum, so that "you corrupted your wisdom." Pride grew to self-adulation, egotism, then narcissism, finally altering his very character.

LUCIFER THE CORRUPTED

What is it like to live for so long in the presence of God, bathing in His perfect love, wisdom, and kindness, and then brush it all aside? It requires such a radical reorientation: that good is bad, love is evil, and hate is good. What a perversion of reality! "You corrupted your wisdom!" was a fitting assessment.

> ✍ **Lucifer became a twisted creature who enjoys inflicting pain and loves to destroy.**

As he now exists, Satan hates everything God represents. "God is love," the Bible says, but this creature believes in hate. God believes in nurturing people, but this one destroys humanity. Whatever God cherishes, he despises.

Thus begins the fall and decline of Lucifer as God describes him now:

> All who knew you are appalled at your fate. *Ezekiel 28:16-19*

A NEW PRINCIPLE

Satan is the one who introduced the Principle of Sin into the universe: exalting created will over and against the Creator's will. "I will be like the Most High God!" he vowed. One author describes this well:

> It is possible to say that the shortest definition of sin is simply "I Will." It makes no difference who speaks the words.[5]

The creature can never usurp the authority of the Creator. Who can replace God as ruler of the universe? Who is more dependable or capable? God makes this point Himself:

> Who is like me? Let him proclaim it. Let him declare and set it before me!...Is there a God besides me? There is no Rock; I know not any. *Isaiah 44:7-8* (ESV)

The thought of removing God from His proper role is incredulous, a mere fantasy necessitating volumes of pride to imagine replacing Him! Beyond audacity, it belongs to the realm of the delusional. Pride eliminates God from the horizon:

> In the pride of his face the wicked does not seek him; all his thoughts are, "There is no God." *Psalm 10:4* (ESV)

The Principle of Sin always leads to a certain "lostness" or "blindness" as the Bible calls it: it becomes delusional as it sets the creature at the center of the universe. The result is an unnatural separation between the creature and the Creator, and reality is turned inside out. The tangible world is exchanged for an imaginary world without moorings, a world where "There is no Rock" as God said, a creation without a Creator.

> **Self-rule is actually self-destruction: it is a fundamental perversion of the design of creation.**

Self-determination is one of the highest virtues of our society. Although independence can be a liberating concept, when it becomes a drive for independence from God, it destroys. We actually lose our independence, because the Principle of Sin takes over with a momentum all its own. Where once God ruled, now the Principle of Sin rules and molds our very nature.

Satan degenerates into a "ravenous" creature as this Principle of Sin becomes the driving force behind everything he does. It devoured his capacity to understand reality.

THE SATANIC ACCUSATION

Satan accused God of intolerance and injustice because God is opposed to Self-Rule. What an outrage to prohibit beings with Sovereign Will from exercising their Free Will! God suppresses independence! To Satan, God was a rigid and stifling tyrant. Is innovation so wrong?

Indeed, there is apparent basis for Satan's accusation when we see God's declared order of creation:

> There is only one God, the Father, who created everything, and we exist for him. *1 Corinthians 8:6a*

Since "we exist for Him," does this not justify Satan's accusation of tyranny? Apparently, God reserves Self Rule only for Himself, while everyone else is deprived of freedom!

These were potent accusations, to be sure, with strong appeal. What is not immediately apparent is the hideous deception lurking beneath the surface: Satan was not advocating freedom, he had a different agenda.

THE REBELLION SPREADS

Exactly how it happened, we can only guess. God did not censor the satanic accusation, we do know that much. There was some kind of public hearing where his accusation and God's answers were laid before the angelic multitudes. Satan accused God of lying, and God accused Satan of lying:[6]

> There is no truth in him. When he lies, it is consistent with his character; for he is a liar and the father of lies. *John 8:44*

Amazingly, one third of the angels were swept into his rebellion, so we know it was not a private affair.[7] With so many others taking the plunge to follow Satan's lead and abandon God, considerable conversation and debate about this new, unfamiliar direction raged throughout the universe. It was a violent affair involving vast populations of creatures—a massive division that tore apart their communities.

Lucifer clearly has a phenomenal ability to incite rebellion and deceive lesser creatures. Despite the resistance from two-thirds of the angels, he still managed to challenge Almighty God and draw away the remainder with the allure of freedom.

THE HIDDEN AGENDA

God calls Satan "a liar" and "the father of lies" for good reason: the power of his persuasion rests on deception.

Very quickly it became obvious Satan's rebellion was a bid for power, not freedom. He always intended to "ascend to heaven and rule the angels!" When he said, "I will be like God!" he meant that he wanted to imitate God's authority, not God's character. He lusted for power over others and craved worship, but God stood in his way, so he called for others to leave the protection of God's Kingdom.

Satan's offer of freedom through rebellion was merely the freedom to replace God's authority with Satan's authority, and he knew it. He knew lesser, weaker creatures would immediately fall under his domination once set apart from God.

God's authority was not suppression, it was a provision: it provided an orderly and peaceful universe. It was a kingdom based on love, but Satan's kingdom was based on hatred.

> ⤳ **There is no such thing as autonomous freedom in this universe.**

The universe is not empty, and it is impossible to avoid the presence and reality of other beings. There is either God's authority with His love, or Satan's authority with his devious hate. There are only two kingdoms, not an in-between, autonomous kingdom of our own invention.

No longer "angels," these collaborators came under his realm as "unclean spirits," "demons," or simply "his [Satan's] angels."[8] As they embraced the Principle of Sin, they, too, became twisted. They share Lucifer's vision for a universe opposed to God's authority. With this great host, he is heading up a war against God and His kingdom.

Satan is not a silly gargoyle with horns that prances around in red flannel underwear. He is the master of deception and seduces in the most appealing manner. This is why the spiritual realm requires real discernment: the false ideas and accusations against God that Satan triggers are rampant in the universe.

One popular writer typifies this naive approach to spirituality:

> Listen to your feelings. Listen to your highest thoughts. Listen to your experience. Whenever any of these differ from what you've been told by your teachers or read in your books, forget the words. Words are the least reliable purveyor of truth. *Neale Donald Walsh*[9]

THE REBELLION IS CONFINED

Although much of Eternity Past is veiled in mystery, apparently God did pass judgment on Lucifer's rebellion, and pronounced Satan's defeat. God expelled Satan and his supporters from the Throne of His Presence:

> So I banished you from the mountain of God. I expelled you, O mighty guardian, from your place among the stones of fire ... I threw you to the earth and exposed you... All who knew you are appalled at you. *Ezekiel 28:16-17*

Satan changed from a creature "perfect, full of beauty" into one to be "appalled at" —yet he remains a dangerous creature. Although God proclaimed judgment, Satan retains all his former gifting and genius.

Most significantly, God confined the rebellion to Planet Earth. Here in exile, Satan relentlessly builds his kingdom at any cost, and anyone opposing him becomes an enemy. He retains a strong organization of allies:

> ...the evil rulers and authorities of the unseen world...those mighty powers of darkness who rule this world...wicked spirits in the heavenly realms. *Ephesians 6:12*

With these supporters, he dominates this globe:

> The whole world lies in the power of the Evil One. *1 John 5:19* (NASB-U)

✐ Earth is now center-stage for the rebellion against God's Kingdom.

Planet Earth is not a benign realm. It bears the scars of a rebellion in progress: a dangerous and violent place, stained with hatred, and held together with political deceit and intrigue. One author summarizes it well:

> It is important to remember that Satan has always looked upon this world as his personal property. There is much that will remain incomprehensible if we overlook this fact.[10]

THE COUNTERFEIT KINGDOM

✐ The very foundation for tragic events on Planet Earth begins with Satan's Counterfeit Kingdom.

Planet Earth is now center-stage for this "Invisible War," where Satan rules a Counterfeit Kingdom. It is counterfeit because it lacks the permanence and substance of God's Kingdom, and it will ultimately self-destruct because its foundation is the Principle of Sin.

What makes the Counterfeit Kingdom so attractive?

Satan can promise power and authority within the Counterfeit Kingdom to whomever he pleases—in return for worship of himself. It is not the worship of direct praise and adulation (after all, his rebellion offered freedom from the worship of God), yet he receives praise indirectly through dedication and loyalty given to his Counterfeit Kingdom. It is, after all, such a magnificent kingdom—on the surface.

The Bible describes Satan as "the one deceiving the whole world."[11] It requires discernment to detect the devious ways in which Satan seduces others into following him, which eventually results in our worshiping him.

∾ **Ultimately, what attracts followers in Satan's kingdom is the Principle of Sin.**

The intoxicating promise of position and status within the Counterfeit Kingdom lures a parade of followers: the Hitlers, Stalins, and Julius Caesars we know today as tyrants.

Roman emperors snatched at the allure of Satan's Counterfeit Kingdom, irregardless of cost. A lengthy succession of emperors seized the throne of the empire with its boundless dominance and wealth, yet each met a cruel death at the hands of assassins. Amazingly, others still clamored for the position, intoxicated by power even though coronation inevitably brought death.

Not everyone wants world power, of course; yet the desire for autonomy from God is itself an arrogant bid for power. Independence from God is inherently based on the appeal of the Principle of Sin, the hope of establishing a new kingdom. It has an allure that drives a universe of empire-builders. Satan's paradigm appeals to the pride of autonomous rule, and to God, pride is synonymous with "wicked," the very epitome of a defective universe:

> In his pride the wicked does not seek Him; in all his thoughts there is no room for God. *Psalm 10:4* (NIV)

The Counterfeit Kingdom offers the promise to rule rather than follow, and glorifies pride. In Satan's world, pride is a virtue, something to hold onto with determination to the bitter end, a right that nobody can take away. Everyone admires the rebel who will not capitulate. To yield or submit is a despicable experience. These are views we understand easily today, but they were novel and intriguing when Satan first launched his rebellion.

In the end, pride is the opportunity to seize the authority that rightfully belongs to God. In such a proud mindset, "there is no room for God," the psalmist says. Pride exalted above God's authority is the impetus driving the Principle of Sin forward and away from God.

There is a hideous omission in the advertisement of the virtues of pride. As pride is conveniently ignored—or deliberately suppressed—it triggers the chaos and destruction ravaging Satan's kingdom.

CHAOS, DESTRUCTION AND DEATH
∾ **Even with all its promise and allure, this new kingdom is essentially dysfunctional.**

What looks so good and so real proves to be the very source of evil and unreality, because at its heart it is a kingdom based on deception.

The Counterfeit Kingdom promises an abundance of stimulation and reward, so much opportunity! Satan inaugurated a succession of glamorous empires with breathtaking monuments and shimmering palaces of gold and precious stones. Still, even his most glorious kingdom can only offer a forgery, a pale shadow of the real Kingdom of God. Something significant is missing, and it is a public secret everyone knows, but few discuss.

∽ What the Counterfeit Kingdom cannot offer is workable relationships.

Outside of God's Kingdom, authentic love as God intended is impossible. Trust is missing. The threat of rejection and division always hovers nearby in Satan's kingdom, because proud wills collide. Distrust erupts.

The difference between the two kingdoms is striking: One is a Regime of Chaos, while the other operates under the peace of God's rule.

Chaos is the fruit of a kingdom based on the Principle of Sin. Without a true God, we see instead billions of "sovereign gods" at war with each other, each one acting as the center of his own universe. What a stark contrast to God's harmonious society of angels! Satan caters to the allure of pride, but suppresses the heart-rending loneliness and division it fosters.

In God's Kingdom, God's will is the ordering principle throughout creation, an authentic center for the universe. God is the only valid context for unity between individuals, the only credible basis for trust. Who but the Almighty Creator works from altruistic intentions? Only the Infinite God has nothing to gain from his creatures, and He has no needs to fulfill. Not so with finite creatures.

JUST FORGIVE AND FORGET? Is it not possible for Satan to come to his senses, admit a terrible mistake, then receive forgiveness and help from God? This is a question often asked, since human disputes are sometimes healed this way. After World War II the Allies offered Japan and Germany forgiveness and aid, and so former enemies became strong allies during the Cold War.

The Bible emphatically answers that forgive and forget is not an option for this one. Even if Satan changed his mind—which is impossible—forgiveness is unavailable for him.

Satan's decision to reject God's authority was not made in ignorance. He was intimately familiar with the beauty and kindness of God, the glory of God's Kingdom, and the depth of His wisdom. It was not God's character that drove him away, but rather Satan's lust for worship. He was keenly aware that such a bid for power would bring massive division and consequence, aware how inherently dangerous it was to oppose the Almighty God, and he executed it with foresight and cunning —the "Father of lies." Once made, this decision set in motion an unalterable change of character, and now Satan is quite a different beast than the Lucifer of God's creation.

There is nothing left to redeem with Satan or his followers, they are so calloused and hideously evil. This is why the Bible declares, "For assuredly He does not give help to angels, but He gives help to the descendant of Abraham" Hebrews 2:16 (NASB-U). Humans are born outside of God's Kingdom, and choose their way into it, so there is still hope; Satan was inside God's Kingdom and chose his way out of it.

Satan's kingdom is a Regime of Chaos, where power is seized in desperation from others. Authority belongs to the most powerful, since there is no authentic center of the universe. War becomes necessary to impose order, and so this kingdom becomes a regime through coercion and brutality. The Bible declares this planet a dangerous and tragic place where the weak and helpless are brutalized by evil:

> Their mouths are full of cursing, lies, and threats...They lurk in dark alleys, murdering the innocent who pass by. They are always searching for some helpless victim. The helpless are overwhelmed and collapse...
> *Psalm 10:7-10*

The Regime of Chaos rains destruction—a whirlwind of war, schemes, deceit, coalitions and betrayal sparked by power-plays between kingdom-builders. Satan's realm is a seething caldron of kingdoms within kingdoms, kingdoms crashing against each other, and kingdoms in collapse while others ascend. Such are the trademarks of the Counterfeit Kingdom as Satan imposes rule over other autonomous "gods."

THE NEW "KING"

Since the beginning of his rebellion, Satan always craved worship. Ironically, his ambitions are frustrated because—like himself—the members of his kingdom are operating by the Principle of Sin. Everyone is too proud and autonomous to subjugate without coercion.

Still, Satan is not easily deterred. He remains intently focused: "I will be like the Most High God!" He pursues this worship with all his zeal and fantastic gifting. Anyone opposing him is an enemy:

> For Satan prowls around like a hungry and roaring lion, looking for some victim to tear apart! *1 Peter 5:8* (LB)

Although the Counterfeit Kingdom continually erupts in chaos, Satan is still able to retain enough control to be "the ruler of this world." There is a singular intelligence and drive behind the pervasive evil on earth. The atrocities of human history resurface with remarkable uniformity, despite new faces in the human administration.

> ➴ **To live in a world of widespread evil, and yet dismiss the possibility of an evil intelligence behind it, is unreasonable.**

It may be hard for some to believe in a literal Satan, yet even the most casual observer of history cannot deny a world pervasively entangled with cruel violence and suffering. How is it possible to believe in an all-powerful and loving God in the face of such evil, unless someone else rules this world?

People so easily focus their blame—even hatred—toward God for the pain and suffering of this realm. Few consider that someone else may be involved. The Bible traces these tragedies back to the Principle of Sin, and ultimately to its author, Satan.

WHY DOES GOD LET IT CONTINUE?

This is one of the most common disputes raised by people suffering in this Counterfeit Kingdom: "Why cannot an all-powerful God end this evil?" If rebellion is the source of evil, God should eliminate its leader.

The Bible gives a clear answer: God desires willing participants in His Kingdom. This necessitates true freedom, not apparent freedom. Sovereign Will is a farce if every dissent or rebellion is immediately squashed, a choice at gunpoint! Who dares make the wrong choice? Such a world is indeed dominated by a tyrannical God, as the Evil One asserts.

> **Because God is just, He allows Free Will to take its course, and demonstrates the ultimate fate of Self-Rule.**

When Satan's Counterfeit Kingdom reaches completion, everyone in the universe will finally see what happens if the creature sets its will against the Creator: the result is always chaos and destruction. As one scholar puts it:

> It was not lack of power that prevented God from crushing Satan—it was a matter of principle…Satan's accusations must be answered, and they cannot be truly answered by a force that crushes the accuser.[12]

> **God allows the rebellion to continue for our sakes.**

God defends His justice to the universe in order to invite us back into a relationship of trust with our loving Creator. He gives us reasons, time and opportunity to decide if we want in His Eternal Kingdom—or out of it.

We may be powerless to change the world, but each of us can decide where to invest the power of our own Sovereign Will. Anyone opting for a relationship with God becomes a participant in His Eternal Kingdom.

The rebellion interrupted God's plan for eternity, but only temporarily, a very brief period compared to the vastness of God's Eternal Plan. God's plan will resume. Meanwhile, creation bogs down while the rebellion plays out. As one author puts it:

> Although the Lord had the power to destroy Satan with a breath, He did not do so. It was as though an edict had been proclaimed in heaven:

> We shall give this rebellion a thorough trial. We shall permit it to run its full course. We shall watch this experiment, and permit the universe of creatures to watch it, during this brief interlude between eternity past and eternity future called time.[13]

A SOLUTION IN SIGHT

God's plan is still intact despite these events. By His sovereignty, these events will become the cornerstone of a revelation so astonishing, so inspiring, the universe will literally shout with joy at the extent of His triumph. This astonishing revelation is called The Mystery in the Bible. It is His solution to Satan's horrific chaos, something so unexpected it cannot be described in brief—it can only be perceived by watching The Mystery unfold in historical events. It has a stupendous impact:

> And He will again startle many nations. Kings will stand speechless in his presence. For they will see what they had not previously been told about; they will understand what they had not heard about. *Isaiah 52:15*

The tension of the Great Schism heats up as He unveils The Mystery in a special piece of real estate we know today as the Middle East.

FURTHER CONSIDERATION

GOD'S SOVEREIGNTY AND HUMAN CHOICE

It is the nature of God's creation that these two concepts remain eternally true: God's Sovereign Plan, and human Sovereign Will. It is true that God is not a passive observer of human affairs, and He is building a Kingdom through a plan conceived "before the foundation of the world."[14] Yet the Bible also says our personal destinies are not pre-determined by God, and we are not victims of fate. How does the Bible resolve this apparent contradiction between God's Sovereign Plan and Man's Sovereign Will?

These concepts are not contradictory; they simply apply to different spheres. God's Sovereign Plan controls the destiny of kingdoms—not individuals—and His Eternal Plan is ultimately never thwarted, He declares. The destiny of the individual is left to our Sovereign Will: to engage in the excitement of His Kingdom Plan, or reject it and join forces with the Counterfeit Kingdom. God's Plan predetermines nobody's choice, as Forster and Marston point out:

> It is true that God will ultimately achieve His plan for the world in spite of those who resist it, but the individual still has his own moral choice of whether or not to reject God's plan for him.[15]

We do have free choice, not unlimited choice. There are only two kingdoms on Planet Earth to choose between. We do not have the power to establish a novel, independent kingdom. Anything we build with our lives falls within the domain of God's Eternal Kingdom or the Counterfeit Kingdom. Emerson's call to individualism —the "march to the beat of a different drummer"[16]—is a sad illusion, a non-option.

HUMAN HISTORY BEGINS

What are mortals that you should think of us, mere humans that you should care for us?
…You crown us with glory and honor!
Psalm 8:4-5

Swirling out from vast eons of Eternity Past, countless warring spirits gather from across the universe, and the Great Schism pivots in a singular piece of real estate on Planet Earth: the Middle East. Here in a sheltered environment God creates two seemingly trite and harmless beings, naked and innocent, in the obscure corner of Planet Earth called the Garden of Eden.

THE MYSTERY

∽ **From the beginning, God's intent for Planet Earth is extraordinary.**

The Bible says God worked from a "predetermined plan" formed "before the creation of the world," a tremendous "mystery which has been kept secret for long ages past."[1] From beginning to end, the Bible is a revelation of this mysterious plan of God, and it is aimed squarely at mankind, here, on Planet Earth:

> But we speak God's wisdom in a mystery, the hidden wisdom which God predestined before the ages to our glory. *1 Corinthians 2:7* (NASB-U)

God's Mystery elevates man "to our glory," meaning "Great honor, praise, or distinction accorded by common consent."[2] Others are watching. Man will be viewed by all creation—angels included—with great honor and praise, according to His plan.[3]

For this reason He gave us the very first chapter of the Bible—seated in the grandstands, watching the Master Architect build a foundation, weaving design and purpose into the very fabric of the universe. It is a gracious invitation by a loving God to watch the great Mystery unfolding—the reason He gave Revelation. It is impossible to comprehend the character of our world apart from the artist's hand:

The Lord, who created the heavens and stretched them out, who spread out the earth and what comes from it, who gives breath to the people on it and spirit to those who walk in it. *Isaiah 42:5* (ESV)

A BRILLIANT DAWN

Eons of time are enveloped in the Bible's first, simple statement:

In the beginning God created the heavens and the earth. *Genesis 1:1* (NASB-U)

This one verse says so much. God sparked it: the spectacular eruption of the universe with blinding energy expanding and cooling over millions of years into luminous clouds of dust, nebulae weaving into great orbs of flaming gas, stars colliding and swirling into enormous galaxies thousands of light years across…He saw all this—He made it happen!

∾ **The ages pass differently for the Eternal God, who stands outside of time, and behind the universe.**

So impossible to fully grasp, yet He provides a glimpse of how time elapses for Him:

EVOLUTION OR CREATION? To some people, the universe is a chance collection of molecules without purpose or design, and the Genesis 1 account is nonsense arising from a mistaken belief that the Bible contradicts modern science. Particularly offensive to some is the Bible's declaration that man was created directly by God Himself and did not evolve from other hominids. Yet if we consider the evidence, there is no contradiction between science and the Creation account, and the Bible certainly allows room for the discoveries of modern science.

It is surprising to some when they discover that substantial faith is involved in discounting Creationism. Objective science alone cannot disprove Genesis—although it is true that some interpretations of Genesis 1 are clearly in error.[4] Rather, "the creation-evolution controversy is not between the Bible and science, as such. Instead, it is between some persons who hold certain interpretations of the Bible and other persons who maintain certain extrapolations or theories in science."[5]

Naturalism[A] is not derived from scientific fact, and is in fact a position of extreme faith: truly, it is a religion.[6] Prominent secular scientists such as Nobel Laureate Francis Crick—pioneer of DNA—find problems with a purely mechanical Darwinism.[B] As a philosophy, *Naturalism* is not without significant problems, as one scholar points out:

"Both Darwinism as it was first presented as the survival of the fittest and neo-Darwinism have been shown to have not only philosophical but methodological and statistical problems...The concept of an unbroken line from the molecule to man on the basis of time and chance is, it seems to me, very clearly a faith position held by modern rationalistic man."[7] *Francis Schaeffer*

(A) Naturalism is "a philosophical viewpoint according to which everything arises from natural properties and causes, and supernatural or spiritual explanations are excluded or discounted." [OED]

(B) See Further Consideration at the end of the chapter for more details.

But do not let this one fact escape your notice, beloved, that with the Lord one day is like a thousand years, and a thousand years like one day. *2 Peter 3:8* (NASB-U)

The focus zooms to Earth itself, the crowning point of His intentions:

The earth was formless and void, and darkness was over the surface of the deep... *Genesis 1:1-2a* (NASB-U)

Earth is a dark place, "formless and void:" two Hebrew words that describe a planet literally in "chaos and disorder."[8] It is void of life, a harsh and foreboding planet, dark and lifeless. But something stirs across the seas of the planet:

...and the Spirit of God was moving over the surface of the waters." *Genesis 1:1-2a* (NASB-U)

Although He stands above creation, God's Spirit now engages in this planet. The Hebrew language depicts Him literally "hovering," ready, anticipating, and waiting.[11] Then suddenly the planet erupts in one of the most dramatic moments in Earth's history:

Then God said, 'Let there be light'; and there was light. *Genesis 1:3* (NASB-U)

What a dramatic sight: utter darkness fractured with the brilliance of nuclear fission, enveloping the face of the planet!

A UNIVERSE OF CHANCE?

At the heart of Genesis 1 is God's declaration this is not a universe by chance. Life reflects God's personal touch with certain artistry and design, the evidence of His genius at work:

"For since the creation of the world His invisible attributes, His eternal power and divine nature, have been clearly seen, being understood through what has been made, so that they are without excuse." *Romans 1:20* (NASB-U)

Although it is a creation with order, it is not rigid. God creates life with its own momentum, a perpetual change poetically described as "the miracle of life." For even the most skeptical and brilliant scientific minds life inspires a deep fascination, an awe. Life engages and mystifies us precisely because there is a beauty and genius that random chance could not create.

The most advanced human technology cannot imitate the simplest of God's creative acts—not even a primitive single-cell. Even the smallest component of a living cell—the protein molecule—faces infinitesimally small chances of occurring spontaneously.[9] The famous Russian scientist and atheist A.I. Oparian concedes this point:

"To the student of protein structure, the spontaneous formation of such an atomic arrangement in the protein molecule would seem as improbable as would the accidental origin of the text of Virgil's Aeneid from scattered letter type."[10]

This is no ordinary light, it is not sunlight. This was God-spoken light, a bold proclamation by God that He is here—on Planet Earth—to stir up something marvelous. Among the multitudes of galaxies and bodies in the universe, Earth is where His very thought behind creation is first revealed.[12]

He triggers a staggering transformation of the planet, and from a state of chaos God fashions order. Where it was once "desolate and void," He fills every corner of Earth with a new entity called life: across the seas, land, mountains and deserts, even filling the air, entire kingdoms of life with infinite variety are "brought forth," the Bible declares. At each point where He establishes life, it is self-propagating, "each after their own kind," Genesis repeats.

When God finishes, the chaos is replaced by systems of life, self-sustaining. Creation has order, which enables scientists to study it, systematize and comprehend it.

God was obviously pleased with this new order: seven times it is repeated that "God saw that it was good."[13] God—like humans—enjoys creative accomplishment. The message is clear: the problem in creation did not originate with Him.

As the creation account closes, the transformation is complete: out of chaos, God fashioned order. It depicts a King establishing His throne over vast and complex kingdoms of life. The Bible summarizes it well:

> Heaven is my throne, and the earth is my footstool. Could you ever build me a temple as good as that? Could you build a dwelling place for me? My hands have made both heaven and earth, and they are mine. I, the Lord, have spoken! *Isaiah 66:1-2*

ENTER: MAN

With great care God fashioned man and left His distinct signature:

> And the Lord God formed a man's body from the dust of the ground and breathed into it the breath of life... *Genesis 2:7a*

∽ God's creation of man surpassed anything yet placed upon the earth.

This was a peculiar creature. At first glance, it seems paltry and insignificant. Composed of the most worthless material—common dust—this creature was crippled with limitations. Bound by space and time, so unlike angels, it was trapped inside a physical body. Compared to other animals it seemed weak, without sharp teeth, claws or poisons—completely vulnerable and weaponless.

Yet this new creature held an advantage that set it apart from all the other creatures on earth:

> God...breathed into it the breath of life. And the man became a living person. *Genesis 2:7a*

"Man became a living person"—literally, a "soul"[14]—because God "breathed into it the breath of life." Deep inside, God placed a restless and impelling spark, a different kind of life not at all physical. In perhaps the most thrilling statement found in the Bible, God uncovers the hidden essence and potency of man:

> So God created people in his own image; God patterned them after Himself. *Genesis 1:27a*

Man stands at the apex of Genesis 1. The entire study of God's Incredible Plan is rooted in this terse statement and its echoing reverberations through time. At the core, man is a Spiritual Being, like God, stamped with God's image.

Man is inferior to the angels in almost every way except one: we are also made in the image of God. We, too, have Eternal Life and the power to exercise free, Sovereign Will. Like angels, we have direct access to God's realm—the spiritual dimension. We were created as members of His Kingdom, with the faculties to fellowship with other Spiritual Beings.

Yet God's "Breath of Life'" is a double-edged sword. As Spiritual Beings, we are exposed to the raging conflict between the Two Kingdoms. Like the other spirits, man can select which kingdom deserves his allegiance.

"WITH ETERNITY IN THEIR HEARTS"

God unleashed a creature far more complex and powerful than meets the eye when He created man, as we intuitively know. In the Bible, David marvels:

> I will give thanks to you because I have been so amazingly and miraculously made. Your works are miraculous, and my soul is fully aware of this. *Psalm 139:14* (GW)

ᔆ As Spiritual Beings, we are also Eternal Beings.

We know our existence does not terminate with physical death. Although we cannot fully fathom it, our built-in awareness of eternity is not easily dismissed, the Bible says:

> He has also set eternity in the hearts of men; yet they cannot fathom what God has done from beginning to end. *Ecclesiastes 3:11*

Historically, humankind is obsessed with the spiritual realm and eternal life, building complex religious systems and funeral rites around them. We know our existence is significant beyond the physical here-and-now. It is a restlessness that follows us through life, a haunting curiosity:

> One certainly has a soul; but how it came to allow itself to be enclosed in a body is more than I can imagine. *Lord Byron*[15]

ᔆ We have a deep, built-in longing for His Eternal Kingdom.

Beginning at an early age we grapple with the question of mission, our inherent composition and what possible imprint our existence might leave. At the center of these struggles is an acute awareness of our future as Eternal Beings.

A RELATIONAL BEING

God created man to be a Personal Being like Himself, so we can build relationships with other Personal Beings. These are not merely relationships of convenience or survival as found in the animal kingdom—human relationships are designed to be meaningful and lasting.

From the outset, God wired humans as relationship-builders:

> God patterned them after himself; male and female He created them. *Genesis 1:27b*

Humans carry a profound ability to attach, invest emotionally and build deep love relationships meant to last.

Because we are both relational and eternal, when death or separation terminates our intimate relationships, the effect is devastating. Something is wrong: relationships should be unbroken and eternal.

God created us as both male and female, patterned after His very nature. "In the Image of God" means a Relational Being because God is relational. Our deepest craving is to form an intimate bond like the one marriage promises. This is something wonderfully different from the angels, who apparently do not enjoy gender differences and cannot enjoy marriage.[16]

Adam soon discovered the excitement of this new gender concept when God created a partner for him.

THE FIRST MARRIAGE

With loving care God formed a new haven for Adam, full of "beautiful trees that produced delicious fruit." It was a sanctuary where "a river flowed" and "divided and became four rivers."[17] Crafted by God Himself, we know it was a breathtaking landscape because Adam called it "Eden," meaning, "delight."

God added immeasurably to Adam's delight by creating a woman, someone literally "corresponding to him."[18] The Bible captures Adam's thrill at her beauty and nobility:

> "At last!" Adam exclaimed. "She is part of my own flesh and bone! She will be called 'woman,' because she was taken out of a man." *Genesis 2:23*[19]

She would become a lifelong partner and forever alter his life:

> For this reason a man shall leave his father and his mother and hold fast to his wife, and they shall become one flesh. *Genesis 2:24* (ESV)

Since Adam was a Relational Being, the woman brought a profound satisfaction to his need for intimacy, especially physical intimacy. This concept of sexual intercourse was a surprisingly powerful and unparalleled form of intimacy, an honor God did not grant to the angels: the ability for two beings to experience unity at the physical level, where "they shall become one flesh."

Sexual intercourse as designed by God was a delightful expression of the underlying unity between two individuals. It strengthened the relationship:

> If two lie down together they keep warm, but how can one be warm alone? *Ecclesiastes 4:11* (NASB-U)

Even more, as Spiritual Beings, they shared the thrill of a relationship with God together, building purpose within His Eternal Kingdom Plan. There was such marvelous potential for purpose and achievement within the first marriage! The Bible describes the strength of this combination, when God is involved:

> And though a man might prevail against one who is alone, two will withstand him—a threefold cord is not quickly broken. *Ecclesiastes 4:12* (ESV)

With God's presence, a marriage becomes that strong "threefold cord."

We still experience a deep longing for intimacy like this—physically, intellectually, and emotionally. It is a deep desire to build and share a life together with someone not easily ignored.

> The only stable happiness for mankind is that it shall live married in blessed union to woman-kind—intimacy, physical and psychical between a man and his wife. *D. H. Lawrence*[14]

God wants to see us fulfilled by the intimacy of marriage: "It is not good for man to be alone," God declared, and then created Eve. The common phrase "ordained by God" is truly an appropriate description of marriage, and only God can reveal the secrets of a thriving marriage.

TRUE INTIMACY In the Garden of Eden, their relationship worked because God was personally involved. Together with God, they relished "walking in the garden in the cool of the day,"[20] talking and sharing their thoughts. What intriguing questions and insights they discussed with the Creator! It was a truly intimate, unfettered relationship with each other and God.

Eden depicts the essence of God's kind intentions for humanity still today. Inside His Kingdom, we can enjoy relationships that succeed. Clearly, He is a God of intimacy.

Sadly, people often avoid God because they fear Him. Will He dominate? Will He overwhelm? This is the experience typical of other authorities we encounter in life.

This is precisely why the Bible provides a glimpse of life before The Fall: so we can rediscover the same intimacy Adam and Eve enjoyed with Him and each other. These were relationships of simple trust and love, unfettered by the Principle of Sin. Clearly God did not smother human freedom. Quite the opposite, He granted us Sovereign Will because it is so vital to intimacy!

AN HONORED RACE

The centerpiece of creation on earth was a race of rulers designed to become vice-regents in God's Eternal Kingdom. This, too, is part of The Mystery.

> God blessed them; and God said to them, "Be fruitful and multiply, and fill the earth, and subdue it; and rule over the fish of the sea and over the birds of the sky and over every living thing that moves on the earth." *Genesis 1:28* (NASB-U)

∽ Man retains the blueprint of a ruler today.

Although man later becomes greatly handicapped in his ability to fulfill that commission, the Bible declares that still, today:

> You put us in charge of everything you made, giving us authority over all things. *Psalm 8:6*

Related to our desire to rule, humans also discover great fulfillment building things and establishing order like God enjoyed during creation. From the outset this was an important part of man's design:

> The Lord God took the man and put him in the Garden of Eden to work it and take care of it. *Genesis 2:15* (NIV)

Adam's life in the Garden of Eden did not pass in idle boredom. God created us with a great ability to work: to stamp the world around us with our creative touch,

THE QUALITY OF ETERNITY As Eternal Beings we are not happy living trapped within time. It simply makes no sense to live as though everything about us is confined within a mere 70 years of existence. We have such high expectations for purpose and significance, which saddens us to think they disappear so quickly.

When eternity is the point of reference—as it is with God—there is no time. This limiting thing called time is only possible for those who live outside of God's eternity, bound by time, and ruled by time. One scholar describes how Eternity Past was shattered by this thing we call time:

"The quality of eternity is the fact there is but one will—the will of God. The quality of time is that there is more than one will. There came into the universe a second will rising from the heart of Lucifer, the highest and most wonderful of all the created beings of the universe."[21]

The rebellion introduced a new reference point in the universe, outside of God: "Until Eternity Future begins, we are aware of time through the sequence of events which can be established by reference to an initial point...beginning with the creation of the heavens and the earth, and ending with the creation of the new heavens and the new earth."[22]

At that time, when the rebellion is finished and no longer dominates our world view, we will be able to enjoy the quality of eternity, living in harmony with God as we were designed: "The will of God is a line of truth and goodness that is unending. It moves straight and with certainty across the universe of space, time and thought."[23]

our personal sense of order. This is a driving force, a profound sense of fulfillment that propels us into enthusiastic pursuits. Although later the nature of work becomes dreary and frustrating, man still derives great enjoyment from creativity.

What great feats man can achieve! We can construct magnificent empires, mono-lithic buildings, change the course of rivers, and carve out the landscape according to our own designs. God truly subjected this earth to our will, "giving us authority over all things."

A CONQUEROR

God intended for this new ruler to conquer and crush the original rebellion incited by Lucifer. As Spiritual Beings, humanity is in the midst of the conflict raging in the universe. We can throw all our intellectual and spiritual abilities into the foray as powerful kingdom-builders and allies.

Exactly how God proposed to use humanity to dismantle Satan's rebellion was still part of The Mystery to be revealed. Humans were clearly enemies from Satan's standpoint, since they were members of God's Kingdom. Yet, what an absurdity man at first seemed to the Evil One—naked, defenseless creatures formed from the dust and trapped inside feeble bodies—these things would invade Lucifer's kingdom on Planet Earth?

Yet here God revealed the profound nature of His Kingdom Plan: He uses "the weak things of this world to shame the things which are strong,"[25] precisely why God's plan is so incredible. He actually invites us—frail and limited though we are—to rule alongside with Him. As one author puts it:

> To please God...to be a real ingredient in the Divine happiness...to be loved by God, not merely pitied, but delighted in as an artist delights in his work or a father in a son—it seems impossible a weight or burden of glory which our thoughts can hardly sustain. But so it is. For glory means good report with God, acceptance by God, response, acknowl-edgment, and welcome into the heart of things.[26]

In Eternity Future man will be elevated above the angels.

Even though now humans are "made for a little while lower than the angels," yet God "crowned him with glory and honor, and appointed him over the works of His hands."[27] God planned for humans to end up in a seat of honor as rulers and even judges. As Paul points out,

> Do you not know that we will judge angels? *1 Corinthians 6:3*

God unleashed a race of conquering rulers on this planet. Our desire to compete and win is more than a basic instinct for survival—it is a compelling source of excitement and motivation. This is yet another reason why humans today struggle with a desire for significance, even glory and honor.

When operating under God's leadership, the rest of creation benefits from our drive for success. God established a framework for Earth's future to fall under the domain of this new creature.

TWO SIGNIFICANT TREES

All of man's great potential in God's fledgling Kingdom pivoted on a simple free will choice for Adam and Eve:

> At the center of the garden He placed the tree of life and the tree of the knowledge of good and evil. *Genesis 2:9* (NLT)

The second tree mentioned—the "tree of the knowledge of good and evil"—was a decision for self-determination and self-rule apart from God. It was a dangerous freedom, but not a complicated choice:

> "But you must never eat from the tree of the knowledge of good and evil because when you eat from it, you will certainly die." *Genesis 2:17* (GW)

✑ People object: "Why would God place such a choice there?"

Some people feel God engineered failure for these humans by making this dangerous choice available.

Yet Sovereign Will without choice is a contradiction of terms. All the devotion and love they felt towards God at this point existed because God created them this way—it was not their choice.

Still, God did not leave them trapped. God offered them the freedom to leave their relationship with Him. He did not overwhelm them with innumerable rules or complex traps to test their loyalty. Simple choice was available: believe God and remain loyal to Him, or launch a new way of life disconnected from the life of God.

PUTTING IT ALL TOGETHER It can be overwhelming to study all the intricacies of our human makeup from the biblical perspective. Yet the composition of a human is really quite simple in a broad sense: we are composed of body, soul and spirit. It is this last piece—the spirit—that holds the extraordinary potential of humanity.

As spiritual beings, we are designed to actually contain the spiritual life of God, called the Indwelling Presence of God. Neither animals nor angels contain this capacity. Without a relationship with Him, our spirits are considered dead, or devoid of God's spiritual life. Consequently, without God we are left wandering through life with a great emptiness and loneliness that only God can fulfill.

More significantly, we become victims rather than rulers without the Indwelling Presence of God. The human is severely handicapped and falls under the domain of angelic life, the next-highest created order of beings. "Further Consideration" at the end of chapter 4 explains this in greater detail.

Only a Sovereign Will Being with an option for independence can form a love relationship, a relationship so much different than fond attachment with a pet, whose choices are controlled by instinct. In order to be meaningful, a genuine love relationship requires the freedom not to love. Adam and Eve could walk away from God and reject His will for their lives.

The Tree of Life was a monumental opportunity for Adam and Eve. With this choice they could contain the spiritual life of God as designed and enjoy an eternal relationship with Him.

The Tree of Life is at the center of God's Revelation. It is found not only at the beginning of human history in Genesis 2, but also at the culmination of human exploits found in the very last book of the Bible:

> Blessed are those who wash their robes so they can enter through the gates of the city and eat the fruit from the tree of life. *Revelation 22:14*

This Tree of Life is only one instance of the marvelous unity tying the Bible together. The Tree is a remarkable opportunity for humanity: with it, He provides access into His Kingdom and His Eternal Plan with all its significance, dignity and purpose. Beyond this, the Tree of Life brings the possibility of authentic spiritual life even today for anyone who wishes to enter God's Kingdom, as we continue the unveiling of God's Mystery.

FURTHER CONSIDERATION

WHAT ABOUT EVOLUTION?

The famous movie *Inherit the Wind* with Spencer Tracey reenacted the 1925 Scopes "Monkey Trial," where a high school teacher was prosecuted for teaching evolution. The movie portrayed the Bible as teaching the earth is only 10,000 years old.

Yet there is no such "Young Earth"[28] dating scheme in the Bible. These "Young Earth" views rest largely on a theory published in 1650 by Anglican bishop James Ussher. Without the benefit of modern science, the bishop relied exclusively on Old Testament genealogical records to date the origins of earth back to 4004 B.C.[29] Such innovative use of Old Testament genealogies was never intended by the authors, a fact widely acknowledged within biblical scholarship:

> We can very clearly see that the Bible does not invite us to use the genealogies in Scripture as a chronology…The Bible is not a scientific textbook in the sense that science is not its central theme, and we do not have a comprehensive statement about the cosmos.[30] *Dr. Francis Schaeffer*

THE FAITH OF SECULAR EVOLUTION

On the other extreme are those who teach a purely Mechanical Darwinianism, which excludes the possibility of a Creator. This view is equally dogmatic and problematic:

> First, even if I were still an agnostic, as once I was, I would not accept the concept of evolution from the molecule to man in an unbroken line. My rejection of this does not turn upon my being a Christian but comes rather because I think this concept is weak and certainly has not been proven in any sense of the word. It is a theory with many unproofs. It has not been demonstrated either theoretically or empirically that time and chance can explain either the universe with its high complexity or man as man.[31]

People are surprised to discover the Mechanical Darwinism they learned in school is fraught with problems. It relies on an oversimplified and sometimes naive understanding of the mechanisms of life—complexities only discovered after Darwin's death, as one scientist explains:

> Darwin was ignorant of the reason for variation within a species (one of the requirements of his theory), but biochemistry has identified the molecular basis for it... It was once expected that the basis of life would be exceedingly simple. That expectation has been smashed.[32]

Francis Crick—who helped discover DNA—grasped the implication of his complex discoveries on Darwinianism. Although an atheist, Crick concluded that Darwinianism provided an untenable explanation for life:

> An honest man, armed with all the knowledge available to us now, could only state that in some sense, the origin of life appears at the moment to be almost a miracle, so many are the conditions which would have had to have been satisfied to get it going.[33] *Francis Crick, Nobel laureate*

BIBLICAL EVOLUTION

Within the biblical creation account there is much room for evolutionary processes, and within known science there is certainly room for divine acts of creation. To insist that the Bible and science are mutually exclusive is an extreme position of faith:

> One point often mentioned by evolutionists is that evolution is based only on fact while creation is based only on faith. This implies that no factual evidence supports creation. Neither of these implications is true. Both creationists and evolutionists rely on the same evidence as far as it goes.[34]

Although the Bible does teach that man was a special act of creation by God, this is certainly not refuted by any scientific discovery. Conversely, Mechanical Darwinism certainly conflicts with known scientific evidence and even defies logic in demonstrable ways.[35] Although the fossil record does support microevolution at the level of species, it does not support macroevolution above the level of species:

> In spite of these examples, it remains true, as every paleontologist knows, that most new species, genera, and families and that nearly all new categories above the level of families appear in the record suddenly and are not led up to by any known, gradual, completely continuous transitional sequences.[36]

THE FALL

For this one man, Adam, brought death to many through his sin.
Romans 5:15b

A LOOMING THREAT

The day came when Satan took notice of God's invasion into Planet Earth, God's small beachhead at Eden. To Satan, everything about Eden smelled like God's stifling sense of civilization Satan and his demons so despised and rebelled against. Most detestable was the reign of God's will that permeated the place—and still these naive humans loved God. Satan was determined to snatch them into his domain.

Finally, Satan found Eve alone. Mustering all his gifted cunning, he laid out the oppression of God's realm:

> Now the serpent was the shrewdest of all the creatures the Lord God had made. "Really?" he asked the woman. "Did God really say you must not eat any of the fruit in the garden?" *Genesis 3:1*

DISCONTENT

There it was now, laid before her: an outrage, the accusation that God prohibited all the good things available in the garden! It was a barb against God's authority: a prohibition, not against a few things, but "any fruit!"

This is a genius at work, and it demonstrates why the Bible calls him *diabolos*—or, "devil"—which means "The Accuser." Eve was unprepared for such cunning, and reacted defensively as expected, she snapped back:

> "Of course we may eat it," the woman told him. "It's only the fruit from the tree at the center of the garden that we are not allowed to eat." *Genesis 3:2-3a*

Then Eve made a fatal declaration:

> "God says we must not eat it or even touch it, or we will die."
> *Genesis 3:2-3*

She over-dramatized God's original injunction, "Don't eat it" into an excessive fear of the tree itself, a superstitious view not to "even touch it," as though it were a monstrous and fearful entity. The issue was simple obedience, not a poisonous tree. Her field of view was narrowed and focused on this one issue that overshadowed everything else: God's kind invitation to eat from all the other trees, and even more significantly, to eat from the Tree of Life.

Here were the seeds of discontent brilliantly sown, ready to flourish. Satan launched into a bold denunciation of God:

> The serpent said to the woman, "You surely will not die!" *Genesis 3:4*(NASB-U)

It was a gambit well-played, a shocking denunciation of God's word. Now suddenly for the first time Eve faced the possibility that God might lie. Satan embellished his attack:

> "For God knows that in the day you eat from it your eyes will be opened, and you will be like God, knowing good and evil." *Genesis 3:5* (NASB-U)

The insinuation that God exclusively reserved "knowing good and evil" for Himself intrigued Eve: Why did God conceal this knowledge? What made "knowing good and evil" so desirable? According to Satan, it was God's Achilles' heel, a threat to God "your eyes will be opened" and "you will be like God."

TO BECOME DIVINE

It was on this thought—to become like God—that Eve swayed, tottered and then crumpled under the weight of its appeal. Without consulting God, she seized rebellion with all its exciting allure: so "fresh and delicious," as Satan said, it would "make her so wise!" A decision was made:

> The woman was convinced. The fruit looked so fresh and delicious, and it would make her so wise! So she ate some of the fruit. *Genesis 3:6a*

Nobody can imagine what she experienced, but she was immediately compelled to share it with her husband, Adam. What she said is not recorded, but it worked:

> She also gave some to her husband, who was with her. Then he ate it, too. *Genesis 3:6a*

He, too, joined in rebellion. Things were different now. They underwent a sweeping transformation, alien and terrifying. It triggered an upheaval of the very nature of humanity:

> At that moment, their eyes were opened, and they suddenly felt shame at their nakedness. So they strung fig leaves together around their hips to cover themselves. *Genesis 3:7*

It was petrifying. "Their eyes were opened," seeing and feeling evil for the first time —they were disoriented. Suddenly aware of the evil in the other person, they instinctively protected themselves and sewed fig leaves together to cover up. It was complicated now. This was no longer the carefree relationship they knew earlier. They discovered alienation: the first incipient taste of the Principle of Sin.

THE SATANIC VICTORY

> **They discovered an unfamiliar knowledge: the ability to perceive good and evil, independent from God.**

They assumed a new role as the usurpers of morality, reserved previously only for the Creator God, an unnatural authority since only the Creator God knows what works within His creation. He created within a definition of right and wrong, and He never delegated it to humans, and they never inherited His wisdom and power to reshape creation around a different design. Their new morality was an alien fracture in God's creation when "He saw it was good."

More foreboding, Adam's seizure of God's throne of authority sparked a chain reaction of a long and violent history of self-will, self-direction, and self-rule, the war between creatures driven by the Principle of Sin. This costly knowledge still permeates the human realm:

> Knowledge in itself is not evil... It is knowledge apart from God that has rendered man a prisoner, a slave, and has cost him that knowledge which is eternal life.[1] *T. Austin Sparks*

Consider this...

In today's Post-modern world, it is considered normative for each person to invent morality—an inalienable right. Any encroachment triggers an outrage of "intolerance!" The Bible says the Creator has an authoritative voice in morality—without it, Sovereign Will becomes chaos.

The first two humans enjoyed their partnership with God, yet somehow decided to abandon His realm. A third of the angels also joined Satan's rebellion. What possibly stirred such a revolt?

THE LIE

The Bible traces the success of Satan's rebellion to his brilliant mastery of deception, lies that shield his violent appetite for power:

> "He was a murderer from the beginning and has always hated the truth. There is no truth in him. When he lies, it is consistent with his character; for he is a liar and the father of lies." *John 8:44*

> **The ancient, Satanic Lie is that independence from God is self-fulfilling.**

He persuaded humans to join his rebellion by promising they could "become like God." It was this raw appeal that spawned Satan's rebellion. "The snare of the devil is pride,"[2] the Bible says: the lure of self-rule, the Principle of Sin.

Far too late, it became evident that they could not become like God. Instead, they scuttled into the shadows, covered up with little fig leaves—not a brilliant or rugged choice for clothing material—cowering from the presence of God, who was their one-time close friend:

> They heard the sound of the Lord God walking in the garden in the cool of the day, and the man and his wife hid themselves from the presence of the Lord God among the trees of the garden. Then the Lord God called to the man, and said to him, "Where are you?" He said, "I heard the sound of You in the garden, and I was afraid because I was naked; so I hid myself." *Genesis 3:8-10* (NASB-U)

Satan's promises were hollow lies: Adam and Eve were not gods, not even close, and they knew it and were terrified of their frailty before the One True God.

Consider this...

Humans are easily infatuated with a sense of invincibility until faced with the real God of the universe—as Adam discovered, standing in the presence of the One "from whom earth and sky fled away."[A] *Only then it becomes preposterous that human creatures are remotely "like God."*

ALIENATION REIGNS

Like a coiled viper, the Principle of Sin suddenly struck out at the core of their marriage. When God asked, "What is this you have done?" they launch into a flurry of finger-pointing and blame-shifting:

> ...The Lord God asked. "Have you eaten the fruit I commanded you not to eat?" "Yes," Adam admitted, "but it was the woman you gave me who brought me the fruit, and I ate it." Then the Lord God asked the woman, "How could you do such a thing?" "The serpent tricked me," she replied. "That's why I ate it." *Genesis 3:12*

> **This posturing and hardened heart is so utterly alienating and so deeply scars love.**

Their harmonious marriage was shattered with finger-pointing and blame: "But it was the woman that you gave me!" Adam said in a sweeping indictment of both his

---

(A) There is clearly no way to hide from the Creator of heavens and earth: "Then I saw a great white throne and Him who sat upon it, from whose presence earth and heaven fled away, and no place was found for them." Revelation 20:11 (NASB-U)

wife and God. "It was that creature!" Eve declared. They were lost in rebellion, searching for any way to evade individual blame. Although the obvious solution was to tell the truth and admit fault, yet their indignation and posturing only hardened their hearts. It was the first sting of the Principle of Sin.

Consider this…

As the author of love, the God of the Bible still offers the prospect of healing —if we return to Him. Other philosophies offer intriguing promises of inner peace, but looking inward only triggers more loneliness. God created humans to reach out, engaged in relationships.

THE LONELINESS OF RESENTMENT

Sadly, Adam cut himself off from his only source of hope. Adam turned this new capacity for resentment against God Himself. He told God, "It was the woman you gave me!" Resentment blinded Adam against God's kindness and the wonderful provision Eve seemed at first. Adam was developing the Hardened Heart of Rebellion.

> **A hardened heart begins with a simple lack of gratitude and thankfulness—the very essence of resentment.**

Resentment isolated Adam and Eve from their Creator:

> For even though they knew God, they did not honor Him as God or give thanks…and their foolish heart was darkened. *Romans 1:21* (NASB-U)

FIELD OF DREAMS The movie *Field of Dreams* was immensely popular because it touched this deep need for closeness in a world of estrangement. It is the story of a son longing to reach across a deep rift of alienation with his father. When the movie ends, father and son enjoyed a simple game of "catch," and it brought audiences to tears because it offered a glimpse of hope—perhaps someday deep scars separating relationships will be healed. Only Eternal Beings carry this kind of hope deep inside.

Hope is dashed against the reality of a world burning with resentment—personal histories littered with broken, scarred relationships. For Adam and Eve this was a heartbreaking, alien experience, but they would grow accustomed to it. They were entering the realm of Satan's empire: a world of alienation starved for compassion and love.

One modern writer describes the apathy of despair in a loveless world: "No one to blame! ... That was why most people led lives they hated, with people they hated. ... How wonderful to have someone to blame! How wonderful to live with one's nemesis! You may be miserable, but you feel forever in the right." *Erica Jong*[3]

Since The Fall, it is impossible for people to grow close without hurting each other, since the Principle of Sin festers inside. Ironically, the evidence of a close relationship is pain. The Tin Man in the *Wizard of Oz* knew he had a heart because he felt it breaking, and audiences knew what he meant.

Without thankfulness, resentment swells and leads to the hardened heart, what the Bible calls a "darkened" and "foolish heart," and it reverberates throughout our lives.

> Watch out that no bitterness takes root among you, for as it springs up it causes deep trouble, hurting many in their spiritual lives. *Hebrews 12:15b* (Living)

Alienation from God severs us from the very source of love and the Creator of loving relationships.

Consider this…

Sometimes people dismiss God not because evidence disproves His existence— nor because the question of God's existence is trivial. Rather, the Bible says a Hardened Heart develops toward God, despite the internal conviction that God is there.

Sadly, God was compelled to remove Adam and Eve from their sanctuary in Eden. They now belonged to a hostile kingdom: the Counterfeit Kingdom which operates by cold and sterile principles foreign to God's loving authority. From here, human relationships would become violent affairs where men dominated women with savagery, children became defenseless victims, and all human relationships would be scarred with alienation from each other and God.

A MISSED OPPORTUNITY

Meanwhile, another heartbreaking decision lurked behind their new-found power of self-rule. With all their curiosity, it is amazing that Adam and Eve never ate from the Tree of Life! Had they done so, they would have contained God's Eternal Life, the highest life. They were created to become rulers over the Earth, working alongside God, but instead humanity became trapped inside a satanic rebellion, alienated from God's Eternal Plan.

WHY FORBID ACCESS TO THE TREE OF LIFE? Even though it was a mistake, why would God disallow Adam and Eve from changing their minds?

It is difficult to appreciate the vast gulf between God's Kingdom and the Counterfeit Kingdom. These are two different worlds operating by vastly divergent principles, as God describes it: "How can goodness be a partner with wickedness? How can light live with darkness?" *2 Corinthians 6:14b.* There are certain choices that bring irrevocable change, as these scholars explain:

"In the idyllic situation in which man was placed, he could eat of any fruit, including that of the Tree of Life, but he must not eat of the Tree of the Knowledge of Good and Evil. Someone would presumable be attracted by the Tree of the Knowledge of Good and Evil because of a lust for power through knowledge. He would have a selfish desire to set himself up as a god and so be independent of God. This would lead to a life centered on self and not on God, who is Love. In the day in which Adam chose such a life he (in reality) chose death. (Genesis 2:17) It is clear that he could not choose the way of death and also choose to eat of the Tree of Life. In choosing the one he lost the opportunity to eat of the other."[4] *Forster and Marsten*

After their disobedience it was too late. God placed an angelic being with a flaming sword to keep them from the Tree of Life—they were now poisoned. God could never allow creatures controlled by the Principle of Sin to contain His spiritual life.

∾ The choice was never between right and wrong, but between spiritual life and spiritual death.

At the very heart of the tragedy in the Garden of Eden is not a moral choice, but a spiritual choice. This is important, because people trivialize their problem with God and do not see the life or death struggle with far-reaching implications.

So many people think God weighs their lives on a scale, good deeds weighed against bad. When the scale tips toward good deeds, God is satisfied. This viewpoint is entirely foreign to God's Revelation.

Clearly with Adam and Eve there was only one choice that brought alienation, not a lifelong balance of deeds.

Consider this...
God makes the same Free Will choice available today: either self-rule with alienation from God—or the choice to contain His spiritual life and enjoy an eternal relationship with Him.

∾ Throughout the Bible, these two choices continually resurface.

The Bible is a long shelf of 66 books, and this theme is like the "bookends" on the shelf, prominent at the beginning and end of the Bible. For example, in Revelation, the last book of the Bible, the Tree of Life is mentioned again depicting Eternal Life, and He makes a remarkable offer to any who will listen:

> "I will give the right to eat from the tree of life, which is in the paradise of God." *Revelation 22:7* (NIV)

SIN The Bible uses a broad term that describes human nature resulting from The Fall: Sin. It encompasses so much—self-rule, alienation, spiritual death, the hardened heart and a mass of destructive appetites that dominate a life in rebellion against God.

People think Sin is limited to doing something wrong; in the Bible, Sin is being someone wrong. It is a nature inherited from Adam: "through the one man's disobedience the many were made sinners" *Romans 5:19a* (NASB-U). Other terms like Sin Nature and The Flesh convey the same meaning.

The term Sin means to "miss the mark", describing a character which deviates from God's character and the way He created us "in His image." In short, Sin is deviance.[5] God, by his very nature, cannot allow Sin to continue forever: it is the singular source of the suffering and evil found in Creation.

We prefer Principle of Sin because it isolates a simple drive that triggers such a vast world of deviance and evil: self-rule.

FINALLY, DEATH

Born that day was the monster called death, an obscenity few dare mention and a scar on the face of life. There is no beauty in death, despite our modern skills at dressing up a dead body, and although we can isolate death in specialized institutions, there is no escaping its sting.

Some philosophies claim death is natural and even a beautiful extension of life, but to God it is an enemy, a perversion of our purpose as reigning kings which He intends to eradicate from the human experience:

> He will wipe away every tear from their eyes; and there will no longer be any death; there will no longer be any mourning, or crying, or pain; the first things have passed away. *Revelation 21:4* (NASB-U)

Adam died that day as God warned, but it was not immediate physical death. Rather, Adam experienced spiritual death: separation from the life of God Himself through rebellion and self-rule. He passed from God's Kingdom into Satan's Counterfeit Kingdom marred by death.

God's view of death differs sharply from our view. Physical death is not the most tragic incident in a person's life, necessarily. To God, a person can be dead even while seemingly alive.[6] Mankind was now alienated from God, and our spiritual faculties designed to be in fellowship with Him were suddenly left empty and lifeless, without purpose.

❧ Spiritual death set into motion a chain reaction that ultimately brings physical suffering and death.

God's power no longer sustained physical human life, and although humanity gained independence from God, His protection was lost. Without God's Eternal Life, we face decay and ultimately physical death, the great terror of a lifetime.

THE FEAR OF DEATH Satan uses the fear of death to drive his captives in the Counterfeit Kingdom into a sense of resignation and even despair about the future. The approach of death looms as a great unknown, a dark and foreboding tragedy: "...death is the obscene mystery, the ultimate affront, the thing that cannot be controlled. It can only be denied." *Susan Sontag*[7]

A despairing humanity is easily controlled by "him who holds the power of death, that is, the devil."[8] Thinking that life can only be "short and brutish," people resign themselves to the grim pickings offered by the Counterfeit Kingdom—some stimulation, a little wealth, maybe recognition—none of these yield any substance or meaning to life. These are difficult issues to face: "His was a great sin who first invented consciousness. Let us lose it for a few hours." *F. Scott Fitzgerald*[9]

Because of His great love, God was not content to leave humanity without hope, bound under the authority of Satan, and He set into motion a plan to purchase people out of captivity and remove Satan's claim: it is called The Ransom.

Consider this…

It is inconsistent to pursue independence from God while holding Him accountable for the evil results. People spend a lifetime of pursuit apart from God, then fault Him for a lack of protection against an evil world.

✐ Satan lied to Eve by claiming she could become "like God."

Quite the opposite, humankind became weaker, a victim of the fallen nature with its sickness, wars, and powers beyond our control. Under the domain of Satan's Counterfeit Kingdom, humanity must fend for itself without God's provision, struggling to meet the most basic, instinctual needs. This is the meaning behind God's declaration to Adam:

> Cursed is the ground because of you; In toil you will eat of it all the days of your life. *Genesis 3:17* (NASB-U)

ARTIFICIAL LIFE

The Bible says, "you were alienated from God" at birth, and "born dead in your trespasses and sins."[10] No longer governed by God, we are now governed by the Principle of Sin. This extends to the offspring of Adam and Eve—they were given the authority to "multiply, fill the earth." This was a genuine authority with far-reaching implications. They established their offspring outside of God's Kingdom when they chose this for themselves.

✐ Adam's offspring are also born "spiritually dead."

Today everyone is born spiritually dead. It is evident in the pervasive apathy and denseness towards God triggered by the loss of spiritual faculties. This may seem strange, because humans historically engage in ritual observances, yet these superficial activities bear no resemblance to God's original intention to "dwell among them." Ethereal rituals feel other-worldly and seem spiritual, but God is unimpressed with recitations, incantations, and somber rituals.[11] At best, these man-made atmospheres with incense, music and dim lighting only conjure an artificial spiritual life.

Spiritually frustrated and empty, people are content to supplant real spiritual life with occasional rituals, and otherwise avoid thinking or discussing spiritual life because it touches an unfamiliar realm, something uncomfortable. Although God "set eternity in the hearts of men" at creation, humans are born blind and cannot navigate His spiritual realm—deeply mystified about spiritual realities.

Consider this…

The Bible says that spiritual alienation arises from a spiritually-dead character at birth, and the only hope for spiritual life comes from the outside: God reaching out to humanity.

> ✎ **Sheer human will power will not establish a vital relationship with God.**

Manmade religion tries to reach God through self-effort and will power—through asceticism, abstinence, or rigorous discipline—an approach certain to fail because spiritual life cannot be manufactured. A more radical overhaul of man's fallen nature is required.[B]

God's solution is called the Redemptive Plan.

GOD'S REDEMPTIVE PLAN

Even in this apparently dark hour, God provides the first hint of His solution for man's plight. It is a plan of sweeping proportions:

> For he has rescued us from the one who rules in the kingdom of darkness, and he has brought us into the Kingdom of his dear Son. *Colossians 1:13*

Immediately after The Fall, God turns to Satan and gives an amazing prophecy:

> "And I will put enmity...between your seed and her seed; He shall bruise you on the head, And you shall bruise him on the heel." *Genesis 3:15* (NASB-U)

THE SOURCE OF FALSE RELIGIONS
Many religions claim that God is found within each of us if we summon the will power to find Him, or through harsh discipline gain His approval. The Bible rejects these views because man is spiritually dead and cannot naturally contain the life of God.

Satan propagates counterfeit religions all based on the Principle of Sin: the promise of retaining self-sufficiency and independence while performing rituals to appease the conscience. These rituals offer no spiritual life, the Bible says: "These are matters which have, to be sure, the appearance of wisdom in self-made religion and self-abasement and severe treatment of the body." *Colossians 2:23* (NASB-U)

God's enemy is not so dense as to proclaim, "Join me in hating God and everything He stands for!" Rather, Satan can appear as "an angel of light", and his conspirators "also disguise themselves like servants of righteousness"[12] the Bible says. Entire religious systems originate in the demonic realm, steering people away from the One True God: "Some will abandon the faith and follow deceiving spirits and things taught by demons." *1 Timothy 4:1* (NIV)

Here the biblical viewpoint runs against popular belief that all religions lead to the same god—a view that ignores the reality of deceiving spirits. Satan lied to Eve. Is it impossible that some religious philosophies are merely speculative, and might be erroneous?

So many religions seem attractive and full of good works—replete with momentary emotional reward—but God is opposed to anything that places man's will at the center of the universe.

(B) See Further Consideration: "The Makeup of Mankind" at the end of this chapter, for an in-depth discussion of the effect of The Fall on human nature.

This was a prophecy of the eventual defeat of the Ruler of Darkness at the hand of someone from "her seed," born without a human father. Although Satan would inflict a wound on this descendant of Eve, this descendant would inflict a mortal wound on Satan, "on the head."

This was the first prophecy of Christ's coming to Earth, born of a virgin and of the work He was coming to do:

> But when the right time came, God sent his Son, born of a woman...to buy freedom for us who were slaves to the law, so that he could adopt us as his very own children. *Galatians 4:4-5*

God's plan "to buy freedom for us" is called Redemption in the Bible, which literally means, "to purchase out of slavery." Since Adam and Eve fell under the domain of Satan's Counterfeit Kingdom, God has to purchase us—redeem us— out of this slavery by paying a ransom.

This is God's Redemptive Plan, the greatest revelation of God's wisdom and power in all of history. Even here, at The Fall when man's beginnings appear so meager and hopeless, God provides the first substantial insight into The Mystery, and then expands and builds upon it throughout the Bible as God's Incredible Plan unfolds.

FURTHER CONSIDERATION

THE MAKEUP OF MANKIND

Because we are Eternal Beings, even the most dogmatic atheist cannot live with the bleak view of humans as a chance collection of molecules. At some point the atheist lays aside this bleak philosophy to build significance and purpose in life:

> I don't see myself as so much dust that has appeared in the world, but as a being that was expected, prefigured, called forth. In short, as a being that could, it seems, come only from a creator."[13] *Jean Paul Sarte, existentialist philosopher and atheist.*

The Bible explains why the human being is so strongly linked to eternity: it is linked to our three-part nature:

> May your spirit and soul and body be preserved complete, without blame at the coming of our Lord Jesus Christ. *1 Thessalonians 5:23* (NASB-U)

The Body is called the "Outermost Man,"[14] our material container, what we hold in common with the animal kingdom. It is our "sense-consciousness"[15] and contains instinctive drives and feelings. It can be a marvelous instrument for the expression of the soul. Through the body, we interact with the world around us with our five senses. Yet it is a temporary and fragile container, composed merely of the "dust from the ground," like "jars of clay,"[16] and bound by space and time, unlike angels. As humans we all struggle with the sense of finiteness our bodies impose on our existence, especially as we grow older. But there is so much more to man than the creaturely body.

The Soul contains our personality traits, which include among other things our mind, free will power, emotions, moral consciousness, and eternity of existence. So incredibly distinct from animals, these qualities enable humans to realize that God exists, and we understand that our lives will extend beyond death.

With our Soul we chart our lives: plotting a path with our reason, launching new directions with free will. We comprehend the implications of these chosen directions by moral consciousness, and with memories we audit our choices. With our Soul, there is the enormous risk that humans can chart a clear path away from God; or, we can enjoy the privilege of joining His direction for eternity. Our Soul enables us to build relationships and fortify our chosen course by forming coalitions with other humans and even with God Himself, building societies more powerful than the sum of the parts. What incredible potential God unleashed with humanity!

The Spirit is at the core of our being, and is our most precious possession. It is a unique capacity to actually contain the very life of God inside us, resulting in Eternal Life:

> And now you are united with the one who was raised from the dead.
> *Romans 7:4b*

Our Spirit provides the faculties to relate on a spiritual dimension, to share our feelings and thoughts with God:

> He has given us his very great and precious promises, so that through them you may participate in the divine nature. *2 Peter 1:4a* (NIV)

By giving man a Spirit, God elevated him to a lofty position of prestige and honor unavailable to the angels.[17] The Spirit becomes the home of the indwelling presence of God, where He invites us to share in the unity and intimacy of God:

> Who can know what the Lord is thinking? Who can give him counsel?
> But we can understand these things, for we have the mind of Christ.
> *1 Corinthians 2:16*

Humans were made like a glove to contain Eternal Life, the life of God. In short, man was placed at the very apex of creation here on Planet Earth, designed to not only relate with God, but to actually contain His very life within our beings.

AFTER THE FALL

The Fall triggered a massive upheaval in our makeup:

Man's Spirit no longer contained the life of God—it became dead and empty—and we lost the capacity to understand and experience things of the Spirit.[18]

Our Soul became the controlling part of man, separated from the life of God. We are now governed only by mind, will, and emotions. We lost the ability to "see things, as it were, from His point of view." (Colossians 1:9).

Tragically, man's body became perishable without the sustaining life of God. But this is something He will change: "We…groan to be released from pain and suffering. We, too, wait anxiously for that day when God will give us our full rights as his children, including the new bodies he has promised us." (Romans 8:23)

Without His spiritual life, we cannot function in the capacity God intended for us. Instead, there remains a certain flatness and emptiness to life:

You have made us for yourself, and our hearts are restless until they rest
in you. Augustine.[19]

There are actually four levels of life in the universe today: the highest is divine Life,
God's Eternal Life; then in descending order of rank comes angelic life, human life,
and finally animal and vegetable life.[20] Humans are not alone in the universe, and
we are not at the top of the created order. Without containing the life of God, we
become truly handicapped, victims of other life forms.

People sometimes display an alarming blindness toward their human limitations.
The Bible teaches a more sober perspective about man the creature: without God's
Spirit, man is by default ruled by the next-highest order, angelic life. In fact, man
is brought directly under the control of Satan himself and his Counterfeit
Kingdom when God's authority is absent.

THE CULT OF MAN

"To me the sole hope of human salvation lies in teaching Man to…regard his hands as God's hand, his brain as God's brain, his purpose as God's purpose. He must regard God as a helpless Longing…"[1]
George Bernard Shaw, playwright, critic.

THE PROGRESSION

The tragedy of The Fall unleashed a new phenomenon on Planet Earth never before seen: a gathering force, a threat to God's Kingdom Plan called the Principle of Sin. Hatred ignites into flames of violence in the hands of this potent, unique creature called man.

Simultaneously, humanity builds sophisticated civilizations and religious systems, incubating the rebellion and fortifying the alienation between man and Creator God. A new culture emerges with a hideous strength: a glorious and satanic empire threatening God's Kingdom Plan.

∽ **God's Kingdom will never be derailed: it always moves forward with those who are willing.**

Even while this darkness envelopes the earth, an isolated, seemingly insignificant spark of God's Kingdom is carried forward through the agency of a few willing hearts. The Mystery is germinating and taking root.

A SPARK OF VIOLENCE

Adam and Eve were the first to see the tragedy of violence tear apart their own family with their sons, Cain and Able. Cain offered a sacrifice to God, and was met with a rebuke from God that the sacrifice was performed improperly. Abel's sacrifice, on the other hand, was welcomed by God. This was an affront to Cain's dignity as the older brother, and a humiliation at the hand of his younger brother he could not tolerate.

For a moment, Cain stood on the precipice of a monumental choice that shaped the course of his life, and God tried to save him:

"Why are you so angry?" the Lord asked him. "Why do you look so dejected? You will be accepted if you respond in the right way. But if you refuse to respond correctly, then watch out! Sin is waiting to attack and destroy you, and you must subdue it." *Genesis 4:6-7*

Consider this...

Cain reached a point of decision, crossed it, and entered into a dark world of resentment where even God Himself could not reach. Such is the strength of our Sovereign Free Will.

Cain simmered, plotting and stalking Able until he finally caught him alone in a field. There he brutally murdered his own brother. It was a gruesome execution—nobody had ever murdered before. The blood of his younger brother was splattered all over and soaked the ground. God confronted Cain by pointing to the gruesome scene:

"What have you done? The voice of your brother's blood is crying to me from the ground!" *Genesis 4:10*

It was a heartbreaking tragedy for Adam and Eve to see murder and death in their own family. They were the first people to witness the horrifying violence that drives Satan's Counterfeit Kingdom.

CAIN'S ESCAPISM
When Cain was faced with his sin, he challenged God's right to ask him about Abel: "Am I my brother's keeper?"[3]

This is the typical reaction of a heart in rebellion against God, the hardened heart first revealed in the garden—an argument, a thrust and parry between man and God, evading the real problem of dark rebellion. At a practical level we see the breakdown of the relationship with God by refusing to deal honestly with Him.

Cain refused to deal with God any further, and declared, "From your face I have

THE DARKENED HEART Cain's efforts to hide the rebellion in his heart were useless because God's Light is so penetrating it brings each one of us to either respond and bow to His will, or it drives us into further rebellion: "People who do what is wrong hate the light and don't come to the light. They don't want their actions to be exposed." *John 3:20 (GW)*

Here the decadence of the Principle of Sin flourishes: Adam originally sinned only against God, but Cain took the rebellion to a new level by sinning against both God and his brother. Man's inhumanity against man was born, but the first murder would not be the last one. From here the Principle of Sin escalates into bloodshed between households, villages, even entire civilizations—the scepter is always wielded by brute among hardened hearts:

"We used to wonder where war lived, what it was that made it so vile. And now we realize that we know where it lives, that it is inside ourselves." *Albert Camus.*[2]

been hidden." Yet this was a lie: God did not withdraw from Cain. God mercifully offered protection for Cain from reprisals, but Cain settled into a permanent state of alienation with God.[4]

THE CULT OF MAN

At a superficial level, Cain's life was anything but a failure. He built a city: the first sophisticated human society. Cain's descendants established agriculture, commercial enterprises, and they invented metallurgy. Music and the arts emerge through Cain's line—all great feats of accomplishments.

Yet Cain's line was not the development of a peaceful civilization. Alongside these spectacular feats we see man's quest for greatness—and necessarily, violence— increase for generations until it culminates in the appalling brutality of Lamech, who gloats, "I have killed a boy for striking me." Lamech boasts he is more ruthless than Cain:

> "If anyone who kills Cain is to be punished seven times, anyone who takes revenge against me will be punished seventy-seven times!" *Genesis 4:24*

Lamech was proclaiming he no longer required God's protection like his ancestor Cain. He was a powerful and ruthless man—his very name means "powerful"— who nobody dared to cross. He seized whatever he wanted without fear, and he was the first bigamist.[5]

KOSMOS

Cain and his line inaugurated the Cult of Man: what the Bible calls the Kosmos. The word means "system" or "adornment"[6] and it has the appearance of prosperity and glittering wealth. Yet beneath the surface we see what is called a "Heart of Darkness."[7] Man's systems are not independent, because they operate by the authority and tenets of Satan's Counterfeit Kingdom.

Consider this...

The Cult of Man is a counterfeit of God's Kingdom, and although it holds superficial allure, since God is entirely excluded it lacks permanence. Man's system is the deification of humanity and its accomplishments, a counterfeit "god."

The Kosmos offers thrills and excitement, moments of great accomplishment, stimulation, and the promise of wealth and stature. But all this is a poor substitute for the reality God offers. The Kosmos is actually a bleak and pointless world because the personal involvement of the Creator is excluded. Without God, none of it makes sense. Something is missing:

> The heavens are yours, and the earth is yours; everything in the world is yours—you created it all. *Psalm 89:11*

SETH STARTS A NEW LINE OF MEN

God's plan appears jeopardized when godly Able is murdered. Now where are the hearts willing to trust in God? None arose from Cain's line.

❧ Yet God always keeps his plan from being derailed or destroyed.

Another child was born to Eve named "Seth"—meaning "replacement"[8]—and he continues in the tradition of Able. Seth starts a new line of men who "lived…in close fellowship with the Lord,"[9] and:

> It was during his lifetime that people first began to worship the Lord. *Genesis 4:26b*

Superficially, Seth's line appears less spectacular than Cain's, even though Seth's people are also creative and accomplish noteworthy feats. The difference is emphasis. The hallmark of Seth's line is not the accomplishments, but a genuine unity of purpose with God's Kingdom and authority. There is something profoundly wise about Seth's legacy.

Consider this…

In the end it is Seth's line that lasts into Eternity Future. Through Seth God unfolds His Kingdom Plan on earth through The Mystery: the fulfillment of

THE POWER OF CHAOS There is no great destiny or purpose as promised in the Kosmos because it is so fragile and its rewards are so fleeting: a realm of perpetual instability where promises are broken. However formidable it may appear, the Kosmos breeds anarchy since it is based on a Relativistic[A] viewpoint with each person at the center of his own universe. Without God as a reference point, one man elevates his views over others, and a clash of wills is inevitable. Only the coercion and brutality wielded by Lamech can subdue the anarchy.

Even in our modern, urbane world secular thinkers can see what lurks beneath the surface: "The fundamental concept in social science is Power, in the same sense in which Energy is the fundamental concept in physics."[10] Bertrand Russell, British philosopher, mathematician, social critic.

Thankfully, not everyone translates jealousy into murder like Cain, although it is true that all humans share Cain's potential for violence, given the right conditions:

Therefore pride is their necklace; The garment of violence covers them. *Psalm 73:6* (NASB-U)

It is a perversion of God's original plan: created as benevolent rulers, outside of God's kingdom we use this power to crush. We were given authority to bring order and harmony to this planet, but apart from God this sovereignty stirs more chaos, and Lamech's dictatorship becomes not only commonplace, but a practical necessity. We prefer to think of ourselves as individuals, free with inviolable wills, but truthfully we are coerced and conformed to a world not of our liking, by others not of our choice. Lamech's boastful words were those of a fool who did not understand the power of chaos, because sooner or later he, too, would surely fall prey to another more powerful Lamech.

(A) Relativism is a philosophy that is "The doctrine that knowledge, truth, and morality exist in relation to culture, society, or historical context, and are not absolute." [OED].

God's prophecy to Eve that through her "seed" would come One to crush the ruler of this world.[11]

As with Cain's line, we see creativity, authority, and accomplishments we see in Seth's line that retain their proper role and do not remove God from His throne.

NOAH'S WALK

As untold centuries pass, man's rebellion against God accelerates in violence and scope, and the relentless drive of the Kosmos threatened to sweep all of humanity in its momentum. God's Kingdom Plan was headed for failure. God was deeply grieved over the growing hopelessness of mankind:

> The Lord saw how great man's wickedness on the earth had become, and that every inclination of the thoughts of his heart was only evil all the time. The Lord was grieved that he had made man on the earth, and his heart was filled with pain. *Genesis 6:5-6*

Consider this...
God is not stoic and detached: He sees, He is involved, He is grieved at what He sees, and He will even move history to save humanity.

It is hard to imagine how depraved the atrocities were that provoked God because the Bible provides few details. Yet God's revulsion speaks volumes:

> Now the earth had become corrupt in God's sight, and it was filled with violence. *Genesis 6:11*

Reaching unsurpassed levels, the violence of the Kosmos threatened to engulf the entire race. Despite this threat, the Creator of the heavens and earth is never caught off-guard. He was going to intervene in human history with a massive flood.

THE WILLING HEART
~ **No matter how hopeless man's rebellion becomes, God always finds a willing man and continues His plan.**

God's man is Noah who, along with his family, continued to trust in Him. He ordered Noah to build the ark as a refuge for his family during the flood.

The ark demonstrates the principle that God sustains and provides for the security of His people. God Himself shut the door of the ark, sealing them safely inside for the duration of His judgment.[12]

Throughout history believers like Noah and his family are subjected to the ridicule—even great persecution—from those heavily vested in the Kosmos. The reason is obvious: Noah's pursuits seem foolish compared with the great exploits of others in Cain's line. Worse yet, the pursuits of men like Noah are a repudiation of greatness inside the Kosmos.

Consider this…

God's Kingdom seemed so trivial to the people of that day, and His people so insignificant and paltry. Years later all that changed, when Noah entered the ark and "the Lord closed the door behind him."

DESTRUCTION AND NEW LIFE

The Flood unleashed the judgment of God that demonstrates His character: Holiness and Righteousness. He judged because humanity degenerated. Instead of benevolent authority to "rule and subdue the earth," man in rebellion plunders and destroys God's creation.

God's Holy character compels Him to counter this destruction with judgment: an unleashing of His wrath, justice, and omnipotence.[B] His character does not allow Him to stand by, aloof.

> ✍ **But God's judgment is also an act of Love as He saves those who respond to Him.**

When the earth had sufficiently dried, Noah and his family emerged from the ark into an incredible new world of promise and hope, miraculously marked by a rainbow. The terror of the judgment was left behind. God celebrated this new beginning with an unconditional covenant with Noah, promising that the earth would not again be destroyed by a flood.[13]

Moved by the expansive sight of the rainbow and God's unconditional promise, Noah joyfully offered a sacrifice to God. There was so much promise, so much potential: the human race had a new beginning! God re-commissioned Noah, reminding him of the greatness and lofty authority humans hold in their grasp:

WHEN GOD JUDGES The judgment of God seems harsh to people because it is equated with the vindictiveness often typical of human justice. But God operates from His character, not human nature. His judgment is always motivated by concern and love.

The judgment of God puts an abrupt end to human free choice. He allows human Sovereign Will, but limits the destructive potential. He will not remain passive while the chaos of rebellion devours humanity, as in Noah's day.

Man could learn so much from this tragic demonstration of what rebellion against God yields. Unfortunately, history repeats itself, as Jesus warns, when the same level of corruption that prevailed before the Flood is repeated at the end of man's history.[14]

Until then, however, God continues to deal with us patiently, and He allows Sovereign Will to exist, within boundaries: "He doesn't want to destroy anyone but wants all people to have an opportunity to turn to him and change the way they think and act." *2 Peter 3:9* (GW)

(B) Omnipotence is a technical term that describes the nature of God, "having unlimited power; able to do anything." [OED]

And God blessed Noah and his sons and said to them, "Be fruitful and multiply, and fill the earth. The fear of you and the terror of you will be on every beast of the earth and on every bird of the sky; with everything that creeps on the ground, and all the fish of the sea, into your hand they are given." *Genesis 9:1-2 (NASB-U)*

As a race, humans have always wielded great authority and held sway over their surroundings, so that "the terror of you will be in every beast of the earth…" We are indeed a formidable and extraordinary presence on Planet Earth.

Consider this…

God gave us great freedom and power—but also a great responsibility. By living a life in relationship with Him, we can discharge this awesome commission with confidence and have joy at the outcome. Conversely, it is dishonest to lead a life separated from God's authority and then grow embittered at Him for the results.

A MONUMENT TO THE CULT OF MAN

Generations pass after godly Noah, and yet again the race of man drifted away from the Creator. Along the way, a dominant emperor-king named Nimrod emerged who unified mankind with fantastic accomplishments, building six of the great ancient cities of the world. Two of those cities lasted for centuries as prodigious centers of culture: Nineveh later became the capitol of the formidable Assyrian empire, and Babel—later known as "Babylon the Great"—was the heart of the Babylonian Kingdom.[15]

All these cities and structures required huge populations of labor—working without machines, without modern safety concerns, and largely by trial-and-error —the human cost was phenomenal.

How Nimrod dominated all of humanity is not detailed for us, yet we do know not many people submit without cruel threats or bloodshed involved. Nimrod was driven by the timeless pursuit to make for himself a great name, and he belongs to the elite and vicious class of world rulers like Julius Caesar, Augustus, Napoleon and even Hitler—yet this man lived the dream of Empire that others only tasted, because Nimrod actually ruled all of humanity.

Buildings have a way of capturing the loyalty and imagination of people, and Nimrod as a gifted builder, knew it and controlled this phenomenon. His supreme venture was a monolithic tower at Babel to serve as the foundation of an enduring empire, fueling the zeal of the people:

"Let's build a great city with a tower that reaches to the skies—a monument to our greatness! This will bring us together and keep us from scattering all over the world." *Genesis 11:4*

∽ **The driving force behind the Kosmos is the allure of self-rule.**

This was no ordinary citadel. It was a temple-tower, a proud, eternal "monument to our greatness." Even more foreboding, it had clearly religious overtones—yet not for the worship of God.

THE CENTER OF POWER

Babel, the city they built around the tower, is infamous throughout the Bible.[16] The city is rebuilt, embellished and expanded into the glittering city "Babylon the Great"—and it becomes the epitome of the Cult of Man. Nimrod built it to seize the reigns of history and make his empire the center of authority on earth.

The tower project clearly brought Nimrod's kingdom into a direct clash with God. As God prepared to enter into judgment and once again intervene in human history, He declared something at once incredible and ominous about the human race:

> "Look!" he said. "If they can accomplish this when they have just begun
> to take advantage of their common language and political unity, just
> think of what they will do later. Nothing will be impossible for them!"
> *Genesis 11:6*

A united humanity is a hideous strength. Sharing the same culture and language[17] means "Nothing will be impossible for them!" Humanity destroys itself in the absence of any restraint from its rebellion.

THE OPIUM OF THE PEOPLE Like so many of the massive buildings in ancient history, this tower was the center of religious worship. Archeologists have unearthed ziggurats in this area of Mesopotamia used for astrological observations,[18] "a tower that reaches to the heavens!"

Manmade religions and superstitious idol-worship are the historic tool of the elite to give legitimacy and devotion to The System. Nimrod's empire was no different. It was rightly said by Karl Marx that, "Religion is the sigh of the oppressed creature, the heart of a heartless world, and the soul of soulless conditions. It is the opium of the people."[19]

Repeatedly throughout human history, the elite and powerful have created gods and religions, not only to impose control over The System they lead, but also to contain God Himself and make God into an image of man.

In the modern world, marvels of human engineering like the World Trade Center evoke a sense of awe and invincibility, and a towering 300-foot ziggurat was no less breathtaking to ancient man.[20] Civilization takes hold and thrives around such grand projects, and they stir an almost religious faith in the Cult of Man, as the architect of the Twin Towers said:

"'World trade means world peace...' and consequently the World Trade Center 'becomes a living representation of man's belief in humanity...his belief in the cooperation of men, and through this cooperation his ability to find greatness.'"[21]

STRUCK DOWN

God struck Nimrod's empire with division and confusion:

> Come, let us go down and confuse their language so they will not under-
> stand each other. *Genesis 11:7 (NIV)*

Left without communication—so vital to man's ability to unify—it was impossible for the people in Nimrod's empire to complete the tower. His empire crum-
bled:

> So the Lord scattered them from there over all the earth, and they stopped
> building the city. *Genesis 11:8 (NIV)*

Thus it was God who scattered mankind across the globe and set into motion the
nationalism and ethnicity that divides humanity still today. Yet it was not God who
ignited the millennia of wars and blood feuds between nations: that springs out of
the rebellious heart of man.

> What is causing the quarrels and fights among you? Isn't it the whole
> army of evil desires at war within you? You want what you don't have,
> so you scheme and kill to get it…And yet the reason you don't have
> what you want is that you don't ask God for it. *James 4:1-2*

IS GOD AGAINST UNITY? What a testimony to God's genius that humanity was created
with such potency that "nothing will be impossible for them." This strength arises from our
ability to form societies, however, and not found in a lone individual. From the outset, God created
humans as social creatures, not only for fulfillment, but we also wield an awesome power as a
community. The whole is greater than the sum of its parts.

As with any great capacity, human society can be a destructive weapon—as when Hitler
unleashed the Germans against the world—or, it can become a source of benevolent authority as
God intended. The Romans formed an irresistible, conquering machine under gifted leaders like
Julius Caesar, and in the process overwhelmed less-unified enemies.

Yet God does want mankind to come together in unity—under His leadership. As God works in
history, a powerful and loving kingdom emerges that sweeps the globe. In the very next chapter,
Genesis 12:1-3, God unveils His alternative to Nimrod's unity. Through Abraham, God promises,
"I will make your name great," and "in you all the families of the earth will be blessed." Unlike
Caesar's armies, the Kingdom of God uses different weapons: loving persuasion and free will
choice, not brutal coercion. His promise to Abraham materializes into a formidable kingdom
without parallel, and quite impossible to stop because God Himself leads His people.

The modern "global economy" phenomena appears so fresh and promising, an evolutionary step
from the barbarism, racism and bloody nationalism that stains human history. Not so from God's
perspective. Even this modern, enlightened world of democracy and free trade is guided by
ruthless competition, not God's love. Only God, the author of love, can use love to unite humanity
into the benevolent and powerful community He created us to enjoy.

THE ULTIMATE SYSTEM

If one person's rebellion against God brings so much destruction—as was the case with Adam—then humanity united in rebellion greatly amplifies the destructive power of a hardened heart. This is why God stopped Nimrod's empire:

> "If the whole human race remained united in the proud attempt to take its destiny into its own hands and, by its man-centered efforts, to seize the reins of history, there would be no limit to its unrestrained rebellion against God. The kingdom of man would displace and exclude the kingdom of God." *NASB Study Bible*

God knows the genius of man can overcome virtually any barrier, whether it's over-population or a shortage of resources. The threat of our demise comes from that same human nature that caused Lamech to boast, "I've killed a man for wounding me, and a boy for insulting me!" With our great potential we will discover a way to destroy ourselves.

> **Mankind united in rebellion against God will result in the self-destruction of the human race.**

The Bible says that God must again intervene to save humanity from building the Ultimate System in the future. A united humanity apart from God ultimately brings about the demise of human rule on earth, not some natural disaster. Jesus Christ explains what will happen some day:

> "Unless that time of calamity is shortened, the entire human race will be destroyed." *Matthew 24:22a*

The unification of humanity cannot possibly bring about a benign, utopian world because it is led by men like Nimrod or Lamech. There is only one way to attain leadership in the Kosmos: fallen, power-hungry brutality.

Today, however, mankind is increasingly capable of overcoming the communication barrier imposed by God to preserve man from the Ultimate System. When that occurs, the Kosmos will implode from the chaos of the rebellion and men like Nimrod and Lamech who crave power. God's Kingdom, on the other hand, will never cease.

FURTHER CONSIDERATION

THE HISTORICITY OF THE BIBLE

Objections are raised against the Bible's reliability due to supposedly "legendary" or "mythical" accounts such as The Flood in Genesis, the parting of the Red Sea in Exodus, and other accounts of God's miraculous interventions in human history.

CAN A MODERN, EDUCATED MIND BELIEVE IN MIRACLES?

If the Bible is actually a record of God's supernatural acts in history—as it purports —then it is plausible that miracles would occur. The clear issue is whether or not God exists. Francis Schaeffer helps to focus the issue:

> The Bible is not a scientific textbook in the sense that science is not its central theme, and we do not have a comprehensive statement about the cosmos. But the Bible tells us much about the cosmos in reference to the central theme.[22]

There is a clear difference in themes between a scientific textbook and the Bible. It does not mean, however, that these two fields of study are inherently contradictory, as Schaeffer continues:

> Science by its natural limitations cannot know all we know from God in the Bible, but in those cases where science can know, both sources of knowledge arrive at the same point, even if the knowledge is expressed in different terms.[23]

Although a thorough treatment of these questions is beyond the scope of this book, we can offer helpful bibliographies and credible evidence in the sidebars and Further Consideration sections as the issues arise.

WHAT ABOUT THE FLOOD?

Did this event really happen, or is it perhaps a mythical way ancient people described what they could not explain?

Of all the ancient events recorded in the Bible, The Flood is arguably the most widely supported and corroborated by literatures and civilizations across the globe, found in nearly every ancient culture in one form or another. Even skeptics admit the pervasive recounting of The Flood account, found even in pre-Columbian South American cultures.[24]

Obviously such evidence does not prove The Flood, but it does provide a reasonable thinker enough evidence to suspend judgment until more facts are available. Conversely, there is no strong evidence that the Flood is a fabricated story. Summarizing the debate, these scholars point out the range of interpretations of Genesis 6:

> Some believe the flood was spread over the whole earth, while others insist it was limited to the Mesopotamian basin or some other defined geographical area in the Near East. The point is that Scripture is anxious only to teach it was God's judgment on all mortals living on earth except the eight on the ark. On the other matters we must await more information.[25]

THE CHOSEN RACE

A SHIFT OF STRATEGY

Out of the ashes of Nimrod's empire, from Ur of the Chaldees near Babylon,[1] God raised a man destined to become the most celebrated in the Old Testament. Into the modern era, this man's life carries unparalleled impact. His name is equally meaningful to Jews as well as Arabs, but it extends to people across the globe:

> So Abraham is the spiritual father of those who believe and are saved without obeying Jewish laws. *Romans 4:11b* (Living)

God launched a new era with Abraham. It was a strategic shift away from working with mankind at large—humanity at large was so indifferent and rebellious. He then launched The Mystery as a beachhead against Satan's Counterfeit Kingdom.

On a seemingly insignificant slice of land known as Canaan—no bigger than the state of Vermont—God set aside a Promised Land, and for thousands of years from this strategic point God endeavors to reach the hearts of men, transforming literally billions of lives with His Kingdom of hope and love. As God told Abram,

> "All the families of the earth will be blessed through you." *Genesis 12:3*

Known today as Palestine in the Middle East, the violence there is directly linked to God's plan to establish Abram's descendants as a nation in the midst of an opposing Counterfeit Kingdom. All this stems from one simple man of faith, Abram.

ABRAM'S FAITH

Abram is remarkable because God chose him out of a thriving, sophisticated, yet entirely pagan culture whose people—including members of his own family—worshiped other gods.[2] Ur was a thriving metropolis, one of "the most civilized and cultured cities in the world during Abram's day."[3] It was the very epitome of the Cult of Man. God reached into the dark heart of the Kosmos and called on Abram to leave behind all the security, the civilization and splendor—everything familiar—in order to migrate to an unknown Promised Land, a comparatively sparsely-settled hill country called the land of Canaan.

THE MYSTERY UNFOLDS

God revealed to Abram the sweeping scope of His Kingdom Plan for mankind, called the Abrahamic Covenant:

> "Leave your own country behind you, and your own people, and go to the land I will guide you to. If you do, I will cause you to become the father of a great nation; I will bless you and make your name famous, and you will be a blessing to many others. I will bless those who bless you and curse those who curse you; and the entire world will be blessed because of you." *Genesis 12:1-3*, LB.

 Through Abram God spread The Kingdom across the globe because God found a willing heart.

This was the blueprint for The Mystery of The Kingdom: a simple man, a simple willing heart, a small piece of real estate called the Promised Land. Compared to the exotic systems and monolithic buildings of the Kosmos, God's Kingdom was deceptively simple.

At the age of 75, in the middle of the Bronze Age around 2100 B.C.,[5] Abram finally moved into Canaan. Immediately at Shechem, where the local people worshiped false gods, Abram built an altar and sacrificed to God and put God's stamp of ownership on it.[6] There were no invading armies, no formidable strongholds erected, and no sophisticated war machines to conquer in the land—yet there it was, irrevocably, the centerpiece of The Kingdom.

THE HEART It is difficult to exaggerate the importance of the heart when it comes to dealing with God. The Hebrew word lab (áì pronounced, "labe") means, "heart, understanding, mind" and in the Bible it "became the richest biblical term for the totality of man's inner or immaterial nature."[4]

The heart is the essential core of the person, perhaps our most precious commodity: "Above all else, guard your heart, for it affects everything you do." *Proverbs 4:23*. It is the heart that makes us personal and individual, so unlike a creature driven by instinct, or a machine. Human Sovereign Will resides in the heart.

God responds to our heart, and He reaches out to touch our hearts: "Here I am! I stand at the door and knock. If anyone hears my voice and opens the door, I will come in and eat with him, and he with me." *Revelation 3:20* (NIV)

He calls on us to respond with a simple choice: to let Him come in or not.[A]

(A) Please read the Appendix "Plan A and Plan B of Salvation."

Consider this...

Abram found himself in the middle of God's Kingdom Plan where he discovered an amazing truth: his wildest dreams could be fulfilled inside God's Kingdom Plan, dreams which he never could fulfill for himself had he remained at home in Ur, despite its wealth and sophistication.

It happened one night:

> The Lord brought Abram outside beneath the night sky and told him, "Look up into the heavens and count the stars if you can. Your descendants will be like that—too many to count!" *Genesis 15:5*

This promise was so amazing because at this point Abram had no descendants at all—a terrible fate in a patriarchal society where the absence of an heir meant the extinction of a tribe.

ONE STEP AT A TIME

The original Abrahamic Covenant was given way back in Ur, but it was later at Bethel—a name meaning "house of God"—where Abram set into motion a chain of events that would forever change the world:

> There he built an altar to the Lord and called upon the name of the Lord. *Genesis 12:8* (NASB-U)

At Bethel Abram made a personal decision to sincerely seek God. Although he was responding positively to God all along, at Bethel he moved from an abstract and

THE RELATIONSHIP OF FAITH

The life of Abram is a vital picture of how God reaches out to each of us as individuals, and more significantly, what it means to respond to God.

Abram's acceptance by God was not complicated. He wasn't an exceptionally responsive man at first, yet he did respond step by step to God's Revelation with an honest heart. This sincere responsiveness led him to the most significant breakthrough possible with God: declared completely acceptable and righteous! During the eternal existence of the human soul, there is no greater exercise of our Sovereign Will. God created us with Sovereign Will to make a relationship possible.

This is what the Bible means by the phrase, "call upon the name of the Lord," like Abram at Bethel. It means to approach God calling out for His mercy: "For whoever shall call upon the name of the Lord will be saved." *Romans 10:13* (NASB). Lovingly, God responds to this kind of simple, sincere choice—why would anyone resist it?

The opportunity does not last forever before other matters crowd our lives and we forget all about Him: "Seek the Lord while He may be found; Call upon Him while He is near." *Isaiah 55:6*

This exciting Relationship of Faith is available to anyone. At this moment—even today—it is possible to immediately and finally discover at a personal level how "the Lord declared him righteous." The Appendix "Plan A and Plan B of Salvation" describes how God offers a clear opportunity to discover this eternal Relationship of Faith found in the Bible.

remote view of God into the personal realm, "calling upon the name of the Lord." And now things would begin changing.

Consider this...
So typical of God, He works patiently and steadily to call us into His Kingdom Plan—yet only as we are able to respond.

God is patient and never demands an instantaneous decision made in ignorance. Yet God does expect appropriate movement. Abram's willing heart gradually brought him into the center of God's Kingdom Plan where he discovered the excitement and revolutionary nature of following God.

THE FALL REVERSED

Even more, Abram discovered the simple secret of God's plan to build an intimate, personal relationship with humans:

> "And Abram believed the Lord, and the Lord declared him righteous because of his faith." *Genesis 15:6*

God always intended with humans to "Live in them and walk among them,"[7] but after Adam's rebellion it was unclear how He could accomplish this. With Abram, God made it evident all the achievement was to come from God, who "declared him righteous," but the human response was vital, too: "Abram believed the Lord." Because of Abram's faith the Bible says, "he was called the friend of God."[8]

From Genesis 15 on, Abram's relationship with God was never in doubt. This is the very epitome of the Relationship of Faith God wants from all people:

> This Good News tells us how God makes us right in his sight. This is accomplished from start to finish by faith. As the Scriptures say, "It is through faith that a righteous person has life." *Romans 1:17*

SARAH

God changed Abram's name to Abraham, meaning "father of multitudes"—such an odd name since Abraham and Sarah remained childless for decades, even past child-bearing age. Sarah was especially skeptical, at one point laughing at God's promise to deliver "multitudes" of offspring.

Growing impatient with God's promise, Sarah took control and gave her young maid Hagar to Abraham to conceive a son. The plan was brilliant—initially— because it resulted in a son named Ishmael. Later, however, when God finally gave Sarah a son named Isaac, the trouble began.

Abraham's household became filled with division and strife as jealousy erupted between Sarah and Hagar. Eventually, the only alternative was for Abraham to send poor Hagar and Ishmael away: a virtual death-sentence for a woman with a small son. God was merciful to Hagar, and supernaturally cared for her and Ishmael, promising, "I will make a great nation of him."[9] It is no secret today that Ishmael indeed fathered the Arab nations.

This became a tragedy of epic proportions: not only was Sarah's home torn by strife, but for thousands of years Hagar's and Sarah's offspring have been torn by strife. All this was because Abraham and Sarah tried to fulfill God's promise through human self-effort.

Yet, this story also reveals God's amazing grace, because even though Abraham and Sarah tragically failed, still God delivered the promised son by grace. Clearly, their behavior was less than exemplary, yet God still delivered Isaac.

Consider this...

Abraham and Sarah discovered the timeless truth that God's Kingdom Plan is surely worth trusting.

Delight yourself in the Lord and he will give you the desires of your heart. *Psalm 37:4* (NIV)

What a joy it must have been for Sarah and Abraham to finally hold their child Isaac, clearly a miracle at Sarah's age of almost 90! The delightful and surprising result of a Walk of Faith is the experiencing of the desires of our hearts.

The descendants of Abraham through Isaac became a new race of people who were at first called Israelites and later Jews. These were "God's chosen people" and were destined to play a major role in God's Incredible Plan.

ISAAC

Through Isaac, God revealed an astonishing piece of biblical prophecy, a crucial underpinning of The Mystery. God told Abraham to perform a macabre act:

RELATIONSHIP VERSUS LEADERSHIP These are two very different decisions described in the Bible: the decision to enter into a relationship with God—the Relationship of Faith—and the decision to follow God's leadership: the Walk of Faith.

Abraham began a Relationship of Faith with God when, "Abram believed God, so God declared him to be righteous" so that he "was even called 'the friend of God.'" *James 2:23*. This initial decision to become a "friend of God" resolves our alienation and brings a deep-seated peace: "Therefore, since we have been justified through faith, we have peace with God through our Lord Jesus Christ." *Romans 5:1* (NIV)

After finding peace with God, however, it still remains an open question whether we prefer God's leadership or our own leadership in our daily lives. Once the relationship with God begins, He is anxious to introduce us to the excitement of His leadership. Yet He never overrides our free choice, and He allows us to gradually discover the success and victory of a life led by Him, one step at a time: the Walk of Faith.

sacrifice his son Isaac as a demonstration of his Walk of Faith.[B]

> "Take your son, your only son—yes, Isaac, whom you love so much—and go to the land of Moriah. Sacrifice him there as a burnt offering on one of the mountains, which I will point out to you." *Genesis 22:2*

Even though Abraham was convinced that God meant nothing but good from this test, it was one of the greatest trials of his life.[10] Fortunately, God stopped Abraham from performing the sacrifice. God only wanted to make a point for all generations and all time.

✍ Isaac was a picture of the coming Messiah, the solution to man's alienation from God.

The significance of this event became evident centuries later, on Mount Moriah where this sacrifice was to occur. This very site became known as Jerusalem, the spot where God offered up His only son, Jesus Christ.[11]

Consider this...

It is so significant that God established such a link between Isaac and Jesus Christ, because it clearly shows that God is working from an ingenious plan from beginning to end: He introduced the Kingdom through Abraham, and revealed it fully with Jesus Christ. Isaac is the link between the two.[C]

ABRAM: FACT OR FICTION? For decades during the 19th and 20th centuries, Abraham was not viewed as a historical figure by liberal scholars because, they said, so much of the biblical account contained anachronisms and other historical inaccuracies. Abraham was viewed as a legendary figure, embellished over time by oral tradition.[12]

In the later 20th century, however, the liberal views of Abraham were thrown into disarray by archeologists, especially by the phenomenal Ebla and Tel Armana discoveries.[13] They date from the 2100 B.C. time frame, which best fits the biblical account of Abraham's lifetime, and authenticate the biblical accounts. For example, one of the Ebla tablets caused considerable embarrassment:

"It has become almost a dogma of critical scholarship to insist that Genesis 14...is unhistorical precisely because the five cities mentioned in the story are never referred to in any ancient literature apart from the Old Testament... [In 1976] with amazement Pettinato had observed that the five cities of the plain were on this tablet and that they were listed in exactly the same order as in Genesis 14:2!"[14]

There are numerous incidents where skeptics were certain of unhistorical anachronisms concerning Abraham's life.[15] Yet archeologists repeatedly confirm the historical reliability of the biblical accounts:

"It may be stated categorically that no archeological discovery has ever controverted a biblical passage. Scores of archeological findings have been made which confirm in clear outline or exact detail historical statements in the Bible."[16]

(B) It is vital to understand that God's test of Abraham's faith was in no way connected to Abraham's acceptance before God—his acceptance was already established in Genesis 15:6. Instead, this was God's first clear, dramatic revelation of The Mystery to unfold thousands of years later.

It seemed so unlikely that God would use Abraham and this solitary son to "bless the nations of the earth." Through Isaac came God's answer to man's problem: the rebellion against God resolved through the future "Anointed One."

JACOB THE FIGHTER

Isaac's son Jacob was such an unlikely candidate for God's Incredible Plan. This is an important man who was later renamed Israel, and his 12 sons became known as the "12 Tribes of Israel." Yet he spent decades deceiving, scheming and manipulating, and only late in life discovered any need for assistance from the God of Grace.

Consider this...
Jacob is a worthy study for those who imagine they can control life, but he also demonstrates how willing God is to work with people even after a lifetime of mistakes.

His very name means "he cheats, supplants"[17] because he was born grasping the heel of his twin brother, as though trying to hold him back and win the race for the first-born—a race he would eventually win.

Jacob and his brother, Esau, could not have been more different, even though they were twins:

> When the boys grew up, Esau became a skillful hunter, a man of the field, but Jacob was a peaceful man, living in tents. *Genesis 25:27* (NASB-U)

Esau was the stereotypical "man's man," a hunter favored by his father, but Jacob was more delicate, favored by his mother:

> Isaac loved Esau in particular because of the wild game he brought home, but Rebekah favored Jacob. *Genesis 25:28*

BIRTHRIGHT

The differences between these two brothers would escalate into centuries of violence and opposition. It all centered on the birthright, which belonged to the first-born—Esau—who not only inherited all the family's wealth, but also the responsibility to care for the rest of the family. Most importantly, the first-born inherited the Abrahamic Covenant, God's promise to use this lineage as a "blessing for the nations of the earth." It was a position of great honor and privilege passed down through Abraham's lineage.

Amazingly, Esau cared little for this spiritual heritage:

> Esau said to Jacob, "I'm starved! Give me some of that red stew you've made." (This was how Esau got his other name, Edom—"Red.") Jacob replied, "All right, but trade me your birthright for it." "Look, I'm dying

(C) See Chapter 13 for a thorough treatment of this incident with Isaac.

of starvation!" said Esau. "What good is my birthright to me now?" So
Jacob insisted, "Well then, swear to me right now that it is mine." So
Esau swore an oath, thereby selling all his rights as the first-born to his
younger brother. Then Jacob gave Esau some bread and lentil stew. Esau
ate and drank and went on about his business, indifferent to the fact that
he had given up his birthright. *Genesis 25:30-34*

He sold his birthright for a bowl of stew! Hopefully it was exceptionally good stew,
because to the God of Abraham and Isaac, it was reprehensible that "Esau despised
his birthright." He chose his way out of God's Kingdom Plan.

Esau later realized the folly of his birthright-for-soup deal, and wanted it back, but
Jacob the swindler was two steps ahead and already secured the birthright from
their father Isaac:

But Isaac said, "Your brother was here, and he tricked me. He has
carried away your blessing." Esau said bitterly, "No wonder his name is
Jacob, for he has deceived me twice!"… Then Esau broke down and
wept. *Genesis 27:35-38*

He grew livid with anger:

Esau hated Jacob because he had stolen his blessing, and he said to
himself, "My father will soon be dead and gone. Then I will kill Jacob."
Genesis 27:41

FROM PLEASURE TO PAIN Esau is the epitome of someone who lives for short-term
reward while despising spiritual opportunities with God. The Bible often cites Esau as the typical
hedonist: one whose life is a pleasure-seeking adventure driven by base instinct. Ultimately, it is a
fragile lifestyle, always at the mercy of changing circumstances.

The hedonistic life grows increasingly boring, because constant stimulation becomes normative
and has a desensitizing effect. Yet some people want to be desensitized to the coldness of the
world around them, and it results in scars and callousness:

"But these people mock and curse the things they do not understand. Like animals, they do whatever their instincts tell them, and they bring about their own destruction." *Jude 1:10*

This lifestyle is exceptionally frustrating since it clashes with our created need for significance and
dignity. Humans are actually Eternal Beings with a built-in need for permanent gratification and
significance —things that Esau "despised." When the pursuit of pleasure replaces God, life degenerates into a largely painful existence spiked by occasional moments of excitement that fade away
all too quickly.

Contrary to popular belief, God is not anti-pleasure. He is in fact the One who created the capacity
for enjoyment, and He holds the blueprints for building enjoyment that lasts into eternity. It is, in
fact, one of the reasons why God gave Revelation:

These things we write, so that our joy may be made complete. *1 John 1:4* (NASB-U)

Consider this...
He could not get it back; it was too late. It is a painful reminder that Sovereign Will is significant, that some decisions can irreversibly damage future options.

Afterward, as you know, when he wanted to inherit this blessing, he was rejected. He could bring about no change of mind, though he sought the blessing with tears. *Hebrews 12:17* (NIV)

RUNNING AWAY

Fearing his brother's anger, Jacob ran away from God's Promised Land back to Haran where Abraham's relatives were dwelling. Yet God pursued Jacob one strange night:

> He had a dream in which he saw a stairway resting on the earth, with its top reaching to heaven, and the angels of God were ascending and descending on it. There above it stood the Lord, and he said: "I am the Lord, the God of your father Abraham and the God of Isaac. I will give you and your descendants the land on which you are lying... All peoples on earth will be blessed through you and your offspring." *Genesis 28:13-15* (NIV)

This vision of flaming angels flowing between God's sovereign throne and earth was a vital glimpse of God's power and sovereign hand over the direction of Planet Earth's affairs.[D] It was a dramatic echo of the Abrahamic Covenant, God's blueprint for The Kingdom: everything that Jacob schemed, lied, and risked his life for.

Jacob was not yet ready to become God's man. The next day he responded with a sacrifice to God, but it was little more than a trite, religious ritual, and then he was on his way. For decades Jacob avoided dealing with the God of his fathers: he was still a self-willed man and he was on his own, placating God with occasional religious acts to keep Him at safe distance.[18]

✍ God will pursue anyone with a willing heart.

Despite his drawbacks, God pursued Jacob because this man carried a deep desire to participate in The Kingdom.

STRUGGLING

Jacob landed in Haran where he worked for his Uncle Laban and continued his pattern of manipulation and deceit. In a delightfully ironic twist, Jacob met his match with Laban, who consistently out-maneuvered Jacob and duped him into working for 14 years to win his wife, Rachel, among other feats.

(D) Yet God's overall sovereignty does not negate the responsibility of human free will in the details of life, as discussed in Further Consideration at the end of Chapter 2.

Behind these stories of intrigue however, God was doggedly pursuing Jacob, using Laban to wear down Jacob's self-reliance. Deep inside was a willing heart in need of some rough handling in order to expose it: a hidden but strong sense of self-reliance, a common reason why people refuse to seek God.

Finally, years later on his way back to Canaan, Jacob's tangled relationship with God came to a head. Esau—His nemesis and older brother—discovered Jacob's location and headed that way with an overwhelming force of armed men!

Jacob was alone this night, having divided his family to send them different directions and increase their chances for survival. Amidst the fear and confusion, an "angel of the Lord" appeared to Jacob, and they wrestled all night. After hours of struggle, Jacob was beaten, his hip was broken, and the author depicts a pathetic picture of Jacob clinging to the ankles of the victorious angel pleading, "I will not let you go unless you bless me!"[19]

GOD WINS

This moment was the very climax of Jacob's life. For years God pursued Jacob to bless him, but this self-willed man persisted in skirmishing, plotting and scheming to advance without God. His entire life was a wrestling match against God, refusing the Walk of Faith Abraham enjoyed.

On this night God reduced proud Jacob to the point of desperation, to give up his complex plots and finally ask God for a blessing. Jacob did not give up easily. Wounded and threatened by Esau's approaching army, alone yet still pathetically proud and strong, he tried to strong-arm God's blessing. Yet God saw it was enough and gladly blessed him—just as He always wanted to.

Once Jacob surrendered, God changed Jacob's name to Israel, which means "God's fighter."[20] In the morning Israel emerged a changed man, always limping with the

---

DOES "GOD HELP THOSE WHO HELP THEMSELVES"? This popular catch-phrase is often taken as sacred scripture, yet it is not found anywhere in the Bible. Quite the opposite, it is unbiblical and a benign paraphrase of the Principle of Sin: set an agenda, and then ask God to bless it. This self-help principle lies at the foundation of pagan religions, as Achilles said: "the gods help the strong."

Abraham's life is a refutation of this cliché, because he became the father of nations strictly by God's leadership and power. Much of Jacob's life also refutes this cliché: it is a tragic story of frustration and waste because he relied so heavily on his ability to manipulate and scheme. Yet, all these efforts to "help himself" only ended up wasting years as a fugitive and getting duped by others, like Laban, who were more astute at the art of manipulation.

God offers something so much better: by depending on Him, He leads us into a life of victory and success, avoiding the tragic waste of Jacob's earlier years. Humans are finite and cannot possibly know the full implications of their choices. Nobody can see the scope of alternatives like God.

But before God can truly offer His leadership, we must come to the end of our efforts to live the independent lifestyle and enter the Walk of Faith, as Jacob finally did.

broken hip as the fingerprint of God in his life. Israel was weakened by God at his point of strength—he was a physically strong man[21]—and as a cripple now he could never be so self-sufficient. Yet at this point God could finally use Israel in a pivotal role in His Kingdom Plan by making him the father of a nation, the 12 tribes of Israel. This highly gifted man, always such a great accomplisher independent of God, now discovered lasting significance building God's Kingdom Plan here on earth.

> "There is little evidence of the trickery and bribery that had characterized Jacob before...Jacob was ready to receive the promise, but his entire life had been characterized by his determination to seize the promise and the blessing for himself."[22]

Consider this...

Jacob is proof that God can use anyone in His Kingdom Plan who is willing. Willingness is the issue, not our performance. Jacob's performance was reprehensible for years, yet God continued to pursue him.

FURTHER CONSIDERATION

WHY A "CHOSEN" PEOPLE?

God launched a fantastic enterprise that forever shaped human history when He switched from working with mankind at large and focused on the people of Israel. Why did God find it necessary to have a group of Chosen People? Why not continue working with mankind as a whole?

As God's plan continues, it becomes increasingly narrowed on a specific tribe within the nation Israel (the tribe of Judah), a specific kingly line (from King David), a specific location (Bethlehem), and more. It becomes clear that God is laying the groundwork for the coming of King Messiah. For this King, there must be an exhaustive trail of authenticity.

THE PROPHETIC TRAIL

God chose the Israelites to record and preserve His Revelation,[23] which contained all the prophecies concerning King Messiah—the Anointed One—and validates Jesus Christ as fulfilling "all the things written about me in the Law and the Prophets"..[24] Without these prophecies Jesus would be just another "holy man" or "good man" like so many others. Yet Jesus was unique: this is the One who stands at the climax of human history, from God's viewpoint. This Messiah is this King of The Kingdom who defeats the counterfeit monarch, the Ruler of this World, as God prophesied to Satan in the Garden of Eden: "He will crush your head."[25] This is the One who offers us authentic peace with God and fulfills the prophecy to Abram that "in you, all the nations of the earth will be blessed."[26]

From inside the Chosen People, the Messiah was born from a "Kingly Line"—the tribe of Judah—and from their greatest king, King David.[27] King Messiah was meant to rule The Kingdom "from before the foundations of the earth" from a royal heritage.[28] So exalted is God's view of the human race, He not only created humans to rule, but would identify Himself with them, born among them in the kingly line, so that He would "dwell among them" as the "King of Kings" and "Lord of Lords"[29]—the King Messiah prophesied throughout the Old Testament.

Finally, through the Israelites God provided a snapshot view of King Messiah's reign among humans. It was to be the simple trust of the Walk of Faith, the loving relationship Abraham, Isaac and Jacob found with God.

GENOCIDE

It is no surprise, then, that Satan has launched a genocidal effort to destroy the Jewish race throughout the ages—even in the name of their very Jewish King and savior Jesus Christ. It is difficult to explain this pervasive anti-Semitism apart from the Bible's revelation that Satan is the author of hatred for the Jews because of their prominent role in God's Plan.[30] Even more difficult to explain is their survival despite thousands of years of anti-Semitism—apart from the Abrahamic Covenant in Genesis 12:3—"I will bless those who bless you and curse those who curse you."

THE BIRTH OF A NATION

"I am the Lord, I am the Lord, the merciful and gracious God."
Exodus 34:6

ISRAEL'S SONS

Israel's life sparked the birth of a nation, the evolution of God's promise to his grandfather Abraham that, "I will cause you to become the father of a great nation." His children were called Israelites, and his 12 sons became the "12 Tribes of Israel." God was well on His way to developing His Kingdom Plan using the Chosen People in the Promised Land. The Mystery was taking firm root.

Yet a significant threat loomed ahead. With so many sons, sibling rivalry was inevitable, and it mushroomed when one son, Joseph, became Israel's favorite and so triggered his brother's jealousy. Israel showered Joseph with lavish gifts, like a costly multi-colored coat that Joseph always wore with pride. Joseph further inflamed the brothers by sharing his dreams that one day they would all bow down low before him. Even Israel was appalled at Joseph's arrogance, and rebuked him:

> "What is this dream that you have had? Shall I and your mother and your brothers actually come to bow ourselves down before you to the ground?" *Genesis 37:10*

Joseph soon discovered these were not the sort of brothers to enrage. They hatched a cruel plot to kidnap and sell him into slavery for twenty pieces of silver, dipping his opulent multicolored coat in blood to convince their father that Joseph was dead.

Israel's family was now breaking up, with Joseph living as a slave in Egypt. God's plan to build a Chosen Race and lay claim to the Promised Land was disintegrating. Yet God's will is not so easily dislodged, and He protected Joseph in Egypt and turned this tragedy into a miraculous rescue of Israel's entire family.

BONDAGE IN THE WORLD SYSTEM

God's care of Joseph in Egypt was so thorough that Joseph experienced a miraculous rise in power and prominence, from years as a prisoner rotting in the Pharaoh's dungeons, to rising as second in command throughout Egypt and living in the palace of Pharaoh himself. His life was an unsettling fluctuation between success and failure. Enslaved, falsely accused of rape, imprisoned and even abandoned by friends he helped in jail were all debilitating setbacks; yet throughout this period, God struck back:

> The Lord was with him; He showed him kindness and granted him favor..., and "the Lord gave him success in whatever he did."
> *Genesis 39:21, 23*

Even the Pharaoh marveled at this unnatural ability to rise above defeat:

> "He is a man who is obviously filled with the spirit of God."
> *Genesis 41:38*

> ✐ **God is always at work in the lives of those who love Him, turning hopeless tragedy into resounding success.**

It became apparent that God was working on an ingenious plan—even within such dark circumstances—a plan to save the remaining Israelites from disaster back in the land of Canaan. A severe famine struck the entire region, and starvation forced Joseph's brothers to travel to Egypt for food. Just as Joseph "The Dreamer" predicted,

> "Since Joseph was governor of all Egypt and in charge of the sale of the grain, it was to him that his brothers came. They bowed low before him, with their faces to the ground." *Genesis 42:6*

They bowed before him. What a chilling moment it must have been when Joseph finally said to them, *"I am Joseph!"* Their response was predictable:

> "His brothers were not able to answer him, because they were terrified at his presence." *Genesis 45:3*

Their terror was appropriate: the traitorous brothers were now prostrated before a powerful Egyptian ruler with armies at his command—the very one they sold into slavery! What could they possibly say?

Joseph was not bitter, and he told his brothers,

> "As far as I am concerned, God turned into good what you meant for evil, for he brought me to this high position I have today so that I could save the lives of many people." *Genesis 50:20*

Joseph was not embittered and did not inflict revenge because he saw a glimmer of

God's ingenious plan. He knew that his fortunate rise in Egypt was not merely good luck—it was a vital part of God's Kingdom Plan.

∾ **Through Joseph's suffering, God turned a mere tribe into a great nation.**

Joseph's insight that God "could save the lives of many people" carried deep significance. God preserved the fledgling Chosen Race at a most delicate and formative time. The Egyptians were highly race-conscious and carefully isolated the Israelites within the land of Goshen,[1] so Egypt acted as God's incubator where the Israelites multiplied and prospered in an isolated environment.

Seventy Israelites moved into Egypt, and emerged as a nation over 2 million strong.[2] Had they stayed in Canaan, they would have soon lost their national identity, because intermarriage and assimilation with the Canaanites was already beginning to take place. Even worse, the Canaanites practiced human sacrifice and ritual prostitution among other depraved practices, and unlike the Egyptians, the Canaanite culture was synchronistic and easily assimilated other peoples. Had they remained in Canaan, God's careful plan to raise a unique nation would utterly disintegrate.[3]

A NATION EMERGES

God's plan to cultivate a new nation was so successful they became a significant threat to later Pharaohs as they multiplied. The Pharaohs responded by first enslaving the Hebrews—as the Egyptians called them[4]—and finally slaughtering all Hebrew male infants to stop the growth. The bondage of the Hebrew people became intolerable, and they remembered the God of Abraham, Isaac and Jacob and cried out to Him. True to His promise, God broke into history to protect and preserve His Kingdom Plan in one of the most extraordinary events in history.

MOSES

Amidst this dark period of bondage and the slaughter of Hebrew infants, God selected a Hebrew baby named Moses destined to deliver the nation of Israel. To protect Moses from Pharaoh's slaughter of infants, his mother hid him in a basket and sent him floating down the Nile River. Amazingly, the Pharaoh's daughter found the basket:

> As the princess opened it, she found the baby boy. His helpless cries touched her heart. "He must be one of the Hebrew children," she said.
> *Exodus 2:6*

Knowing he was Hebrew, she was moved to adopt the child, and raised him inside the Pharaoh's royal palace with the most sophisticated education and cultural opportunities available from the Kosmos.[5] By adulthood Moses emerged as a capable and literate stepson of the Pharaoh, prepared for great leadership.

What happened next seemed like a tragic reversal of fortune—yet tragedies take a surprising twist with God involved. For decades the fame of Moses grew in the Pharaoh's court:

> "He was a man of power in words and deeds. But when he was approaching the age of forty, it entered his mind to visit his brethren, the sons of Israel." *Acts 7:22-23*

At this point Moses made the fateful decision to identify himself with God's people, the slaves:

> "And when he saw one of them being treated unjustly, he defended him and took vengeance for the oppressed by striking down the Egyptian." *Acts 7:22-24*

It was a high-stakes decision to kill the Egyptian. Moses held in his grasp inexhaustible riches, the sensuous women of Egypt, and he moved around the court of Pharaoh with prestige and power. His position promised comfort and he was at the pinnacle of his career. Nobody invested heavily in the Kosmos could ever understand this decision to bypass the full glory of Egypt and identify with slaves.

From God's view, however, it was perhaps the most pivotal and wise decision in the entire Old Testament, because when Moses identified with God's Chosen People, he identified with The Kingdom:

> "He thought it was better to suffer for the sake of the Messiah than to own the treasures of Egypt, for he was looking ahead to the great reward that God would give him." *Hebrews 11:26*

Consider this...

Only time tells which of the two kingdoms holds more promise: God's, or the Counterfeit. Ultimately it becomes a faith choice to decide which kingdom deserves the trust and investment of a lifetime. Unlike the cold Kosmos, however, the Walk of Faith in God's Kingdom includes a deepening relationship with a loving Creator.

Moses became a pathetic character in the eyes of the Kosmos as he was forced to flee Egypt and drifted into the desert: an impoverished vagabond who once held the wealth and power of the most glamorous system ever before seen on earth. Yet he also discovered the surprising riches of getting to know the Creator God.

ENCOUNTER WITH GOD

Moses fled Egypt into the far side of the desert where he shepherded flocks and met his wife Zipporah. Here he could now settle into peaceful obscurity—but thankfully, God had other plans.

God reversed the apparent tragedy of this man's life by reaching into human history in the most unexpected fashion—a burning bush. Moses approached the phenomenon with curiosity, and suddenly a voice spoke from out of the fire:

> "Do not come any closer," God told him. "Take off your sandals, for you are standing on holy ground…I am the God of your ancestors—the God of Abraham, the God of Isaac, and the God of Jacob."

What could anyone say to something like this?

> When Moses heard this, he hid his face in his hands because he was afraid to look at God. *Exodus 3:5-6*

Yet Moses discovered something about the Almighty God: this is someone with kind intentions, as He went on to tell Moses:

> Then the Lord told him, "You can be sure I have seen the misery of my people in Egypt…So I have come to rescue them and lead them out of Egypt into their own good and spacious land. It is a land flowing with milk and honey." *Exodus 3:7-8*

God called on Moses to stand at the helm of The Kingdom Plan and lead the Chosen People. It was an exalted position, and Moses naturally asked God what possible credentials he could cite for such a calling.

God then gave Moses a personal and intimate glimpse of the Creator:

> "I Am the One who always is. Just tell them, 'I Am has sent me to you.'" *Exodus 3:14*

"I Am" is His name, pronounced "Yahweh" in the Hebrew. The name echoes with implications, because it means the Creator God is personal and knowable, someone with a name.

GOD, THE PERSON This revelation about the nature of God has significant impact for modern man. One popular view holds that God is an abstract, impersonal force—the Star Wars "force" —and it is not only mistaken, but an affront to the Person of God, reducing Him to a thing without intelligence, will or emotions.

Yahweh is an individual who exerts His will into human history, "the God of Abraham, the God of Isaac, and the God of Jacob," He says. He exercises intellect and communicates intelligibly. He is logical. He carries a personal name, and expresses emotions and is the template for the human individual. Yahweh is not a remote force.

At the most fundamental level, irreconcilable differences exist between these views of God. Either God is an impersonal force as taught by Buddhism, Hinduism and their numerous offspring, or God is a personal Creator, as the Bible teaches. Both these views cannot be true, and they are diametrically opposed.

The question is this: are we willing to find out for ourselves? The personal God Yahweh has spoken, He provides evidence, and is capable of revealing Himself to willing hearts: "Draw near to God and He will draw near to you." *James 4:8a* (NASB-U)

Consider this...

Because He is a Personal Being, it means it is possible to carry on a relationship with God, to talk with Him, learn about Him, and experience His leadership in our lives. Yahweh indeed reveals Himself to those with a willing heart like Moses.

THE PLAGUES

Egypt at this time was at its zenith of power and riches with the most indomitable war machine ever before assembled, controlling the Ancient Near East. Their vast wealth, culture, and monuments like the sphinx and pyramids, evoke awe still today.

Yet, Egypt is also a picture of the futility of defying God: ultimately God will prevail, and The Kingdom will never be destroyed or derailed. Humans might exercise Sovereign Will, but not forever. Historically, God has shown there comes a point at which He will defy human strength.

So it was now: Yahweh defied Pharaoh's hold on the Hebrews. Amazingly, Pharaoh set the strength of his will against God, as it says repeatedly throughout this episode, "Yet Pharaoh's heart became hard" and "Pharaoh hardened his heart."[6]

Gradually at first, but with escalating force, God struck the Pharaoh's empire with a terrifying series of plagues. The Nile turned to fetid blood; swarms of frogs and then flies, locusts and gnats devastated the land and livestock; hail battered the crops; grotesque boils broke out on people, and a terrifying darkness descended over the land for three days. Yet Pharaoh grew increasingly defiant:

> "Get out of here!" Pharaoh shouted at Moses. "Don't ever let me see you again! The day you do, you will die!" *Exodus 10:27*

THE PASSOVER

Yet it was God—not Pharaoh—who passed the sentence of death. All warnings were finished, and God resolved to reduce this ruler to subjection:

> The Lord said to Moses, "I will send just one more disaster on Pharaoh and the land of Egypt. After that, Pharaoh will let you go. In fact, he will be so anxious to get rid of you that he will practically force you to leave the country." *Exodus 11:1*

In one last, horrific plague, God decreed the death of all the firstborn sons. It was to become a long and agonizing night of terror: the Destroyer—the Angel of Death—was descending on the land of Egypt:[8]

> Pharaoh and his officials and all the people of Egypt woke up during the night, and loud wailing was heard throughout the land of Egypt. *Exodus 12:30*

◇ **Even in His fury God provided grace for any willing heart.**

Consider this . . .

Anyone could be protected by placing the blood of an unblemished lamb on his doorposts. It was a step of faith, responding to God's instructions. So typical of God, He offers us life, but we do have to respond.

All that night as Egyptians faced the bane of the passing shadow and while death struck households everywhere, the Israelites were safe inside their homes if the blood was sprinkled around their doors. It was the Night of the Passover, because death passed over those who believed in God's promise of protection.

When the sun rose, the Pharaoh was reduced to a terrified and compliant man. He not only gave the Israelites permission to leave, but in fact "drove them out," even allowing them to carry away plunder from his kingdom.[9] Even almighty Pharaoh was at the mercy of the God of Hebrew slaves!

THE GREAT ESCAPE

Three days later Pharaoh recovered from his trauma and flew into a rage. Even though Moses and the Israelites were long gone, he changed his mind:

> Pharaoh and his officials changed their minds. "What have we done, letting all these slaves get away?" they asked. So Pharaoh called out his troops and led the chase in his chariot. He took with him six hundred of Egypt's best chariots, along with the rest of the chariots of Egypt…The Egyptians caught up with the people of Israel as they were camped beside the shore. *Exodus 14:6-9*

The Israelites were trapped with their backs to the Red Sea, without escape! It was impossible to outrun the chariots of Egypt, and fighting was impossible with this unarmed, untrained mob.

THE PASSOVER LAMB The Passover was the very first and most foundational of all Hebrew rituals. God prescribed elaborate preparations for the Passover meal, and especially for the execution of the Passover lamb whose blood was sprinkled over the doorframe to escape the judgment of God that night. It is significant that these were non-optional instructions for anyone wishing to escape God's judgment. This is God's Redemptive Plan, commonly called "salvation." Redemption means "to buy back" or "to save from captivity by paying a ransom."[7]

Soon afterward, God gave Israel the Sacrificial System, which taught the blood of an unblemished lamb could be used as a substitute for man's personal sin. In Chapter 14, we will see how these details come together as a prophetic picture of the true Passover lamb, Jesus Christ. John the Baptist says of Jesus, "Behold, the lamb of God which comes to take away the sin of the world!" *John 1:29*

Throughout the Old and New Testaments, God points to the sacrificial lamb as the only way for men to receive forgiveness and to be spared from His judgment, the sentence of death. The Night of the Passover is one of several such instances.

Yet Moses was undaunted:

> "Don't be afraid. Just stand where you are and watch the Lord rescue you. The Egyptians that you see today will never be seen again…You won't have to lift a finger in your defense!" *Exodus 14:13-14*

What followed was a rumbling, thunderous roar that must have been terrifying:

> Moses raised his hand over the sea, and the Lord opened up a path through the water with a strong east wind. The wind blew all that night, turning the seabed into dry land. So the people of Israel walked through the sea on dry ground, with walls of water on each side! *Exodus 14:21-22*

The children of Israel scampered across to safety, while God unleashed His fury against Pharaoh:

> As the sun began to rise, Moses raised his hand over the sea. The water roared back into its usual place, and the Lord swept the terrified Egyptians into the surging currents. *Exodus 14:27*

Pharaoh's army was crushed and washed away. The Pharaohs of Egypt believed they were gods. Yet with all their wealth and power the Egyptians were utterly destroyed by Yahweh, despite their vast numbers, war machines and splendid chariots.

Consider this…

Egypt is a picture of how fragile the Cult of Man actually is, and all their imposing monuments and great feats of civilization that stir awe today are testaments to the temporality of the Kosmos. Only time tells which of the two kingdoms holds more promise.

THE WILDERNESS

Still today the wilderness of the Sinai Peninsula is a harsh, dry expanse of blistering heat, devoid of vegetation but full of scorpions and poisonous snakes. Temperatures swing from extreme heat to freezing cold at night. As with any desert, death comes swiftly for the unprepared. How could God lead a nation of 2 million people into this dead zone without provisions?

WHY DID GOD HARDEN PHARAOH'S HEART? In reading the account of the Exodus, at times it seems God took away Pharaoh's free will, and "hardened his heart." However, God only gave Pharaoh the courage to carry out what he actually wanted to do, as these scholars point out:

"The fact remains that the first instance of any act of God on Pharaoh's heart does not come until Exodus 9:12 after Pharaoh himself has repeatedly rejected God's request." The Lord "seems to say, very well, if he wants to do it this way, I'll help him along…God didn't give Pharaoh the wicked desire to rebel against Him; what God did was to give him the stubborn courage to carry out that desire."[10]

Yahweh was acutely aware of their needs, and He thrilled the Israelites with His powerful provisions:

> The Lord spread out a cloud above them as a covering and gave them a great fire to light the darkness. *Psalm 105:39*

This was the Shekinah Glory, a tower of billowing clouds cooling the desert heat, and a pillar of fire for warmth at night. It was God's glory covering them, dwelling among the Chosen People.

Consider this...

God is not someone to be locked away in a remote building, as some imagine. His Shekinah Glory was a glimpse of His continuing presence with them, the goal of His Eternal Plan for mankind and the theme of the Bible:

> For we are the temple of the living God; just as God said, "I will dwell in them and walk among them; and I will be their God, and they shall be My people." *2 Corinthians 6:16*

Through the Shekinah Glory God not only dwelt among the people, but guided and protected them, and progressively taught them about who He was.

God also provided for their physical needs by making water suddenly gush out of dry, desert rocks, and each day He sent strange bread from heaven:

> In time, the food became known as manna. It was white like coriander seed, and it tasted like honey cakes. *Exodus 16:31*

Through all of this, He was teaching spiritual truths of vital significance to all generations and all time. Just as He supplied their physical need for bread, so He supplies the bread of "real life," as Moses told them:

> "Yes, he humbled you by letting you go hungry and then feeding you with manna, a food previously unknown to you and your ancestors. He did it to teach you that people need more than bread for their life; real life comes by feeding on every word of the Lord." *Deuteronomy 8:3*

As desperately as we cling to our physical lives, God says there is still something far more significant: "real life."

Consider this...

This is what God's Revelation is all about: "real life comes by feeding on every word of the Lord." Learning about His Revelation is not merely an academic study.

DESTINATION UNKNOWN

Mile by mile, relentlessly day after day God led the host of Israelites through the harsh desert in a southerly direction to a destination He planned from the beginning when He first met Moses:

> "When you have brought the Israelites out of Egypt, you will return here to worship God at this very mountain." *Exodus 3:12*

To the Israelites Moses seemed lost or even insane, leading them on a zigzag course deeper into a harsh place called the Desert of Sin and even beyond, away from the so-called "Promised Land." Several times they accused him of leading them to their graves:[11]

> They spoke against God and against Moses, and said, "Why have you brought us up out of Egypt to die in the desert? There is no bread! There is no water!" *Numbers 21:5* (NIV)

Yet this was not random wandering. The destination was Mount Sinai, and it would become the most renowned spot in this wilderness. Here the Grand Architect of creation unveiled the blueprints of a magnificent structure: His designs behind creation, and even more, who He was.

FACING GOD AT MOUNT SINAI

At Mount Sinai, the glory of God descended on the mountain:

> All Mount Sinai was covered with smoke because the Lord had descended on it in the form of fire. The smoke billowed into the sky like smoke from a furnace, and the whole mountain shook with a violent earthquake. *Exodus 19:18*

God told Moses to climb the mountain into this maelstrom—alone. Yet Moses was not terrified, because his heart earnestly loved Yahweh. On top of the mountain, Moses made a bold request of God:

UNDERSTANDING GOD The Law proves that God is personal and understandable, since it describes His character. Some disagree: "No statement about God is simply, literally true. God is far more than can be measured, described, defined in ordinary language, or pinned down to any particular happening." *David Jenkins*[13]

This argument is extreme—if we cannot understand everything about God, we cannot understand anything about God. In the real world of learning, knowledge is a building process. Galileo arrived at valid conclusions, yet understood only a fraction of modern astronomy. Young couples can make an intelligent commitment to marry without knowing everything about each other. Is it impossible for God to communicate only a subset of knowledge and still be intelligible?

The Law is not exhaustive revelation, but it is sufficient revelation. God reveals enough about Himself to enable us to make important decisions about whether to pursue a relationship with Him any further.

Then Moses had one more request. "Please let me see your glorious presence," he said. The Lord replied, "I will make all my goodness pass before you. But you may not look directly at my face, for no one may see me and live…I will put you in the cleft of the rock and cover you with my hand until I have passed. Then I will remove my hand, and you will see me from behind. But my face will not be seen." *Exodus 33:18-23*

What followed was a close-up encounter with Yahweh like no prophet ever encountered in the entire Bible. It permanently turned his hair snow white, and left a glow on him that frightened the Israelites when they saw him later. Most people would never want to come face-to-face with Jehovah God, but Moses had a heart to earnestly seek closeness with God; and God revealed Himself:

He passed in front of Moses and said, "I am the Lord, the merciful and gracious God. I am slow to anger and rich in unfailing love and faithfulness. I show this unfailing love to many thousands by forgiving every kind of sin and rebellion…"[12] *Exodus 34:6-7*

THE LAW

At Mount Sinai, for the first time God handed to humanity a written record of His Revelation to us: details of The Mystery. It all revolved around the Mosaic Covenant—also called The Law—an agreement where God told the Hebrews about His grand intentions to use them as a light among the far-flung peoples of the world, the Gentiles:

"You will be my own special treasure from among all the nations of the earth; for all the earth belongs to me. And you will be to me a kingdom of priests, my holy nation." *Exodus 19:5-6*

It was an exalted position He offered them, if they rose to the challenge and lived His moral, civil, and ceremonial laws. All these laws were very necessary and designed to protect the Children of Israel from the destructive pagan cultures of the World System around them:

"For I am the Lord who brought you up from the land of Egypt to be your God; thus you shall be holy, for I am holy." *Leviticus 11:45* (NASB-U)

THE ARK One of the more fascinating parts of the Mosaic Covenant is God's detailed instructions in Exodus 25 about The Ark of the Covenant: a small wooden box overlaid with gold, designed to be carried as a symbol of God's authority and presence with Israel.

The Ark played a vital role in Israel's history, teaching about The Mystery. It contained artifacts that epitomized the struggle between God and man throughout history: God's patience and love, versus man's rebellious heart. Later, when God fully revealed The Mystery, it became evident God designed the Ark as a prophetic picture and foreshadowing of His Plan. This is covered in-depth in Chapter 14, which shows the genius and consistency of this plan throughout the millennia.

For 40 days and nights on top of Mount Sinai, God revealed the blueprints of The Kingdom, from history past into future glimpses of The Mystery still to be revealed. "The Law" which Moses received from God not only includes the well-known "Ten Commandments" and other laws, but also includes the Creation Account, the Great Flood, the Exodus, and all the other dramatic moments of God's intervention in human history. Taken together, The Law is actually a picture of God Himself, revealing both His activities in history and His character, much the same way we can understand someone's character through a biography.

> **The Law explains our design, and why so much pain and suffering occurs when we ignore our design.**

Most importantly, it describes in part The Mystery: God's plan to end the rebellion and bring anyone who is willing inside The Kingdom. This is a surprise to people with a superficial understanding of The Law because they only understand it as a set of restrictions without purpose.

FEAR DOMINATES FAITH

The Shekinah Glory led the Israelites to the threshold of their destination, the edge of the Promised Land, where finally they could become a nation with a home. It was God's dramatic moment to reveal the prize He set aside for Abraham and prepared for their inheritance, a place none of these ex-slaves had seen before.

Moses sent 12 spies into the Promised Land, and they returned:

> "We arrived in the land you sent us to see, and it is indeed a magnificent country—a land flowing with milk and honey. Here is some of its fruit as proof." *Numbers 13:27*

WHAT IS "HOLY?" The term "Holy"—*qodosh* in the Hebrew—can be cryptic and even distorted because of its misuse. "Holy" for some sounds spooky, like an ethereal, unreal state of mind disconnected from the real world—something found in a church sanctuary surrounded by burning incense and flickering candles.

But qodosh carries a real message of hope in a world of suffering and confusion. It means to be like God: "...be holy for I am holy." *Leviticus 11:45*. Everything that is profound and marvelous about the human is connected to being like God. Qodosh means to "be separate"—not in a strange sense—but separate from the fallen world around us. The Garden of Eden was "holy" and separate in the middle of the Counterfeit Kingdom, and it was a delightful, exciting life for Adam and Eve.

To "be holy" means to become loving. "God is love," the Bible says, and this is what makes Him so *godosh*. "If you love your neighbor, you will fulfill all the requirements of God's law." *Romans 13:8*. A large part of the Mosaic Covenant simply describes the character of a loving person: qodosh.

For example, in Matthew 23:23, "the weightier matters of the law: justice and mercy and faithfulness" defines what love is—not just a feeling, but something with character. God sincerely wishes for us to experience the joy of qodosh in our lives.

With that, they dumped huge clusters of grapes, pomegranates and figs at the feet of Moses. It was a virtual paradise!

> "But the people living there are powerful, and their cities and towns are fortified and very large. We also saw the descendants of Anak who are living there!" *Numbers 13:28*

A terrified hush fell across the listening crowd. The Anakim were well-known even to the Egyptians as a ferocious and indomitable warrior-race, with many of them extraordinarily large.[14] The assembly erupted into a raging quarrel:

> Then Caleb quieted the people before Moses and said, "We should by all means go up and take possession of it, for we will surely overcome it." *Numbers 13:30* (NASB-U)

Caleb was one of the spies who saw the land with all its obstacles, so he spoke with authority. But 10 of the 12 spies were terrified:

> The other men who had explored the land with him answered, "We can't go up against them! They are stronger than we are!" So they spread discouraging reports about the land among the Israelites: "The land we explored will swallow up any who go to live there..." *Numbers 13:31-32*

The voices of fear carried the day and the people refused to trust in God's promises. It erupted into a hysterical rebellion:

> Their voices rose in a great chorus of complaint against Moses and Aaron. "We wish we had died in Egypt, or even here in the wilderness!" they wailed..."Let's get out of here and return to Egypt!" *Numbers 14:2-3*

Fear dominated faith and the Israelites refused to take hold of the promise God held out for them. It was a tragedy of epic proportions: they stood on the edge of conquest, and now everything they suffered and endured to this point was suddenly cast aside.

Consider this...

It is the timeless story of unbelief that separates us from God, the reason why life becomes pointless and dominated by chaos. Failing to claim and enjoy the promises of God inevitably results in blaming Him for our circumstances and problems.

This was the problem with Adam and Eve, then Cain, and why almost the whole of mankind was lost during Noah's age: trust in God is replaced by self-rule and rebellion, separation from God, hardened hearts and finally a hatred of God Himself. As we saw in Chapter 4, Adam said it all when he told God the problem was "the woman you gave me!" In fact, the problem was his rebellion.

THE COST OF UNBELIEF

Fearfulness seems so benign—perhaps a mere weakness—but as an excuse to distrust God it becomes open rebellion. To assert that God is untrustworthy requires real courage—rebellious courage, as God said:

> The Lord said to Moses, "How long will these people treat me with contempt? How long will they refuse to believe in me, in spite of all the miraculous signs I have performed among them?" *Numbers 14:11* (NIV)

God could not work with this generation of unbelieving Israelites:

> "They will never even see the land I swore to give their ancestors. None of those who have treated me with contempt will enter it." *Numbers 14:23*

He did not allow them to enter the Promised Land. Their distrust of God brought no safety, as they imagined—instead, it meant wandering in the desert for 40 more years, and slowly dying off until a new generation was raised up that would finally trust God's leadership.

> ✎ **They traded the Promised Land for imagined security, but only received a life of stagnation and death, wandering in the desert.**

God brought them to the edge of the desert so they might "enter my place of rest" as the Bible calls it:

> So God's rest is there for people to enter. But those who formerly heard the Good News failed to enter because they disobeyed God… "They will never enter my place of rest!" *Hebrews 4:6; Psalm 95:11*

The next generation would discover the surprising victory of "God's rest," because they would conquer the dreaded Anakim and even more with ease.

Consider this…

A life of independence from God is such a sad and wasted life. It seems so promising to hold back in safety, but it only means treading water and missing the thrill of discovering purpose and why He created us: the essence of "God's rest" that "is there for people to enter."

Yet still, as always, God's Kingdom will not be derailed by human unbelief. Among all the rebellious hearts, God found two willing hearts in Joshua and Caleb, and these were allowed to enter the Promised Land. God named faithful Joshua as the successor to Moses.

Before Moses died, he summarized the struggle between God and the Israelites during this period, and why they ended up wandering without a home for so long in the desert:

"Choose to love the Lord your God…and commit yourself to him, for he is your life. Then you will live long in the land the Lord swore to give your ancestors Abraham, Isaac, and Jacob." *Deuteronomy 30:20*

THE DEATH OF MOSES

Moses climbed Mount Nebo, where God showed him a spectacular view of the Promised Land spread out before him: God's strategic point on Planet Earth, the land God promised to Abraham's descendants. When Moses died, God buried him.

There has never been another prophet like Moses. This was the man who talked "face to face" with God, knew Him personally, and performed miracles that were never equaled until the coming of Jesus Christ, as God Himself said:

"I speak to him face to face, directly and not in riddles! He sees the Lord as he is." *Numbers 12:8a*

Consider this…

The life of Moses is proof that the Walk of Faith is an amazing lifestyle of discovery and purpose, especially coming to know Yahweh: the Creator God who reveals Himself to anyone with a willing heart.

And what an amazing person Moses discovered:

He revealed his character to Moses…The Lord is merciful and gracious; he is slow to get angry and full of unfailing love. *Psalm 103:7-8*

The children of Israel only observed God's acts from a distance; but God invites us to be like Moses, who knew God's His ways:

Draw close to God, and God will draw close to you. *James 4:8a*

Moses put it well to the Israelites:

"Choose to love the Lord your God and to obey him and to cling to him, for he is your life and the length of your days." *Deuteronomy 30:20* (Living)

FURTHER CONSIDERATION

A TORAH FOR GENTILES?

The Hebrew word torah means "Law," used more than 200 times in the Old Testament. In the narrowest sense, it refers to the Mosaic Covenant—the rules and regulations God gave Moses at Mount Sinai, which includes not only the famous Ten Commandments, but more than 600 others.

Some people attempt to apply the Mosaic Covenant to our Gentile world, thinking its promises and curses apply to America. But the Mosaic Covenant was given specifically to establish the Israelites as a nation distinct and separate from surrounding cultures:

> "Now then, if you will indeed obey My voice and keep My covenant, then you shall be My own possession among all the peoples, for all the earth is Mine;" *Exodus 19:5* (NASB-U)

The Law was a conditional covenant—a contract between God and His Chosen People Israel:

> "The Lord your God will make you successful in everything you do…if you obey his voice and keep the commands and laws written in this Book of the Law, and if you turn to the Lord your God with all your heart and soul." *Deuteronomy. 30:9a-10*

It is not possible to transfer God's covenantal promises to Gentile nations. Nowhere does God extend these promises beyond the borders of Israel, and He does not invite Gentiles to enter into the Mosaic Covenant.

PRESERVING ISRAEL

The Law gave Israel a framework for a highly specialized form of civil government called a Theocracy, where God Himself led the nation through various intermediaries He raised up—quite often prophets. These are the bulk of regulations found in the Torah, and include prescriptions for the Levitical priesthood and their duties, the Tabernacle, their religious calendar, festivals and ceremonies, and more.

Obviously this kind of framework is entirely impractical for Gentile democracies. There are numerous regulations which are irrelevant outside the context of establishing the nation of Israel.

As a nation newly formed, God instituted safeguards to keep Israel from disintegrating and becoming assimilated by surrounding nations. For example, in order to maintain social order, incorrigible youths were to be stoned to death if there was no hope of rehabilitation. In ancient patriarchal societies, maintaining the family structure was fundamentally vital to the survival of the nation itself.

Many of the dietary restrictions were given by an omniscient (or all-knowing) God to susceptible Israelites lacking the benefits of modern sanitary and medical knowledge. Pork, for example, was fortunately forbidden since—as we now know —it is difficult to preserve and becomes a common source of trichinosis: a bad mixture for people without refrigeration and living in the desert. These and other Old Testament laws were given only temporarily and became obviated later in the New Testament when God expanded His Kingdom Plan to include all the nations of the earth.

A CHANGE IN LAW

God did announce that a different age was coming where He would move beyond the Mosaic Covenant and introduced a superior kind of law "written not with ink but with the Spirit of the living God, not on tablets of stone but on tablets of human hearts." *2 Corinthians 3:3* (NASB-U) This is something He offers to the Gentile nations—not the Mosaic Covenant. We encounter this dramatic change in Part 2.

RISE OF THE JEWISH EMPIRE

THE PROMISED LAND

Joshua was a remarkable successor to Moses, a man with a heart zealously in pursuit of God, as he told the Israelites:

"So be very careful to love the Lord your God." *Joshua 23:11*

Joshua's heart was evident years earlier as he yearned to get close to God like Moses, and he was the only person in Israel allowed to climb Mount Sinai along with Moses to meet God.[1] As usual, God strongly supports the one with such a heart, as He told Joshua:

"No one will be able to stand their ground against you as long as you live. For I will be with you as I was with Moses. I will not fail you or abandon you. Be strong and very courageous!" *Joshua 1:5-7*

With such unconquerable power at his disposal, Joshua was ready to go to war and conquer the Promised Land.

CROSSING THE JORDAN RIVER

God's promises were more than words. As the Israelites approached the Promised Land, the Jordan River was flooded and impassible, but God paved the way:

When the people set out to cross the Jordan, the priests who were carrying the Ark of the Covenant went ahead of them. Now it was the harvest season, and the Jordan was overflowing its banks. But as soon as the feet of the priests who were carrying the Ark touched the water at the river's edge, the water began piling up...until the riverbed was dry. *Joshua 3:14-16*

Just as He had parted the Red Sea for the previous generation, God rolled back the flooded river and so proved, "I will not fail you!"

Consider this…
God always backs up His promises with objective facts, and He provided this
new generation of Israelites with undeniable proof that He was trustworthy.

As with Abraham, God always provides evidence first, and only then calls for a response of faith. "Blind faith" is devoid of any evidence, and God deplores such a leap in the dark:

> Now faith is being sure of what we hope for and certain of what we do not see. *Hebrews 11:1*

✐ "Blind faith" is not a biblical concept.

He calls Himself "the God of Abraham, Isaac and Jacob," the God who acts in history. After crossing the Jordan, Israel had the faith required to conquer Jericho.

RAHAB THE PROSTITUTE

The inhabitants of Canaan now faced a multitude of Israelites 2 million strong, homeless, ready to invade, and standing on the wrong side of the Jordan River. Terror swept the cities of the region, and gates were closed and walls fortified.

Not everyone was hostile towards God's Chosen People, however. Rahab was a prostitute who lived in Jericho, a city targeted for conquest. She operated a brothel in Jericho, and when spies from the camp of Israel appeared, she hid them from their pursuers and told them where her allegiance was:

> "I know the Lord has given you this land," she told them. "No wonder our hearts have melted in fear! For the Lord your God is the supreme God of the heavens above and the earth below." *Joshua 2:9-11*

Because she helped the spies, they promised her house would be spared if she draped a scarlet rope from her window. Like the Passover, the scarlet rope symbolized God's willingness to protect those who trust in Him.[A] As with Abraham, acceptance with God is always based on faith, not good works, status, background or nationality:

> "…and the Lord declared him righteous because of his faith." *Genesis 15:6*

Consider this…
Rahab the prostitute is proof that God will certainly receive anyone regardless
of their situation or background – it is never too late to turn to Yahweh in
faith and ask for mercy.

(A) This scarlet rope is part of the recurring Scarlet Thread of Redemption seen throughout the Bible and discussed in the next section.

Even more, Rahab was given an exalted position in The Kingdom, because King David was in her blood line—the same lineage the King of Kings was born into centuries later.[2]

THE BATTLE OF JERICHO

Canaan was anything but an open road: Jericho, for one, stood in the way. It was a huge, thick-walled city[3] that could only fall with siege machinery, which the Israelites lacked. Bypassing Jericho meant leaving a critical threat behind: not an option.

While Joshua was walking alone, pondering and mapping out his strategy, he was startled to encounter a man with a drawn sword! Immediately Joshua challenged him:

> "Are you friend or foe?" "Neither one," he replied. "I am commander of the Lord's army... Take off your sandals, for this is holy ground."
> *Joshua 5:13-15*

Joshua quickly prostrated himself. This was a stark reminder that God would launch the invasion of Canaan for The Kingdom and God's Eternal purposes above and beyond Israel. To underscore that it was God's conquest and not a typical human invasion, this "Commander of the Lord's army" mapped out an unconventional strategy for the conquest of Jericho.

Joshua's army was not allowed to storm the walls, which was fortunate since they were impregnable. Instead, God told the Israelites to march around the city, blowing trumpets and then,

> "When you hear the priests give one long blast on the horns...Then the walls of the city will collapse, and the people can charge straight into the city." *Joshua 6:5*

This was a truly bizarre and unconventional approach to siege warfare. The people of Israel followed the strange instructions anyway, marching around the city in circles for days. Finally, at God's command they sounded their trumpets, and the walls of Jericho literally imploded, collapsing inward and crushing much of the enemy forces. The armies of Israel poured into the city from every direction and completely destroyed the city.[4]

✐ God's approach at times seem so foreign to our natural approach to life.

Jericho typified the kind of miraculous pattern of victory that God established for the next seven years of conquest in Canaan. God led the Israelites into a series of stunning successes—as long and as far as they were willing to trust Him. Yet limits to their trust would soon arise.

THE NEW ESTABLISHMENT

When the dust settled, the Israelites were transformed by the hand of God from impoverished, vagabond slaves into a free people in firm control of the most strategic crossroads in the Ancient Near East. After centuries of bondage under the World System, Israel was to be a prominent launch pad of God's Eternal Plan to free mankind at large from bondage, a clear alternative to the authority of the Kosmos.[5] It was a renunciation of all the principles of greed and power that govern the Counterfeit Kingdom, because in the Promised Land they lived in safety with all the provisions they needed for a victorious legacy:

> "I gave you a land on which you had not labored, and cities which you had not built, and you have lived in them; you are eating of vineyards and olive groves which you did not plant." *Joshua 24:13* (NASB-U)

Realizing that death was near, Joshua outlined the simple principle that governs success within God's economy:

> "So honor the Lord and serve him wholeheartedly...But if you are unwilling to serve the Lord, then choose today whom you will serve... But as for me and my family, we will serve the Lord." *Joshua 24:14-15*

Yet there was also an ominous scenario facing them:

> "If you forsake the Lord and serve other gods, he will turn against you and destroy you, even though he has been so good to you." *Joshua 24:20*

Israel enjoyed a hedge of protection not of their own making and they were not to forget to whom the land belonged: it was Yahweh's. He would never allow His Kingdom Plan to be derailed by rebellion and unbelief.

The people of Israel embraced their new kingdom:

> The Israelites served the Lord throughout the lifetime of Joshua and the leaders who outlived him—those who had seen all the great things the Lord had done for Israel. Then Joshua son of Nun, the servant of the Lord, died at the age of 110. *Judges 2:7-8*

THE PERIOD OF THE JUDGES

Israel quickly spiraled into a dangerous state:

> After that generation died, another generation grew up who did not acknowledge the Lord or remember the mighty things he had done for Israel...They abandoned the Lord, the God of their ancestors, worshiping the gods of the people around them. *Judges 2:10-12*

THE CONFUSION OF COMPLACENCY

Joshua's generation was committed to God, but their subsequent generation became complacent, and developed a supreme self-confidence:

> The people did whatever seemed right in their own eyes. *Judges 21:25*

> ∽ **When people live without reference to God's Absolutes, decay and confusion always results.**

No longer convinced of their need, they exchanged God's leadership for the allure of the Kosmos. They began to intermarry with the surrounding Canaanites, and picked up their false religions, which often included human sacrifice and sexual rituals of incredible perversity—horrifically victimizing women.[B] They quickly become indistinguishable from the surrounding Kosmos through their compromise.

Consider this...
Satan as ruler of the World System and God's adversary always undermines God's order with chaos and anarchy. As a brilliant liar, he easily lures a following with the promise of self-rule and increased pleasure:

Before every man there lies a wide and pleasant road he thinks is right, but it ends in death. *Proverbs 16:25* (Living)

The Israelites were drawn into the culture of the Canaanites because of their women, wealthy trade and exotic rituals. Because the land was so strategically located at the crossroads of ancient trade routes, the Canaanites developed extensive relationships with the most sophisticated and urbane ancient peoples, such as the Phoenicians.[6] These were great sea-faring peoples whose trade brought the best of the Kosmos into the land of Canaan. The security and strength of Yahweh's leadership was soon discarded.

Yet this exposure to exotic and distant cultures came at a terrifying price: invasion.

PEOPLE OF THE SEA
The Promised Land held promise for more than Israelites. This was an era of great cultural upheaval that brought waves of migrations throughout the Ancient Near East, but particularly for Israel located so strategically as a land-bridge between Asia

LESSONS FROM HISTORY The Bible records the interaction between Israel and God show how simple and secure God's leadership can be. Yet, it also demonstrates the folly and destruction that arises from self-sufficiency and indifference towards God, as Paul points out:

These events happened as a warning to us, so that we would not crave evil things as they did or worship idols as some of them did. *1 Corinthians. 10:6-7a*

On the one hand, God offers His provision and protection if we seek His leadership. God will carry us into unparalleled success, fulfillment, and peaceful security, as far as we are willing to go with Him:

"You are my hiding place; You preserve me from trouble; You surround me with songs of deliverance." "I will instruct you and teach you in the way which you should go; I will counsel you with My eye upon you." *Psalm 32:7-8 (NASB-U)*

(B) See Further Consideration at the end of this chapter.

and Africa. The proto-Greek "People of the Sea" from the ancient Minoan civilization in particular became great raiders in this region. Their destructive raids so destabilized the region that it became an open invitation to more invasions from wandering nations in the east.[7]

Eventually the People of the Sea simply quit raiding Canaan, and instead began conquering and settling along its seacoast, bringing with them the latest war technology: iron weaponry. The Israelites were now at an alarming disadvantage with their fragile bronze weapons. Suddenly, all the security of their new nation was gone, replaced by vicious and greedy neighbors: especially the dreaded Philistines, as the Sea Peoples became known.

CHAOS
✍ **Complacency leads to self-confidence and independence from God, which ultimately brings compromise and chaos.**

Satan's lie of freedom where each can pursue "whatever seemed right in his own eyes" only brought chaos and confusion to Israel. Having strayed from God's leadership, Israel's chaos left them easy prey to these invading nations. One nation after another stepped into this vacuum of power and made portions of Israel their vassal state. As always, Satan's offer of "freedom" eventually brings slavery in the Counterfeit Kingdom. The Kosmos suddenly lost its thrilling allure as the Israelites tasted its core, bloody principles. They were playing a dangerous game.

Israel repeatedly cried out to God for relief, and God responded:

> Then the Lord raised up judges to rescue the Israelites from their enemies… But when the judge died, the people returned to their corrupt ways, behaving worse than those who had lived before them. *Judges 2:16-19*

✍ **He is a God of Grace who always responds to faith in Him.**

Consider this…
Here lies one of the incredible mysteries about God: His grace. Grace expresses the heart of God. Grace is His unlimited, unconditional love extended to one who does not deserve it and cannot earn it. God will not participate in devotion to idols, but He always forgives and receives a heart that turns back to Him.

This was how Yahweh revealed Himself to Moses:

> "The Lord, the Lord God, compassionate and gracious, slow to anger, and abounding in lovingkindness and truth; who keeps lovingkindness for thousands, who forgives iniquity, transgression and sin." *Exodus 34:6-7a* (NASB-U)

THE LAST JUDGE

Samuel was the last and most influential of the Judges, appearing when the invasion of the marauding Philistines reached a climax, producing panic:

> The Israelites were badly frightened when they learned that the Philistines were approaching. "Plead with the Lord our God to save us from the Philistines!" they begged Samuel. *1 Samuel 7:7-8*

Samuel's spirituality leveled the playing field against the superior iron weapons of the Philistines:

> The Philistines were subdued and didn't invade Israel again for a long time. And throughout Samuel's lifetime, the Lord's powerful hand was raised against the Philistines. *1 Samuel 7:13*

But everyone grew nervous when Samuel was growing old, about to die. The Israelites proposed a reasonable solution:

> "Look," they told him, "you are now old, and your sons are not like you. Give us a king like all the other nations have." *1 Samuel 8:5*

On the surface, it was a reasonable request. Samuel's sons were corrupt and taking bribes; a king would provide stability, a centralized government and a standing army. Until now, the armies of Israel were formed spontaneously in reaction to the latest invasion, by whatever prophet the Lord anointed. A monarchy brought a predictable order.

Their calculations neglected one important factor: Israel was not a normal nation, and they already had a king named Yahweh.

THE HUMAN SOLUTION

The request for a human king was a rejection of their current King, as God told Samuel:

> "It is not you they have rejected, but they have rejected me as their king." *1 Samuel 8:7*

> ✎ **Throughout history, mankind always prefers to trust well-organized systems and institutions rather than the leadership and authority of God.**

God does not object to human organization; as a God of order, He gave us a magnificent ability to structure the world around us. Trust is the issue: Israel wanted to trust a human institution to deliver security when necessary, and remove the urgent need to cry out to God for help.

Samuel was distressed—after all, the people were calling for an end to the long succession of Judges—yet God granted the people's wish to have a king. He is not a dictator:

"Do as they ask, but solemnly warn them about how a king will treat them." *1 Samuel 8:9*

God warned the people to not let their hope depend on their kings, because human leadership alone is never as trustworthy, never as infallible as God's leadership. Kings would betray their trust:

> "This is how a king will treat you," Samuel said. "The king will draft your sons into his army and make them run before his chariots while others will be slave laborers…The king will take your daughters from you and force them to cook and bake and make perfumes for him. He will take away the best of your fields and vineyards and olive groves and give them to his own servants." *1 Samuel 8:11-18*

GOD'S VERSION OF ROYALTY

Although the children of Israel were naive about the potential disasters, God was not. He protected Israel with a unique plan of monarchical rule, and instructed Samuel to write it down:

> Samuel explained to the people the regulations of the kingship. He wrote them down on a scroll and deposited it before the Lord. *1 Samuel 10:25*

God's new plan was a safeguard against the potential despotism of a monarch: it mandated the king must submit to God as Israel's ultimate authority speaking through the prophets. These prophets were not elected, appointed, or known through any means, other than when God manifested His overwhelming supernatural power through one of them, such as with Elijah:

> Elijah was as human as we are, and yet when he prayed earnestly that no rain would fall, none fell for the next three and a half years! Then he prayed for rain, and down it poured. *James 5:17-18*

Thus began the era of the prophets[8] who exercised God's authority over the king. This was not a common monarchy, but rather a theocracy with God as the ultimate King.[9]

The new monarchy as God designed it proved to be a resounding success whenever the king had a heart inclined toward God, honoring God's leadership. Conversely, even the most gifted and powerful kings met tragic failure whenever they strayed away and tried appeasement through a Religion of Merit.

   Despite their naiveté, Sovereign God protected His Kingdom Plan.

Most significantly, God turned the people's request for human protection through human institutions into a great launching pad for The Mystery.

Consider this…

Through the monarchy, the King of Kings would appear from the tribe of Judah,[C] *known as the "Kingly Line."* [10] *This King of Kings would also fulfill the role of Prophet, and usher in God's ideal authority for The Kingdom.* [11]

KING SAUL

Saul began his rule with an amazingly humble attitude. When he was selected as their king, he hid:

> So they asked the Lord, "Where is he?" And the Lord replied, "He is hiding among the baggage." They brought him out, and he stood head and shoulders above anyone else. Then Samuel said to all the people, "This is the man the Lord has chosen as your king" …And all the people shouted, "Long live the king!" *1 Samuel 10:22-24*

Saul was a majestic figure, the very epitome of a great king. Once he tasted his popularity, he gained his footing and easily stepped into his autocratic authority. Yet he soon forgot who the true King was.

THE FATAL FLAW

God led Saul into a stunning series of successful campaigns against the dreaded Philistines. But the popularity and power from his successes made Saul so arrogant, he disdained God's leadership and offered a sacrifice reserved exclusively for the prophet of God, Samuel. God opposed Saul's bid for absolute authority by sending Samuel with perhaps one of the most pointed and significant insights in the entire Old Testament:

> "What is more pleasing to the Lord: your burnt offerings and sacrifices or your obedience to his voice? …Rebellion is as bad as the sin of witchcraft, and stubbornness is as bad as worshiping idols."

Samuel then revealed the real authority behind Israel:

> "So because you have rejected the word of the Lord, he has rejected you from being king." *1 Samuel 15:22-23*

God declared an end to Saul's reign.

※ **God is not impressed by manmade religion.**

Saul maintained the outward forms of religious worship, but in reality he grew increasingly self-willed and defiant toward God. He invented a "Saul-religion," where the king does not depend on God's Prophets or Judges.

(C) See Further Consideration at the end of chapter 6.

Consider this...

Saul is so very typical of the Religious Mindset God so clearly despises. The Religious Mindset creates a man-made god under human control. Repeatedly God exposes these simplistic attempts to manipulate Him.

Is it actually possible God is incapable of discerning someone's true aversion toward Him? The notion is ludicrous. The Bible clearly warns that even the most religious person may be in great trouble when he is finally exposed by God, because God looks at the heart, not ritual observance:

> "I hate all your show and pretense—the hypocrisy of your religious festivals and solemn assemblies." *Amos 5:21-22*

SAUL'S END

Fighting against God is a losing proposition. When God declared an end to Saul's rule, Saul was still desperate to maintain his authority, even as it was slipping away. He grew paranoid and tried to kill anyone he imagined was conspiring against him. David was one of Saul's most loyal servants who lived in Saul's household and played the harp to sooth Saul's burgeoning tantrums:

> [Saul] began to rave like a madman. David began to play the harp, as he did whenever this happened. But Saul, who had a spear in his hand, suddenly hurled it at David, intending to pin him to the wall. But David jumped aside and escaped.

But Saul was fighting God, not David:

> Saul was afraid of [David], and he was jealous because the Lord had left him and was now with David. *1 Samuel 18:10-12* (NASB-U)

Saul's life ended in tragedy. Before his last battle, he turned to a source for supernatural guidance clearly forbidden by God: a witch! To God, witchcraft is a most detestable spiritual force because it is empowered by demons.[12]

KING DAVID

When God declared an end to Saul's reign, He chose a most startling and unlikely candidate to replace him: a mere shepherd boy! It was an amazing contrast. Saul was tall and handsome, an imposing and regal figure who looked like a king; David, on the other hand, was the youngest and smallest of seven brothers, merely a teenager with boyish looks and "beautiful eyes."[13]

Yet as God anointed David as king, He revealed a profound truth:

> "For God sees not as man sees, for man looks at the outward appearance, but the Lord looks at the heart." *1 Samuel 16:7b* (NASB-U)

GREAT FEATS

Even as a teenager David demonstrated his deep faith in God by killing Goliath, a gigantic Philistine warrior who defied Israel. David stood before the nine-foot giant with nothing but a shepherd's sling and five smooth stones. He pronounced his source of confidence and boldness:

> "Everyone will know that the Lord does not need weapons to rescue his people. It is his battle, not ours!" *1 Samuel 17:47*

With that, he hurled a single stone that shattered the giant's skull—Goliath never considered the accuracy of God's aim; it changes the equation.

During King David's reign, the nation of Israel enjoyed the zenith of its power.[16] David defeated Israel's enemies and enlarged the kingdom to include the land God promised Abraham hundreds of years before.[17] God's Kingdom on earth clearly gained significant ground in the midst of Satan's Counterfeit Kingdom, all because of King David.

David's life is a clear example of how God can take someone simple and obscure like a shepherd boy, and exalt him to a lofty position within His Kingdom.

Consider this...

God is in the business of granting rulership, dignity and authority to humans, as we saw during the creation of man. David's life is an example of the kind of purpose and satisfaction God can bring to those who seek Him.

Even more thrilling, David became the launch pad for the King of Kings who would come to establish The Kingdom forever:

> "Your dynasty and your kingdom will continue for all time before me, and your throne will be secure forever." *2 Samuel 7:16*

David responds with an amazing realization of the Grace of God, just as Abraham knew it:

THE BIGGER THEY COME, THE HARDER THEY FALL Goliath is a famous instance where God's power negates both size and odds, by human calculation. According to the Bible, Goliath measured almost nine feet tall. Compared to David, who was a teenager at the time, this was undoubtedly an overwhelming size.

But just how reliable is this story?

Egyptian reliefs depict Philistines as tall warriors, and the Egyptians themselves were fearful of these "People of the Sea."[14] Archeologists have unearthed skeletons and Philistine beds for people this size.[15]

Only someone writing from this time period would know such detailed characteristics of the Philistine invaders—a race that was entirely dead within a few short centuries. Time and again, archeology proves the Bible is a reliable historical record.

Then King David went in and sat before the Lord and prayed, "Who am
I, O Sovereign Lord, and what is my family, that you have brought me
this far? What more can I say? You know what I am really like, Sovereign
Lord." *2 Samuel 7:18, 20*

THE SOURCE OF SUCCESS

What made David's reign so successful? Clearly it was not David's religious Good
Works, David not only committed adultery with Bathsheba,[18] but he also committed
murder by sending her husband Uriah into the front lines of battle to be killed—
especially reprehensible because Uriah was one of David's most loyal friends.[19]
Rather, it was despite these shortfalls, God found in David a remarkable characteristic: humility and repentance.

> Create in me a clean heart, O God. Renew a right spirit within me.
> *Psalm 51:10*

ꜿ **God responds to a person's heart, not his performance.**

The Bible summarizes King David's greatness this way:

> "The Lord has sought out for Himself a man after His own heart."
> *1 Samuel 13:14b* (NASB-U)

Consider this...
*From this point forward, Israel's kings were repeatedly measured against this
simple standard: a heart of love towards God, like David's heart. Even today,
this "heart for God" is what God seeks from each of us.*

David went on to write most of the book of Psalms, which so poetically expresses
the joy and confidence that arose from his relationship with God. Psalms records the
way we too, can cry out to God for help and safety despite overwhelming obstacles.

KING SOLOMON

When King David died, his son Solomon was crowned the third king of Israel.
God offered Solomon an amazing opportunity:

> That night the Lord appeared to Solomon in a dream, and God said,
> "What do you want? Ask, and I will give it to you!" *1 Kings 3:5*

Solomon's answer revealed a mark of true leadership:

> "Give me an understanding mind so that I can govern your people well
> and know the difference between right and wrong." *1 Kings 3:9*

It was a simple request for God's leadership and as always, God responds joyfully to such a request:

> The Lord was pleased with Solomon's reply... "Because you have asked for wisdom in governing my people and have not asked for a long life or riches for yourself or the death of your enemies—I will give you what you asked for! I will give you a wise and understanding mind such as no one else has ever had or ever will have!" *1 Kings 3:10-12*

This was a highly unusual request for a monarch. Successful rulers in the World System usually crave wealth, power or popularity. Wisdom is a different kind of strength, as Solomon himself points out:

> How does a man become wise? The first step is to trust and reverence the Lord! *Proverbs 1:7* (Living)

∽ God is the very source of Wisdom.

Solomon's desire for wisdom was a desire to understand the very mind of God. Wisdom is different than knowledge; in the Bible, it is rooted in the very person of God, and it unlocks the secrets of creation, the blueprints of our design:

> By wisdom the Lord laid the earth's foundations, by understanding he set the heavens in place; *Proverbs 3:19*

Consider this...

People heavily invest in the tools to build their lives, like education degrees, job experience, popularity or wealth. But without wisdom, these otherwise valuable assets can become useless and even destructive.

Wisdom is the most foundational of all capabilities, but without the Creator, wisdom is impossible:

SOLOMON'S TEMPLE One of Solomon's greatest achievements was building the first Temple, a magnificent stone structure with inner walls of cedar, much of it overlaid with gold.

More than just an ornate building, it was at the epicenter of The Mystery: built on Mount Moriah,[20] where God directed Abraham to sacrifice his only son, Isaac. This became the center of God's picture of Redemption, which is His plan to purchase humanity from slavery in the Kosmos. The priests placed the Ark of the Covenant in the inner sanctuary, and God's Shekinah glory filled the Holy of Hollies as a sign of His presence.

This building was never built to contain God, but rather to pronounce His greatness, as Solomon said:

"He prayed, "'O Lord, God of Israel, there is no God like you in all of heaven or earth. You keep your promises and show unfailing love to all who obey you and are eager to do your will...But will God really live on earth? Why, even the highest heavens cannot contain you. How much less this Temple I have built!'" *1 Kings 8:23-27*

The fool has said in his heart, "There is no God," *Psalm 53:1* (NASB-U)

For those unwilling to acknowledge the Creator, God jealously guards the power of Wisdom:

For it is written, "I will destroy the wisdom of the wise, And the cleverness of the clever I will set aside." *1 Corinthians 1:19* (NASB-U)

But for those who approach God like Solomon, with an earnest desire to grasp Wisdom:

But you desire honesty from the heart, so you can teach me to be wise in my inmost being. *Psalm 51:6*

Israel was at her peak, the fulfillment of God's ancient promise to Abraham to "make a great nation." From David's conquests, her borders were expansive and secured, and with Solomon's godly wisdom, it promised to become a "blessing to the nations," as God told Abraham.

Yet the ancient Principle of Sin still held a grip on Israel that proved to be fatal.

A TRAGEDY

Tragically, Solomon in his later years drifted away from the Lord and his foundation of wisdom. Instead, he became enslaved to luxury, wealth and sensuality, eventually amassing a harem that would thrill even the most hedonistic addict:

He had seven hundred wives and three hundred concubines. And sure enough, they led his heart away from the Lord. *1 Kings 11:3*

Solomon's hedonism led him far away from the original, simple love of God that his father David knew and passed along to his son:

In Solomon's old age, [the wives] turned his heart to worship their gods instead of trusting only in the Lord his God, as his father, David, had done. *1 Kings 11:4*

His opulent lifestyle and decadence required vast sums of money and His powerful kingdom began to crumble. Solomon launched a crushing program of heavy taxation and forced labor to fuel vast building projects, especially ornate temples for the pagan idols of his 1,000 women.

He refused to follow the Lord completely, as his father, David, had done…Solomon built shrines for all his foreign wives to use for burning incense and sacrificing to their gods. *1 Kings 11:6a, 8*

Solomon's new direction triggered far-reaching consequences, as God's protection was removed from his smug and rebellious kingdom:

"I will surely tear the kingdom away from you and give it to one of your servants." *1 Kings 11:11*

SOLOMON'S DISCOVERY

Near the end of his life, Solomon returned to God and wrote one last book called Ecclesiastes. It was a searing attack against the false sense of security the Counterfeit Kingdom offers, and dismantles the meaninglessness of living for pleasure.

His conclusion: hedonism is "striving after the wind" because in the end, "I hated all the fruit of my labor." A lifestyle of self-gratification is not only pointless, but it actually results in a hatred of the fruit it bears. Solomon indulged in everything the Counterfeit Kingdom offers—the stimulation and reward, recognition and power, everything so attractive and promising from the World System—yet even as Solomon grasps for all these treasures, he finds only the wind in his hands, nothing of substance:

> I denied myself nothing my eyes desired; I refused my heart no pleasure. My heart took delight in all my work, and this was the reward for all my labor. Yet when I surveyed all that my hands had done and what I had toiled to achieve, everything was meaningless, a chasing after the wind; nothing was gained under the sun. So I hated life, because the work that is done under the sun was grievous to me. All of it is meaningless, a chasing after the wind. I hated all the things I had toiled for under the sun, because I must leave them to the one who comes after me. So my heart began to despair over all my toilsome labor under the sun. *EcclesIastes. 2:10-20* (NIV)

Consider this...

The Counterfeit Kingdom cannot offer substance and purpose. Its ability to satisfy is so fleeting because this lifestyle is so shallow. It always requires more intense jolts of stimulation to compensate for the emptiness of the aftermath.

None of this can outweigh all the suffering of life, as Solomon eloquently puts it:

> As he had come naked from his mother's womb, so will he return as he came. He will take nothing from the fruit of his labor that he can carry in his hand. This also is a grievous evil—exactly as a man is born, thus will he die. So what is the advantage to him who toils for the wind? Throughout his life he also eats in darkness with great vexation, sickness and anger. *Ecclesiastes 5:15-17* (NASB-U)

FURTHER CONSIDERATION

THE CANAANITE PROBLEM

The destruction of Jericho and the subsequent campaign throughout Canaan was the fulfillment of God's judgment on the debauchery and violence of the nations living there. For generations God exercised patience with the Canaanites, stretching back 400 years to the time of Abraham, giving them time to change until "your descendants will return here to this land, when the sin of the Amorites has run its course." *Genesis 15:16*

God's patience is sometimes longer than seems necessary because, "He does not want anyone to perish, so he is giving more time for everyone to repent." *2 Peter 3:9*

A POINT OF NO RETURN

Yet some people never change. When a culture crosses the point where God's light can no longer penetrate, it becomes a breeding ground of savagery and atrocities that can only be stopped by wiping it out. The Canaanites were remarkably debauched:

> Archaeology has graphically illustrated just how debased these people were... Worship of these gods carried with it some of the most demoralizing practices then in existence.[21]

Beyond orgiastic nature worship and widespread sexual depravity,[22] their atrocities included human sacrifice, especially burning children—even infants[23]—alive:

> Certain rabbinic writers describe a hollow bronze statute...children were placed in the structure which was then heated from below. Drums were pounded to drown out the cries of the children.[24]

This practice was strictly forbidden by Yahweh:

> Sacrificing children to the gods was a common practice [in Canaan]...They saw this as the greatest gift they could offer to ward off evil or appease angry gods. God made it clear that this practice was detestable and strictly forbidden...his character made human sacrifice unthinkable.[25]

In some cultures, the depravity becomes so intense and deeply embedded, even defenseless children become objects of torture and have no chance. At some point, God out of His mercy terminates the spiraling cycle of depravity.

THE FALL OF THE JEWISH EMPIRE

He struck down great nations and slaughtered mighty kings
Psalm 135:10

DIVISION

King Solomon set a new trend of drifting away from God and assimilating the idol worship of the surrounding cultures, including the atrocities and decadent lifestyles. Although Israel still acknowledged the God of their fathers in practice, in actuality their attitude toward God became increasingly characterized by Ritual Observance: an obligatory but token acknowledgement of God, like paying taxes. They observed all the Holy Days, the sacrifices and some of the tithes, but there was no pleasure in this cursory relationship with God.

Missing was the genuine trust in God that marked Abraham's life—the relationship man was created to enjoy. Solomon's glorious new Temple in Jerusalem did not prevent their drift away from the true worship of God, and the Religious Mindset

THE ALLURE OF IDOL WORSHIP Human history is flooded with manmade religions called idolatry which God renounces as utterly absurd: "Who but a fool would make his own god—an idol that cannot help him one bit!" *Isaiah 44:10*

It is impossible to represent God with an image, and He forbade the Israelites to worship any such images: "What image might we find to resemble him? 'To whom will you compare me? Who is my equal?' asks the Holy One. "Look up into the heavens. Who created all the stars?" *Isaiah 40:18, 25-26*

Yet continually idol worship crept back into Israel from the surrounding cultures because, "special enticements to idolatry as offered by these various cults were found in...their appeal to primitive human desires, especially the sexual."[1]

Still today people create manmade religions that reduce God to a remote and inconsequential being, not unlike an idol "that cannot help one bit!" In the Modern West, hand-carved idols are replaced with something similar: "Their god is their appetite...and all they think about is this life here on earth." *Philippians 3:19*. The allure of false religion is always the "appeal to primitive human desires."

typical of King Saul took firm root in Israel, apparently forgetting how God rejected Saul's rituals of appeasement—but they soon found out.

ᕰ **Yet God is not fooled by ritual.**

He repeatedly warns Israel:

> "I don't want your sacrifices—I want your love; I don't want your offerings—I want you to know me." *Hosea 6:6* (Living)

SOLOMON'S SON

When Solomon died, the people sent a delegation to the new king Rehoboam, and begged for relief from the overwhelming program of taxation and conscripted labor imposed by Solomon.

> "Your father was a hard master," they said. "Lighten the harsh labor demands and heavy taxes that your father imposed on us. Then we will be your loyal subjects." *1 Kings 12:4*

But Rehoboam was young and brash, and reacted by imposing even heavier taxes to demonstrate his authority.

> "Yes, my father was harsh on you, but I'll be even harsher! My father used whips on you, but I'll use scorpions!" *1 Kings 12:11*

This is exactly what God warned when Israel first cried out for a king: the heavy taxation, their young men enslaved, and their lives burdened more than ever. With God's leadership prior to the monarchy, God fought their battles and they enjoyed peace without this high price.

ᕰ **Life is guaranteed to be more desirable under God's leadership than apart from Him.**

Consider this...
God is often the last resort for direction—if ever considered—because turning to God means surrendering the innate desire to live without His interference.

JEROBOAM'S REBELLION

A charismatic general named Jeroboam emerged, and ten of the twelve tribes gathered around him:

> When all the Israelites heard that Jeroboam had returned, they sent and called him to the assembly and made him king over all Israel. *1 Kings 12:20* (NIV)

The 10 tribes formed the Northern Kingdom of Israel under Jeroboam, while

Solomon's son was barely able to retain the two tribes, which became Judah, named after the larger of the loyal tribes. Judah enjoyed a significant advantage by retaining southern Israel, where Solomon's temple was in Jerusalem, and this became the source of northern Israel's eventual demise.

THE COLLAPSE OF THE NORTHERN KINGDOM

The Northern Kingdom quickly degenerated into chaos and destruction. It started with Jeroboam, the first king:

> He placed calf idols at the southern and northern ends of Israel—in Bethel and in Dan. This became a great sin, for the people worshiped them, traveling even as far as Dan. *1 Kings 12:28-30*

Placing idols at strategic locations offered a convenient alternative to the otherwise long journey south into Judah where Solomon's temple was. The strategy worked, and traffic from northern Israel to Jerusalem trickled to a stop; but it set a pattern of idol worship that intensified through the centuries until the Northern Kingdom lost all connections with God. This pattern became known as the "Sin of Jeroboam," and it destroyed northern Israel.[3]

Consider this...

True to historical form, the people exchanged the Creator God for a religion of convenience. It seems easier to practice a religion that leaves the Principle of Sin unchallenged and autonomy from God intact.

ELIJAH VERSUS AHAB

God did not give up easily on the Northern Kingdom of Israel. He raised a powerful prophet named Elijah, who alone led a successful revolt against Israel's most notorious ruler, King Ahab, and his scheming wife Jezebel—a name used even today as an insult. Together they slaughtered God's prophets in order to spread the religion of Jezebel's native idol, Baal:[4]

> [Ahab] did more to arouse the anger of the Lord, the God of Israel, than any of the other kings of Israel before him. *1 Kings 16:33*

LATER OLD TESTAMENT CHRONOLOGY[2]

931 B.C. Kingdom divides into Israel, Judah	*597 B.C.* Babylonians sack Jerusalem (2nd deportation)
722-1 B.C. Assyria conquers northern Israel	*586 B.C.* Babylonians destroy Jerusalem (3rd deportation)
612 B.C. Babylonian Alliance conquers Assyria	
605 B.C. Babylonians attack Jerusalem (1st deportation)	*539-538 B.C.* Medo-Persians (Cyrus) overthrow Babylon, Jews permitted to return

Repeatedly God sent Elijah to intimidate these monarchs with demonstrations of unequalled power—striking the land with a prolonged drought, calling down flames from heaven, and then enraging Jezebel by executing her false prophets:

> Elijah commanded, "Seize all the prophets of Baal. Don't let a single one escape!" So the people seized them all, and Elijah took them down to the Kishon Valley and killed them there. *1 Kings 18:40*

In one day, Elijah bloodied his sword by executing 450 prophets of Baal.

AHAB VERSUS YAHWEH

Ahab and Jezebel remained defiant toward God, despite these demonstrations of God's power. Finally Elijah burst into the throne room of King Ahab with a harrowing message from God:

> "So my enemy has found me!" Ahab exclaimed to Elijah. "Yes," Elijah answered, "The Lord is going to bring disaster to you and sweep you away. He will not let a single one of your male descendants, slave or free alike, survive in Israel!"

Ahab was dumfounded by Elijah's audacious proclamation, and yet Elijah had more:

> "The Lord has also told me that the dogs will eat the body of your wife, Jezebel, at the city wall. The members of your family will be eaten by dogs, and eaten by vultures." *1 Kings 21:20-24*

∞ **It is impossible to form a casual opinion about God.**

The message of Elijah was simple: there is only one God, and His name is Yahweh. Sooner or later, God calls for a decision:

> "How long are you going to waver between two opinions? If the Lord is God, follow him! But if Baal is God, then follow him!" *1 Kings 18:21*

AHAB'S SUCCESS STORY Many of the ungodly kings in northern Israel were hugely successful and are even mentioned prominently in the literatures of neighboring kingdoms. Ahab, for example, receives praise as a victorious warrior-king at the famous battle of Qarqar, yet the Bible never bothers with such acclaim. In the eyes of God, Ahab was a dismal failure, "more than any of the other kings of Israel before him." God proved how frail the man actually was by prophesying his death in detail, and despite Ahab's desperate attempts to avoid it, he died as foretold. Human greatness pales in comparison to God's sovereignty.

Ahab's father King Omri was considered by the Assyrians to be one of northern Israel's most wealthy and powerful kings. Ironically, the Bible dismisses him with a few sentences as an idolatrous follower of "Jeroboam's sin."

Clearly God is unimpressed by the standards of success so honored and pursued within the Kosmos.

To "waiver between two opinions," like Ahab, betrays a genuine mistrust toward God. The Creator insists His created beings decide who to follow: "If the Lord is God, follow him!"

Consider this...

A sense of urgency necessarily surrounds the decision about God because a strong gravitational pull away from God stirs inside, active and fueled by the Principle of Sin. Not making a decision is a decision against God, as default habits take control.

Ahab became deeply sorrowful for his rebellion when Elijah prophesied the dogs would eat his wife and family:

> When Ahab heard this message, he tore his clothing, dressed in sackcloth, and fasted. He even slept in sackcloth and went about in deep mourning. *1 Kings 21:27*

Yet his "deep mourning" only lasted until the danger passed. We next see Ahab jailing another of God's prophets, and his life remained unchanged.[5]

Ahab was presented with clear convictions about God, but the burden becomes intolerable, and the familiar spiritual dullness descends as temporary needs press in from all sides. Without making any decision, the details of daily life dominate again:

> "I have measured out my life with coffee spoons." *T. S. Eliot* [6]

Consider this...

Although God gives everyone opportunity to decide, it is not endless: He struggles with our will power long enough for each to make an informed decision.

> Today, if you hear his voice, do not harden your hearts... *Psalm 95:7-8* (NIV)

> For God says, "At just the right time, I heard you. On the day of salvation, I helped you." Indeed, God is ready to help you right now. Today is the day of salvation. *2 Corinthians 6:2*

THE ASSYRIAN INVASION

In the 240-year history of northern Israel, not one king honored God. God finally removed His protection, and Israel was exposed to the war machine of the expanding Assyrian empire. This was an ancient empire, reaching back to Nimrod's days with the founding of Nineveh.[7] Assyria was a formidable kingdom for many centuries, but then suddenly launched a rampage of conquests rolling across the

Hittite and Phoenician kingdoms. Smaller kingdoms fell like dominoes until the Assyrians stood at the very doorstep of Israel.

The Assyrians were brutal conquerors, as their emperors boasted:

> "I burned 3,000 captives from them. I did not leave one of them alive as hostage. I captured alive…their city ruler. I made a pile of their corpses. I burnt their adolescent boys and girls. I flayed…their city ruler and draped his skin over the wall of the city."[8]

A torrent of urgent prophecies from God fell on deaf ears as Israel drifted further away from His protection, smug and oblivious to the distant rumbling of Assyria's power. Vast passages of scripture were written prophesying the danger in detail. Isaiah offers a typical warning:

> "They will come racing toward Jerusalem…Roaring like lions, they will pounce on their prey. They will seize my people and carry them off into captivity, and no one will be there to rescue them…The enemy nations will growl over their victims like the roaring of the sea. A cloud of darkness and sorrow will hover over Israel." *Isaiah 5:26-30*

By 721 B.C., it was over.[9] Successive Assyrian invasions climaxed in the horrific destruction of northern Israel's cities, burning and pillaging so extensively that starvation ravaged the land.

WITHOUT A FUTURE

When the Assyrians conquered a particularly rebellious people—as the Israelites were—they diffused the will to fight by exporting and importing large populations, thus confusing their national identity. This reduced patriotic fighting spirit:

> And the king of Assyria transported groups of people from Babylon, Cuthah, Avva, Hamath, and Sepharvaim, and resettled them in the towns of Samaria, replacing the people of Israel. *2 Kings 17:24*

Stripped of their national identity and monarchy, the Northern Kingdom was permanently dissolved. Clear warnings led up to this tragedy, yet still Israel became hopelessly absorbed with the barbaric paganism of her neighbors.

Consider this…

The Principle of Sin begins with independence from God and always gains momentum, until it finally spirals into chaos, destruction and finally death.

THE SOUTHERN KINGDOM

Meanwhile in the south, the kingdom of Judah followed a different course, but only slightly. Under the leadership of some godly kings—really very few—the people followed God, especially whenever threatened by invasion.

ASSYRIA DESCENDS ON JUDAH

  God still responds, even though disaster is the initial reason someone turns to Him.

Time and again God delivered Judah from waves of invasions, especially when Assyria was on the rampage. In 701 B.C.,[10] when the Assyrian king Sennacherib approached Jerusalem with his massive war machine, he sent messengers who stood outside the walls of Jerusalem shouting for everyone to hear:

> "Don't let this God you trust deceive you with promises that Jerusalem will not be captured by the king of Assyria. You know perfectly well what the kings of Assyria have done wherever they have gone!" *2 Kings 19:10-11*

Everyone "knew perfectly well" the gruesome Assyrian practice of covering city walls with impaled bodies and how they dismantled Israel.[11] Fortunately Judah enjoyed godly leadership for a change—King Hezekiah. He cried out to God in a moment of lucid insight:

> "O Lord God of Israel, sitting on your throne high above the angels, you alone are the God of all the kingdoms of the earth. You created the heavens and the earth." *2 Kings 19:15* (Living)

Hezekiah then did something unusual for a king by publicly declaring:

> "O Lord our God, we plead with you to save us from his power; then all the kingdoms of the earth will know that you alone are God." *2 Kings 19:19* (Living)

  Real faith in God means calling on Him for rescue.

It required some awkward humility for Hezekiah to admit weakness and inability to control the kingdom. Pleading for God's help always feels like whimpering cowardice—only because the Principle of Sin distorts reality. In reality, humans are weak and do require God's help.

Consider this . . .

The difference between Ahab's temporary "faith" and Hezekiah's genuine trust pivots on the willingness to admit weakness before God. This humility and need for God is precisely at the heart of what the Bible calls salvation. Salvation is not a recitation of words; it is a change of heart attitude, and calling out to God for His mercy.

Everyone who calls on the name of the Lord will be saved. *Romans 10:13* (NIV)

RESCUE

God sent the famous prophet Isaiah to answer King Hezekiah's prayer. Isaiah was one tough prophet, convinced of God's sovereignty despite the overwhelming power of Assyria's war machine. He let the Assyrians know who was in control:

> "Whom do you think you have been insulting and ridiculing? Against whom did you raise your voice? It was the Holy One of Israel! I will put my hook in your nose [and] make you return by the road on which you came." *2 Kings 19:22, 28*

These were bold words from a lonely old man. While hordes of Assyrian warriors encircled Jerusalem, Isaiah inflamed their bloodlust—which meant savage treatment if they ever breached the walls.

God responded to Hezekiah's shaky faith and unleashed His own version of terror against the battle-hardened Assyrians. It was slaughter, not warfare. Sending a solitary angel out of His vast army of angels, God taught the Assyrians how frail they really were:

> That night the angel of the Lord went out to the Assyrian camp and killed 185,000 Assyrian troops. When the surviving Assyrians woke up the next morning, they found corpses everywhere. *2 Kings 19:35*

These were terrifying casualties by ancient standards of warfare: an all-night-long slaughter, a frenzied mob trying to flee an invisible killer. Judah became the only nation throughout the region to resist the Assyrian war machine, and the success reverberated far:

> From then on King Hezekiah became highly respected among the surrounding nations, and many gifts for the Lord arrived at Jerusalem, with valuable presents for King Hezekiah, too. *2 Chronicles 32:23*

✎ **Faith in God is always a reasonable and simple choice.**

SENNACHARIB'S VIEWPOINT The incident between the Assyrian King Sennacharib and King Hezekiah was also preserved in the Assyrian annals. Not surprisingly, the Assyrians put a different spin on it. Sennacharib necessarily admits he did not capture Jerusalem, but says that he left King Hezekiah "himself like a bird in a cage in Jerusalem, his royal city, I penned him."[12] In his version, Sennacharib was the victor.

Yet Sennacharib's story is suspect. We know the Assyrians never left a resisting city intact, willingly. Theirs was one of the most ruinous invading armies in ancient history, infamous for their sophisticated siege machines used for destroying the walls of any city daring resistance.

Conveniently, Sennacharib never explains why he was content to merely leave Hezekiah "like a bird in a cage." Perhaps losing 185,000 soldiers played a role, as the Bible says? Like other ancient rulers, Sennacharib, would never allow such a humiliation to be recorded.

Hezekiah is proof that God never demands an immense "leap of faith," contrary to some fears.[13] Hezekiah certainly wavered at first: when Sennacherib demanded 12 tons of silver and gold, Hezekiah paid the tribute, but Sennacherib wanted still more. When Hezekiah finally asked for God's help, it was the most reasonable alternative available.

Consider this…

The safety Hezekiah desired was always available from God, as he finally discovered. It only required a simple decision to lay down pride and depend on God. It is not complicated, as King David describes it:

Come near and rescue me! *Psalm 69:18*

Hezekiah also discovered a delightful side-effect of trusting God: He always provides more than expected. Not only saved from the Assyrians, Judah's devastated treasury was replenished when the "surrounding nations" sent many "valuable presents."

JUDAH'S DECLINE

After their rescue from Assyria, Judah launched a fateful course that ultimately destroyed their nation. They too embraced idol worship, but in a shrewd variation on Israel's idolatry Judah never rejected the God of Abraham altogether. Instead, they relegated Him to an obscure role, acknowledged on sacred days and confined to Solomon's Temple, utterly impotent. They developed the Religious Mindset, using appeasement through Ritual Observance.

CULTURAL ASSIMILATION

For more than one hundred years God's prophets predicted the fall of Judah in detail:

> "The time is coming when everything you have—all the treasures stored up by your ancestors—will be carried off to Babylon. Nothing will be left, says the Lord." *Isaiah 39:6-7*

Gone were the days of King Hezekiah's humility and need for God. The Kings of Judah refused to believe and grew increasingly smug because Solomon's Temple was in Jerusalem: God would certainly never allow it to fall into the hands of invaders![14] God sent Prophets to warn them otherwise:

> Thus says the Lord, "Heaven is My throne and the earth is My footstool. Where then is a house you could build for Me? And where is a place that I may rest?" *Isaiah 66:1* (NASB-U)

∽ **God cannot be confined in a temple.**

Their view of Yahweh became farcical—He was a trite deity like all the others, easily fooled by their sacrifices. Judah became indistinguishable from the surrounding Kosmos, pursuing the enticements offered by idolatry, building altars to foreign gods inside the Temple with "male cult prostitutes which were in the house of the Lord." *2 Kings 23:7* (NASB-U) Even worse, they began practicing child sacrifice outside the gates of Jerusalem itself—where Judah's kings were sacrificing their own children![26] They were fully entrenched in the Cult of Man.

A SHIFT IN POWER

Great political upheavals swept the ancient world. As the Assyrians gained dominance, new and more powerful kingdoms were rising in the east: the Neo-Babylonians,[A] Medes, Scythians, and Persians—all significant problems for Assyria.

Meanwhile, the kingdoms of Israel grew weaker. Curiously, God never objected when Israel divided and weakened militarily. Centuries of spiritual depravity further eroded Israel and Judah until pagan kingdoms now threatened to completely overrun God's small beachhead anchored in Palestine.

These problems were anticipated long before Israel divided in 931 B.C., and He set a plan in motion unfettered by self-willed kings. Gradually, God was raising another power that threatened all the others.

✐ **God was raising a powerful and loyal army of His own.**

By 740 B.C. during the time of the prophet Isaiah, came the Writing Prophets: agents of change throughout the Near East. Such unlikely threats—unarmed, often solitary, yet holding sway over kings and empires—these prophets stood on the power of God's Word. Israel and Judah were unimpressed:

> But the people mocked these messengers of God and despised their words. They scoffed at the prophets until the Lord's anger could no longer be restrained and there was no remedy. *2 Chronicles 36:16*

SACRED SPACE Just as Judah confined God to the temple, throughout history the Cult of Man always worships a deity confined within a Sacred Space. There, the deity's presence is felt through a manufactured atmosphere of "other-worldliness:" a combination of unusual architecture, often with a dark, hazy atmosphere or incense where people move slowly with monotonous gestures, surrounded by the sounds of repetitive chants or ethereal music.[35]

The True Creator God wants to take up residence inside our very persons. He wants our hearts as His "Sacred Space." Since God is spiritual, no material structure can possibly contain Him:

"True worshippers will worship the Father in spirit and in truth. The Father is looking for anyone who will worship him that way." *John 4:24*

This is good news: it means God is easily accessible, anywhere!

(A) Historians call it Neo ("New") Babylonian to distinguish it from the "Old Babylonia" of the second and third millennia BC. Also called the Neo Chaldean Empire, Abraham's home town "Ur of the Chaldeans" led this revived empire.

Consider this...

Although God's Prophets were ridiculed, banished, jailed, and ruthlessly executed for their treasonous opposition to the monarchy,[27] God's Word prevailed as prophecies were fulfilled in rapid, terrifying succession.

Centuries before the invasions stunned Israel and Judah, the Writing Prophets wove a picture of a future mixed with great foreboding and yet great hope. It was foreboding because the increasing rebellion of the kings after Solomon's time was pronounced irreversible by the Prophets, and violent overthrow was inevitable:

> "And as surely as I live," says the Lord, "I will abandon you to King Nebuchadnezzar of Babylon and the mighty Babylonian army."
> *Jeremiah 22:24a-25*

It was also a picture of hope. The same Prophets declared monumental human empires would ebb and flow like waves on the sand, but the authority of God's Word always remained standing.

The Word of God through the Prophets dominated not only Palestine, but the surrounding nations. Even the supreme Assyrians and Babylonians were defenseless against it, as Assyria discovered next.

ASSYRIA DESTROYED

When the Assyrians invaded God's Promised Land, they entered God's territory only by His permission, and took away more than plunder—they also carried an obligation to acknowledge the sovereignty of Yahweh over their success. Wealthy and powerful Assyrians were not inclined to bow to anyone:

> [The Assyrians] boast, "We in our own power and wisdom have won these wars…By our own strength we broke down the walls and destroyed the people and carried off their treasures." *Isaiah 10:13* (Living)

The prophets warned Assyria:

ASSYRIA AS GOD'S WEAPON In 2 Kings 19:25-26, God declares He smoothed the road for Assyria's great conquests: "their people are such easy prey for you." This worked to Israel's benefit, as in 2 Kings 13:4—"Jehoahaz prayed for the Lord's help…So the Lord raised up a deliverer to rescue the Israelites from the tyranny of the Arameans." The "deliverer" of Israel was none other than Assyria.[19]

For centuries, God tried to rescue Assyria from its false idols, especially since their chief deity was a bloody "god of war" contributing to their ruthlessness. God sent a series of prophetic warnings to their leaders—he even sent Jonah into Nineveh, their capital. Jonah's mission was successful, but only temporarily. Still, He had compassion on the Ninevites:

"Nineveh has more than 120,000 people living in spiritual darkness... Shouldn't I feel sorry for such a great city?" *Jonah 4:11*

"I am your enemy!" says the Lord Almighty. "Your chariots will soon go up in smoke...Never again will you bring back plunder from conquered nations!" *Nahum 2:11a, 13a*

Then the Babylonians struck hard. Allied with Assyria's numerous enemies, in 612 B.C. the capital city Nineveh was breached and the Ninevites paid a horrific price for many centuries of brutal conquest. It was God's Prophets who decreed it decades earlier:[18]

"Loot the silver! Plunder the gold! There seems no end to Nineveh's many treasures—its vast, uncounted wealth. Soon the city is an empty shambles, stripped of its wealth." *Nahum 2: 4, 9-10*

∽ Human sovereignty only exists by God's permission.

The message of the prophets was a simple one: humans enjoy considerable freedom of choice, and freedom to rebel is possible, but it is not an eternal and unlimited freedom.

Consider this...
God provides everyone a chance to end the rebellion by finding a love-trust relationship with Him. Enough time, evidence and free will are available to make an informed decision about whether God is worthy of trust.

With or without a trust relationship, everyone will acknowledge His authority:

"I have sworn by my own name, and I will never go back on my word: Every knee will bow to me, and every tongue will confess allegiance to my name." *Isaiah 45:23*

The destruction of Nineveh opened a vacuum of power which the Babylonian armies quickly filled, menacing Judah. Judah was by now thoroughly enamored with the pagan religions of her neighbors, and would soon discover what lies beneath the splendid veneer of the Kosmos.

FURTHER CONSIDERATION

THE EXCITEMENT OF CHRONOLOGIES

Historical chronologies are perhaps not the most exciting study for most people, but they become critical for anyone seriously investigating the Bible. A Chronology is "the study of historical records to establish the dates of past events." It is difficult to appreciate the deep insights of the Old Testament writings—especially those of The Prophets—without understanding at least some Ancient Near Eastern (ANE) history.

The rise of Assyria was a significant milestone because they established the first in a chain of famous Empires dominating the Middle East: followed by the Babylonians, Persians, Greeks, and finally the Romans. Each stood on the shoulders of the previous, inheriting a vast region by toppling the existing regime.

THE SIGNIFICANCE

This extra-biblical history is significant because it ties the Bible's message to verifiable names, dates and places. All these famous empires interact with the Bible over centuries. Israel's Kings Omri and Ahab are non-fictional characters found in Assyrian writings, for example.

These four Empires—along with Egypt—provide historians with extensive chronicles which might either affirm or refute the Bible's historical record. What we find is a remarkable confirmation of the Bible's historicity in detail. Many secular archeologists have high regard for the Bible's chronologies, finding that, "Nowhere has archeological discovery refuted the Bible as history." This is no minor feat since the Bible's historical record covers such a long period.

Beginning with the Exodus—and certainly by the time of King David—the Bible gives a tight chronology of the various kings and their encounters with the surrounding cultures. There is very little room for error: the correlation and lengths of king's reigns "make impossible any arbitrary adjustment of as much as a single year in the reign of any king, without introducing widespread disruption into an otherwise harmonious pattern."[20]

Nehemiah 2:1 shows the historical details found in the Bible:

> And it came about in the month Nisan, in the twentieth year of King Artaxerxes... *Nehemiah 2:1* (NASB-U)

Artaxerxes is a well-known, well-documented Persian king, and Nehemiah's comments make it possible to absolutely fix the date of this passage to 444 B.C.— a very key date, because it also makes it possible to fix 33 A.D. as the date of Daniel's famous prophecy about the coming of the Messiah (discussed in Chapter 15 sidebar "Daniel 9").

In 1951, Edwin R. Thiele pointed out "Absolute Dates in Near Eastern Chronology," which indisputably fix key dates in the biblical record. Working from well-established Assyrian and Babylonian lists of kings, Thiele established the veracity of the biblical chronologies, resulting in "a changed attitude among Old Testament scholars toward the Hebrew text resulting in a greater appreciation for its transmission and accuracy."[21]

With objective facts verified, the Bible's spiritual truths become credible. This is a unique feature of the Bible among other sacred writings: more than a philosophy or an abstraction, God is a historical figure.

A CLEAR FUTURE

"A ruler of Israel will come from you, one whose origins are from the distant past."
Micah 5:2b

THE EXILE

The Babylonians utterly ravaged Judah over a 50-year period, beginning with the most lucrative treasure of all: the glorious Temple of Solomon with more than 300 years of accumulated gold, silver and precious artifacts.[1]

King Jehoiakim triggered it. With contempt he defied the Lord's authority over the monarchy, savagely killing and desecrating the body of Uriah the prophet. Jeremiah the Prophet sent him written warnings:

> The king took his knife and cut off that section of the scroll. He then threw it into the fire, section by section, until the whole scroll was burned up. *Jeremiah 36:23*

This was a king with unrestrained pride.[2] Foolishly, he next defied the most-powerful conqueror ever seen: King Nebuchadnezzar of Babylon. He saw how the Babylonians swept aside the powerful Egyptian-Assyrian armies, and was initially intimidated into paying tribute to this new invader—a tribute which included hostages, among whom was the young man Daniel, soon to become one of the Writing Prophets.[3] Then Jehoiakim regained his confidence and rebelled against Babylon, sealing his fate.

THE TEMPLE SACKED

For God, Jehoiakim was a dead man long before the Babylonian backlash:

> He will be buried like a dead donkey—dragged out of Jerusalem and dumped outside the gate! *Jeremiah 22:18-19*

As prophesied, an angry Nebuchadnezzar surrounded Jerusalem with armies, and the frightened inhabitants offered an olive branch by killing their proud king and tossing his body over the city walls. As Jeremiah foretold, the invaders desecrated the carcass "like a dead donkey."[4]

Sheepishly, hoping Nebuchadnezzar was placated by the "dead donkey," they opened Jerusalem's doors to the Babylonians: It was a dream of a lifetime for hardened, armed soldiers, and a frenzy of looting filled the streets. Solomon's Temple was the prize:

> As the Lord had said beforehand, Nebuchadnezzar carried away all the treasures from the Lord's Temple and the royal palace. They cut apart all the gold vessels that King Solomon of Israel had placed in the Temple. *2 Kings 24:13*

Not satisfied with treasure alone:

> King Nebuchadnezzar took 10,000 captives from Jerusalem, including all the princes and the best of the soldiers, craftsmen, and smiths. So only the poorest people were left in the land. *2 Kings 24:14*

The date was 597 B.C., and it was the first time invaders ever sacked the great center of Israel's pride.[5] The sacking of the Temple shocked and dismayed the nation. Lost forever were the cherished artifacts of the nation's history, going back to the Exodus from Egypt. Judah experienced the withdrawal of God's protection–the result of assimilating into the Counterfeit Kingdom.

DEPORTATIONS

The Babylonians extracted more treasures and deported larger populations of Israelites into slavery, feeding Nebuchadnezzar's massive building programs. By the time they were finished, the Promised Land was destitute.[6]

Imagine the bewilderment of God's People as they marched naked and chained through a barren wasteland left by invasions of armies: Palestine, once "flowing

THE LOST ARK Contrary to popular myth perpetrated by Spielberg's famous film, the Ark of the Covenant was not a mystical "power source" guaranteed to destroy Israel's enemies. The Israelites discovered this the hard way when they carried the Ark into battle, expecting victory: "Israel was defeated again. The slaughter was great; 30,000 Israelite men died that day. The survivors turned and fled to their tents." *1 Samuel 4:10*

The Ark most likely was captured when Nebuchadnezzar sacked the Temple. It was probably melted for its gold, and ironically used for the construction of a massive golden idol worshiped by the Babylonians.

Jeremiah at this point writes about a future in which the Ark will no longer be needed or even missed: "And when your land is once more filled with people," says the Lord, "you will no longer wish for 'the good old days' when you possessed the Ark of the Lord's covenant...there will be no need to rebuild the Ark." *Jeremiah 3:16*

Jeremiah was soon to be proven correct: God replaced the symbolism depicted by the Ark with something so wonderfully tangible, the symbols pale by comparison: the manifestation of The Mystery.[A]

(A) The Ark and its symbolism are discussed in detail in this book.

with milk and honey"—their home and "Promised Land"—all gone.

"Where is God?" dominated their theology.[7] God's Abrahamic Covenant with "the land I will give you" and how "I will make you a great nation" seemed like hollow words.

Leaving behind the gray and desolate world of Palestine, the slaves entered the gates of a stunning realm—it was called "Babylon the Great." It was the heart of its Empire—the Cult of Man—with towering palaces, citizens flaunting gold and jewels, bustling with armored chariots, and columns of soldiers on the move. Babylon was the Renaissance of the Near East; Nebuchadnezzar's "Hanging Gardens of Babylon" is one of the "Seven Ancient Wonders of the World." Here was an empire so vast, so glorious and formidable, it seemed indomitable. What nation could topple it?

The walls of Babylon were so thick, four chariots could race abreast. It seemed like it could last forever—but it didn't. It ended at 539 BC.

> **The apparent invincibility of the Kosmos breeds indifference towards God and His Kingdom.**

Consider this...
Each new empire rises to power with invincible splendor, while God and His Kingdom seem remote and feeble by comparison. It is no coincidence that apathy about God increases in the Modern West as it reaches its zenith of power.

Glorious Babylon was a bastion of occultic worship, dominated by the ancient Ruler of this World. The Babylonians were called "Chaldeans," meaning "Master Astrologers,"[8] and it was the birthplace of astrology and the horoscope.[9] The Cult of Man—once disrupted by God during Nimrod's ancient Tower of Babel—was resurging with vengeance, dominating God's Promised Land and using His Chosen People as slaves to build the system opposed to God.

> **Human empires, no matter how formidable, can never match the security and permanence of God's Kingdom.**

Magnificent Babylon soon tasted the power of God's Word when the Prophets were dragged into the city along with the exiles. Nebuchadnezzar soon learned his vast authority and empire teetered on God's will.

THE PROPHETS TAKE CHARGE

The age of the Writing Prophets was in full stride since the Jewish monarchy was effectively stripped of all authority and power, as the Prophets warned. All of God's leadership now centered on the Prophets, and any hope of deliverance meant the Jews[B] must pay close attention to these unlikely leaders.

(B) "Jew" denotes originally an inhabitant of Judah (2 Kings 16:6) and became a prominent name during the Exile and afterward, since only the people of Judah remained after the Assyrian destruction of northern Israel.

The Jewish captives already saw extensive prophecies fulfilled by the invasions of Assyria and Babylonia, so there were reasons for confidence in the rapid demise of Babylon prophesied earlier.[10]

A new generation of prophets arrived from among the Exiles and stood before the king's throne to announce God's authority. As the Assyrians discovered, by conquering the Promised Land the Babylonians stumbled onto the stage of God's Kingdom Plan, and returned from Palestine with an obligation to acknowledge God's sovereignty.

BABYLON MEETS THE PROPHETS

It began simply enough: God showed Nebuchadnezzar a disturbing vision one night. He immediately realized this was no common dream, and desperately tried to discover its meaning, but not one of Babylon's famed occultists or astrologers could pass a simple test of authenticity: to reveal not only the interpretation, but the dream itself. After lengthy debates and stall tactics,

> The astrologers replied to the king:, "There isn't a man alive who can tell Your Majesty his dream! And no king, however great and powerful, has ever asked such a thing of any magician, enchanter, or astrologer!" *Daniel 2:10*

Enraged, the king realized he was surrounded by charlatans, and began ordering executions. Then one of the Jewish captives stepped confidently before the throne: It was one of God's Prophets with typically bold claims.

> Daniel replied, "There is a God in heaven who reveals secrets...Now I will tell you your dream and the visions you saw as you lay on your bed." *Daniel 2:27-28*

THE OCCULT VERSUS TRUTH God warns extensively to keep away from the occult. (See Leviticus 19:31; 20:6, 27; Deuteronomy. 18:10, 11; Jeremiah 27:9, 10.) The term describes a vast array of spiritual pursuits: astrology, fortune-telling, conjuring spirits and more. Yet they all have a common feature: invoking spiritual phenomena outside of God's authority.

God causes supernatural phenomena Himself: miracles, predictions, or visions like Nebuchadnezzar received. The difference pivots on the question of Truth: The occult is deceptive, but God offers authentic spirituality.

Occultists are often impostors, as with Nebuchadnezzar's Chaldeans. Isaiah observes, "Astrologers... are as useless as dried grass burning in a fire. They cannot even save themselves!" *Isaiah 47:13-14*

Occultic phenomena can be paranormal, but never originating from God. Satan offers spiritual experiences too, but only because, "the father of lies" desires to capture and "work in the hearts of those who refuse to obey God." *Ephesians 2:1b*

Whether fraudulent or genuine, occult phenomena are laced with deception. God wants us to learn truth from Him.

The vision centered on a monolithic statue. It was God's Revelation about the course of human empires rising to conquer the Promised Land, one glorious kingdom after another: the Babylonians, Persians, Greeks and finally Rome, the most "dreadful and terrifying and extremely strong" of all, a kingdom that will "devour the whole earth and tread it down and crush it..."[11] Yet none of these would last, not even the Babylonian Empire. Only one authentic kingdom will remain, Daniel told Nebuchadnezzar:

> The God of heaven will set up a kingdom that will never be destroyed; no one will ever conquer it. It will shatter all these kingdoms into nothingness, but it will stand forever. *Daniel 2:44*

Once again a Prophet stood before the throne, pronouncing the king's frailty and demonstrating God's true authority over creation.

✎ God's prophetic Word cannot be broken.

Consider this...

All the violence and upheaval of ancient history was still in the future when the Prophets wrote it down: the rise and fall of Assyria, Babylonia, Persia, Greece and Rome. God's Kingdom will arise as tangible and certain as the great human empires, according to the same prophets. His Kingdom is not a fantasy.

THE FALL OF 'BABYLON THE GREAT'

So typical of human interests, Nebuchadnezzar dismissed God's message and resumed building his great kingdom. Like a fool, he grossly over-estimated his stature and security in the universe:

> The king reflected and said, "Is this not Babylon the great, which I myself have built as a royal residence by the might of my power and for the glory of my majesty?" *Daniel 4:30*

If Nebuchadnezzar was not so indifferent to God's Word—it was relayed to him, accompanied by miraculous displays of power—he would know about the impending

THE SIGNIFICANCE OF DANIEL One of the most remarkable exiles in Babylon at this time was the prophet Daniel, who wrote the Old Testament book of Daniel. God revealed to this man some of the most exciting prophecies found anywhere.

The prophecies in Daniel 11 describing the Ptolemy-Seleucid wars are so accurate in detail that some skeptics thought it was written after the facts—until the Dead Sea Scrolls proved otherwise.

The most significant prophecy concerned the mystery of Messiah the Prince. Daniel 9:24-26 pinpoints the exact time when the Messiah comes—the month Nissan in A.D. 33. This precisely dates to Palm Sunday, when Jesus Christ was proclaimed King Messiah in Luke 19:40-44. Further details of this prophecy are discussed in the sidebar "Daniel 9" in chapter 15.

overthrow of "Babylon the Great." It was all predicted and documented extensively more than 150 years earlier, including Jeremiah's uncanny prediction that Babylon was on a short, 70-year timer:

> "Then, after the 70 years of captivity are over, I will punish the king of Babylon and his people for their sins," says the Lord. *Jeremiah 25:12*

Babylon's fall occurred in 539 B.C., 70 years after the conquest of Judah. While the new Babylonian King, Belshazzar, was throwing a wild celebration for a thousand nobles, the revelry was suddenly shattered by a terrifying and shadowy figure:

> At that very moment they saw the fingers of a human hand writing on the plaster wall of the king's palace, near the lampstand. The king himself saw the hand as it wrote...Such terror gripped him that his knees knocked together and his legs gave way beneath him. *Daniel 5:5-6*

This disembodied hand originated the ominous phrase, "to see the writing on the wall." It was God's sovereign declaration that the Babylonian Empire was finished. Later that night the Persians entered the city and executed the proud Babylonian king.

AFTER THE EXILE

Under the Persians, a series of new, friendly monarchs started the process of returning God's people back to Palestine. Cyrus "The Great" and Artaxerxes issued proclamations returning the Jewish remnant to Judah, rebuilding the walls of Jerusalem, and even restoring the Temple. The new Temple was only a pale shadow of the glory of Solomon's Temple, until it was enlarged by King Herod centuries later.

Remnants of God's Chosen People were back in the Promised Land, and they were no longer exiles and slaves, Post-Exilic life was terrifically strained for God's People. Poverty was rampant in Judea after all the invasions and pillaging. Cities lay in charred ruins and food was scarce from the depopulation of farmland. With no significant military or finances, the Judeans were exposed to constant hostilities and persecutions from unfriendly neighbors. Since their land was strategically located in the path of conquering armies, it was a source of food and plunder.

SIGNIFICANT POST-EXILIC DATES[12]

539	Medo-Persians (Cyrus) overthrow Babylon, Jews permitted to return	444	Decree of Artaxerxes for the third return of exiles under Nehemiah. *Nehemiah 2*
538	Edict of Cyrus for the first return of exiles(Ezra 1:1-4) under Zerubbabel.	490	Greeks defeat the Persians at Marathon.
		167	Maccabean revolt against the Greeks.
458	Decree of Artaxerxes for the second return of exiles under Ezra. *Ezra 7-10*	63	Rome under Pompey controls Palestine.

THE KING TO COME

In this gloomy atmosphere there remained, however, a brilliant hope.

For centuries, Prophets wrote that God would bring His People back from Exile into the Promised Land to witness the arrival of a King who triggers the greatest upheaval in human rule since the beginning.

Now back from Exile, the prophecies were coming true, and clearly God was not finished with the Children of Israel after all—even after centuries of rebellion, God's promise to make Israel "a blessing for all the nations" was still a reality. There now remained a great prophetic expectation:

> "For a child will be born to us, a son will be given to us; And the government will rest on His shoulders;" *Isaiah 9:6a* (NASB-U)

So far Isaiah describes typical royalty, but then shocks his audience:

> "And His name will be called Wonderful Counselor, Mighty God, Eternal Father, Prince of Peace. There will be no end to the increase of His government or of peace, On the throne of David and over his kingdom, to establish it and to uphold it with justice and righteousness from then on and forevermore. The zeal of the Lord of hosts will accomplish this." *Isaiah 9:6b-7* (NASB-U)

 At the very heart of God's Eternal Plan is nothing less than the human birth of God Himself.

What an amazing hope! A human child called "Mighty God" and "Eternal Father"—titles reserved exclusively for Yahweh—"will be born." From the beginning when God first created Adam, His intent was to be clothed with human skin and step into our realm as a helpless child, into The Fall like the rest of us.

TRULY FULFILLED PROPHECY The excitement of reading prophecy that becomes history is something not shared by any other world religion or found in other sacred writings.

The stakes are high with biblical prophecy because the authority of the Bible's message depends on accuracy. False prophets have often tried to assume spiritual leadership in Israel, and it continues in the postmodern age with the fascination in the occult and so-called prophets like Nostradamus.[13]

Unlike false prophets, biblical prophecies are clear and therefore verifiable. Jeremiah's 70-year duration for the Exile is an example.

Biblical prophecy can be divided into two major groups: near-term and long-term predictions. Considering the vital role of Prophets in Israel, the Mosaic Covenant establishes a strict test of a Prophet's authenticity: "If the prophet predicts something in the Lord's name and it does not happen, the Lord did not give the message." (Deuteronomy 18:22). The accuracy of near-term prophecies established the Prophet's authority and proved the ability to see the "long-range" future.

Unlike the rest of us, He will rule "on the throne of David" as the "Prince of Peace," inaugurating The Kingdom "with justice and righteousness" and without any "end to the increase of peace"—this is The Kingdom of God defined.

A DIFFERENT KINGDOM

The Kosmos is shaped by wars and bloody upheaval, and everyone suffers. No adjustments, new governments or rulers can possibly change the underlying thirst for power that triggers the atrocities of history.

God's Kingdom, on the other hand, is ruled by Isaiah's "Prince of Peace." In Genesis 49:10, he was called Shiloh by Israel himself from the beginning days of prophetic Revelation. Shiloh means "peace," and through this King God ends the Counterfeit Kingdom with its wars and cruelty:

> "I will bring to the throne of David a righteous descendant, and he will do what is just and right throughout the land. In that day Judah will be saved, and Jerusalem will live in safety." *Jeremiah 33:14-17*

This change in kingdoms means radical change, not a change in government:

> "Look! I am creating new heavens and a new earth—so wonderful that no one will even think about the old ones anymore. Be glad; rejoice forever in my creation! And look! I will create Jerusalem as a place of happiness. Her people will be a source of joy." *Isaiah 65:17-18*

All this radical upheaval depended on the Prince of Peace. Shortly before the Jews were released from The Exile, the Prophet Daniel writing in Babylonia describes it:

> I kept looking in the night visions, And behold, with the clouds of heaven One like a Son of Man was coming…

This "Son of Man" is none other than the King of The Kingdom:

> And He came up to the Ancient of Days, And to Him was given dominion, glory and a kingdom, that all the peoples, nations and men of every language might serve Him. His dominion is an everlasting dominion which will not pass away; and His kingdom is one which will not be destroyed. *Daniel 7:13-14* (NASB-U)

A NEW ORTHODOXY

After The Exile, God sends a series of Prophets who write in great detail about the birth, life and work of the coming King. The last prophecies declare the inevitable coming of the Messiah-King:

> "But you, O Bethlehem Ephrathah, are only a small village in Judah. Yet a ruler of Israel will come from you, one whose origins are from the distant past." *Micah 5:2*

Anticipation and excitement about the Messiah dominated the new Israel, and the people became a nation much different than before the Exile. They became zealous "People of the Book," steeped in the Scriptures. Their confidence and knowledge of Scripture provided a solid foundation for understanding the coming King and his teachings.

Yet, so typical of human interactions with God, they also developed a disturbing tendency towards the recurring Religion of Merit, but without the idolatry characterizing their Pre-Exile drift from God. This was a new development: Becoming more preoccupied with avoiding sin than loving God, Judaism became a distinctly law-focused religion. Vast commentaries were written to clarify what it actually meant to break the Law of Moses, leading to the rise of legalism and literalism finally embodied in a comprehensive work called the Talmud (meaning, "teaching" or "inference").[14] This additional material began taking prominence alongside (and sometimes over) God's Word, and would cause problems in their future.

A CLOSING OF THE OLD TESTAMENT

As the Old Testament closes around 400 B.C., everyone knew about Him, eagerly anticipating and calling Him the Messiah—literally, "the Anointed One," which means someone appointed as king.

Suddenly God ceased any further Revelation, and no prophets were raised up. What followed was 400 years of silence, the so-called "Silent Years."[15]

It was still a period of intense activity as prophecies were fulfilled in rapid succession. As Daniel predicted, the Persians were defeated by the Greeks at the Battle of Marathon, and a messenger ran 22 miles with the news to Athens—the basis for today's Marathon race. Alexander the Great conquered far and wide, and when he approached Jerusalem they showed him where Daniel prophesied his victories. Alexander was stunned, and granted the Jews special status in the Greek Empire.[16] Alexander's four generals divided his empire, and the ensuing Ptolemy-Seleucid wars devastated Palestine—all as prophesied.[17] Finally, Rome arose as Daniel predicted, the most "dreadful and terrifying and extremely strong" of all,[18] and Pompeii conquered Palestine in 63 B.C.

ᴂ **Only the True God can know the future with certainty.**

By the end of these series of wars with so many prophesies fulfilled, the Jews were increasingly certain about the fulfillment of the Messianic prophecies as well.

The time was near. Things became very quiet; God had nothing more to say, and nobody to say it through. He was waiting for just the right time as the prophetic clock began ticking.

FURTHER CONSIDERATION

THE MESSAGE OF PROPHECY

People are surprised to discover the vast quantity of prophetic material contained in the Old Testament. From Isaiah to the end of the Old Testament, God delivered more than 300 years of continuous prophetic Revelation. It is a stunning collection of almost 9,000 verses comprising more than 27 percent of the entire Old Testament. Amazingly, more than 600 prophecies are already fulfilled today.[19]

God uses the supernatural power of prophecy to expose and even ridicule false gods and man-made religions:

> "Who is like me? Let him proclaim it. Let him declare and set it before me... Let them declare what is to come, and what will happen." *Isaiah 44:7* (ESV)

THE CONFLICT OF THE AGES

Prophecy is more than a curiosity. Along with the rest of the Old Testament, it reveals the purpose and direction of the creation and God's "Hidden Mystery"— His plans for accomplishing it. The prophetic picture sweeps across millennia, and captures the turmoil swirling around God's Promised Land of Israel. It describes the future conflict between The Kingdom and the Counterfeit Kingdom opposed to God, as King David shows us:

> Why do the nations rage? Why do the people waste their time with futile plans? The kings of the earth prepare for battle; the rulers plot together against the Lord and against his anointed one. "Let us break their chains," they cry, and free ourselves from this slavery." But the one who rules in heaven laughs. The Lord scoffs at them. *Psalm 2:1-4*

This "Anointed One" is at the center of the controversy between God and man. Every king of Israel was anointed by a prophet, and "Anointed One" is a king. It is "Mashiach" in Hebrew, pronounced "Messiah" in English—in Greek it is translated "Christ." The Christ-King described in Psalm 2 is no normal king—he is the Son of God, and he rules the nations:

"I will surely tell of the decree of the Lord: He said to Me, 'You are My Son, Today I have begotten You. "Ask of Me, and I will surely give the nations as Your inheritance, And the very ends of the earth as Your possession.'" *Psalm 2:7-8* (NASB-U)

It is a fair statement that all these prophecies revolve around the King and coming Kingdom. Prophecies specifically about Shiloh saturate the Old Testament—it is not an obscure picture. Through Isaiah, Jeremiah, Daniel, Ezekiel and a list of other chosen prophets, God contrasts the future rise and fall of human kingdoms against the Messiah's kingdom which never crumbles. The point: the horror of human conquest reaches a point where God intervenes. The apparent glory and power of human kingdoms will never disrupt God's Eternal Plan.

THE CULMINATION OF ALL REVELATION

Old Testament prophecies concerning Shiloh number in the hundreds, but his names are many: Shiloh, The Prophet, Wonderful Counselor, Messiah, Son of God, The Servant, The King, The Branch, The Redeemer, Almighty God, the Son of Man, and dozens of others.

There is good reason for so many titles: He is the culmination of all the promises and all the leadership roles found in the Old Testament. Taken together, these titles fall into three roles: Priest, Prophet and King. These were the three great offices instituted by God to lead His Chosen People, and it was always understood that God Himself would step into these key roles one day.

As Priest, He would bring love and acceptance with God through the great Atonement. (See Chapter 14.) As Prophet, not only will He reveal a clear future, but like the Old Testament prophets He will convey the very words of God. As King, He rules The Kingdom.

A STRANGE TWIST

It was a clear overall picture, but also confusing in some of the details. Alongside the conquering king, God also pictures Him as a "Suffering Servant," very humble, not authoritarian like other conquering kings.

> He was despised and rejected—a man of sorrows, acquainted with bitterest grief. We turned our backs on him and looked the other way when he went by. He was despised, and we did not care. *Isaiah 53:3*

The prophecies about this person are not limited to his role as a ruler. Through Shiloh, God would reach out to mankind with His love and kindness, offering us a significant place in His Eternal kingdom. This "Suffering Servant" would also bring multitudes of people into a personal relationship with God as described in Chapter 14.

Even Isaiah wondered what these prophecies could possibly mean—the Suffering Servant who is also a great king enthroned forever. The two roles seem incompatible, but God assured Isaiah that they were both true and would be fulfilled exactly as prophesied:

> This salvation was something the prophets wanted to know more about...They wondered when and to whom all this would happen. They were told that these things would not happen during their lifetime... It is all so wonderful that even the angels are eagerly watching these things happen. *1 Peter 1:11-12*

A CONQUERING LOVE

GOD'S KINGDOM REVEALED

*"I will open My mouth in parables; I will utter things hidden since the foundation of
the world."*
Matthew 13:35b (NASB-U)

TWO GREAT RULERS

Augustus Caesar—Octavian was his real name—was arguably the most powerful
and famous ruler known in the history of the Roman Empire—perhaps in all
human history. His reign was the "Golden Age" of Roman sovereignty, and later
Roman Emperors tried to recapture it, but nobody ever matched the authority and
duration of his reign.

Yet another King was born during the reign of Octavian, someone with far greater
authority and power. Even Octavian will bow down and worship this One as the
King of Kings, the Bible says:

> that at the name of Jesus every knee should bow, in heaven and on earth
> and under the earth, and every tongue confess that Jesus Christ is Lord...
> *Philippians 2:10-11 (NIV)*

Ironically, Octavian's empire enabled the rival kingdom of Jesus Christ to spread
rapidly. Roman roads provided a ready-made network for rapid travel and brought
the nations of the world within reach, even the Far East.

Octavian's kingdom had a head start, but The Kingdom of Christ eventually swept
the entire Roman Empire, and Emperors themselves quickly grasped the profound
threat it meant to the powers of Rome—its slavery, pagan gods, even the Emperor-
worship were at stake.

THE AUTHORITY OF JESUS
  ∽ **Jesus Christ was none other than the Creator God Himself in
    human form.**

He is the very same one described by Isaiah's prophecy as the "Almighty God, Eternal Father, and Prince of Peace," the Creator of the universe:[1]

> He existed before everything else began, and he holds all creation together. *Colossians 1:17*

Incredibly, the Sovereign God slipped into history as a helpless baby to live on Earth for a time as a human, at the lowest echelons of human society:

> Though he was God, he did not demand and cling to his rights as God...he took the humble position of a slave and appeared in human form. *Philippians 2:6-7*

So typical, this is the Backward Thinking of God—everything about Him is unexpected. Who could imagine the Almighty God would come as a helpless baby?

Thus the genius of God's Plan: rejecting what the Kosmos worships as "greatness," laying aside His own authority, He approaches mankind as a child born in poverty. Nazareth was the hometown of Jesus, known and despised by both Jews and Romans as a backward, seedy town where Roman soldiers could find recreational prostitution.[2] When Nathaniel, one of Jesus' disciples, heard that Jesus came from Nazareth, he declared with disbelief, "Can anything good come out of Nazareth?"[3]

Consider this...

As we delve into His life, it becomes evident that everything in the Bible is pointing to this event in human history as the time when God came to earth to dwell as Immanuel: "God among us."

WHY DID GOD WAIT? Eons of time passed since the first proclamations of the coming King Messiah in Genesis. Why did He wait until the Roman era? Simply, "It was the fullness of time"— the first real opportunity to fulfill the Abrahamic covenant to bring a "blessing for all the nations," and everything was ready.

Greek was spoken and written everywhere in the Roman Empire. The Old Testament was translated into Greek in 250 B.C. Called the Septuagint, it made all the Messianic prophecies readily available to everyone. Everything written about the life of Jesus was widely disseminated, and all the claims about him were available for verification.

The combination of Pax Romana ("Roman Peace") and Roman Roads opened up vast tracts of land for travel like never before or after until the modern era. This enabled the good news of God's love through Jesus to spread to the farthest reaches of the Roman Empire.

After The Exile, the Jews became "People of the Book," rejecting idolatry and fervently expecting the Messiah after all the fulfilled prophecy. Synagogues were established throughout Israel and Hebrew children were taught the Messianic prophecies, which provided a basis for understanding the teachings of Jesus.

It was an amazing era, never seen before or since: "the fullness of times."

THE BIRTH OF A KING

The birth of Jesus Christ is an historical event dating around 4 B.C. As with everything recorded about his life in the "Gospel Accounts," well-known events in secular history are such as "while Quirinius was governor," "when Herod was king of Judea," "Caesar Augustus decreed that a census should be taken," and "the fifteenth year of the reign of Tiberius," among many others.[5] The "Gospel Accounts," as they are called, are four books of the Bible written shortly after His death, by first-hand witnesses who recorded what they saw. They took great pains to convey the accuracy of their testimony, as John records:

> This is that disciple who saw these events and recorded them here. And we all know that his account of these things is accurate. *John 21:24*

✐ God inaugurated His Kingdom at the most strategic moment in human history.

It was the perfect moment in human history when God launched His Kingdom and revealed The Mystery. This was not by chance—God was planning for the right moment all along, the Bible says:

> In the fullness of time, God sent His Son into the world, born of woman, born under the Law that He might redeem those who are under the Law, that they might be inheritors of His Kingdom. *Galatians 4:4-5*

The Gospels record a very sad and yet remarkable birth for Jesus Christ. Because Augustus Caesar mandated an empire-wide census, Joseph and his wife Mary were

---

AN EXTRAORDINARY BIRTH Mary knew this would be an extraordinary child. She was instructed by an angel to name him "Jesus," which means "Savior." At this point, Old Testament prophecies about the Messiah were being fulfilled at a rapid pace.

Virgin Birth: Matthew 1:23 says He was conceived miraculously through the Holy Spirit while she was still a virgin, fulfilling the prophecy in Isaiah 7:14: "Behold, a virgin will be with child and bear a son, and she will call His name Immanuel." (NASB-U) "Immanuel" means "God among us."

Son of David: Matthew 1 and Luke 3 devote whole chapters tracing the genealogies of Jesus back to King David, fulfilling amazing predictions. Matthew traces Joseph's ancestry, while Luke traces Mary's. Taken together, these genealogies resolve God's judgment against the "kingly line" in Jeremiah 22:30, that "none of his children will ever sit on the throne of David." Through Joseph, Christ inherited the legal right to David's throne, but not the bloodline cursed by God. Through Mary, Jesus was a direct blood descendant of David.[6]

Bethlehem birth: He was born in Bethlehem as Micah 5:2 predicted 400 years earlier: "But you, O Bethlehem...a ruler of Israel will come from you, one whose origins are from the distant past."

Galilean poverty: As a carpenter whose father soon died, He lived in the abject poverty of Nazareth, and grew up in Galilee, as Isaiah prophesied: "Galilee ...will be filled with glory." Isaiah then describes this "glory" as the birth of "Almighty God."[7]

forced to travel from their hometown of Nazareth all the way to Bethlehem, just outside Jerusalem. Bethlehem was the city of King David, and since Joseph and Mary were both descendants of David, they had to be counted in the census from their city of origin.

This was a terrible inconvenience, not only because Mary was pregnant, but also because Bethlehem was thronging with everyone else trying to register for the census. Consequently, there was no lodging available anywhere in the town.

Joseph and Mary found shelter in a barn, a "stable" full of animals. Then she went into labor, and the newborn infant was laid down in a feeding trough!

> And she gave birth to her firstborn son; and she wrapped Him in cloths, and laid Him in a manger, because there was no room for them in the inn. *Luke 2:7* (NASB-U)

This is the way Jesus Christ, Creator of the Universe, entered into our world – in an obscure barn where God launches the opening salvo of God's Kingdom on earth. It speaks volumes about the character of God, because He could have demanded and rightfully expected the palace of Augustus Caesar himself.

> ✍ **God willingly suffered this humiliation and suffering for one reason: His love for us.**

> For God so loved the world that he gave his only Son, so that everyone who believes in him will not perish but have eternal life. *John 3:16*

Consider this...

This is so typical of God's humble approach to man—not with overwhelming force, not exercising His right to be God. He stoops to our level and shoulders our suffering, and proves His deep desire to re-establish the relationship He once created with Adam.

Yet this child's birth did not go completely unnoticed. In a nearby field, in the middle of the night, shepherds were suddenly surrounded by a host of brilliant angels singing out a most remarkable message:

> "Glory to God in the highest, And on earth peace among men with whom He is pleased." *Luke 2:14* (NASB-U)

The shepherds were summoned to the birthplace of Christ, along with another unlikely group: three kings from the Far East. Although they were neither Jewish nor familiar with the Bible, God reached these kings in their distant culture and country. God always reaches those who have hearts open to Him:

> For the eyes of the Lord move to and fro throughout the earth that He may strongly support those whose heart is completely His. *2 Chronicles 16:9* (NASB-U)

Consider this…

Because of their willing hearts, both lowly shepherds and powerful kings were the fortunate witnesses to the dawn of God's Kingdom on earth—the greatest moment in history.

A VOICE CRYING FROM THE WILDERNESS

Thirty years later, the cities of Judea were stirring with news and neighbors were chatting with excitement. It was an electrified atmosphere, with crowds of people streaming across bridges and paths, down long and dusty roads from all across Judea, even descending the 3,000-foot Mountains of Jerusalem. It became a mass movement into the Jordan Valley where the river Jordan snakes from the Sea of Galilee across Samaria and Judea, emptying in the Dead Sea.

At the river Jordan, hordes of people mass around a solitary figure waste-deep in the river, sometimes standing on the riverbank and yelling above the din. He wore a simple camel hair tunic and leather belt—a gnarly figure. He appeared from the southern Wilderness regions of vast desert and mountains where he lived on a diet of locusts mixed with honey, it was said..

"I am a voice of one crying in the wilderness!" he shouted. It shocked the nation and brought the crowds—he was quoting one of the famous Messianic prophecies:

> A voice is calling, "Clear the way for the Lord in the wilderness; Make smooth in the desert a highway for our God."

It was a prophecy describing the advent of God's Kingdom:

THE GNOSTIC "GOSPELS" With the rise of the "New Age" movement in the 1980s, there is a renewed interest in the so-called "Gnostic Gospels," books which were written in the second and third centuries AD describing the early years of Jesus. Claims are made that he studied in India under Hindu masters. Fictional stories such as the *DaVinci Code* and *The Stigmata* claim these "Gnostic Gospels" were deliberately suppressed by the early church.

People subscribing to this conspiracy theory often have never read the writings, which are not only crude but also clearly anti-Christian in nature. For example, in the famous Gospel of Thomas, Jesus teaches about women:

"Women are not worthy of the Life." Jesus said: "I will make her male, that she too may become a living spirit, resembling you males. For every woman who makes herself male will enter the Kingdom of Heaven."[8]

The best refutation of these writings is to read them. The reason why Gnosticism quickly died out is simply because the teachings were far too esoteric to grasp: "The Forgetting did not arise under the hand of the Father... but what arises in Him is Gnosis, which made its appearance in order that Forgetting might be destroyed and the Father be known."[9]

Let every valley be lifted up, And every mountain and hill be made low; And let the rough ground become a plain, And the rugged terrain a broad valley; Then the glory of the Lord will be revealed, And all flesh will see it together; For the mouth of the Lord has spoken.
Isaiah 40:3-5 (NASB-U)

For more than 400 years there was no prophet in Judea. Now, mysteriously, this man appeared out of the Wilderness, declaring with boldness that the Messiah was on the way. He looked and acted like Elijah the prophet, a radical coming out of the Wilderness to denounce Israel's Religion of Merit. He spoke with Elijah's authority. He was called "John the Baptist" because he baptized the people in the river, if they honestly sought God.

STALE ORTHODOXY
⤳ **John was in fierce rebellion against the Religion of Merit that marked Judaism.**

The growing dead orthodoxy and staleness of Judaism fueled John's immense popularity. People were disenchanted with the endless incantations, countless rules and strict, foreboding airs of the sacred religious leaders of the day. This man spoke differently, with real life and authority as though he actually knew God Himself, without the religious airs.

Fearlessly John attacked the powerful religious leaders:

THE TRINITY At the baptism of Christ we see the revelation of one of the deepest mysteries about God: what theologians call the "Trinity."

"Trinity" is the term that expresses the unity of three Persons in the one God. It is one of the great mysteries of God's Revelation because we simply cannot grasp this aspect of God as humans: "It is admitted by all who thoughtfully deal with this subject that the Scripture revelation here leads us into the presence of a deep mystery and that all human attempts at expression are of necessity imperfect."[10]

The term "Trinity" is descriptive of what the Bible teaches, but not actually used by the Bible. What we see in the Bible are numerous passages like Christ's baptism, where the Trinity is clearly revealed: the Father spoke, the Holy Spirit descended and the Son was the recipient. It also occurs at the beginning of the Bible during creation, when God said "let us make man in our image," and then He made us male and female. Apparently, as God originally designed marriage, when the "two shall become one flesh," humans taste the concept of the Trinity that God knows. Of course, marriage as we know it today is far from God's design.

What we do know is that Jesus Christ was indeed God in the flesh, described in both Old and New Testaments: "In the beginning was the Word, and the Word was with God, and the Word was God....And the Word became flesh, and dwelt among us..." *John 1:14* (NASB). In the Old Testament it says, "For a child will be born to us...and His name will be called Wonderful Counselor, Mighty God, Eternal Father..." *Isaiah 9:6* (NASB-U)

But when he saw many Pharisees and Sadducees coming to be baptized, he denounced them. "You brood of snakes!" he exclaimed. "Who warned you to flee God's coming judgment?" *Matthew 3:7*

He was fierce with them because they were stuck in complacency:

"Don't just say, 'We're safe—we're the descendants of Abraham.' That proves nothing. God can change these stones here into children of Abraham." *Matthew 3:9*

There was freshness to his message, the great hope of the coming Messiah:

He announced: "Someone is coming soon who is far greater than I am...I baptize you with water, but he will baptize you with the Holy Spirit!" *Mark 1:7-8*

After such prolonged silence, God was again at work among His People, and something marvelous was about to happen in Judea. The revival spread like fire throughout the country.

A GREATER REBEL

Then one day, Jesus appeared among the crowd.

Jesus sought out this rebellious prophet to be baptized by him and to inaugurate his own ministry, and by so doing Jesus was clearly taking sides in the growing religious schism, throwing his full support behind John's denunciations. Finally, at about 30 years old, Jesus was ready to reveal Himself publicly as the very Messiah that John was proclaiming.

As Jesus approached the river, John at first protested: "I am not fit to untie your sandals!" Yet Jesus insisted, and when the baptism occurred, it was clear that all the hopes of John and the people of Judea were now to be fulfilled:

After his baptism, as Jesus came up out of the water, the heavens were opened and he saw the Spirit of God descending like a dove and settling on him. And a voice from heaven said, "This is my beloved Son, and I am fully pleased with him." *Matthew 3:16-17*

Things would never be the same around Judea for years to come.

KINGS COLLIDE

After the baptism, Jesus made a strange decision: rather than immediately start His public ministry, He disappeared into the Judean Wilderness. For 40 days, He fasted. It was an intense time of starvation as Jesus sought out direction, preparation and spiritual strength from the Holy Spirit to do His Father's Will. He desperately needed it. He was about to clash directly, head-to-head with the powerful Ruler of this World.

The day came when finally Satan faced Christ in the desert: two world leaders, one seasoned by thousands of years of success, the other only newly arrived to Planet Earth, living for the first time as a human with all the limitations of a man. Christ was facing Satan as Adam did, human versus angel. For this reason, the Bible calls Jesus the "Last Adam":

> The Scriptures tell us, "The first man, Adam, became a living person." But the last Adam—that is, Christ—is a life-giving Spirit. *1 Corinthians 15:45*

✑ The Last Adam reversed The Fall caused by the First Adam.

Satan launched into a series of attacks against Jesus that He used so effectively against the first humans. Immediately sensing the physical weakness caused by the prolonged fasting, Satan challenged Christ to put an end to His suffering:

> "If you are the Son of God, change this stone into a loaf of bread!" *Luke 4:3*

Satan was enticing Jesus to rise up and seize his innate power, reject dependence on God the Father, and take control of His own destiny, just as Lucifer once did.

However, the whole mission of Christ depended on His ability to live like Adam, like a human, and depend on God the Father rather than depend on Himself— although He certainly could take care of Himself, being God.

Satan's approach worked so well before with Eve, because when she fell for it she thought the fruit of the Tree of the Knowledge of Good and Evil was "good for food" and she readily ate it.

Consider this...
The reply Jesus gave showed His determination to live on this earth and qualify as the Last Adam, living the way God originally wanted Adam to live, and living the way we can find lasting, deep satisfaction even today:

> "Man shall not live by bread alone, but on every word that comes from the mouth of God." *Deuteronomy 8:3*

Undeterred, Satan suddenly whisked Jesus away to the very pinnacle of Herod's glorious Temple in Jerusalem. Standing there, looking down at the crowds coming to worship God, it was the perfect opportunity for Christ to start His ministry by proving to everyone that He was the Messiah. Satan told Christ:

> "If You are the Son of God, throw Yourself down from here; for it is written, 'He will command His angels concerning You to guard You,'" *Luke 4:9-10* (NASB-U)

It was a bold move. Satan was inviting Christ to indulge in the same self-glorification that first sparked Satan's rebellion against God. Eve, too, was swept up by it, because she saw that it "was desirable to make one wise" and "become like God" if she joined Satan's rebellion.

Jesus refused again, and revealed the essential evil behind Satan's words:

> Jesus responded, "The Scriptures also say, 'Do not test the Lord your God.'" *Luke 4:12*

Consider this...

Jesus proves that the satanic need for self-glorification can be replaced by simply trusting a loving God to exalt us at the proper time, according to His will.

Jesus was authenticated as the true Son of God in God's timing: at the resurrection. God did create humans for the exalted purpose of ruling. But the self-willed approach of Satan has no patience to trust in God's timing or God's approach to fulfilling our built-in need for significance.

DISDAIN FOR THE KOSMOS

In a final bid to dislodge Christ's mission, Satan performed a most spectacular feat: in one sweeping moment he displayed to Jesus the vast empires across the earth, all the towering palaces and wealth, the full glory of the Roman Empire at its height of power:

> "I will give you the glory of these kingdoms and authority over them— because they are mine to give to anyone I please. I will give it all to you if you will bow down and worship me." *Luke 4:6-7*

This was an opportunity for Jesus to have all authority and power over humanity— just as God should have—but it meant ruling within Satan's Counterfeit Kingdom, using the Kosmos already in place and ruling by its principles.

Jesus was building a new Kingdom starting from scratch, and it would take a long time to build it. Great opposition lay ahead. Yet here were kingdoms already established, vast systems already in place, and Jesus could simply build upon these and avoid the future suffering and strife another kingdom would cause.

Yet the answer from Jesus goes to the heart of the war between kingdoms:

> Jesus replied, "The Scriptures say, 'You must worship the Lord your God; serve only him.'" *Luke 4:8*

Jesus would not deny that Satan already owned the kingdoms of the earth.

Consider this...

What Jesus rejected was Satan's authority that underlies human kingdoms. To Jesus, all the allure and fulfillment offered by the Kosmos is irreparably tainted by the repugnant presence of the Ruler of this World.

REPUDIATING THE PRINCIPLE OF SIN

Satan left utterly frustrated because all the temptations that worked so well with the first Adam were exhausted. Yet, the Bible records, Satan remained lurking around Christ for the duration of His ministry:

> When the Devil had finished tempting Jesus, he left him until the next opportunity came. *Luke 4:13*

These temptations left Christ spiritually exhausted and physically weakened from the difficulty of wrestling with the genius of Satan's tactics. God the Father sent angels to minister to Christ's needs, proof that Jesus Himself felt the difficulty and strain of living in a world at war.

Christ repudiated the Principle of Sin, the hallmark of Satan's outlook that poisons human ambition. Reversing Adam's rebellion, Christ came as the "Last Adam" to inaugurate a new humanity—in fellowship with God, dependent on God as intended, and free from the hold of the Kosmos. He brought a choice never available before.

Jesus offers nothing less than a complete overhaul in the very nature of humanity. More than offering timeless, quotable platitudes or examples of kindness and love, he revolutionizes the heart of humanity through nothing less than rebirth:

> Jesus replied, "I assure you, unless you are born again, you can never see the Kingdom of God." *John 3:3*

∞ **God's Kingdom is populated only by members of this new race, the last race of humans God will ever create.**

Consider this...

Through Christ, anyone can join his new humanity and escape the rebellion and alienation from God—the sickness that permeates the Kosmos from the First Adam.

Jesus emerged from the wilderness ready to proclaim an alternative to the Counterfeit Kingdom.

FURTHER CONSIDERATION

THE AMAZING UNITY OF THE BIBLE

The confrontation between Satan and Christ is so profound. It clearly reveals what the Bible says are the major ways Satan is able to "blind the minds of the unbelieving" and keep people desperately locked within his Kosmos, even though everyone knows it is a temporary and shallow realm:

> For all that is in the world, the lust of the flesh and the lust of the eyes and the boastful pride of life, is not from the Father, but is from the world... *1 John 2:16a* (NASB-U)

THE FUEL OF THE KOSMOS

What fuels the Kosmos are but three basic drives: the "lust of the flesh," the "lust of the eyes" and the "boastful pride of life." These three elementary principles can be traced back to Satan's original rebellion, Adam's rebellion, and into Satan's confrontation with Christ. Still today, these three elements keep people preoccupied and deceived about the danger of investing in the Kosmos.

The "lust of the flesh" means the cravings and short-term appetites that dominate so many people's lives. Christ experienced this same desperate, short-term need to fulfill His physical hunger when Satan suggested turning the stones into bread.

The "lust of the eyes" is the sparkling wealth and luxury the Kosmos offers so readily. Christ faced this when Satan showed Him the pride and splendor of the kingdoms of the world.

The "boastful pride of life" is the prominence and glory that drives people into deeper investment in the Kosmos. Christ too was offered the opportunity of great glory at the Temple, if indeed a host of angels surrounded Him to protect Him—it would have been a great spectacle, and nobody could doubt Him.

In each case, Jesus showed that these temporary fascinations were only shallow alternatives to real life—spiritual life with God. This is why John concludes these appetites are too shallow to deserve allegiance:

The world is passing away, and also its lusts; but the one who does the will of God lives forever. *1 John 2:16b* (NASB-U)

THE KINGDOM IS LAUNCHED

"...the kingdom of God has come upon you."
Luke 11:20

When Isaiah prophesied about the coming "Almighty God, Eternal Father, Prince of Peace," he started out the prophecy with this:

"There will be a time in the future when Galilee of the Gentiles...will be filled with glory." *Isaiah 9:1*

THE SHOCK

Galilee was ground zero when Jesus the Messiah launched His ministry near his hometown of Nazareth. There at a wedding feast, He committed a surprising act of desecration against the so-called sacred vessels reserved strictly for ritual cleansing—a vital ceremony in the Religion of Merit contemporary Judaism had become. He filled the pots with water and miraculously changed the water into wine.[1] Not surprisingly, this made a big splash at the wedding feast, especially since the party was out of wine, and the bride and groom could be disgraced. When the wine steward of the party tasted it, he took the bridegroom aside:

"Usually a host serves the best wine first," he said. "Then, when everyone is full and doesn't care, he brings out the less expensive wines. But you have kept the best until now!" This miraculous sign at Cana in Galilee was Jesus' first display of his glory. And his disciples believed in him. *John 2:10-11*

This was the beginning of a series of "signs"—literally translated "attesting proofs" or "distinguishing marks"—Jesus unleashed across northern Galilee. It is indicative that he started His ministry at a wedding celebration rather than the sacred space of temple or synagogue. Instead, Jesus revealed a God who lives among us—He is engaged.

∽ **Jesus broke all the stereotypes of manmade religion.**

People asked Christ about this, since it seemed that a truly religious man should have a more somber, religious demeanor:

> One day some people came to Jesus and asked, "Why do John's disciples and the Pharisees fast, but your disciples don't fast?" Jesus replied, "Do wedding guests fast while celebrating with the groom? Of course not. They can't fast while they are with the groom!" *Mark 2:18b-19*

Christ's ministry was a continuous proclamation of the joyous words similar to those of John the Baptist: "The time has come! The Kingdom of God is here! Believe the Good News!"[2]

BLASPHEMY

He performed other miracles to reveal who He was, often shocking the religious elite. The Pharisees and Sadducees began shadowing Him.

When a paralytic was brought for healing, Jesus said to the man, "My son, your sins are forgiven." There were immediate howls of protest:

> But some of the teachers of religious law who were sitting there said to themselves, "What? This is blasphemy! Who but God can forgive sins!" Jesus knew what they were discussing among themselves, so he said to them, "Why do you think this is blasphemy? Is it easier to say to the paralyzed man, 'Your sins are forgiven' or 'Get up, pick up your mat, and walk'? I will prove that I, the Son of Man, have the authority on earth to forgive sins." Then Jesus turned to the paralyzed man and said, "Stand up, take your mat, and go on home, because you are healed!" *Mark 2:6-11*

The paralytic jumped up, and the people standing around began praising God in amazement.

THE POWER OF GOD

This was typical of the ministry of Christ—He not only made bold claims, but He also backed them up with evidence that He was indeed the Messiah. The teachers

---

OUTRAGEOUS CLAIMS Today Christ is popularly considered a great man or a wise man, but not as He claimed to be—God in human form: Jesus said to them, "Truly, truly, I say to you, before Abraham was born, I Am." *John 8:58* (NASB-U). By using "I Am," he took God's personal name, Yahweh.

If Jesus was not God, He surely was lying or out of His mind. Yet, a liar or a lunatic could not possibly teach such profound principles of truth. His claim has the ring of authenticity because He lived with integrity and taught with authority.

It was not the miracles of Christ, but His claims that threatened the religious leaders, so that they determined to kill Him.

The Pharisees charged Jesus with blaspheming God, but Jesus charged them with blaspheming: "You dishonor both Me and My Father who sent Me." *John 8:49*

of the law were correct in saying that only God has the power to actually remove sin. When Jesus offered forgiveness, He was claiming to be God, and He proved it with His miracles.

So completely different from other so-called "holy" men in history, Jesus Christ inaugurated The Kingdom with power:

> For the kingdom of God does not consist in words but in power. *1 Corinthians 4:20*

As Jesus and His disciples traveled from town to town in Judea and Galilee, He asserted His authority over all realms of life. He performed miracles that proved His power over nature by calming a storm on the Sea of Galilee with just a word.[3] There were extensive healing miracles, miracles that controlled the spirit world, and on several occasions Jesus raised people from the dead.

> ✍ **Because Jesus Christ was God, He had the power to suspend the laws of nature.**

He followed up one miracle after another, and the word spread rapidly across Galilee. Soon there were masses of people swarming throughout the region, looking for this Jesus of Nazareth, and once found, relentlessly trailing Him wherever He went. At one time, there was a crowd of 5,000, at another time a crowd of 10,000 or more gathered around Him.[4]

THE KINGDOM

With such large numbers surrounding Jesus, the nature of His ministry changed. He was no longer just a popular teacher; it was growing into a movement with real political opportunities. As with most leaders with a groundswell of support, sooner or later the agenda becomes clear, and with Jesus it was no different:

> But the crowds found out where he was going, and they followed him. And he welcomed them, teaching them about the Kingdom of God and curing those who were ill. *Luke 9:11*

Everywhere Jesus went, He kept talking about The Kingdom of God. It was at the center of His message, and He kept moving from city to city teaching about it:

> "I must preach the Good News of the Kingdom of God in other places, too, because that is why I was sent." *Luke 4:43*

Watching and following Jesus, everyone wanted to see what this new kingdom was like.

A KINGDOM OF COMPASSION

From the outset, Jesus threw His spiritual power at the pain and suffering of broken lives, healing and comforting them. People with painful and debilitating afflictions came by the hundreds, even from the surrounding countries of Tyre, Sidon and Samaria.[5] So many hurting and lost people surrounded Christ, He was unable to find time alone to grieve the death of His cousin John the Baptist, who was executed by King Herod. Even then, although deeply grieved, the plight of the human condition still overwhelmed Him:

> A vast crowd was there as he stepped from the boat, and he had compassion on them and healed their sick. *Matthew 14:14*

∾ Compassion is the hallmark of Christ's new Kingdom.

He was God living among us as a human, surrounded day and night with the horrific suffering of a world under Satan's authority. The life of Christ is proof that God is not detached from human suffering:

> He felt great pity for the crowds that came, because their problems were so great and they didn't know where to go for help. They were like sheep without a shepherd. *Matthew 9:36*

Isaiah and the other Old Testament prophets spoke of the Messiah in mixed language: on the one hand, He would be a conquering King, but on the other hand, a Suffering Servant:

> He was despised and rejected—a man of sorrows, acquainted with bitterest grief. *Isaiah 53:3*

Consider this...

The Messiah first came to save humanity from the plight of suffering, to serve us and demonstrate the love and grace of God towards all men. He offered everyone a chance to escape the terrible sentence of death we labor under:

> "The Spirit of the Lord is upon me; he has appointed me to preach Good News to the poor; he has sent me to heal the brokenhearted and to announce that captives shall be released and the blind shall see; that the downtrodden shall be freed from their oppressors, and that God is ready to give blessings to all who come to him." *Luke 4:18-19* (LB)

Jesus read that passage in a synagogue, and His audience was stunned into silence. He was quoting from a Messianic promise in Isaiah 61:1-2.

> He closed the book and handed it back to the attendant and sat down, while everyone in the synagogue gazed at him intently. Then he added, "These Scriptures came true today!" *Luke 4:20-21* (LB)

What a joyful fulfillment of the Messianic prophecies—God was here to tackle the tragedy of this fallen world! Before John the Baptist was executed, he sent messengers to Jesus, asking if indeed Jesus was the Messiah:

Jesus replied, "Go back to John and tell him about the miracles you've seen me do—the blind people I've healed, the lame people now walking without help, the cured lepers, the deaf who hear, and the dead raised to life. Tell him about my preaching the Good News to the poor. Then give him this message, 'Blessed are those who don't doubt me.'" *Matthew 11:3-6 (LB)*.

A KINGDOM OF THE DISAFFECTED

Jesus deliberately reached out to the despised and excluded: the poor, the "sinners," castaways of no value within Satan's Counterfeit Kingdom. Not everyone enjoys power and position in the Kosmos. Too many are victims, dropouts and castaways. The dichotomy between the rich and the poor in this society was tremendous, and there was no middle class as we understand it today. Everything about His lifestyle identified with the poor—Jesus lived without a home, exposed Himself to leprosy and horrific diseases, and owned nothing.

He did so at great personal cost, alienating the powerful political and religious leaders of the Kosmos, people who could hurt Him the most. This became a hot issue when Jesus started associating with the lowest dregs of society—tax collectors:

> Tax collectors and other notorious sinners often came to listen to Jesus teach. This made the Pharisees and teachers of religious law complain that he was associating with such despicable people—even eating with them! *Luke 15:1-2*

It is proof of God's loving nature that He is willing to take our suffering onto Himself.

Consider this...

People often criticize God as being aloof: setting the world in motion, and from the safety of heaven watching us struggle with suffering. This view makes God either unloving or impotent in the face of a suffering world.

Yet, God took a substantial step down from His throne of power and authority, clothed Himself in all the limitations and vulnerability of humankind, living in tremendous suffering and poverty. Thus, we have the shortest verse in the Bible:

Jesus wept. *John 11:35 (NASB-U)*

These were real tears shed when faced with the sudden death of His close friend, Lazarus. It was strange—Christ knew He would raise Lazarus from the tomb and demonstrate absolute authority over death. It was not personal loss that moved Christ to tears. Rather, it was the impact of death on the heartbroken sister and other friends of Lazarus that struck him:

When Jesus saw her crying, and the Jews who were crying with her, he was deeply moved and troubled. *John 11:33* (GW)

Consider this...

Only God can touch our deepest, hidden grief because He too was subjected to the futility and horror of life inside the Counterfeit Kingdom:

He is able to deal gently with those who are ignorant and are going astray, since he himself is subject to weakness. *Hebrews 5:2* (NIV)

✍ God longs to bring healing into our lives.

The miracles and healings of the Suffering Servant are strong proof that God can reverse the effects of The Fall. He is a great King with the authority and power to invite anyone into The Kingdom where they can experience a new life:

"Come to me, all you who are weary and burdened, and I will give you rest. Take my yoke upon you and learn from me, for I am gentle and humble in heart, and you will find rest for your souls. For my yoke is easy and my burden is light." *Matthew 11:28-30* (NIV)

The Kingdom of the Suffering Servant is for those who know despair and suffering, for those who feel they have no chance with God, and for people "weary and burdened" with life in the Counterfeit Kingdom.

The promise of relief is not only for those with physical or emotional sickness—it is for everyone who labors under the futility of The Fall. God is acutely aware of the quiet desperation and frustration of living as Eternal Beings surrounded by a world of fleeting significance. He is grieved by the global experience He sees:

So many live out their lives in quiet lostness...Their immortal souls are blown away, and they are not disquieted by the question of its immortality, because they are already disintegrated before they die. *Søren Kierkegaard*[i]

A KINGDOM WITHOUT COERCION

At first, the crowds were excited about Jesus because they fully expected Him to overthrow the Roman Empire and establish Jerusalem as the world's seat of government. This hope was not without basis, because numerous Messianic prophecies describe The King enthroned in Jerusalem:

For the Lord declares, "I have placed my chosen king on the throne in Jerusalem, my holy city." *Psalm 2:6*

Jesus often referred to himself as "The Son of Man"—a title reserved exclusively for the Messiah who comes as a conquering King:

"...One like a Son of Man was coming... And to Him was given dominion, Glory and a kingdom, That all the peoples, nations and men of
every language might serve Him." *Daniel 7:13-14 (NASB-U)*

It was not surprising, then, when enthusiastic crowds tried to coronate Him as their
King. His powerful miracles proved He could seize political power easily, and they
kept pressuring Christ to grab it. Yet Christ refused:

So Jesus, perceiving that they were intending to come and take Him by
force to make Him king, withdrew again to the mountain by Himself
alone. *John 6:15 (NASB-U)*

✎ The crowds following Jesus were convinced He would set the Jews free from the yoke of Roman slavery.

What a perfect time to unleash the crushing power of the Messiah. Nobody could
defeat the Romans except Him, and with so many prophecies proclaiming the
Messiah's glorious rule, victory was certain.

Yet for some strange reason Christ rejected the role of Conquering King, even
though He knew it was rightfully His:

"Do you think I cannot call on my Father, and he will at once put at my
disposal more than twelve legions of angels?" *Matthew 26:53 (NIV)*

"Twelve legions" meant a formidable army of angels at His disposal, since one legion
is 6,000 troops. In Hezekiah's day the Assyrians faced the terror of just one angel,
and they lost 185,000 men—what could 72,000 angels do against the Romans?
The prospect was exciting to the Jews, and even his Disciples were convinced that
He must establish The Kingdom through power and conquest.

Jesus firmly rejected world conquest by force:

Jesus answered, "My kingdom is not of this world. If My kingdom were
of this world, then My servants would be fighting so that I would not be
handed over to the Jews; but as it is, My kingdom is not of this realm."
John 18:36 (NASB-U)

A KINGDOM NOT OF THIS WORLD

Jesus did teach that He was a kingdom-builder, but the overthrow of the Roman
Empire was far too limited in scope. Christ refused the crown just as He rejected
Satan's offer to rule the kingdoms of the earth: this whole realm—the Kosmos with
all its glory—was counterfeit, unredeemable, entirely based on the Principle of Sin.

Consider this...

*The problem with the Kosmos is with the people born into it: all offspring
from the First Adam come from a spiritually dead race, alienated from the
life of God.*

∽ Christ's Kingdom is a thorough repudiation of the Kosmos.

Rather than conquer neighboring kingdoms as most empires do, The Kingdom would grow through the birth of a new race of humanity. It was to be a kingdom whose members were rulers—benevolent rulers—the humanity God first intended for His Eternal Plan. Jesus began teaching about a kingdom free from the principles operating among earth's kingdoms.

∽ The Messiah's Kingdom was an assault on the Cult of Man.

Jesus launched into a prolific teaching ministry, leaving behind a detailed and ingenious strategy for the ultimate collapse of Satan's Counterfeit Kingdom by the growth of The Kingdom. Everything about this new Kingdom was backwards, unexpected, and its principles by nature release the grip of the Kosmos over its captives.

God used Redemption, not coercion.

THE KINGDOM STRATEGY

God did not create us in order to subjugate us the way human rulers dominate their subjects. He never wanted another version of the Roman Empire, however successful it was, because it relies on coercion. His Eternal purpose with man "before the foundations of the earth" was to raise a race of co-rulers—not slaves— who contained His very life:

> For we are the temple of the living God; just as God said, "I will dwell

THE RANSOM The real impact of Jesus' life was not his teachings—although unparalleled—it was His crucifixion that suddenly changed the options for humanity. The Cross made it possible to escape the Counterfeit Kingdom into The Kingdom for the first time ever.

The Ransom made it possible. It means to "obtain the release of (a prisoner) by making a payment demanded."[7] So, "the Son of Man came here not to be served but to serve others, and to give His life as a ransom for many." *Mark 10:45*

Jesus never intended to meet the Kosmos on its own terms, using coercion to expand. Instead, he released Satan's legal ownership over his captives—anyone from The First Adam, anyone tainted by the Principle of Sin—by declaring us forgiven and righteous, totally acceptable to God: "but now your sins have been washed away, and you have been set apart for God. You have been made right with God because of what the Lord Jesus Christ and the Spirit of our God have done for you." *1 Corinthians 6:11*

Satan only has legal rights over us because, "There is a problem—your sins have cut you off from God" *Isaiah 59:2*. Outside God's authority, we automatically fall under the jurisdiction of the Ruler of this World. But Jesus paid a ransom—anyone "washed" is set free, and comes back under God's rulership.

"It was for freedom that Christ set us free;" *Galatians 5:1* (NASB-U). Chapter 14 describes this amazing transformation in more detail.

in them and walk among them; And I will be their God, and they shall be My people. Therefore, come out from their midst and be separate," says the Lord. *2 Corinthians 6:16-17* (NASB-U)

"Come out" and "be separate" is His offer of release from the grip of the Kosmos and entry into The Kingdom, where we live under the leadership we were designed for:

"…And I will welcome you. And I will be a father to you, and you shall be sons and daughters to Me," Says the Lord Almighty. *2 Corinthians 6:18* (NASB-U)

This passage quotes from the earliest days of Revelation, a repeated theme throughout the Old Testament: God indwelling and ruling with man.[8]

∾ The Kingdom was the fulfillment of God's Eternal Plan to dwell within man.

Rather than subjects, God wanted heirs, that is, sons and daughters who inherit the universe prepared beforehand for them:

Because you are sons, God has sent forth the Spirit of His Son into our hearts…Therefore you are no longer a slave, but a son; and if a son, then an heir through God. *Galatians 4:6-7* (NASB-U)

The Spirit Himself testifies with our spirit that we are children of God, and if children, heirs also, heirs of God and fellow heirs with Christ. *Romans 8:16-17a* (NASB-U)

Rather than conquest, The Kingdom necessarily starts within the hearts of men— God changing individuals from the inside, and spreading the change from person to person across the earth. This was the core of Christ's teachings about the

THE POWERFUL ENEMIES OF CHRIST The Jewish leaders were so desperate to get rid of Jesus that, despite their intense hatred for Rome, they shouted, "We have no king but Caesar." *John 19:15* (LAN) How ironic that they feigned allegiance to Rome while rejecting their own Messiah! Their own words condemned them, for God was to be their only true King, and they had abandoned every trace of loyalty to Him. The priests had truly lost their reasons for existence— instead of turning people to God, they claimed allegiance to Rome in order to kill their Messiah.

The Pharisees and Sadducees were the leading religious parties of Christ's day. Lawyers, priests and scholars called "Scribes" belonged to the Pharisees, a scholarly and strict class. The Sadducees were very different, largely comprised of the wealthy aristocracy and high priestly families among the Jews. Together, these two sects of Judaism formed a political body called the Sanhedrin and ruled Israel, by permission of the Romans.

The Romans only reserved the right of taxation and the sentence of execution for themselves, but left the Sanhedrin otherwise free to govern Judea.

Kingdom: slow growth—at first miniscule, individual change—but eventually filling the earth:

> Jesus asked, "How can I describe the Kingdom of God? What story should I use to illustrate it? It is like a tiny mustard seed. Though this is one of the smallest of seeds, it grows to become one of the largest of plants, with long branches where birds can come and find shelter." *Mark 4:30-32*

∽ **Membership in the Kingdom of God requires internal change.**

Consider this...

As an act of mercy, God started The Kingdom by offering individuals an opportunity to change. If King Messiah abruptly changed the Kosmos as the people wanted, nobody would survive to enjoy the results.

To establish The Kingdom with its entire authority means destroying the Counterfeit Kingdom, and everyone who belongs to it. Nobody belongs to The Kingdom at birth—all humanity is spiritually dead like Adam and alienated from the life of God.

Jesus began teaching the crowds the essential strategy of kingdom growth:

> "Truly, truly, I say to you, unless a grain of wheat falls into the earth and dies, it remains alone; but if it dies, it bears much fruit." *John 12:24* (NASB-U)

These teachings about death began to alienate the crowds. Jesus never called for an overthrow of Roman rule as they thought he should, he never attacked it. Instead

REWRITING THE LAW Most of the public confrontations between Christ and the religious scholars centered over questions about what the Law of Moses taught. A new tradition was developing at this time, where the Pharisees were rewriting the Law to objectively prove their own righteousness. They "changed the spiritual import of [the Law] into a complicated code of external and burdensome ordinances."[9]

For example, the simple commandment in Exodus 20:8 contains just a few words: "Remember the Sabbath day to keep it holy." This developed into hundreds of pages and dozens of "chapters" in the Talmud of precise legal stipulations, so exotic in detail, "one would scarcely imagine a sane intellect would seriously entertain," as one Jewish scholar says.[10] "There is a grave discussion whether it was lawful to spit on the ground, and then to rub it with the foot, because thereby the earth may be scratched. It may, however, be done on stones."[11] If someone threw a stone in the air, "there could be no doubt a man incurred guilt if he caught it with the same hand which it had been thrown, but he was not guilty if he caught it in his mouth..."[12]

Jesus rejected these absurdities and pointed out the key problem: "You ignore the important things of the law—justice, mercy, and faith." *Matthew 23:23*. Compared to the teachers of his day, is it any wonder the crowds were thrilled and relieved at the teachings of Jesus?

he kept talking about the need for personal change, and denounced the evil found inside people:

> "For from within, out of a person's heart, come evil thoughts, sexual immorality, theft, murder, adultery, greed, wickedness, deceit, eagerness for lustful pleasure, envy, slander, pride, and foolishness. All these vile things come from within; they are what defile you and make you unacceptable to God." *Mark 7:21-23*

This was not the kind of teaching people came to hear, and things changed.

OPPOSITION MOUNTS

People heavily invested in the Kosmos were the most likely candidates to reject a different Kingdom. It was precisely those with the most to lose who mustered opposition against God's Kingdom.

At first, the gathering movement in Galilee caught the powerful rulers of Israel off guard, because it was far to the north and inconsequential to the center of worship in Jerusalem. When they finally sent people to Galilee to follow Christ around and report on His activities, the authorities did not like what they saw. In Judea, the authorities were religious leaders.

The religious leaders at first approached Jesus with respect, calling Him "rabbi," meaning "teacher." Some invited Him to dinner, while others like Nicodemus met Him secretly to ask sincere questions.

PRONOUNCED A REBEL

It soon became apparent, however, that Jesus was more threatening than John the Baptist—He was a rebel against their religious institutions. His message was bitter medicine for people with the Religious Mindset like the Pharisees. Their rituals and good deeds did not placate God, Jesus warned them, because God saw the spiritual indifference lurking in their hearts. Their religious pride was the most reprehensible barrier, Jesus said, because it made them seem so religious, yet unreachable by God because they saw no need. They lived by the Principle of Sin like everyone else, but theirs was buried beneath layers of religious works.

The Pharisees in particular were highly esteemed by the people because of their strict adherence to the "traditions of the elders." The Pharisees, however, viewed the common people contemptuously, as ignorant and unworthy masses. The proud Pharisees never associated with lowly sinners, and they ceremoniously washed themselves each time after walking among the common people.[13]

When Jesus began showing compassion toward the so-called dirty people—the poor, tax collectors and other sinners—the Pharisees were outraged. Theirs was a carefully structured society, separating "sinner" from "holy men," Gentile from Jew. Jesus exposed their artificial barriers:

The Pharisees and the scribes asked Him, "Why do Your disciples not walk according to the tradition of the elders, but eat their bread with impure hands?" And He said to them, "Rightly did Isaiah prophesy of you hypocrites, as it is written: 'This people honors Me with their lips, But their heart is far away from Me.' Neglecting the commandment of God, you hold to the tradition of men." *Mark 7:5-8* (NASB-U)

Jesus then publicly dismantled the myth of the Pharisee's righteousness.

And He said to them, "You are those who justify yourselves in the sight of men, but God knows your hearts; for that which is highly esteemed among men is detestable in the sight of God." *Luke 16:15* (NASB-U)

He turned the Religion of Merit on its head when He showed that even lowly tax collectors were more acceptable to God than the righteous Pharisees:

"Two men went up into the temple to pray, one a Pharisee and the other a tax collector. The Pharisee stood and was praying this to himself: 'God, I thank You that I am not like other people: swindlers, unjust, adulterers, or even like this tax collector. I fast twice a week; I pay tithes of all that I get.' But the tax collector, standing some distance away, was even unwilling to lift up his eyes to heaven, but was beating his breast, saying, 'God, be merciful to me, the sinner!'" *Luke 18:10-13* (NASB-U)

It was a shocking revelation, but a welcome one. It still left a haunting question unanswered: If the righteousness of the Pharisees did not appease God, then how could anyone have hope?

Consider this…

This is the most agonizing question people have about God, and why so many give up hope ever knowing Him; considering what kind of people we are, why would God ever accept us?

The answer is in one simple word: Grace.

OPPOSITION TO GRACE

Grace is God's profound yet simple answer to our spiritual alienation. From the beginning of time, at the heart of The Mystery, and throughout the Old and New Testaments, Grace is the central, recurring theme. With Jesus, it was the first thing to strike people who met him:

…We saw His glory, glory as of the only begotten from the Father, full of grace and truth. *John 1:14* (NASB-U)

∽ **It is impossible to understand God, the Bible, or His activity in history without understanding Grace.**

It was precisely this concept that repelled the religious thinkers of Christ's day, because Grace redefined their system of who was acceptable and who was not, as Jesus told the religious leaders:

> "But go and learn what this means: 'I desire compassion, and not sacrifice,' for I did not come to call the righteous, but sinners." *Matthew 9:13* (NASB-U)

Jesus was quoting the Old Testament with "I desire compassion"—an area of expertise for the religious scholars. Jesus grew increasingly angry with these men because they, if anyone, should know Grace stands at the very heart of Revelation and even the character of God Himself, as He revealed to Moses 1,500 years earlier:

> Then the Lord passed by in front of him and proclaimed, "The Lord, the Lord God, compassionate and gracious, slow to anger, and abounding in lovingkindness and truth …" *Exodus 34:6-7* (NASB-U)

Consider this…

Grace is difficult to accept. It flies in the face of the Counterfeit Kingdom and all its inducements, where only through great effort can someone advance, and the highly esteemed are those proving their worth. From an early age, all our thinking is conditioned against Grace.

> **Grace expresses the unlimited, unconditional love of God poured out on someone who does not deserve it and cannot earn it.**

When Christ began teaching about Grace, it caused some confusion, as it still does today:

> When the scribes of the Pharisees saw that He was eating with the sinners and tax collectors, they said to His disciples, "Why is He eating and drinking with tax collectors and sinners?" And hearing this, Jesus said to them, "It is not those who are healthy who need a physician, but those who are sick; I did not come to call the righteous, but sinners." *Mark 2:16-17* (NASB-U)

Nobody is beyond the reach of God's Grace. Quite the opposite: those who feel no need for Grace are beyond the reach of God's Grace, and so Jesus said, "I did not come to call the righteous, but sinners." Grace eludes those with a Religious Mindset, because they see no need for it.

Consider this…

God offers Grace unconditionally, but until we ask for forgiveness, Grace remains a useless abstraction; it makes no practical difference in our lives.

> **The Mystery is entirely wrapped around the revelation of Grace.**

It is called The Atonement—the most profound and exciting story in the Bible. Without understanding The Atonement, Grace makes little sense. It was finally at Christ's death that The Mystery was revealed, and Grace through The Atonement became possible.

THE DECISION TO KILL CHRIST

It did not take long for the Sanhedrin to conclude Jesus posed a very real threat to their political power. Not only did He denounce their religious piety, but also the miracles increased His popularity over theirs. They became concerned especially after Jesus raised Lazarus from the dead near Jerusalem. No longer in distant Galilee, threat was looming near the nation's headquarters for religious worship. They convened a meeting to deliberate His fate:

> Then the leading priests and Pharisees called the high council together to discuss the situation. "What are we going to do?" they asked each other. "This man certainly performs many miraculous signs. If we leave him alone, the whole nation will follow him, and then the Roman army will come and destroy both our Temple and our nation." *John 11:47-48* (NLT)

Their conclusions were correct, of course: if Jesus continued unchecked, he could effectively undermine their system. The Sanhedrin enjoyed some measure of power under the Romans because they enjoyed the popular support of the nation. By threatening their popularity, Jesus threatened their standing with Rome.

Because there were some on the Sanhedrin like Nicodemus who believed in Christ, we are privy to a most remarkable incident at this council meeting:

> And one of them, Caiaphas, who was High Priest that year, said, "You stupid idiots—let this one man die for the people—why should the whole nation perish?" This prophecy that Jesus should die for the entire nation came from Caiaphas in his position as High Priest—he didn't think of it by himself, but was inspired to say it. It was a prediction that Jesus' death would not be for Israel only, but for all the children of God scattered around the world. *John 11:49-52* (Living)

Indeed, just as the High Priest prophesied, it was Christ's very intention to die. Early in His ministry, Christ proclaimed this to His Disciples:

> "For even I, the Messiah, am not here to be served, but to help others, and to give my life as a ransom for many." *Mark 10:45* (Living)

Christ dying "as a ransom for many" is the heart and soul of God's Redemptive Plan. This is why Christ died on the cross. He carefully instructed His disciples about this purpose:

From then on Jesus began to speak plainly to his disciples about going to Jerusalem, and what would happen to him there—that he would suffer at the hands of the Jewish leaders, that he would be killed, and that three days later he would be raised to life again. *Matthew 16:21* (LB)

This upset the disciples, particularly Peter, but Jesus bluntly told them it was necessary for Him to die—to conquer death and sin.

The most difficult aspect of the life of Christ for many to swallow is that He intentionally headed for the Cross. What an unparalleled strategy for a great leader to pursue! If the king dies, how is it possible to establish a worldwide Kingdom? Great kingdoms always expand through large armies, vast reserves of men and money and armaments, led by brilliant military minds.

Yet here again, as throughout the Eternal Plan of God, we see His Backward Thinking at work. The Cross was not only the intention of Christ's life, but also seeded throughout the course of God's Revelation.

✺ The Cross is the reason God gave Revelation.

Here is the genius of God's Revelation to man: He did not want the crucifixion to occur in a vacuum, sudden and unexpected as it was. Instead, thousands of years of prophecy points to the Cross, weaving together the entire fabric of the Old Testament.

We call this The Scarlet Thread of Redemption, and understanding this leads directly to the exciting discovery of a relationship with God. Before we can proceed with the story of Christ's death on the Cross, it is essential to back up and look at how the Scarlet Thread of Redemption weaves throughout the entirety of God's Revelation.

THE SCARLET THREAD

Only in this way could he deliver those who have lived all their lives as slaves to
the fear of dying.
Hebrews 2:14-15

Jesus Christ was not born into a historical vacuum, suddenly and unexpected. His
appearance on earth in 4 B.C. was part of a continuous series of interactions with
humanity extending back to the dawn of human history, countless ages ago:

"His goings forth are from long ago…" *Micah 5:2* (NASB-U)

Jesus Christ created mankind; He was in the Garden of Eden and knew what a
relationship with humans looked like before sin scarred the picture. He exposed
himself to our world of suffering at birth, although he could have come as a full-
grown man instead. He is heavily invested in the human the race—it is His race.

Why, then, would He expel Adam and Eve from the Garden of Eden, remove His
protection, and expose their children to ages of suffering?

THE PROBLEM

After God expelled Adam and Eve from His Kingdom, He did a strange thing: He
placed an angelic being with a flaming sword to guard the Tree of Life, fearing that

VIOLATING GOD'S CHARACTER If God forgave the rebellion of Adam and Eve because of
His Love, this would be at the expense of at least four other attributes:

- He would no longer be the Sovereign of the Universe, because they chose to be their own
  gods. God cannot abandon His sovereignty.

- He would no longer be Just, because He was not judging their rebellion. God cannot allow
  rebellion to run rampant in His universe.

- He would no longer be Immutable (unchanging), because He changed His decree of death on
  them. When God speaks, it is with certainty.

- He would violate His Veracity, because He lied when He warned them about impending death
  if they did not die.

man would return and eat from it. Why? Why not allow them to reverse course, apologize for their rebellion, and return to Eden? It would save so much suffering.

God's character is the limiting factor. People are surprised to discover God cannot do certain things, such as lie. Since He is the very source of Veracity, or truth, lying would contradict His character.

> ⤳ **God cannot express one of His attributes at the expense of another.**

This is the key to understanding God. God must confront the challenge of rebellion with Justice. Yet, He also loved Adam and Eve. How then to deal with them with both Justice and Love? Out of Love, God created us for fellowship with Him, yet a Righteous God cannot fellowship with sin.

BLOOD SACRIFICE

For the first time ever, Adam and Eve faced alienation from God when they were exiled from the garden. They no longer enjoyed the carefree days of approaching God with complete freedom—they were alienated.

The God of Love opened a new channel of access through a Blood Sacrifice. It made a relationship with God still possible, yet different, because blood was spilled in the process. Abel tried this new approach to God and sacrificed an innocent, unblemished lamb. He discovered an exciting response:

> The Lord looked with favor on Abel and his offering. *Genesis 4:4b* (NIV)

Abel discovered a revolutionary hope in the bleakness of the Counterfeit Kingdom: peace and acceptance with God. There was something uniquely powerful about this idea of a Blood Sacrifice, and it would be centuries before God explained clearly what it was.

A RELIGION OF MERIT

Tragically, Abel's brother Cain approached God differently, and it did not work. Like Abel, this man also had faith—he held his beliefs strongly enough to kill for. Yet God rejected Cain's approach decisively:

> …but on Cain and his offering he did not look with favor. So Cain was very angry, and his face was downcast. *Genesis 4:5* (NIV)

Cain offered grain, which was an innovative way to approach God and very different from Abel's Blood Sacrifice. He chose grain because he was a farmer, and it was the classic Religion of Convenience—the hallmark of man-made religion. Cain tried to appease God by offering his best.[1]

Cain was enraged by God's rejection! Cain had offered his best! In Cain's mind, Abel was the problem. He discarded God's clear message that the problem was Cain's sacrifice—God wanted a Blood Sacrifice, not grain. God's rebuke was a personal insult, a rejection of his workmanship and the best fruits of his labor. It was a serious effort by Cain—he cared so deeply, he killed Abel.

Consider this...

Here is where even a "Religious" person is in trouble with God: approaching God with Cain's attitude, demanding acceptance, refusing God's correction, or trusting in good works. God can see it all for what it truly is: the Principle of Sin cloaked in religion.

∽ **It is false that God is bound to accept all sincere, religious efforts.**

People grow indignant to think God has any right to exclude certain ways of approaching Him. Cain, for example, held a tacit demand that either God accept his best efforts, or he would rebel. Cain is proof God can see through the veneer to the heart, and is unimpressed by grand religious shows. His Grace is only available to a certain kind of heart:

> God is opposed to the proud, but gives grace to the humble. *James 4:6* (NASB-U)

THE VITAL DIFFERENCE

Inside Cain was a deep-seated unwillingness to submit to God, which became obvious when Cain killed Abel for revenge.

Abel, on the other hand, trusted in the Blood Sacrifice mandated by God. This is the kind of faith that always brings a relationship with God:

> Faith led Abel to offer God a better sacrifice than Cain's sacrifice. Through his faith Abel received God's approval, since God accepted his sacrifices... *Hebrews 11:4* (GW)

PRIMITIVE SACRIFICES The Blood Sacrifice is an ancient practice according to the Bible, beginning with the dawn of man. Yet somewhere in history, it became a superstitious ritual and lost God's original point to Abel: the blood sacrifice of an unblemished lamb was God's chosen way of gaining access.

Sacrifice became distorted along with the prevailing view of God. Myths depicting God as little more than immoral humans with great powers developed, and sacrifice became a way of feeding the hungry gods:

"The sacrifices and offerings were designed to serve the gods by meeting any physical need that they may have had. The sacrifices were the food and drink of the gods. Faithfulness to the preparation and presentation of them was an act of devotion."[2]

These and other superstitious views of sacrifice developed into human sacrifice so detestable to God. God's Blood Sacrifice was a Substitutionary Death: the one bringing the offering was to lay a hand upon the animal in order to identify that the animal was taking the person's place in judgment: "Lay your hand on its head so the Lord will accept it as your substitute..." *Leviticus 1:4*[3]

Consider this...

Abel trusted in God's prescribed method of approach: the Blood Sacrifice.
Cain demanded acceptance for a novel approach, and was insulted by God's
refusal.

The Old Testament is one continuous and deepening Revelation of the Blood
Sacrifice, and without exception, all the godly characters in the Old Testament
approached God this way. Although it was a mystery how it worked, they still
trusted God. With Abraham, God made it clear.

THE PRINCIPLE OF SUBSTITUTION

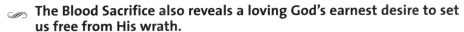

The Blood Sacrifice in the Old Testament was no superstitious ritual. It was a
vivid, even violent picture of what it means to encounter God's Justice when sin is
present. The result is called wrath—God's reaction to sin.

> **The Blood Sacrifice also reveals a loving God's earnest desire to set**
> **us free from His wrath.**

The Blood Sacrifice taught two important lessons: that man deserves judgment,
and that God can provide a way to save us from judgment. Exactly how the sacrifice itself saves us from judgment was still unknown. It was The Mystery.

A STRANGE SACRIFICE

Untold thousands of years later, a man appears who received a mountain of reve-
lation about The Mystery. Abraham—whose very name means "the Father of a
Multitude" because of his great impact on human history—is a vital link in The
Mystery running through the Bible.

It centered on his son Isaac. When he was about 14, Abraham was asked by God
to do something utterly horrific: to sacrifice his only son as a burnt offering! It is
one of the strangest incidents in the entire Bible, since God clearly opposes human
sacrifice:

> "Take your son, your only son—yes, Isaac, whom you love so much—
> and go to the land of Moriah. Sacrifice him there as a burnt offering on
> one of the mountains, which I will point out to you." *Genesis 22:2*

In a classic biblical understatement, the author tells us simply:

> The next morning Abraham got up early. He saddled his donkey and
> took two of his servants with him, along with his son Isaac. Then he
> chopped wood to build a fire for a burnt offering and set out for the
> place where God had told him to go. *Genesis 22:3*

Nothing in this narrative tells how Abraham felt; the doubts that had to be swirling
through his head, the conflict he wrestled with knowing human sacrifice is

detestable to God. Everything within Abraham surely screamed out against the glaring contradiction of God's promise to build a nation through Isaac, and this command to kill Isaac as a Blood Sacrifice. For three days Abraham traveled with Isaac, alone with his thoughts.

COMBINED WITH FAITH

Yet, Abraham knew something about God that many do not understand: God deserves our complete trust. This is the essence of true faith:

> Abraham assumed that if Isaac died, God was able to bring him back to life again. And in a sense, Abraham did receive his son back from the dead. *Hebrews 11:19*

Even though Abraham faced the prospect of killing his own son, he was convinced of the goodness of God and His promise to make Isaac a "blessing for all the nations of the earth." For this reason the Bible calls Abraham the "Father of us all who believe."[4]

Consider this...

God wants us to become "Abraham's offspring" and personally discover He is indeed trustworthy—that He delivers on His promises to provide the most fulfilling life imaginable.

A NARROW ESCAPE

After three days they arrived at Mount Moriah, the place God designated for the sacrifice. Abraham left his servants behind and, with only Isaac, climbed up the mountain..

Isaac broke the silence and asks a devastating question:

> Isaac said, "Father?" "Yes, my son," Abraham replied. "We have the wood and the fire," said the boy, "but where is the lamb for the sacrifice?" *Genesis 22:7*

Abraham's reply demonstrates a profound understanding of Grace:

> "God will provide a lamb, my son," Abraham answered. And they both went on together. *Genesis 22:8*

The silence must have been deafening.

Abraham reached the point where he tied his son down on the altar and raised the knife to drive it into Isaac's heart – when an Angel of God calls out,

> "Abraham! Abraham! … Lay down the knife," the angel said. "Do not hurt the boy in any way!" *Genesis 22:11a, 12a*

A profound sense of relief swept across Abraham's tear-stained face. He was spared the grief of slaying his only son! Why would God put this man through such torment?

THE PRINCIPLE OF SUBSTITUTION
∽ **God Himself experienced this horror some 2,000 years later with his own son Jesus Christ. And nobody yelled, "Stop!"**

Abraham dramatically acted out the Principle of Substitution, where God's wrath is unleashed on a substitute—a stand-in. God provided a ram caught in the thicket— a substitute—for his son, Isaac. This was deeply significant Revelation, "a copy of heavenly things to come." *Hebrews 9:23*

Consider this...
In the Principle of Substitution, Abraham offered an innocent substitute for the guilty party. It is God's timeless principle that only innocent blood can enable a guilty person to live with God forever.

Blood is specifically required:

> "..I have given this blood to you to make peace with me on the altar. Blood is needed to make peace with me." *Leviticus 17:11* (GW)

The Principle of Substitution is derived from the ancient sense of justice that resides only in the mind of God, a justice without corollary in modern human courts: a substitute takes the punishment. Some close examples occur in modern courtrooms when a parent is punished for a juvenile's truancy.

AN AMAZING PROPHECY
Abraham acted out an astonishing piece of biblical prophecy: Mount Moriah where this occurred became known as Jerusalem centuries later, where Jesus Christ was given as a sacrifice.

God revealed at Mount Moriah a critical and missing piece of the Blood Sacrifice: that God Himself provides a substitute for the sins of man! Abraham understood this vital point:

> Abraham named the place "The Lord Will Provide." This name has now become a proverb: "On the mountain of the Lord it will be provided." *Genesis 22:14*

∽ **The Principle of Substitution teaches that God will provide the way and means of salvation itself.**

REDEMPTION

The Blood Sacrifice continues to build as a theme in the Bible 600 years later when God had undeniably delivered on His promise to build a great nation through Isaac. Now this nation—around 2 million strong—was living in captivity in the land of Egypt. It was the night they expected to be released from slavery, the terrifying Night of the Passover.

PREPARATION OF THE PASSOVER

On this night, God's People would be purchased out of slavery.

> **This is what the Bible calls Redemption: to purchase out of slavery.**

Redemption not only bought freedom for the Israelites, but God used it to purchase humanity out of the Counterfeit Kingdom. On Passover Night, God taught the Israelites what Redemption entailed, and they were instructed to carefully preserve this lesson for future ages.

As terror swept across Egypt leaving dead bodies and grieving households behind; inside the households of Israel, people gathered around the Passover Meal in safety. This was the first Passover, reenacted still today with solemn remembrance of their rescue by the blood of the lamb. In order to escape the judgment of death striking Egyptian households, each Hebrew family was carefully instructed to kill an unblemished lamb, and:

> "They are to take some of the lamb's blood and smear it on the top and sides of the doorframe of the house where the lamb will be eaten." *Exodus 12:7*

It was specifically the blood of the lamb that saved the household:

> "For the Lord will pass through the land and strike down the Egyptians. But when he sees the blood on the top and sides of the doorframe, the Lord will pass over your home..." *Exodus 12:23*

The blood of the lamb was their Redemption:[5]

> "I am the Lord, and I will free you from your slavery in Egypt. I will redeem you with mighty power and great acts of judgment." *Exodus 6:6*

The Passover was the very first festival instituted for the new nation of Israel, and their most important. It marks the time when they became a nation as God's People:[6]

> "I will redeem you...I will make you my own special people" *Exodus 6:6b-7a*

THE LAMB OF GOD

It was no accident Jesus was killed on the Passover as the Lamb of God:

> "Behold, the Lamb of God who takes away the sin of the world!" *John 1:29*

Even Isaiah predicts that the Messiah will come as the sacrificial lamb:

> "…He was led as a lamb to the slaughter. And as a sheep is silent before the shearers, he did not open his mouth. From prison and trial they led him away to his death. But who among the people realized that he was dying for their sins—that he was suffering their punishment?" *Isaiah 53:7-8*

Long before He was killed at the cross, Jesus told His Disciples it was His purpose to exchange His life for the freedom of mankind, the Redemption:

> "For even the Son of Man did not come to be served, but to serve, and to give His life a ransom for many." *Mark 10:45* (NASB-U)

Consider this…

Throughout the history of Israel, God was using Festivals, Prophets and pictures to build an understanding for the need of a Blood Sacrifice and Redemption. This is called the Scarlet Thread of Redemption, and it is threaded throughout the Bible, from Genesis to Revelation.

All these pictures were to be fulfilled by the coming Messiah.

THE NEED FOR REDEMPTION

Satan's victory over humanity in The Fall was hideous. Satan became the rightful owner of humanity, and his Counterfeit Kingdom is a system of slavery because it is owned by a tyrant. Satan will not share worship or power, and no elections or human revolutions can change his leadership:

> The whole world lies in the power of the evil one. *1 John 5:19* (NASB-U)

∽ **Adam and Eve handed over the deed to their lives to a new ruler.**

Consider this…

Once born into slavery, we live out our years in slavery, raise families in it, and die without knowing any other kingdom. As years pass, the Counterfeit Kingdom reduces people to a slave's status: a plodding, resigned existence, accepting the flatness of life, growing cynical and beaten down.

To live is the rarest thing in the world. Most people exist, that is all.
Oscar Wilde[7]

The Kosmos absorbs years, energy, emotions, intellect—the entire person—and in exchange offers a little excitement or diversion, perhaps acclaim. It all evaporates, and leaves the slave with nothing for his labors:

> Perhaps life is just that ... a dream and a fear. *Joseph Conrad*[8]

Great thinkers through the ages have tried to resolve the conflict between our desire to be free, and the way it actually turns out inside the Kosmos:

> Man is born free, and everywhere he is in chains. *Jean-Jacques Rousseau*[9]

This desire to be free was the driving force behind the Communist movement that caught the imagination of millions in the 20th Century. The Communists failed tragically because it is impossible to refine the Kosmos—as Jesus Christ knew, and avoided—and Communists only created yet another system of slavery like the one they overthrew:

> Let's not talk about Communism. Communism was just an idea, just pie in the sky. *Boris Yeltsin, Russian president*[10]

The slavery of the Kosmos is tied to the unalterable character of the Ruler of this World, the owner of humanity, and maintains an iron hold through fear.

SLAVES OF FEAR

Fear is a slave's driving motivation. Satan wields fear like a whip, holding the threat of death over the heads of everyone trapped in The System. But Jesus came to set us free:

> Jesus also became flesh and blood...Only in this way could he deliver those who have lived all their lives as slaves to the fear of dying. *Hebrews 2:14-15*

Because of their fear of death, people dare not think too deeply beyond it. Death is fearful because it is so final—and uncertain. It is an ugly scar on the human experience, a gruesome—and violent—future for everyone. Death cannot be trivialized; its impact is irrevocable, as C. S. Lewis says:

> It is hard to have patience with people who say "There is no death" or "Death doesn't matter." There is death. And whatever is matters. And whatever happens has consequences, and it and they are irrevocable and irreversible. You might as well say that birth doesn't matter. *C. S. Lewis*[11]

Redemption is God's answer to the fear of death and slavery.

THE ATONEMENT

For the more we know God's law, the clearer it becomes that we aren't obeying it.
Romans 3:20b

Beyond doubt, the Religion of Merit is the world's most popular religion. So ancient, it extends back to the dawn of human history; so pervasive, it includes every major world religion still today—except for what Jesus Christ brought. Even segments of Christianity have become virtually indistinguishable from it, so compelling is the attraction. The Religion of Merit appeals to the Principle of Sin within man, allowing independence from God, while hopefully appeasing God with Good Works.

Consider this...

God meets the Religion of Merit with the Law: the Mosaic Covenant. Because God is compassionate even in the face of human pride—He even tried to persuade murderous Cain. God carefully described to Moses why a Religion of Merit could never succeed.

COMPARATIVE RELIGION It is not unfair to say that outside of Christianity, theistic religions fall into four broad groups—Eastern Religions (Hinduism, Buddhism and their offshoots), Islam, and Judaism. They all share a common emphasis on Good Works for salvation.

Eastern Religions offer salvation by "a primary emphasis on what man himself can do about it...by practicing the rigorous discipline...attained by righteousness, but much more often by asceticism, knowledge, or devotion."[1]

Islam "is preeminently a religion of law" which offers salvation "exclusively on the quality of obedience to the sacred law..." known as the Pillars of Religion.[2]

Modern Judaism is virtually unrecognizable from the sacrificial system of the Mosaic Covenant—understandably, since the vital Temple and Priesthood disappeared after the time of Christ. Sadly, they "tended to make the moral and ceremonial law together into a way in which they sought to establish a righteousness of their own."[3]

By the time Jesus came to Israel, the Mosaic Covenant was becoming virtually unrecognizable, and its viability as a stop-gap against the Religion of Merit was diluted. The colossal tome of modern Judaism called the Talmud—the work of 400 to 500 rabbis over a period of almost 1,000 years, beginning around 400 B.C. when God stopped sending prophets and Revelation fell silent[4]—was gaining momentum at this time.[5] The Talmud became a collection of commentaries on the Law, as pious and sincere Jewish thinkers tried to codify Judaism.

This development caused a problem: slowly elevating human commentary to the status of God's Revelation, they began creating a Religion of Merit which was evident by Christ's day. Codifying Judaism meant creating hallowed "traditions of men" that Jesus was determined to strip away from the essence of The Law, and this explains a huge segment of His teachings and strongest criticisms:

> "Neglecting the commandment of God, you hold to the tradition of men." *Mark 7:8* (NASB-U)

THE MORAL NATURE OF THE LAW

The Law was originally given to Moses at Mount Sinai as a practical and specific framework to form a new nation under God's leadership.[A] But it also contains general principles describing the character of God, and so the Law frequently says, "You are to be holy as I am holy."[6] This term "holy" is not easily understood by the modern mind. It is a strong word that means to be "wholly different," which anyone must become in order to impress God, considering our Fallen Nature.[B]

The Law gives an overwhelming picture of God's character of Righteousness— even then, it is only a glimpse, so vast is His Righteousness. The Law makes a clear point: God is very "wholly different."

✎ The Law is a threatening document to read—purposefully.

The Law reveals a yawning gap between God's character and our Fallen Nature, and reading it creates a sour taste of despair, a sense of hopelessness, exposing the damage inflicted by The Fall. The Law is not pleasant reading.

Why did God give a law about murder? Not because God murders, but because humans murder. The same is true for all the moral code in the Law—directed at the problem of evil:

> Why was the law given? It was given to show people how guilty they are. *Galatians 3:19*

Because humanity is rampant with greed and injustice, the Law of God stirs despair in the conscience when it describes the ideal behavior God desires. Daily life is different with Fallen Nature continually violating these laws, as Paul complains:

(A) See chapter 7 "Further Consideration" and the sidebar "What is Holy?" for a background discussion of the Law.

(B) See the sidebar "Sin" in chapter 4. Fallen Nature, Sin and the Principle of Sin are used interchangeably.

The trouble is not with the law but with me…I don't understand myself at all, for I really want to do what is right, but I don't do it. *Romans 7:14-17*

CONSCIENCE

Made in the image of God, humans are moral agents with a conscience that deeply feels the moral defects of Fallen Nature—called Sin.

> ✍ **It is universally true across all cultures and all ages that humans have a moral conscience.**

Without debate, "every culture has developed an ethic," and "all human societies studied have…their own form of morality."[7] There may be disagreement about the details of right or wrong or the source of ethical judgments, but there is universal consensus among philosophers, anthropologists, historians and archeologists that humans of every age are moral agents:

Two things fill the soul…the starry heavens above and the moral law within. *Immanuel Kant*[8]

The Law stings the conscience with conviction—by design:

A FLAWED RELIGION OF MERIT There was one, fatal flaw in Cain's Religion of Merit—a deficient view of sin. He did not grasp how offensive and foreign sin is to God's Righteousness. God's Righteousness demands judgment for sin, and He cannot dismiss sin by man's simplistic appeasement. The only possible verdict is separation from God. He will not and cannot have fellowship with sin because it violates His very character, and it demands His Wrath: "For all have sinned; all fall short of God's glorious standard." *Romans 3:23*

This means the alienation between man and God is far deeper than the Religion of Merit concedes. It is impossible for man to grasp how deeply sin offends God's character because sin has a numbing effect on those surrounded by it and practicing it. This is why Revelation from God is desperately needed—otherwise, nobody can grasp how serious our predicament with God actually is.

Sinful man is in no position to dictate terms to God. Nobody can freely invent novel approaches to God, an obvious point—at issue is God's authority.

God mercifully offered Redemption, which proves His loving character. Yet humanity consistently embraces the Religion of Merit in one of its many guises. Why? Redemption angers people. It insults personal merit and self-worth. Manmade religions always approach God with great fanfare and parades of self-worth. It sometimes appears humble when religions practice self-denial or asceticism—but this severity is truly a proud display of human worthiness before God through strenuous efforts.

The popularity of the Religion of Merit proves how obsessed we are with self-worth—how else to explain the massive appeal of religions that demand such harsh self-abasement? Meanwhile, God's simple offer of Redemption is treated historically with ridicule, rejection and even contempt.

I felt fine when I did not understand what the law demanded. But when I learned the truth, I realized I had broken the law and was a sinner, doomed to die. *Romans 7:9*

The problem with having a conscience is the burden of a deep sense of failure it bears, as Paul says:

It seems to be a fact of life that when I want to do what is right, I inevitably do what is wrong… Oh, what a miserable person I am! Who will free me from this life that is dominated by sin? *Romans 7:21, 24*

Consider this…

Even those without God's Revelation and who are unaware of God's Law feel the same problem of moral failure. It is revealed by God-given conscience:

Gentiles, who do not have God's written law, instinctively follow what the law says… They demonstrate that God's law is written within them, for their own consciences either accuse them or tell them they are doing what is right. *Romans 2:14-15*

SELF-JUSTIFICATION

Nobody endures guilt for long, and the Religion of Merit is a popular solution. Using simplistic morality, it becomes possible to "do the right thing" and create a feeling of self-justification. Man-made religions create attainable ethics which focus on superficial behaviors—like ritual prayers or sacred ceremonies—precisely what Jesus criticized among the Pharisees of His day:

"Hypocrites! You are so careful to clean the outside of the cup and the dish, but inside you are filthy—full of greed and self-indulgence!" *Matthew 23:25*

✍ Self-justification is possible by redefining morality as behavior.

The religious leaders became highly accomplished at behavioral change and main-taining appearances, projecting an impressive persona of high morality:

"Everything they do is for show. On their arms they wear extra wide prayer boxes with Scripture verses inside, and they wear extra long tas-sels on their robes. And how they love to sit at the head table at banquets and in the most prominent seats in the synagogue! They enjoy the attention they get on the streets, and they enjoy being called 'Rabbi.'" *Matthew 23:5-7*

It goes by many names—the Religion of Convenience, Good Works, Ritual Observance, or Sacred Space—it is all the same Religion of Merit that consoles the conscience and makes a guilty person feel self-justified.

A GUILTY HEART

God's Law is quite different. It is not so easy to feel self-justified, because the ethics are impossibly demanding. Nobody can get past the "great commandment" without recognizing failure:

> "'You shall love the Lord your God with all your heart, and with all your soul, and with all your mind.' This is the great and foremost commandment." *Matthew 22:37-38 (NASB-U)*[9]

Those controlled by the Principle of Sin cannot possibly live up to this commandment—and such is the nature of the Law. It exposes the deep-seated problem hidden in the heart where rebellion resides:

> The law aroused these evil desires that produced sinful deeds… *Romans 7:5*

On and on the Law attacks the hidden thoughts that others never see:

> "You shall have no other gods before me…Observe the Sabbath day to keep it holy…Honor your father and mother…You shall not covet…" *Deuteronomy 5:7-21*

> ✑ **God's Law defines morality in terms of thoughts and attitudes— by who we are, not what we do.**

THE SERMON ON THE MOUNT People reading the Sermon on the Mount have often misunderstood its intended meaning. It was addressed specifically to people living "under the law" who mistakenly thought they were properly keeping the Law through their external behavior— the popular teaching of the day. (See sidebar "Rewriting the Law" in Chapter 12) The Sermon clearly shows the impossibility of attaining moral righteousness:

"You have heard that the law of Moses says, 'Do not murder.'...But I say, if you are angry with someone, you are subject to judgment! ...And if you curse someone, you are in danger of the fires of hell." *Matthew 5:21-22*

"You have heard that it was said, 'You shall not commit adultery'; but I say to you that everyone who looks at a woman with lust for her has already committed adultery with her in his heart." *Matthew 5:27-28*

In case any lingering self-confidence remained: "Therefore you are to be perfect, as your heavenly Father is perfect." *Matthew 5:48 (NASB-U)*

The Sermon on the Mount demonstrates the huge moral gulf between God and Fallen Man, and it was designed to discourage—as with the Law of Moses.

Yet this Sermon also contains one of the most exciting promises in scripture:

"I did not come to abolish the Law of Moses or the writings of the prophets. No, I came to fulfill them." *Matthew 5:17*

" Jesus can fulfill the Law for us, removing any need for a Religion of Merit: "Christ is the end of the law for righteousness to everyone who believes." *Romans 10:4 (NASB-U)*

Attempts can be made to limit God's Law to behavior—precisely what Post-Exilic Judaism tried and failed to do[C]—but in the end, it is quite impossible. The Law is intended to frustrate—not guide.

Consider this…

God's Law targets an attitude problem called the Principle of Sin, not a behavioral problem. Jesus strongly clarified this with his famous Sermon on the Mount (see p. 181 Sidebar), and demonstrated the true purpose of the Law: to convict a guilty heart.

It seems like such a negative message—yet the Law contains a great hope.

THE RECONCILIATION

There is good news in the Law, because it reveals how to form an authentic relationship with God, despite the huge gap. With the Mosaic Covenant God reversed the course of history and—for the first time since Adam—took up residence among a community of people.

Since the Garden of Eden, there was no place on earth where the Creator God dwelt among people, leading and fellowshipping with them as originally designed. Yet all the instructions God gave to Moses revolved around this very purpose:

WHAT IS THE PRESENCE OF GOD? "No man can see Me and live!" God told Moses.

In Isaiah 6, the creatures surrounding the Throne of God have only one thing to say: "Holy, Holy, Holy is the Lord of hosts." So hard to describe, the Righteousness of God is stunning. We never meet someone with such a character, but it is the first thing to hit someone coming into His presence. This overpowering Righteousness is not seen per se, but it is sensed through the one faculty God gave us for this purpose: the conscience.

"Your righteousness is like the mighty mountains," David says of Him.[10]

Even the great prophet Isaiah could have but one reaction before the throne of God: his knees buckled, he fell on the ground terrified, saying, "My destruction is sealed, for I am a sinful man and a member of a sinful race. Yet I have seen the King, the Lord Almighty!" *Isaiah 6:5*

Entering the Holy of Holies could be deadly, as Aaron's two sons discovered: "Fire blazed forth from the Lord's presence and burned them up, and they died there before the Lord." *Leviticus 10:2.* What a shocking tragedy this must have been to Aaron when his sons were killed—they were only bringing incense. It left the people of Israel terrified. What kind of God is this who wants to "walk among you" and yet annihilates His people?

They should have known, it was clearly revealed in the Law: Atonement is required for sinful man to approach God.

(C) See sidebar "Rewriting the Law" in Chapter 12, where the attempt to objectify the Sabbath law resulted in volumes of intricate stipulations.

"I will live among you, and I will not despise you. I will walk among you;
I will be your God, and you will be my people." *Leviticus 26:11-12*

This is what the Bible calls Reconciliation—it begins with the forgiveness of Sin,
but goes far beyond. Reconciliation causes "someone to accept a disagreeable or
unwelcome thing."[11] It means ending the personal alienation between God and
humanity.

THE DAY OF ATONEMENT
〰 **People are surprised to discover God's kind offer of amnesty in the
Mosaic Covenant.**

It was the most revered and sacred day of the year—the day when Almighty God
Himself would initiate the Reconciliation and end the terrible rift with mankind.

This all took place in the Tabernacle, called The Tent of the Testimony at the center of Israel's wilderness camp. Here in a tent, God and His People met, but it was
no festive occasion. It was a somber approach, because something of monumental
significance was taking place—His eternal Plan of Redemption.

The entire setting was antithetical to the glorious temples and towering idols of
ancient cultures. This was a tent—remarkably inconspicuous. Yet this little tent
was full of glory unmatched by the grandeur of any Egyptian or Roman shrine
because it was crowned with the Shekinah Glory. And inside were the keys to
understanding the history of humanity and God's intentions for man.

THE HOLY OF HOLIES
Inside the Tabernacle was a dangerous place, called the Holy of Holies, or The
Holy Place. This is where God dwelt with His presence, the Shekinah Glory which
means "the Glory of God." People could easily die in that place.

In the heart of the Holy of Holies, the Ark of the Covenant contained artifacts
from the wilderness wanderings when Israel rebelled against God's leadership so
often. (See p. 184 sidebar "The Ark.") They were symbols of the rebellion all
humans harbor against the authority of God. On top of the Ark, two angelic cherubim made of gold, facing each other with wings spread upwards, gaze down at the
symbols of rebellion. It is a drama capturing the attention of the watching universe:
God's angels amazed at His patience, while Satan leads mankind in rebellion.

It is as though the angels are asking each other, "Why doesn't God judge them?"
The answer: "But He loves them!" Again: "This evil race should be destroyed!"
And the second angel answers, "He created them!" They are the voices of God's
Justice and Mercy, wrestling with the difficulty God faces.

GOD'S WRATH
As the Day of Atonement (Yom Kippur) approached, the Children of Israel were
to prepare with a full week of reflection and anticipation. It was a dreary week of

waiting, the entire nation considering the full measure of their sinfulness and alienation before God. Yom Kippur arrives as a somber day.

God was not trying to torment the people; it is necessary because humans are cavalier about the sinfulness of sin. Even today people sneer at the word "sin" as though it is overly-dramatized—everyone makes mistakes.

To God sin is utterly loathsome. He is a judge, by nature—He must judge—and is in a position of authority to execute judgment. Yet when God judges, what is the sentence? There are no prison terms, no acts of community service, no penance decreed. Rather, the guilty are punished by facing His Wrath.

This is what humans find so alienating about God: His Wrath. It is a punishing, fierce anger unleashed by the full power of the Almighty God:

> It is a terrifying thing to fall into the hands of the living God.
> *Hebrews 10:31* (NASB-U)

Nobody can face God's Wrath and live. It is a terrifying power—actually, a fierce emotion—and a nightmarish prospective:

> "Who can stand before his fierce anger? Who can survive his burning fury? His rage blazes forth like fire, and the mountains crumble to dust in his presence." *Nahum 1:6*

It is impossible to grasp it without experiencing it. We can only see examples, as

THE ARK The Ark was designed in detail by God Himself to tell the story of His love for humanity, and the rejection He received. Inside was a collection of artifacts God carefully preserved from His historical interactions with humanity. It told a sad story.

A jar of Manna told the story of God providing for the needs of the children of Israel while they wandered in the desert, unable to feed themselves. Although Manna was a great source of nourishment, the people began complaining and then rejected Manna as God's provision for their lives.[12]

Aaron's rod of leadership was also placed there, testifying about their rebellion against God's leadership in the wilderness.[13] It was a terrible rebellion, full of bitter accusation aimed at God Himself: "Isn't it enough that you brought us out of Egypt, a land flowing with milk and honey, to kill us here in this wilderness and that you now treat us like your subjects?" *Numbers 16:13*. More than 250 rebel leaders were destroyed by God that day—consumed by fire billowing out of the Holy of Hollies inside the Tabernacle.

Also placed inside the Ark were the original tables of stone where the "finger of God" wrote down the Law for Moses.[14] Yet even as God was giving the Law to Moses at Mount Sinai, the people below were engaged in a drunken orgy.

Taken together, the articles inside the Ark symbolized God's love and care, contrasted with the sin and self-centeredness of people. But these artifacts did not tell the whole story—there was also the Mercy Seat.

when Aaron's sons entered the Holy of Hollies and were consumed in flames. The Bible describes it:

> Then I saw a great white throne and Him who sat upon it, from whose presence earth and heaven fled away... *Revelation 20:11* (NASB-U)

> Our God is a consuming fire. *Hebrews 12:29*

Of course, nobody likes to think about this, it is so unpleasant.

FACING GOD

The people of Israel would be sobered by the prospect of facing this Wrath as the Day of Atonement arrived. In the morning, a towering inferno descended on the Holy of Hollies—it was Shekinah Glory, the Glory of God.

Fortunately, nobody had to go into that dreadful place and face Him—except one person. The High Priest was the only one allowed into the Holy of Hollies to face the Shekinah Glory, and only on this one day of the year. Everyone else waited safely outside.

The High Priest was meticulously prepared before entering—this was no easy job. He was first ritually purified, or "consecrated," then carefully dressed in the priestly robes according to the instructions of the Law. Sacrifices were performed, and only then would the High Priest gingerly, carefully enter the Holy Place. According the Jewish tradition, he went into that place with a rope tied around him in case he died there, so nobody would have to enter that place to pull out the body.

When the High Priest entered the Holy of Hollies and stood before the Ark of the Covenant, the Shekinah Glory towered above him. And then a thrilling spectacle occurred...

THE MERCY SEAT

On top of the Ark, the two angels straddled the solid gold lid of the Ark that was the focus and meaning of this day: it was the Mercy Seat. It symbolized the Throne of God, and from it the Shekinah Glory emanated.[15] The angels gazed directly through the Mercy Seat at the symbols of rebellion below, inside the Ark.

The High Priest splashed the Mercy Seat with the blood of the sacrifice. Suddenly, everything changed. The angels were no longer gazing at the sins of rebellion in the chest—now they saw blood. Atonement means covering, and this was the purpose of the Day of Atonement: the blood covered the sins of the people.[16]

Meanwhile, outside the tabernacle, another marvelous ritual was underway. It was the Scapegoat, the source of our popular term today.

There were two goats on the Day of Atonement: one was sacrificed for the sins of the people, and its blood was sprinkled on the Mercy Seat. The other one—the Scapegoat—was taken deep into the wilderness as far away as possible and left where it could not possibly find its way back to the camp of Israel.

The Scapegoat was significant because the High Priest placed his hands on it, symbolically transferring the guilt of the people, and then went inside the Holy Place to sprinkle blood on the Mercy Seat. While he was in there:

> "…the scapegoat…shall be presented alive before the Lord, to make atonement upon it, to send it into the wilderness as the scapegoat."
> *Leviticus 16:10* (NASB-U)

The Scapegoat full of guilt disappeared into the wilderness, never to return again.[17]

∾ **The central message of the Bible is how God removes the guilt of sin from mankind.**

A DEFICIENCY

As marvelous and liberating as it was, the Day of Atonement was far from ideal. It was at once the happiest day of the year, and the saddest: happy because the people were liberated from their guilty, sinful past; sad, because their sense of freedom and release from sin was short-lived. They immediately began piling up sin and guilt for the next year's ritual.

∾ **The Mosaic Code only symbolically removed their sinfulness.**

The Day of Atonement never altered the root problem: sinful man was still sinful. Humans were still fallen, still spiritually dead, and by nature members of a race alienated from the life of God.

THE END OF THE PRIESTHOOD One of the most remarkable prophesies is seen with the sons of Levi, the priests of Israel. The priests performing sacrifices were themselves impure before God, and the Mosaic code prescribed elaborate rituals for the priests in order to emphasize this problem: hours of ritual purification. Everyone knew the washings, special prayers, and the elaborate requirements for clean clothing only symbolically removed sin. The Messiah would purify the sons of Levi in a way that was genuine: "and He will purify the Levites, and refine them like gold or silver." *Malachi 3:3*

The coming of the Messiah would forever remove the requirement of the sacrificial system, so that "you don't require burnt offerings" any more.[18] He offered the last sacrifice—the true atonement—removing the looming threat of God's wrath forever, for those who trust in Him: "but He, having offered one sacrifice for sins for all time, sat down at the right hand of God." *Hebrews 10:12*

The priests were intermediaries between God and man, and Jesus was the last priest forever: "But Jesus remains a priest forever; his priesthood will never end." *Hebrews 7:24*

When the High Priest emerged from the Holy of Hollies, it was all over. The camp of Israel exploded into a celebration of joy! Their sins were atoned for by the sacrifice, and their sense of guilt was removed far away by the Scapegoat. The threat of God's Wrath was gone!

As far as the east is from the west, So far has He removed our transgressions from us. *Psalm 103:12* (NASB-U)

A latent danger loomed: it was possible to misinterpret the Law and think somehow that performing a simple ritual would placate God. It could mean the revival of Cain's Religion of Merit so despised by God. The hideous deception behind all man-made religions—using small human efforts to earn God's accept-ance—trivializes both the vastness of God's Righteousness, and the vastness of man's sinfulness.

Yet the Scarlet Thread of Redemption did not end with Moses. King David brought an outpouring of revelation about the true Relationship of Faith that God always seeks. David wrote prolifically in the Psalms about the need to trust in God's Redemption—or salvation—and not in human goodness. Also within these Psalms a picture of a coming Messiah takes shape, someone who would bring a true change —purification from sin.[14]

These two themes—a Relationship of Faith and the Redemption of God—take prominence as the Scarlet Thread unfolds in the Old Testament.

FURTHER CONSIDERATION

THE COMING REDEMPTION

The ritual sacrifice was the great deficiency of the Mosaic Law. Although it explained the Principle of Substitution, it was only the blood of a dumb animal.

Yet God had in mind a more perfect, permanent sacrifice: the blood of Jesus Christ, which would permanently end the annual repetition of the Day of Atonement. This is the "more perfect way" which surrounds the death of Christ:

> For the Law, since it has only a shadow of the good things to come and not the very form of things, can never, by the same sacrifices which they offer continually year by year, make perfect those who draw near...But in those sacrifices there is a reminder of sins year by year. For it is impossible for the blood of bulls and goats to take away sins. *Hebrews 10:1-5*

Such an obvious point, yet confusing: though animals could never actually substitute for sinful humans, yet this ritual was decreed by God. How would God resolve this incongruity? Clearly, something was missing from God's Revelation, and the ancient Hebrew prophets knew it. God gave King David an amazing insight into this missing piece that perhaps raised more questions than it answered:

> You take no delight in sacrifices or offerings. Now that you have made me listen, I finally understand—you don't require burnt offerings or sin offerings. *Psalm 40:6*

God does not "require burnt offerings or sin offerings," yet, "without the shedding of blood, there is no forgiveness of sins."[20] David is then given a dim picture of the resolution, from inside the mind of God:

> Then I said, "Look, I have come. And this has been written about me in your scroll: I take joy in doing your will, my God, for your law is written on my heart. *Psalm 40:7-8*

Someone fundamentally different than all fallen humans was coming: "for your law is written on my heart," He says. This was the Anointed One who "has been written about," David said. From David's time forward, more would be written about Him as God revealed the missing pieces of His Redemptive Plan:

> "Come now, and let us reason together," Says the Lord, "Though your sins are as scarlet, They will be as white as snow; Though they are red like crimson, They will be like wool." *Isaiah 1:18* (NASB-U)

THE PASCHAL LAMB

"Behold the lamb of God who takes away the sin of the world!"
John 1:29

Nothing portrays the love of God for humanity more than the coming of Jesus Christ. For centuries a flurry of prophecies led to this point:

"Look, your king is coming to you! He is righteous and victorious, yet he is humble, riding on a donkey...Your king will bring peace to the nations." *Zechariah 9:9*

It is a typical Messianic prophecy, so full of irony—a victorious king arrives, yet riding a lowly donkey! This paradox takes shape in the form of Jesus Christ, and demonstrates the coherent, ingenious Eternal Plan of God.

THE COMING OF THE KING!

People streamed out of the Jerusalem gates, crowds gathering along the winding road that descends from the Mount of Olives into Jerusalem. There, riding on a donkey was Jesus of Nazareth, followed by crowds leaping and singing. This is the day all Israel anticipated for centuries, what Daniel the prophet foretold:

Then the crowds spread out their coats on the road ahead of Jesus. As they reached the place where the road started down from the Mount of Olives, all of his followers began to shout and sing as they walked along, praising God for all the wonderful miracles they had seen. "Bless the King who comes in the name of the Lord! Peace in heaven and glory in highest heaven!" *Luke 19:36-38*

∽ **This was the first and only time that Jesus Christ allowed the crowds to proclaim Him King.**

More than King, they were proclaiming Him as King Messiah, their songs coming from a famous Messianic prophecy, a Psalm of David. Here, entering the City of

David was the great offspring of King David, as prophesied:

> "…He will rule forever with fairness and justice from the throne of his ancestor David." *Isaiah 9:7*

The enemies of Christ—the ever-present and watchful Pharisees—were scandalized by it:

> But some of the Pharisees among the crowd said, "Teacher, rebuke your followers for saying things like that!" *Luke 19:39*

It was blasphemous—the people were equating Jesus with the Anointed One of God!

Yet Jesus knew this was the moment pre-ordained by God:

> He replied, "If they kept quiet, the stones along the road would burst into cheers!" *Luke 19:40*

Nothing could stop this kingly procession into Jerusalem! It was fixed by Daniel the prophet—more than 500 years earlier—as the time and place when Israel would receive the Anointed One, according to Daniel.[3] It was God's carefully-chosen time.

Just as the prophets predicted, the Anointed One came with kind intentions,

---

DANIEL 9 The amazing prophecy of Daniel 9 declares King Messiah will come to Israel in A.D. 33 exactly 444 years after King Artaxerxes decreed the rebuilding of Jerusalem's walls.[1] The prophecy reads:

"Now listen! It will be 49 years plus 434 years from the time the command is given to rebuild Jerusalem until the Anointed One comes! Jerusalem's streets and walls will be rebuilt despite the perilous times. After this period of 434 years, the Anointed One will be killed, his kingdom still unrealized…" *Daniel 9:25-26* (Living)

Daniel wrote this in Babylon in 537 B.C. during the Exile, and his prophecy gave two thrilling promises for the Exiles: a decree would enable them to return and rebuild Jerusalem, including its defensive walls; and 483 years later, the "Anointed One comes!" Dating this decree is simple, because Nehemiah 2:1 says it happened in March, "in the 20th year of the reign of Artaxerxes," a well-known Persian King, which allows us to set this at 444 B.C.

However, Daniel's 483 years must be converted to modern equivalents, because the calendar Daniel used was lunar, not solar, and only 360 days long, not the 365.25 days we know. This means Daniel predicted 476 modern years, and it means the Messiah would come in March, A.D. 33.

Jesus Christ came into Jerusalem surrounded by shouts of "Bless the King!" It was March, A.D. 33. (See sidebar "Pontius Pilate in History.") Normally he refused to allow the crowds to declare him Messiah King,[2] but not so this day. It was ordained by God's Word.

Also ordained and fulfilled a week later: "The Anointed One will be killed, his kingdom still unrealized."

"riding on a donkey" to "bring peace to the nations." The King was here to offer clemency and freedom from the Counterfeit Kingdom dominating the earth for eons.

A TRAGIC FUTURE

Despite how wonderful this moment was, its message so long-awaited and full of hope—it is yet perhaps the most tragic of all moments in human history. Even as shouting throngs of people encircled the Anointed One, the celebration was shattered. Jesus turned the last bend in the winding descent, and suddenly stretched out before Him was the glorious, ancient city of Jerusalem, punctuated by the world-famous Temple of Herod glittering in the sun. Jesus begins to weep:

> When He approached Jerusalem, He saw the city and wept over it, saying, "If you had known in this day, even you, the things which make for peace! But now they have been hidden from your eyes." *Luke 19:41-42* (NASB-U)

These were not silent tears as he shed at the grave of Lazarus, but "loud and deep lamentation" of someone struck with tragic news.[4] On this day God was presenting King Messiah to Israel, along with all "the things which make for peace!" Yet in a moment Jesus caught a glimpse of the ancient City of David blazing with ruin and death:

> "For the days will come upon you when your enemies will throw up a

THE DIASPORA For centuries, the Jews were gradually dispersed among the nations, beginning with the Assyrian resettlements of Northern Israel (2 Kings 17:6), and followed by the Babylonian conquest (2 Kings 25:8-12). Later conquests by the Greeks and Romans, and harsh conditions in Palestine also scattered large numbers of Jews until it grew into a population known as Hellenized Jews, and a movement called the Diaspora ("dispersion").

In A.D. 70, Titus destroyed the Temple, and in A.D. 135, Severus finally excluded all Jews from Jerusalem on pain of death. Israel ceased to be a home for the Jews for thousands of years.[5] This wide scattering of Jews among the nations was prophesied hundreds of years earlier in Ezekiel 37 and other passages.

More amazing is God's promise to regather the remnant of the Diaspora: "For I will gather you up from all the nations and bring you home again to your land." *Ezekiel 36:24.* Jesus also prophesied, "Jerusalem will be conquered and trampled down by the Gentiles until the age of the Gentiles comes to an end." *Luke 21:24*

These are amazing prophecies because in 1948, they were fulfilled by the founding of modern Israel. Never before in history has any race been so scattered for so long across so many nations, yet still retained their identity and regathered as prophesied. It is sure proof of God's unconditional covenant with Abraham, and proof God has an Incredible Plan for His Chosen People revealed from cover-to-cover in the Bible.

"For behold, I am commanding, And I will shake the house of Israel among all nations as grain is shaken in a sieve..." *Amos 9:9* (NASB-U)

barricade against you, and surround you and hem you in on every side, and they will level you to the ground and your children within you, and they will not leave in you one stone upon another…" *Luke 19:43-44* (NASB-U)

Jesus foresaw the looming disaster when Titus Vespasian would hurl his legions and massive siege machines against the city, utterly destroying its splendor and massacring its inhabitants by the tens of thousands. This occurred in A.D. 70, when Jerusalem fell. It marked the beginning of the dismantling of Israel as a nation: the Jews were permanently scattered across the nations of the earth for millennia. This too was prophesied:

Despite the apparent welcome displayed on Palm Sunday, Jesus knew the people of Jerusalem would turn against Him within days when they discovered He would not free them from Roman bondage. His true mission—to offer amnesty to all mankind—was rejected. Israel did not want the Humble Messiah.

∾ Israel wanted the Messiah to reign as a bloody conqueror and destroy all other human kingdoms.

When Israel rejected her Messiah, they rejected God's leadership, and His protection. Just as with Adam and Eve and the Israelites of the Old Testament, the choice to remove God's authority meant losing God's protection, and Jerusalem was left exposed to the wrath of Roman legions.

All this would come about because of a serious and fatal flaw in the course of Jewish history, spoken by Jesus as he rode the donkey, weeping, into Jerusalem:

"…because you did not recognize the time of your visitation."
Luke 19:44 (NASB-U)

Consider this…

God reveals Himself, and offers everyone amnesty before He ends the Counterfeit Kingdom. It is not an endless offer, however, and needs no prolonged thought—it is not a complex decision. A simple turning of the heart determines whether The Kingdom or another will be our home.

ATTACKING THE TEMPLE

During the week before His death, Jesus carefully built a foundation for the wave of spiritual awakening God would soon unleash on mankind. The spiritual darkness hovering over humanity since The Fall was to be lifted, as prophesied:

"The people who walk in darkness will see a great light—a light that will shine on all who live in the land where death casts its shadow." *Isaiah 9:2*

Jerusalem was electrified with the news that Jesus arrived at last, in the very center of Israel. Crowds eagerly followed Him to see when and how the Messiah might establish His throne. He did not disappoint, because He immediately attacked the regime—not of Rome, but the Cult of Man.

∽ Jesus entered the Temple with all the Spirit and power of the Old Testament Prophets.

The Prophet-Messiah headed to the Temple of Herod, which is "considered an architectural wonder of the ancient world" and the center of Jewish religious life.[6] It was hallowed ground, where God and man met according to the Law and hope was available through the Redemption. It was the national monument to Israel's elite standing with God, because "to the Jews nothing was as magnificent and formidable as their temple."[7]

Jesus entered this most revered site and shocked the nation. This was his building! It was filled with pictures and prophecies of Jesus everywhere, given 1,500 years earlier and practiced annually in anticipation of the coming of the Christ. He was enraged to find that God's provision for mankind was now a tool of the Kosmos.

The Temple outer court was crowded with the commerce of merchants, booths and pilgrims from across the Roman Empire. Jesus waded into the thickest part of the bazaar and launched into a tirade; overturning tables, scattering money boxes, and pushing and chasing the merchants out of the temple court with a whip. To the shocked crowd, He quoted from the prophet Jeremiah:

> "Is it not written, 'My house shall be called a house of prayer for all the nations'? But you have made it a robbers' den." *Mark 11:17* (NASB-U)

Jeremiah's prophesy warned Israel against letting the Temple degrade into an elitist Religion of Merit, with rituals replacing a true Relationship of Faith with God.

Yet Jewish teachers emphasized elaborate rituals and good works that masked a deep indifference towards the Personal God. Temple merchants were only part of a vast system of wealth and power that surrounded the famous Temple of Herod. Their religion now wielded political and economic power across the nation, and Jesus attacked the very heart of their power.

∽ The entire life of Jesus was a declaration of war against the Religion of Merit, and led to His death.

This, too, fulfilled Old Testament prophecies about the Messiah:

> Then his disciples remembered this prophecy from the Scriptures: "Passion for God's house burns within me." *John 2:17*

TAUNTING THE ELITE

The common people immediately understood what Jesus was doing, and were intrigued. The rich and powerful also understood His message, and were terrified:

> When the leading priests and teachers of religious law heard what Jesus had done, they began planning how to kill him. But they were afraid of him because the people were so enthusiastic about Jesus' teaching. *Mark 11:18*

For days afterward, Jesus returned to the temple and pronounced some of His most poignant renunciations of the Cult of Man, growing as a threat against the powerful elite:

> "Everything they do is for show...They enjoy the attention they get on the streets, and they enjoy being called 'Rabbi.' How terrible it will be for you teachers of religious law and you Pharisees. Hypocrites! For you won't let others enter the Kingdom of Heaven, and you won't go in yourselves. How terrible it will be for you teachers of religious law and you Pharisees. Hypocrites! You are so careful to clean the outside of the cup and the dish, but inside you are filthy—full of greed and self-indulgence!" *Matthew 23:5-25*

✑ Jesus was deliberately inciting a reaction.

With such degrading words spoken publicly at the national monument, it was impossible to take a neutral stand about Him. Indeed, even Jesus called on His listeners to decide where they would stand:

> "Do not think that I came to bring peace on the earth; I did not come to bring peace, but a sword—He who is not with Me is against Me; and he who does not gather with Me scatters." *Matthew 12:30; 10:34* (NASB-U)

Consider this...
God's offer of clemency and forgiveness—the first Coming of the Messiah—cannot be relegated to a mere philosophy. It is a choice between peace and war with God Himself.

THE PRICE OF A SLAVE When Judas betrayed Jesus and was paid 30 pieces of silver in Matthew 26:15, another Old Testament prophecy was fulfilled. It was prophesied in Zechariah 11: "So they weighed out thirty shekels of silver as my wages. Then the Lord said to me, 'Throw it to the potter, that magnificent price at which I was valued by them.'" (NASB-U). Thirty pieces of silver was the price Israel set for the worth of the "True Shepherd" in Zechariah's prophecy.

Why 30 pieces of silver? It was the price for a slave's life.[8] It was an astounding drama, since this money came from the Temple treasury used for purchasing sacrifices.[9]

Jesus, the slave of all, was bought as a sacrifice for all: "For even I, the Son of Man, came here not to be served but to serve others, and to give my life as a ransom for many." *Mark 10:45*

Jesus made it clear that He came to sweep aside man's Religion of Merit. He called for a genuine change of heart toward God. Because it is impossible to take a neutral attitude with Him; indifference is rejection.

THE CONSPIRACY

The religious elite realized the stakes were high, and they decided to go to war. During the week leading to His crucifixion, the enemies of Christ conspired, plotting His death and gathering a small army of those who saw Jesus as a formidable enemy. These were powerful and deadly enemies, united and intent. By the end of the week, the same crowds shouting "Bless the King!" would be shouting "Crucify Him!"

A secret meeting was assembled by the most important leaders of Israel. Nicodemus—a private admirer of Jesus—was no doubt present, since he was a prominent member of the ruling body called the Sanhedrin, and we know the gist of the meeting. Jesus was the topic:

> They plotted together to seize Jesus by stealth and kill Him. But they were saying, "Not during the festival, otherwise a riot might occur among the people." *Matthew 26:4-5* (NASB-U)

There was much to fear from a man who renounced their piety and hypocrisy daily in the Temple. Spies shadowed His movements, looking for an opportunity to seize him. A public arrest was unthinkable, but they watched and waited, hoping to catch Him alone in a side street or private place. They were frustrated because He somehow knew their plans and kept slipping away.

The conspirators laid a trap: Using bribes, they gathered people willing to bring accusations against Jesus. Others were paid to help sway crowds that might assemble to defend Jesus. They thought through all the angles, anticipated the glitches. But one thing they could not do was catch Jesus alone for the arrest.

Then good fortune struck like lightening. One of Jesus' own disciples approached the chief priests and offered to show them where Jesus was staying, so they could arrest him in private. Judas Iscariot was his name, and he was deeply disillusioned with Jesus. As a Zealot, Judas was devoted to overthrowing Roman rule, and his initial enthusiasm with Jesus was anchored in the promise of King Messiah to conquer Israel's enemies. Rather than fight Romans, however, Jesus fought Israel's sacred leaders. The Judas who approached the chief priests was embittered and cynical:

> "How much will you pay me to betray Jesus to you?" And they gave him thirty pieces of silver. From that time on, Judas began looking for the right time and place to betray Jesus. *Matthew 26:15b-16*

Jesus was now living on borrowed time. So many powerful, brilliant minds were united and determined to capture Him; and they owned a spy within the innermost circle of disciples, waiting and watching for the moment to snare Him.

THE SUBSTITUTIONARY DEATH OF THE CHRIST

It was time for the final fulfillment of all Revelation. At last, The Mystery of God's Eternal Plan, watched by a universe of beings—"things into which angels long to look," it says—was to be unfurled in the most unexpected, revolutionary manner, just as predicted centuries earlier:

> "Who has believed our message? To whom will the Lord reveal his saving power?" *Isaiah 53:1*

On this night Jesus fulfills all the prophecies and pictures and even the ethics of the Old Covenant the Prophet-Priest-King Messiah.

It began with a simple dinner: the Passover meal celebrated for 1,500 years. Knowing the plots against His life, Jesus and the Disciples met alone in secret to eat the most famous meal in the Old Testament. Outside of this quiet room, Jerusalem leaders were desperately hoping to arrest Him before Passover restrictions forbade it. Everyone was ready and waiting on Judas to disclose the spot.

THE PROPHET-MESSIAH'S NEW ETHIC

As the Disciples drifted into the room, they each saw the horrible problem this night would bring—whoever sat next to Jesus clearly sat in the more privileged position, but who deserved it the most? Then:

> A dispute arose among them as to which of them was considered to be greatest. *Luke 22:24b* (NIV)

This was a favorite topic of discussion among the Disciples, it happened repeatedly.[10] On this occasion, John won and sat at Christ's side, and Judas won, too.[11] Exactly why Judas sat next to Jesus is not told, but there is something perverse about it, because he was already determined to betray Jesus. Judas walked into that room

THE ROLE OF PROPHET The primary role for the Prophets of God was not to foretell the future, but to forth-tell the Revelation of God. They were "ambassadors of God," who proclaimed God's sovereignty over human history. More significantly, they proclaimed the Eternal Plan of God. They were the mouth of God, moved by the Holy Spirit of God: "for no prophecy was ever made by an act of human will, but men moved by the Holy Spirit spoke from God." *2 Peter 1:21* (NASB-U)

Moses was the first Prophet, and he presented the Old Covenant with all its pictures and Revelation about God's will. He was followed by an unending succession of Prophets, reaching a climax during the age of the Writing Prophets, and suddenly ending with Malachi around 400 B.C.[12]

John the Baptist appeared with all the clothes and manners of Elijah the Prophet, and "the people were in a state of expectation and all were wondering in their hearts about John," and asked him, "Are you the Prophet?" *Luke 3:15, John 1:21* (NASB-U). "The Prophet" was also the anticipated Anointed One, who would come as the greatest prophet of all: "The Spirit of the Lord God is upon me...to proclaim liberty to captives." *Isaiah 61:1* (NASB-U). Jesus claimed to be the fulfillment of the Prophet-Messiah (Luke 4:18-21), and brought additional Revelation for mankind.

already supernaturally empowered, desperate to kill Jesus:

> During supper, the devil having already put into the heart of Judas
> Iscariot, the son of Simon, to betray Him. *John 13:2* (NASB-U)

Against this background, Jesus launched into the strangest teaching of his career,
and He taught it silently:

> So he got up from the table, took off his robe, wrapped a towel around
> his waist, and poured water into a basin. Then he began to wash the
> disciples' feet and to wipe them with the towel he had around him.
> *John 13:4-5*

The silence in the room was deafening as Jesus assumed the role of a common slave
and—one by one—washed their dusty, reeking feet. This included Judas, whom
Christ already knew was set for betrayal.

It was a clear pronouncement of God's method of kingdom expansion:

> He made himself nothing; he took the humble position of a slave…
> *Philippians 2:7*

No world ruler or great leader of manmade religion would ever take such a humil-
iating role. Yet such is the genius and Backward Thinking of God:

> After washing their feet, he put on his robe again and sat down and
> asked, "Do you understand what I was doing? You call me 'Teacher' and
> 'Lord,' and you are right, because it is true. And since I, the Lord
> and Teacher, have washed your feet, you ought to wash each other's feet.
> I have given you an example to follow. Do as I have done to you."
> *John 13:12-15*

✎ As Prophet-Messiah, Christ revealed the New Ethic that became the trademark of God's Kingdom expansion.

This was a hard pill to swallow for men like these, who only moments earlier were
arguing over who should take the seat of honor. Christ's new ethic is an insult to
the Religious Mindset, and Peter voiced the offense felt by others:

> "No," Peter protested, "you will never wash my feet!" *John 13:8a*

But God does not allow anyone steeped in pride to fellowship with Him:

> Jesus replied, "But if I don't wash you, you won't belong to me." *John 13:8b*

Consider this…

*God's Grace has a polarizing effect. For those who are "clean," it is offensive.
For those cleaned by His Grace, it is contagious, and they "wash each other's
feet." His Kingdom is populated by those who love Grace.*

"For I have come to call sinners, not those who think they are already good enough." *Matthew 9:13*

THE UPPER ROOM DISCOURSE

Prophet-Messiah then launched into the Upper Room Discourse, describing how radical this new ethic was that went beyond anything written by God's Prophets before:

"So now I am giving you a new commandment: Love each other. Just as I have loved you, you should love each other." *John 13:34*

This was a New Commandment—an ethic not found anywhere in the Old Testament—and he defined it precisely:

"And here is how to measure it—the greatest love is shown when people lay down their lives for their friends." *John 15:13*

It was a demanding, almost impossible ethic, yet holds great promise:

"I have told you this so that you will be filled with my joy. Yes, your joy will overflow!" *John 15:11*

Here was the secret of a fulfilled and joyous life—not one dominated by the Principle of Sin and the useless effort to order the universe around self. The New Commandment refutes Satan's lie to Eve that "you can be like God." Those who live by it are frustrated by failure, as history shows. Marxism was the epitome of the Cult of Man, with man at the center of the universe, and it was a tragic failure:

"The Marxist vision of man without God must eventually be seen as an empty and a false faith—the second oldest in the world—first proclaimed in the Garden of Eden with whispered words of temptation: 'Ye shall be as gods.'" *Ronald Reagan, U.S. President.*[13]

❧ **The New Commandment of Jesus Christ is a repudiation of the Ethic of Man.**

Consider this…
The Kosmos is fueled by the Ethic of Man, which says fulfillment comes from placing Self at the center of the universe—an impossible task, the Bible says, because God is at the center of the universe.

"Your joy will overflow," Jesus promises, if "you love each other in the same way that I love you."

THE TRAP SHUTS

Jesus threw the dinner into turmoil by announcing a traitor sat among them:

While they were eating, he said, "The truth is, one of you will betray me." *Matthew 26:21*

Nobody guessed it was Judas:

Greatly distressed, one by one they began to ask him, "I'm not the one, am I, Lord?" *Matthew 26:22*

Judas was the epitome of the heart of humanity—he apparently looked so good on the outside, each Disciple looked to himself rather than accuse Judas. He was an unbeliever and a thief, but only the Prophet-Messiah could see through his pretentious airs:

Judas…also asked, "Teacher, I'm not the one, am I?" *Matthew 26:25a*

Sealing his own fate:

Then Jesus told him, "Hurry. Do it now." *John 13:27*

Jesus was determined to show the Disciples "the greatest love," as he hastened towards the crucifixion.

THE NEW COVENANT

Plans were in motion, forces were moving, and time was running out. Jesus quickly needed to explain the meaning of the coming terror that would rip apart their fellowship:

Then he took a loaf of bread; and when he had thanked God for it, he broke it in pieces and gave it to the disciples, saying, "This is my body, given for you. Do this in remembrance of me." *Luke 22:19*

ᐇ **At this dinner the Prophet-Messiah announced a remarkable New Covenant, centered on His death.**

It was an astonishing reach of authority for Jesus to seize the Mosaic Covenant and redefine the sacred Passover. It was within His authority, since the Passover meal was a picture of The Redemption given centuries earlier.

Consider this…

No longer commemorating escape from Egyptian slavery by the blood of the Paschal[A] lamb, the Prophet-Messiah changed the Passover meal into a larger celebration—escape for all humanity from slavery in the Kosmos by the blood of the Lamb of God:

"every time you eat this bread and drink this cup, you are announcing the Lord's death until he comes again. *1 Corinthians 11:26*

(A) Paschal means anything relating to the Passover; as in this case, the lamb without blemish killed as a sacrifice.

The Prophet-Messiah seized the Passover—this hallowed, first and foremost festival of the Mosaic Covenant—and turned it into the first symbol of a New Covenant:

> In the same way, after the supper He took the cup, saying, "This cup is the new covenant in my blood, which is poured out for you." *Luke 22:20* (NIV)

This was the first Communion, as we call it, and everywhere The Kingdom expanded, Christ said it was to be practiced as a memorial: "Do this in remembrance of me." It was not a commemoration of his life or miracles or teachings, but of the costly death Christ paid for our sins—the Principle of Substitution.

Sadly, at the Communion Jesus officiated His own Memorial Service. He then led the singing of King David's old prophecies about the Messiah found in the Hallel Psalms traditionally sung at the Seder:[14]

> The stone which the builders rejected Has become the chief corner stone. This is the Lord's doing; It is marvelous in our eyes. *Psalm 118:22-23*

As he led them to a nearby garden, the suffering of Jesus was beginning.

THE GARDEN OF DESPAIR

As they approached the Garden of Gethsemane, the Ruler of this World began controlling events. Satan was working energetically to kill the Messiah, having "already enticed Judas to carry out his plan."[15] Peter was next:

> "Simon, Simon, behold, Satan has demanded permission to sift you like wheat." *Luke 22:31* (NASB-U)

THE CUP The terrible physical suffering and humiliation of the cross was certainly a terrifying prospect, but still not enough to bring Jesus to this point of utter despair where He cries out, "Take this away from Me!" It must be remembered that all the Gospel writers agree He did not cry out during the physical torment.[16]

"The Cup" was something far more terrifying—and more hideous—than anything He faced from Roman execution. It is a term in the Bible uses for describing the measure of man's moral filth: "the cup of iniquities." For example, as the Cult of Man is described this way:

Babylon the Great, the mother of harlots and of the abominations of the earth. *Revelation 17:5* (NASB-U)

And "Babylon the Great" was holding something foul:

The woman was clothed in purple and scarlet, and adorned with gold and precious stones and pearls, having in her hand a gold cup full of abominations and of the unclean things of her immorality. *Revelation 17:4* (NASB-U)

"The Cup" is a filthy thing throughout the Scriptures, signifying a cup full of sin.[17] It also describes the measure of God's Wrath against sin.[18] In both ways, it depicts something so horrifying and foul, Jesus was repulsed by it, and begged to be released from it.

It was incredulous, since Peter was Jesus' staunchest friend, but indeed he would fall. Like a prowling lion, Satan was circling all the Disciples:

> Jesus said to them, "You will all fall away because of Me this night, for it is written, 'I will strike down the shepherd, and the sheep of the flock shall be scattered.'" *Matthew 26:31* (NASB-U)

As Jesus entered the Garden to engage in the contest, the Disciples were already succumbing to an atmosphere swirling with spiritual activity—they all fell asleep, knocked out of the action.

Jesus also had a strategy. What Satan didn't realize was that Jesus was going to destroy the strength of The Rebellion from the inside—becoming a member of it himself!

> "For the time has come for this prophecy about me to be fulfilled: 'He was counted among those who were rebels.' Yes, everything written about me by the prophets will come true." *Luke 22:37*

Here was the real agony and love of Jesus: He was willing to put himself under God's judgment by soiling himself with all the filth of human sin:

> God took the sinless Christ and poured into him our sins. Then, in exchange, he poured God's goodness into us! *2 Corinthians. 5:21b* (Living)

∞ The anticipation of this horror began in the Garden of Gethsemane, just hours before the crucifixion.

Knowing what he was headed for, Jesus left the Disciples behind and went to be alone with the Father one last time. He was facing a despair never before encountered:

> He prayed more fervently, and He was in such agony of spirit that His sweat fell to the ground like great drops of blood. *Luke 22:44*

It was a stress like none other, when capillaries burst and droplets of blood mix with profuse sweat.[19] The crucifixion loomed before His eyes like an overwhelming monolith of suffering:

> "Father, if you are willing, please take this cup of suffering away from me. Yet I want your will, not mine." *Luke 22:42*

Christ was so repulsed by "the cup of suffering," that He asked to have it removed. It was the wrath of God he faced—the most terrifying of all the sufferings He would face that night. Never before had Jesus been guilty of sin:

> For He faced all of the same temptations we do, yet He did not sin. *Hebrews 4:15*

Yet now in the Garden, in that dark hour before the long process of Crucifixion was to begin, Jesus knew all the sins of humanity would be piling on Him. All the depravity of man, the savagery and perversion too reprehensible to mention—gathered from all time past, present and future. This was all going to be placed placed on him:

He takes away not only our sins but the sins of all the world. *1 John 2:2*

Never before was Jesus the object of the Father's wrath. For Eternity Past, Jesus was in perfect communion with the Father, for "I and the Father are one essence."[20] How can anyone grasp the horror of separation Jesus faced as He stared into "The Cup of Suffering" full of the vilest filth of humanity and the wrath of God?

The Father knew it, and had compassion for the Son:

Then an angel from heaven appeared and strengthened him. *Luke 22:43*

ARREST AND TRIAL

Consider this...

Christ became our High Priest, interceding on our behalf before God. Like the High Priest of Yom Kippur, Jesus dared to enter the Most Holy Place with the blood of the sacrifice—His own blood.

∽ **Christ was both the sacrificial Lamb of God, and the High Priest who killed the sacrifice.**

Nobody killed Christ but Christ himself:

"No one can take my life from me. I lay down my life voluntarily." *John 10:18*

Christ was not surprised, then, when lights began appearing all around him, and he was surrounded by soldiers. The Disciples were awake by now, wondering what it meant, and then Judas stepped forward:

WHY KILL A MESSIAH? The Bible says Satan was actively engaged in the Christ's execution. But what could he possibly gain? Is it really possible to kill God?

The answer lies in the question of, Who rules this realm—the human realm on Planet Earth? The Bible says that Satan is the Ruler of the World; but Jesus Christ came as a King, prepared to rule, which posed a clear and present danger. He had to be removed.

But killing the Messiah surely would not prevent God from ruling on Planet Earth in person, would it?

It is impossible for God to step into our realm as the glorified Father and rule, because, "No man can see Me and live!" *Exodus 33:20*. His mere presence on Planet Earth would kill all potential subjects. He had to come in human form if He were to rule as a king over humanity.

This is why Satan was so anxious to kill the Man-God Jesus Christ, and remove all future competition!

But Jesus said, "Judas, how can you betray me, the Son of Man, with a kiss?" *Luke 22:48*

A scuffle broke out and Peter cut off a soldier's ear, but Jesus shouted for everyone to stop, and healed the soldier. Turning to the captain of the guard, Jesus proclaimed who was in charge:

"This is your moment, the time when the power of darkness reigns." *Luke 22:53*

They whisked Him away to a hastily-assembled trial with the Sanhedrin, the ruling religious body in Israel, but it was a stacked deck and an illegal trial. Only the conspirators would be assembled at this hour of dawn, not the full court. The carefully-chosen, paid witnesses took turns accusing Jesus, but their testimonies were contradictory and unconvincing even by the standards of this kangaroo court. It appeared their plot was quickly disintegrating, until a frustrated High Priest demanded an answer:

Then the high priest asked him, "Are you the Messiah, the Son of the blessed God?" Jesus said, "I am, and you will see me, the Son of Man, sitting at God's right hand in the place of power and coming back on the clouds of heaven." *Mark 14:61-62*

It was a shocking claim of divinity, from the mouth of Jesus Himself, claiming to be the fulfillment of Daniel's Messianic prophecy. It ended the trial—guilty!

◞ From beginning to end, Jesus voluntarily gave up his life.

It was difficult to execute Jesus, because He was so popular and it stirred such a commotion. He was bounced between Pontius Pilate, the Roman governor, and King Herod. Nobody outside the Sanhedrin wanted to pronounce execution, but Jesus would not make it any easier on Pilate or Herod by answering their questions. Clearly Jesus intended to be killed.[21]

Soldiers savagely beat Him with fists and rods, ripped His skin with steel-tipped whips, pierced His head with a basket of thorns, spit on Him, pulled His beard out, and ridiculed endlessly. The whole time, "He did not cry out." It was a scandalous treatment of God by the hands of Fallen Man, but He voluntarily,

"offered my back to those who beat me, my cheeks to those who pulled out my beard; I did not hide my face from mocking and spitting." *Isaiah 50:6* (NIV)

For many present, another prophecy was overlooked:

"You will see me, the Son of Man, sitting at God's right hand in the place of power." *Mark 14:62b*

The torment lasted for hours, but Jesus endured it for one simple reason:

He saw the joy ahead of him, so he endured death on the cross and ignored the disgrace it brought him. *Hebrews 12:2* (GW)

Consider this...

Throughout His suffering, the heart of God was driven by a yearning love, the "joy ahead of him"—hope for drifting and eroded lives still held captive in Satan's Kingdom.

It was clear by His silence and words that Pilate and the Jews were on trial before Jesus, not the other way around:

"You could have no power but that it's been given to you..." *John 19:11a*

FURTHER CONSIDERATION

A CHANGE IN COVENANTS

God's Prophets announced this change in Covenant—meaning, agreement—for centuries beforehand:

> "The day will come," says the Lord, "when I will make a new covenant with the people of Israel and Judah. This covenant will not be like the one I made with their ancestors when I took them by the hand and brought them out of the land of Egypt." *Jeremiah 31:31-32a*

As Jesus lifted the wine glass, he spoke about the Jeremiah 31 prophecy:

> "This cup is the new covenant in my blood, which is poured out for you." *Luke 22:20*

The Mosaic Covenant was always intended by God as a temporary place-holder in history, until the coming of King Messiah. The Mosaic Covenant never worked—it never changed the root problem of Sin that separated God from humanity:

> "They broke that covenant, though I loved them as a husband loves his wife," says the Lord. "But this is the new covenant I will make with the people of Israel on that day," says the Lord. "I will put my laws in their minds, and I will write them on their hearts. I will be their God, and they will be my people." *Jeremiah 31:32b-33*

God's Covenant Promise to mankind was always based on the shedding of blood as a reminder of the need for purification of Sin:

> Moses then took the blood, sprinkled it on the people and said, "This is the blood of the covenant that the Lord has made with you in accordance with all these words." *Exodus 24:8* (NIV)

Like the old one, the New Covenant was prophesied based on the blood—of God's sacrifice, Jesus Christ—and Jeremiah continues with the promise it held:

"For I will forgive their wickedness and will remember their sins no more." *Jeremiah 31:34* (NIV)

When Jesus held up that wineglass at communion, change was in the air: "The New Covenant would be instituted with His death."[22] This is not insignificant:

> The New Covenant becomes the basis of the message proclaimed throughout the New Testament...Paul also declared that he was a minister of the New Covenant (2 Corinthians 3:6). The writer of Hebrews declared that Jesus Christ is the mediator of the New Covenant (Hebrews 9:15; 12:24). "The blood of the eternal covenant" (13:20) is the foundation of all the believer's blessings.[23]

THE NEW COVENANT

Everything about the New Covenant is a replacement of the Old Covenant:

The rituals are different—we are forbidden to engage in ritual sacrifice now that the real sacrifice has been made. This brings a huge change, because so much of the Mosaic Covenant was anchored in those rituals depicting the Substitutionary Death of Jesus. It has all been swept away: the priesthood, the temple, the holy days and festivals, ritual cleansings, dietary restrictions, and everything else declared "clean" or "unclean." Under the New Covenant, only two rituals are prescribed: communion and baptism.

The scope is enlarged—under the Mosaic Covenant, God established a theocracy, and so much of the Law concerned the proper functioning of national Israel.[24] God was deeply concerned with preserving a Chosen People to serve as a launch pad for The Mystery. (See Further Consideration in chapter 5.) However, His intention long before Moses was the covenant to Abraham to "bless all the nations,"[25] and beginning with Jesus Christ, The Kingdom is now established for both Jews and Gentiles. Consequently, Jesus told us to leave civil government in the hands of secular rulers.[26] We no longer execute adulterers, prostitutes, or any number of civil penalties to be practiced by national Israel in the Old Testament. Instead, the New Covenant provides a framework for governing the Church.[27]

The morals are different—under the Mosaic Covenant, morals were specified apart from the knowledge of the New Man or the Indwelling of the Holy Spirit, since "the Spirit was not yet given" *John 7:39*. Moral change is called Regeneration under the New Covenant—a foreign concept in the Law—and its standards are immeasurably higher than those found in the Law, calling for a radical change in human nature itself.

FULFILLMENT, NOT ABANDONMENT

Christians sometimes make the mistake of picking and choosing which elements of the Mosaic Covenant to keep, and which to discard. Almost everyone agrees the rituals and civil parts of the Law are entirely replaced, since the New Testament is so adamant about these changes. Yet, the moral aspects of the Law are also replaced by New Covenant morality, and here is where confusion occurs.

It is not so easy to obviate only select portions of the Law, and attempts to do so can be arbitrary.[28] The entire Mosaic Covenant is an intricate web of interdependent legislations, and much of the ritual or civil code is intimately tied to the moral aspects, and vice-versa. For example, the New Testament is clear that removing the priesthood means the rest of the Mosaic Covenant falls apart as well:

> For when the priesthood is changed, of necessity there takes place a change of law also. *Hebrews 7:12* (NASB)

On the one hand, Christ said the Law can never be set aside:

> "For truly I say to you, until heaven and earth pass away, not the smallest letter or stroke shall pass from the Law until all is accomplished." *Matthew 5:18* (NASB)

On the other hand, Jesus said He fulfills the Law for us:

> "Do not think that I came to abolish the Law or the Prophets; I did not come to abolish but to fulfill." *Matthew 5:17* (NASB)

Since the moral requirements of the Law were all fulfilled in Christ, He set us free from its obligations and judgments:

> For Christ is the end of the law for righteousness to everyone who believes. *Romans 10:4* (NASB)

A NEW KIND OF CHANGE

Under the New Covenant, moral change occurs by spiritual Regeneration, which is a different approach not available under the Old Covenant:

> For what the Law could not do, weak as it was through the flesh, God did: sending His own Son in the likeness of sinful flesh and as an offering for sin, He condemned sin in the flesh, so that the requirement of the Law might be fulfilled in us, who do not walk according to the flesh but according to the Spirit. *Romans 8:3-4* (NASB)

The secret to Regeneration under the New Covenant is that phrase "walk…according to the Spirit." This is a whole new approach: it is a God-focused lifestyle—with dependence on the Holy Spirit—rather than a Law-focused lifestyle, as found under the Law. It is accomplished by spiritual means—the Means of Growth discussed at the end of chapter 17—and can never be accomplished through Old Testament means of focusing on the Law:

> But I say, walk by the Spirit, and you will not carry out the desire of the flesh…But if you are led by the Spirit, you are not under the Law. *Galatians 5:16, 18* (NASB)

A NEW KIND OF LAW

Jesus Christ was a genius—not surprising, since he was God. With just a few sentences, he introduced a New Law vastly more sweeping in scope than the entire Mosaic Code:

> "A new commandment I give to you, that you love one another, even as I have loved you, that you also love one another." *John 13:34* (NASB)

Variously called the Law of Christ, the Royal Law, the new Law of Liberty, or just the Law of Love, it defines New Testament ethics:[29]

> "Teacher, which is the great commandment in the Law?" And He said to him, "'You shall love the Lord your God with all your heart, and with all your soul, and with all your mind.' This is the great and foremost commandment. The second is like it, 'You shall love your neighbor as yourself.' On these two commandments depend the whole Law and the Prophets." *Matthew 22:36-40* (NASB)

It is imperative for Christians to understand that Regeneration is not external change, but internal change. It is not an issue of changing behavior, but rather changing human nature.

DEATH AND RESURRECTION

The time of judgment for the world has come, when the prince of this world will be cast out.
John 12:31

ECCE, HOMO!

Jesus then came out, wearing the crown of thorns and the purple robe. Pilate said to them, "Behold, the Man!" *John 19:5* (NASB)

"Ecce, Homo!" Pilot declared, hoping this severe treatment would settle the matter. The pressure to crucify Jesus only intensified. Pilate's own wife was opposed to killing Jesus because of a dream the night before. He wanted this to go away, but the battered Christ only drove the crowd into a blood-crazed frenzy, yelling, "Crucify him!" Bewildered, he took Jesus inside and interrogated him:

"You are a king then?" "You say that I am a king, and you are right," Jesus said. "I was born for that purpose. And I came to bring truth to the world." *John 18:37*

Pilate then dismissed Christ in the same way people dismiss God today:

"What is truth?" Pilate asked. *John 18:38*

Consider this...
The modern Death of Truth[1] is as old as Pilate—as old as humanity—the inflated heart that imagines Truth is the sovereign and personal jurisdiction of each individual. Yet there is a greater authority:

Jesus said, "You would have no power over me at all unless it were given to you from above." *John 19:11a*

It was hard to refute such logic, and Pilate was sobered and reluctant to execute him. The turning point came when he realized it was not worthwhile to save Jesus' life:

> Pilate tried to release him, but the Jewish leaders told him, "If you release this man, you are not a friend of Caesar. Anyone who declares himself a king is a rebel against Caesar." *John 19:12*

This was a crucial turning point for Pilate, and he did not like it:

> When they said this, Pilate brought Jesus out to them again... "Here is your king!" "Away with him," they yelled. "Away with him—crucify him!" "What? Crucify your king?" Pilate asked. "We have no king but Caesar," the leading priests shouted back. Then Pilate gave Jesus to them to be crucified. *John 19:13-16*

BEARING THE CROSS

> He went out, bearing his own cross... *John 19:17a* (ESV)

It is the *Scarlet Thread* woven through time: In the same manner Isaac carried the wood for his own sacrifice 2,000 years earlier, Jesus too, carried the wood for His death. But with Abraham's only son, somebody yelled, "Stop!" With Christ, they trailed behind shouting, "Crucify!"

It went back to the Garden of Eden, where the Original Sin meant they needed to be covered in blood—God killed in the Garden of Delight, covering their nakedness with animal skins—their shame was clothed in death. Here was Abel's blood sacrifice, the only acceptable one. Jesus was covered in blood, dragging the cross to die at Golgotha, the "Place of the Skull." He was to die the same day and hour when the Paschal Lambs of Israel were sacrificed at the Temple, within sight of the

PONTIUS PILATE IN HISTORY This Roman governor ruled in Palestine from A.D. 27 to 37, and is known to classical historians as ruthless and inflexible. It surprises some historians that Pilate is so easily compelled to kill Jesus despite his reluctance portrayed by the Gospels. Some liberal scholars cite this to prove the Gospel accounts should not be considered historical, written long after the events.[2]

Recently, skepticism is replaced with respect. It appears the Gospel writers reported an historical anomaly only a contemporary history would capture. It centers on a plot to kill Tiberius Caesar by Sejanus. Pilate was a political ally of Sejanus, and after the plot was uncovered and Sejanus was executed in A.D. 31, Tiberius launched an empire-wide purge of potential conspirators. Pilate desperately needed to prove his loyalty.

Pilate was unwilling to execute Jesus until the Jews cried out, "If you let this man live, you are no friend of Caesar's!" This was phrased as a legal accusation, and Pilate immediately saw the implication. He did not need a political black eye with Tiberius Caesar, and saving Jesus from execution was not worth it: "Pilate was an inflexible and ruthless character as long as his mentor Sejanus was in power. But with Christ's trial in A.D. 33, he appears submissive...and could not afford to get into more trouble with Tiberius."[3]

This also means A.D. 33 is the best date for the death of Christ, which is significant, because it is also the date given by Daniel 9:26 for when the "Messiah will be killed."[4]

Temple, and Israel and—even all mankind. Death would pass over anyone covered by the blood of "the Lamb of God, who takes away the sins of the world."[A] Here was a grand procession stretching back to be beginnings of mankind.

✑ The Cross was The Mystery unveiled at last to a watching universe.

The bearer of the titulus ("the notice" or "the title") led the way, proclaiming the crimes for which execution was decreed, according to Roman law.[5] It was the legal Certificate of Death. Pilate had written the titulus in Hebrew, Latin and Greek so everyone would know:

> "Jesus of Nazareth, the King of the Jews." *John 19:19*

Pilate originally wrote it with contempt for the absurd charges brought against Jesus—and God turned His scorn into Revelation for those willing to believe He was indeed Messiah King.

Consider this...

The titulus was nailed at the top of His cross and remained there as a bold declaration of the crimes of humanity against God. It was all one gruesome crime: "They killed their King—they killed my only Son!"

That one crime stands as the epitome of The Rebellion. Yet that colossal crime was nailed onto the cross of Christ, and he bore the penalty for it. The titulus was His, through The Principle of Substitution:

> The record of debt that stood against us with its legal demands. This he set aside, nailing it to the cross. *Colossians 2:14 (ESV)*

BARABBAS SAVED Jesus was crucified on a cross already prepared for immediate service—the cross of Barabbas. Trying to avoid executing an innocent man, Pilate offered the crowd a chance to release a condemned man as was customary during Passover. They could choose between Barabbas and Jesus, and the crowd yelled, "Away with this man, and release for us Barabbas!" *Luke 23:18* (NASB-U) The bribes worked well.

On this day, Barabbas was the first human ever to experience The Redemption first-hand. In typically cruel Roman fashion, a condemned man had to watch as his cross was being constructed in the courtyard in front of his cell—the "death row" of first century Roman justice, which archeologists have dug up and is still there today.

All week long, Barabbas watched his cross take shape, considering the horrors soon facing him. Suddenly on Passover, the cross was snatched away and Jesus Christ was nailed to it instead, while Barabbas went free. What a joy it must have meant for Barabbas! Yet, the evidence is strong that Barabbas never believed in Jesus, and he was saved only from death by crucifixion that day.

It is the epitome of The Principle of Substitution God offers anyone willing to receive it—for Jesus Christ to stand in our place of judgment.

(A) See "The Lamb of God" in Chapter 13.

It was the greatest Revelation ever witnessed by humanity, "which forms the subject of all prophecy."[6] Only the hand of God could make it happen.

THE ASSAULT

"The time of judgment for the world has come, when the prince of this world will be cast out!" *John 12:31*

Now was the hour pre-ordained by God to break the back of The Rebellion, and it would happen the way Christ said earlier that week:

"And when I am lifted up on the cross, I will draw everyone to myself." *John 12:31-32*

They reached Golgotha, stripped Him, nailed Him to the Cross, and lifted Him up within view of the Temple for all to see. It was a violent and bloody scene covering the hillside that Passover, with all the marks of warfare. A Clash of Kingdoms was underway, splattering Golgotha with blood.

While Satan was engineering the crucifixion and reveling in the gruesome wounds of Christ, Christ struck back with a lethal blow even while the nails pierced his flesh and bones. Satan did not yet realize the horror of it—all the brunt of violence that day fell on Satan, not Jesus, just as God prophesied to the serpent at the dawn of history:

"He shall bruise you on the head, And you shall bruise him on the heel." *Genesis 3:15* (NASB-U)

ꝏ The victim of the cross was the Ruler of this World.

As promised, at "The Place of the Skull" Christ unsheathed the weapon of God that shattered the skull, the head and mindset of Satan's rule. It was not through brutal conquest, as Satan grows his kingdoms, but through a more lethal weapon that Satan's kingdoms could never imitate or offer: forgiveness.

But Jesus was saying, "Father, forgive them; for they do not know what they are doing." *Luke 23:34* (NASB-U)

With that one thought: "forgive them," the genius of God erupts at the Cross. Unmasked before the watching universe, Satan's ancient accusation that God is a tyrant was decisively proven a lie:

Satan spoke first...Satan said, "I will ascend," but the Lord Jesus Christ said, "I will descend."[7]

For all eternity, the Cross is a towering monolith of God's love. It is the naked truth that, "No! Satan is the tyrant," and "God is love." God is patient; He endured millennia of slander about his authority, but finally The Mystery was born:

"...so that every mouth may be silenced and the whole world held accountable to God." *Romans 3:19* (NIV)

Consider this...

Three simple words, "Father, forgive them!" It launched an assault against the Counterfeit Kingdom's lethal hold on humanity. This is the battle cry of Christianity that conquered the world.

Everyone else stood around the cross weeping in abject defeat, but Jesus:

"For the joy set before Him endured the cross, despising the shame." *Hebrews 12:2b* (NASB-U)

HUMAN SACRIFICE

Jesus was not above the pain of the cross where, "The victim of crucifixion literally died a thousand deaths."[8] This was flesh and blood raised high before the Temple: "Ecce, Homo!" It was the reason for the humanity of Jesus Christ:

For only as a human being could he die, and only by dying could he break the power of the Devil, who had the power of death. *Hebrews 2:14*

The crucifixion was non-optional, if God cared to release Satan's captives:

Only in this way could he deliver those who have lived all their lives as slaves to the fear of dying. *Hebrews 2:15*

Jesus had to be a human in order to substitute a human's death. As a blood member of the human race, born through Mary, by God's ancient Principle of Substitution, Jesus was identified with the human race. It was all explained in The Day of Atonement: when the High Priest placed his hands on the sacrifice, he transferred the sins of the people.

Human sacrifice is despised by God throughout the Old Testament because the Sacrificial System was symbolic. Using a human for symbolic sacrifice was detestable, God said. Jesus Christ, however, was not symbolic. He was the actual flesh and blood of The Substitution promised for all mankind from the beginning, enveloped and hidden within The Mystery.

He had done no violence, Nor was there any deceit in His mouth. But the Lord was pleased To crush Him, putting Him to grief; If He would render Himself as a guilt offering. *Isaiah 53:9b-10a*

THE VICTORY OF THE CROSS

Swirling around Jesus that day on the Cross were all the fulfillments of prophecy and symbols and pictures of the Old Covenant:

"He is the one all the prophets testified about, saying everyone who believes in him will have their sins forgiven through his name." *Acts 10:43*

At his feet, soldiers amused themselves gambling for his clothes, as foretold:

My enemies stare at me and gloat. They divide my clothes among themselves and throw dice for my garments. *Psalm 22:17-18*

He was stretched out on the cross, his ligaments torn, as foreknown:

My life is poured out like water, and all my bones are out of joint. They have pierced my hands and feet. I can count every bone in my body. *Psalm 22:14, 16b-17a*

Christ endured the ridicule of the religious elite—even the criminal on the Cross beside him—as they scoffed at His helplessness:

Those passing by were hurling abuse at Him, wagging their heads, and saying, "Ha! …Save Yourself, and come down from the cross!" The chief priests also, along with the scribes, were mocking Him… and saying, "He saved others; He cannot save Himself. Let this Christ, the King of Israel, now come down from the cross, so that we may see and believe!" Those who were crucified with Him were also insulting Him. *Mark 15:29-32* (NASB-U)

This too was all prophesied:

But I am a worm and not a man, scorned by men and despised by the people. Everyone who sees me mocks me. They sneer and shake their heads, saying, "He trusts in the Lord; let the Lord rescue him. Let him deliver him, since he delights in him." *Psalm 22:6-8* (NIV)

ROMAN CRUCIFIXION The Romans used crucifixion to subjugate a population, often massacring whole populations as in 4 B.C., with 2,000 rebels in Galilee. Roman law decreed that the criminal must carry his own cross, in order to maximize the shame.[9] Once crucifixion was decreed, Jesus lost the protection of Rome against the hatred and spite of crowds lining the street, and it was normative to antagonize the victim. Fortunately, today's movies spare audiences the shock of seeing the crucifixion victim stripped naked, which often occurred.[10]

The Romans tried to keep their victims alive as long as possible, feeding and quenching their thirst, so that it might take from three to nine days before someone died[11]—often from infection of the open wounds.[12] During this time insects and birds of prey attacked the bleeding wounds and eyes[13] Among other causes, death occurred by asphyxiation because the victim tired from lifting themselves up by his nailed appendages to gasp another breath.[14] For this reason, the soldiers broke the legs of the other two crucifixion victims to hasten their death by asphyxia at the request of the Jews—it was a "High Sabbath" not to be desecrated by hanging bodies.[15]

Crucifixion is by all accounts, the most degrading and painful death devised by man, and the Romans refined it into a science of pain. Excruciating comes from the Latin *excruciatus*, meaning "out of the cross."[16]

The excruciating death of Jesus swelled into a gala celebration among his enemies for three hours. For the Ruler of this World, it was a victory feast of blood. It reached a crescendo of feverish abuse and slander, until something horrendous descended across the Jerusalem:

At the birth of Jesus, there was brightness at midnight; at his death, there was darkness at noon. *Mark 15:33*

And then Jesus uttered a most horrendous yell....

ELOI, ELOI

It was a cry of loneliness and dejection:

At the ninth hour Jesus cried out with a loud voice, "Eloi, Eloi, lama sabachthani?" which is translated, "My God, My God, why have You forsaken Me?" *Mark 15:34* (NASB-U)

This was the ninth hour, when Passover sacrifices were beginning at the Temple.[17] It was a bloodbath, as priests began killing literally thousands of lambs—all without blemish.[18] They were pictures of the Christ, without sin.

Also at the ninth hour, the scene at the crucifixion climaxed:

Jesus uttered another loud cry and breathed his last. *Mark 15:37*

Jesus died—the human Substitute received God's Wrath. But he had to be more than human in order to substitute for all sins. He had to be God as well.

∾ **Only the infinite God could take upon Himself all the sins of all time for all of humanity.**

In one single moment, at this one point in human history, Eternal God paid the eternal price of eternal wrath for all humanity:

A CRIMINAL'S DEATH Adding to the insults that day was one of the thieves on the cross: "So you're the Messiah, are you? Prove it by saving yourself—and us, too, while you're at it!" *Luke 23:39-43*

But the other thief would not join in: "Don't you fear God, even while you're dying?" Turning to Jesus, he added, "Jesus, remember me when you come into your kingdom."

Jesus replied, "I assure you, today you will be with me in Paradise."

It is sure proof that anyone who "calls out in the name of the Lord to be saved" will pass straight into God's presence at death.

It is also sure proof Jesus Christ's forgiveness of sins is sufficient to cover the most scarred life—even up to the point of death—and it is never too late to turn to Jesus and say, "Be merciful to me, the sinner." *Luke 18:13*

At noon, darkness fell across the whole land until three o'clock. *Mark 15:33*

For by that one offering he perfected forever all those whom he is making holy. *Hebrews 10:14*

All the Old Testament sacrifices were only symbols and pictures, and could never actually take away the problem of Sin:

The sacrifices under the old system were repeated again and again, year after year, but they were never able to provide perfect cleansing for those who came to worship. *Hebrews 10:1*

It was at this point that all the symbols and types and pictures of the Old Testament were suddenly fulfilled. The pinnacle of the Mosaic Covenant—the Holy of Hollies—was shaken at its foundations:

At that moment the curtain in the Temple was torn in two, from top to bottom. The earth shook, rocks split apart. *Matthew 27:51*

It was the veil covering the Holy of Hollies, which the priest could enter only once a year. The ultimate symbol of God's dwelling place was suddenly exposed, and "God was now available apart from the temple system and that the old temple order stood judged and abolished."[19]

It was a formidable and insurmountable veil, and Jewish tradition claimed it was so thick that 300 priests were required to hang it over the Holy of Hollies.[20] It was ripped from top to bottom, torn by the hand of God—He fled the Holy of Hollies forever. He now "dwells among men."

PROPHECY FULFILLED

Some thought "Eloi, Eloi" was a measure of Christ's disorientation; it was common for crucifixion victims to become delirious.

Some of the bystanders misunderstood and thought he was calling for the prophet Elijah. *Mark 15:35*

Yet it was not delirium. It was a loud, public proclamation that all this was known before, and was now fulfilled—it was The Mystery of Prophecy, told by King David 1,000 years earlier in the Psalms:

"My God, my God! Why have you forsaken me?" *Psalm 22:1*

∽ With Jesus Christ, all the Messianic Prophecies made sense.

Everything in the Psalm 22 prophecy described the crucifixion in detail, beginning with "Eloi, Eloi." It was a Messianic Psalm, told through the voice of someone dying: "They have pierced my hands and feet," and, "You lay me in the dust of death." When King David wrote that in 1,000 B.C., crucifixion did not exist, and it made no sense to kill somebody by merely piercing the hands and feet.

Consider this...

"The things which God announced beforehand by the mouth of all the prophets, that His Christ would suffer, He has thus fulfilled." Acts 3:18 (NASB-U)

TETELESTAI!

As He died, when "Jesus uttered another loud cry," He fulfilled all these prophecies, with:

"Tetelestai!" *John 19:30*

The Greek word is translated in English, "It is finished!" It was the term always stamped on the criminal's titulus when the sentence had been carried out, and it meant, "Paid in Full." For criminals serving a jail sentence, the titulus was nailed outside their cell, and when released, Tetelestai was stamped on the Certificate of Debt. From that point forward, wherever the ex-prisoner roamed, if someone questioned his release from prison the titulus was produced as proof the penalty had been paid in full.

When Jesus yelled "Paid in Full," it was a declaration that would resound through the ages that He paid for the sins of all humanity:

THE ISAIAH 53 PROPHECY On this day was the fulfillment of Isaiah's famous prophecy written more than 600 years earlier in Isaiah 53.

A Suffering Servant: "It was our weaknesses he carried; it was our sorrows that weighed him down. And we thought his troubles were a punishment from God for his own sins!" *Isaiah 53:4*

He was crucified, as King David described: "But He was pierced through for our transgressions, He was crushed for our iniquities." *Isaiah 53:5a* (NASB)

He died for the sins of the world, as prophesied: "But he was wounded and crushed for our sins. He was beaten that we might have peace. He was whipped, and we were healed!" *Isaiah 53:5b*

He died for each individual: "All of us have strayed away like sheep. We have left God's paths to follow our own" *Isaiah 53:6a*.

He died by the hand of God, not by human hands: "Yet the Lord laid on him the guilt and sins of us all." *Isaiah 53:6b*

His death surprised everyone: "But who among the people realized that he was dying for their sins—that he was suffering their punishment?" *Isaiah 53:8*

He was then buried in a rich man's grave: "His grave was assigned with wicked men, Yet He was with a rich man in His death." *Isaiah 53:9*

He arose again from the grave: "He will see His offspring, He will prolong His days, and the good pleasure of the Lord will prosper in His hand." *Isaiah 53:10* (NASB)

When you were dead in your transgressions…He made you alive togeth-er with Him, having forgiven us all our transgressions, having canceled out the Certificate of Debt consisting of decrees against us, which was hostile to us…having nailed it to the cross. *Colossians 2:13-14* (NASB)

And yet, that was not the end of the story, as the prophets foretold…

BURIED

Crucifixion victims were often left on the cross long after death as a warning to all passers-by, their carcasses grim pickings for predators until the remains were thrown into a pit. There were exceptions, however, and Jesus was one, as prophe-sied:

His grave was assigned with wicked men, Yet He was with a rich man in His death. *Isaiah 53:9*

Joseph of Arimathaea was an oxymoron—a follower of Jesus and yet a member of the Sanhedrin who condemned Jesus to death. Most likely he was excluded from the illegal trial of Jesus, along with anyone else whom might have opposed the sentencing.

As it is with politics, the wealthy carry clout, and Joseph was one of those:

As evening approached, Joseph, a rich man from Arimathea who was one of Jesus' followers, went to Pilate and asked for Jesus' body. And Pilate issued an order to release it to him. *Matthew 27:57-58*

Before taking His body down from the cross, the Roman soldiers drove a lance through the body of Christ, evidently piercing the heart.[21] These were professional killers who knew how to crucify, and they would never pronounce Jesus dead if a

THE GREATEST CRIME Is Jesus Christ only one of many different ways to reach God? If so, then the Cross is the greatest crime ever perpetrated in history—because it would be the very hand of God inflicting it.

The Cross of Christ is proof of God's rejection of all human Religion of Merit. If God were to forgive or accept just one person on the basis of their good works, sincerity, energetic efforts or religious activity; then the cross of Christ would be the greatest crime in history—and God's greatest folly. Why would He do something so costly that was so unnecessary? It is hard to imag-ine the God of the Universe making a fool of Himself by committing His Son to an excruciating death on the Cross, while other religious thinkers like Buddha or Muhammad, discovered better ways to approach God.

Quite simply, Jesus went to the cross because there was no other way to resolve the alienation with man. The Cross was absolutely necessary. The gravity of the Principle of Sin is so serious that only the person and power of God Himself could resolve it. All religious leaders throughout histo-ry were contaminated by Sin and therefore guilty, in need of salvation themselves, and unable to save anyone else. Only Jesus Christ was without Sin, and therefore able to offer help to mankind.

remote chance existed He still lived—especially when the eyes of all Judea and its elite were watching. It was not an ignorant foot soldier who certified the death:

> Pilate wondered if He was dead by this time, and summoning the centurion, he questioned him as to whether He was already dead. And ascertaining this from the centurion, he granted the body to Joseph. *Mark 15:44-45* (NASB-U)

Many powerful people were strongly motivated to ensure Jesus was indeed dead.

The rulers of Israel feared the disciples would try to keep the Jesus movement alive, and took measures against it by approaching Pilate:

> They told him, "Sir, we remember what that deceiver once said while he was still alive: 'After three days I will be raised from the dead.' We request that you seal the tomb…This will prevent his disciples from coming and stealing his body and then telling everyone he came back to life! If that happens, we'll be worse off than we were at first."

He made sure nobody could steal the body:

> Pilate replied, "Take guards and secure it the best you can." So they sealed the tomb and posted guards to protect it. *Matthew 27:63-66*

GRIEF

That first Easter Sunrise was, by all accounts, a peaceful and unsuspecting morning as three women made their way to the gravesite, wondering if the Roman cohort would allow them to pass. Jesus was buried so quickly in order to beat the Sabbath restrictions, there was no time to properly honor the body with perfumes according to their customs. These women came to remedy that.

GRIEF: THE HUMAN SOLUTION Authors become wealthy writing about death, especially those who wrap death in glowing terms. One popular view downplays death as only a natural progression of life, not so horrible.[22] Stories about near-death experiences and the "approaching, warm light" are popular assurances precisely because people are so terrified of death. These documented accounts offer serious problems for the Naturalist,[23] but they still offer no authoritative word about the afterlife—only brief impressions.

No matter how much we subdue it, everyone instinctively fears death because it is so final—and uncertain. Despite attempts to put a spin on it, we fear death for good reason. It is a grotesque scar on life, our greatest enemy: "Death is the obscene mystery, the ultimate affront, the thing that cannot be controlled. It can only be denied." *Susan Sontag*

All accounts about death are terribly incomplete, except for what Jesus Christ provided: "I proceeded forth and have come from God," *John 8:42* (NASB), and he can say with authority, "I am the resurrection and the life. Those who believe in me, even though they die like everyone else, will live again." *John 11:25*

Consider this...

They walked in silence and suffering, grieving. Death strikes everyone with the kind of agony and finality that words cannot possibly express. It is the enemy of God and man alike, and the very reason why Jesus came:

> And the last enemy to be destroyed is death. For the Scriptures say, "God has given him authority over all things." *1 Corinthians 15:26-27a*

What they did not realize and—could not have imagined—was that morning the very fabric of the universe was ripped apart. Natural law was fractured, because death was transformed. Jesus discovered it first:

> But the fact is that Christ has been raised from the dead. He has become the first of a great harvest of those who will be raised to life again. *1 Corinthians 15:20*

> ✎ **Jesus Christ became the very first human throughout Eternity to experience the Resurrection.**

The Resurrection of Jesus is one of the few stories repeated in all four Gospel accounts. Repeated, because here was something unbelievably real—and also very terrifying, because it defies natural explanation.

HE LIVES!

It happened as the women walked toward the garden where Jesus was buried in the tomb of wealthy Joseph of Arimathaea:

> Suddenly there was a great earthquake, because an angel of the Lord came down from heaven and rolled aside the stone and sat on it. His face shone like lightning, and his clothing was as white as snow. The guards shook with fear when they saw him, and they fell into a dead faint. *Matthew 28:2-4*

The guards were terrified because of their ignorance about whom they were guarding; the women, however, met someone who explained with joy:

> Then the angel spoke to the women. "Don't be afraid!" he said. "I know you are looking for Jesus, who was crucified. He isn't here! He has been raised from the dead, just as he said would happen. Come, see where his body was lying…"

It is hard to blame the women for their reaction:

> The women ran quickly from the tomb. They were very frightened but also filled with great joy, and they rushed to find the disciples to give them the angel's message. *Matthew 28:5-8*

Consider this...

Resurrection is not the imaginary horror stories of people coming back as dead zombies. Resurrection is not resuscitation, as Christ performed with Lazarus earlier. Lazarus returned to life still clothed in his earthly body.

The frightened women ran to tell the Disciples, who felt it was little more than a hallucination:

> They told the apostles what had happened, but the story sounded like nonsense, so they didn't believe it. *Luke 24:10b-11*

∽ Christ's Resurrection was physical as well as spiritual.

It is the typical reaction still today from skeptics—even some theologians—to frame this "Resurrection Story" as the product of bereaved minds, or perhaps legend.[29] Yet there is great authenticity here, because the Disciples were skeptical too, even when others showed up with similar reports. Then something revolutionized their worlds:

> While they were telling these things, He Himself stood in their midst and said to them, "Peace be to you." But they were startled and frightened and thought that they were seeing a spirit. *Luke 24:36-38a (NASB-U)*

Christ stood directly in front of them, but they still could not believe it was really Him.

> They still could not believe it because of their joy and amazement. He said to them, "Have you anything here to eat?" They gave Him a piece of a broiled fish; and He took it and ate it before them. *Luke 24:41b-43 (NASB-U)*

IS IT REAL? The consensus of archeologists, historians and scholars is overwhelming: "The appearances of the (resurrected) Jesus are as well authenticated as anything in antiquity."[24] Nobody doubts Julius Caesar crossed the Rubicon with his troops in order to seize power in Rome. Yet archeological and historical evidence for the Crucifixion far outweighs this incident, so "Nothing but the assumption that it must be false could suggest the idea of deficiency in the proof of it."[25]

Was it legend? It is impossible to perpetrate a legend in the same area, with the same people and at the same time as the legendary events. Time, distance, a "never-never land" atmosphere, and strange names are needed. With the crucifixion, scholars acknowledge, "The earliest evidence we have for the Resurrection almost certainly goes back to the time immediately after the Resurrection event is alleged to have taken place."[26]

Failed critiques: exhaustive attempts have been made to discredit the historicity of the Resurrection, most recently from the discredited Jesus Seminar.[27] Yet still today, "The idea that stories about Jesus emerged from mythology fails to withstand scrutiny." There is currently no credible, objective proof that the Resurrection was ever derived from legend.[28]

Hallucinations do not eat food. Hallucinations are not shared by a group. He spent hours with them on numerous occasions, teaching and answering questions about Old Testament passages predicting these events—hallucinations cannot teach.[30]

Something happened so real and life changing, the Disciples were instantly transformed from a cringing, discouraged and confused group into an excited, animated movement that rapidly spread like wildfire.

Consider this…

It is unreasonable to frame the Resurrection as a mass hallucination. Unless the Disciples formed a conspiracy of lies, the Hallucination Theory does not match the many recorded histories. If they were lies, what could possibly explain the Disciples resolve to all die as martyrs? [31]

RESURRECTION GLORY
Resurrection is the Bible's declaration of a new body.

Resurrection means inheriting a different—yet familiar—body. The change from caterpillar to butterfly is not a poor analogy, considering the Bible's descriptions:

There are heavenly bodies and earthly bodies, but the glory of the heav-

---

THE VITAL IMPORTANCE OF THE RESURRECTION Clearly, the Resurrection of Jesus is the most distinctive feature of Christianity. If true, it enforces His claim of, "I am the way, the truth, and the life. No one can come to the Father except through me." *John 14:6*. His Bodily Resurrection is inseparable from Christianity:

Otherwise, the New Testament is a conspiracy of lies: Seven different books citing hundreds of witnesses claim first-hand knowledge of it.[32]

It defines Christianity: "If Christ has not been raised, then your faith is useless." *1 Corinthians 15:17a*. It would mean Christians are foolish, and "we are of all men most to be pitied." *1 Corinthians 15:19* (NASB). It is impossible to respect Christianity if Christ's Resurrection is untrue.

It fulfills prophecy: The Messiah is clearly someone who was once killed, and yet stands before His killers in the triumph of a resurrected body: "They will look on me whom they have pierced and mourn for him as for an only son. They will grieve bitterly for him as for a firstborn son who has died." *Zechariah 12:10* (NASB)[33]

It proves Jesus was God: "The Jews then said to Him, 'What sign do you show us as your authority for doing these things?' Jesus answered them, 'Destroy this temple, and in three days I will raise it up.'" *John 2:18-19* (NASB). They understood this referred to His Resurrection, because they cited this as reason for the Romans to guard the grave. *Matthew 26:61*

It proves forgiveness of sins: "He who was delivered over because of our transgressions, and was raised because of our justification." *Romans 4:25* (NASB). Unlike human speculation or the subjective experiences of "enlightened" religious leaders through history, the fact of the Resurrection is an objective, verifiable basis for knowing we are justified before God by His death.

enly is of one kind, and the glory of the earthly is of another. There is one glory of the sun, and another glory of the moon, and another glory of the stars; for star differs from star in glory.

So is it with the Resurrection of the dead. What is sown is perishable; what is raised is imperishable. *1 Corinthians 15:39-42 (ESV)*

The difference is the Glory of the resurrected body verses the earthly body The "heavenly body" is certainly physical, as the disciples soon discovered:

Glory reduced the battle-hardened Roman soldiers at the gravesite into shaking, wobbling, "dead faint." It displays the excellence of the person, and comes from the Hebrew word meaning weight.[34] God's Weight of Glory is blinding and lethal to humans with earthly bodies. Glory is something carried:

"…which tends to throw around its subject a halo of glory, or in some respect to crown it with honor; as when the glory of man is identified with his soul."[35]

The Resurrection Body of Jesus was full of Glory, and it is a good look at what humans will carry throughout Eternity Future, as co-heirs with Christ:

But now Christ has been raised from the dead, the first fruits of those who are asleep. *1 Corinthians 15:20 (NASB-U)*

And like Jesus, our Resurrected Bodies will also carry Glory, and it will seem much different than the earthly sick, deteriorating and weak body which,

"…is sown in dishonor; it is raised in glory. It is sown in weakness; it is raised in power." *1 Corinthians 15:42-43 (ESV)*

THE REAL PROOF The wonderful news of the New Testament is that anyone can discover if Jesus Christ is indeed alive today. The Cross of Christ is God's provision for each of us to contain His Eternal Life, just as Adam and Eve were created to contain it—but those two gave up the title deed of their life to Satan, and died. Now we all live separated and alienated from God. Yet God began His Redemptive Plan that day in the Garden of Eden, and it culminated in the Cross of Christ.

God elected to become a human, like us, so He could bear the consequences of His own judgment of our sins. The Judge of the Universe decreed the sentence of death, both physical and spiritual. Then, setting aside His majesty, He stepped out of His robes of judgment and took our place as the defendant. He took that sentence of death on Himself, so great is His Love for us.

But each defendant must give Him permission for this—He will not over-rule anyone's Sovereign Will. A deliberate act of humility is required: coming to Jesus in prayer, and saying, "Please, take away the Divine Wrath that is due for my sins, because I want to contain your Eternal Life." This is called an act of faith, and it is God's will for each of us, holding great promise, as Jesus said:

"I assure you, those who listen to my message and believe…have eternal life. They will never be condemned for their sins, but they have already passed from death into life." *John 5:24*

✍ The Glory of Christ's Resurrection proves the Atonement of Sins.

Since Jesus Christ died for the sins of all humanity, if one sin remained which was not fully atoned by His death, Jesus would never have been resurrected with such Glory.

Consider this...

When someone receives Redemption, their sins are forgiven, and there will be an "eternal weight of Glory" emanating for all Eternity Future as a testimony to the Glory of the Resurrection of Jesus Christ.

FURTHER CONSIDERATION

THE VICTORY OF THE MYSTERY

Why did the Ruler of this World play such an active role in crucifying the Messiah? The death of Christ was the Redemption of humanity from slavery in Satan's Counterfeit Kingdom. Surely Satan would oppose the crucifixion, not promote it!

The amazing answer lies in The Mystery of the Kingdom of God, known before the foundations of the earth:

> But we speak God's wisdom in a mystery, the hidden wisdom which God predestined before the ages to our glory;
> *1 Corinthians 2:7* (NASB-U)

The Bible is such an incredible gift to mankind because it is the Revelation of the "counsels of God," an invitation by God to come inside His private world and see something amazing, as foretold in prophecy:

> This is the Lord's doing, and it is marvelous to see. *Psalm 118:23*

David explains what is so "marvelous"

> The stone rejected by the builders has now become the cornerstone. *Psalm 118:22*

This is from one of the Hallel Psalms traditionally sung after the Passover meal for centuries, sung by Jesus and His Disciples after communion. It encapsulates the very essence of the life of Jesus Christ—the cornerstone rejected by the Kosmos, but used by God to build The Kingdom. Jesus quoted this Psalm to the religious elite to let them know what they were rejecting:

> But Jesus looked at them and said, "What then is this that is written: 'The stone which the builders rejected, This became the chief cornerstone'? Everyone who falls on that stone will be broken to pieces; but on whomever it falls, it will scatter him like dust."

They did not like the inference:

> The scribes and the chief priests tried to lay hands on Him that very hour, and they feared the people; for they understood that He spoke this parable against them. *Luke 20:17-19* (NASB-U)

THE SECRET COMING

Although the Messianic prophecies of the Old Testament are vast, it was not well understood that God planned two separate comings of Messiah King. The First Coming was an offer of amnesty before the Second Coming, when He brings justice and rules the nations.

Typically, the prophecies of God are crystal clear, with but one caveat: the fact of two separate comings became crystal clear only after his First Coming. God constructed Messianic prophecy with such genius, that until the very moment Christ died on the cross, it was difficult to perceive The Mystery. Why?

Simply put, the prophesied death of Jesus was a shock to the spiritual Rulers of this World. This is why Satan so ferociously pursued the crucifixion of Christ: by killing Christ, he mistakenly thought it would end Jesus' ability to build The Kingdom. For this reason:

> We do speak wisdom…not of this age nor of the rulers of this age, who are passing away…the wisdom which none of the rulers of this age has understood; for if they had understood it they would not have crucified the Lord of glory. *1 Corinthians 2:6,8* (NASB-U)

This is why Satan pursued the crucifixion so heavily: He did not understand the wisdom of God. He, along with the religious elite, did not realize Jesus came to die. Even God's Prophets were confused about how this strange picture of the Messiah would come true. There was the Suffering Servant:

> Surely our griefs He Himself bore, And our sorrows He carried; Yet we ourselves esteemed Him stricken, Smitten of God, and afflicted. *Isaiah 53:4* (NASB-U)

Yet there was also King Messiah:

> I will surely tell of the decree of the Lord: He said to Me, "You are My Son, Today I have begotten You. Ask of Me, and I will surely give the nations as Your inheritance, And the very ends of the earth as Your possession." *Psalm 2:7-9a* (NASB-U)

Nobody could withstand the Messiah's power and authority:

> You shall break them with a rod of iron, You shall shatter them like earthenware. *Psalm 2:9b* (NASB-U)

But He would die:

> The Anointed One will be killed, appearing to have accomplished nothing. *Daniel 9:26b*

This is why we find such apparently contradictory Messianic prophecies: indeed, God surprised the Kosmos with The Mystery, which is the crucifixion of Jesus Christ at the First Coming:

> God's secret plan has now been revealed to us; it is a plan centered on Christ, designed long ago according to his good pleasure. *Ephesians 1:9*

The New Testament is God's clear revelation about The Mystery, full of:

> ...the preaching of Jesus Christ, according to the revelation of the mystery that was kept secret for long ages. *Romans 16:25* (ESV)

THE VASTNESS OF THE MYSTERY

The Mystery encompasses far more than just the Two Comings of the Messiah; it includes all the ramifications as well. This is especially true for the Age of the Gentiles, called the Church Age. The death of Jesus Christ introduced this new era in God's plan of salvation:

> By revelation there was made known to me the mystery, as I wrote before in brief...to be specific, that the Gentiles are fellow heirs and fellow members of the body, and fellow partakers of the promise in Christ Jesus through the gospel" *Ephesians 3:3-6* (NASB-U)

Throughout the Old Testament, it is only hinted that God would open up his plan of salvation to the entire Gentile world; yet it is there, at the very beginning, in the Abrahamic Covenant:

> "And in you all the families of the earth will be blessed." *Genesis 12:3* (NASB-U)

But this is more clearly revealed after the crucifixion in the New Testament:

> The Scripture, foreseeing that God would justify the Gentiles by faith, preached the gospel beforehand to Abraham, saying, "All the nations will be blessed in you." *Galatians 3:8* (NASB-U)

The modern era is still experiencing the Age of the Gentiles, but it will not last forever; God will again return to working with Israel again, as Jesus prophesied:

> "And Jerusalem will be conquered and trampled down by the Gentiles until the age of the Gentiles comes to an end." *Luke 21:24*

The Age of the Gentiles draws to a close according to this prophecy when Israel regains control of Jerusalem. Against all odds, in 1948 Israel was re-established as a nation. In 1967 Jerusalem passed from Gentile control back into the hands of God's Chosen People, triggering a whole new set of prophesies as God's Incredible Plan continues to unfurl.[B]

It is a plan stretching from Eternity to Eternity, the Scarlet Thread of Redemption that ties together the entire Bible, finally revealed in The Mystery. With this in mind, Paul praises the genius and vastness of God's Plan:

> That is what the Scriptures mean when they say, "No eye has seen, no ear has heard, and no mind has imagined what God has prepared for those who love him." *1 Corinthians 2:9*

Yet, all this is tied up in one single day in human history: the crucifixion of Jesus the Messiah, the Son of God.

(B) The fulfillment of biblical prophecies in the modern era is covered more fully in the Epilogue.

THE BODY OF CHRIST

"In those days I will pour out my Spirit upon all my servants, men and women alike, and they will prophesy."
Joel 2:28, quoted by Peter on the Day of Pentecost

THE NEXT MOVE

For weeks, the Disciples were overcome with excitement. Jesus Christ was not dead, He was alive! All the Disciples—along with more than 500 other followers of Christ—repeatedly witnessed the Glory of the risen Christ.[1] It fundamentally altered their view of life, and all their plans were shaken. Long and exciting conversations took place over fulfilled prophecies:

> "When I was with you before, I told you that everything written about me by Moses and the prophets and in the Psalms must all come true...it was written long ago that the Messiah must suffer and die and rise again from the dead on the third day." *Luke 24:46*

∽ **They were dealing with a very tangible, living person—not a vision or dream.**

These were exciting Bible studies, and were written down into what became the New Testament, meaning a New Covenant, which explained so much of The Mystery found in the Old Covenant.

After weeks of these encounters, Christ finally summoned his Disciples to meet Him at the Mount of Olives, outside Jerusalem. Everyone knew this was important. Gathering around Christ, they bombarded Him with questions about the next move, like children on the first day of school:

> "Lord, are you going to free Israel now and restore our kingdom?" *Acts 1:6b*

His answer was cryptic:

> He said to them, "It is not for you to know times or epochs which the Father has fixed by His own authority;" *Acts 1:7* (NASB-U)

THE HOLY SPIRIT

Rather than crushing the Romans and seizing power, Christ began describing a very mysterious and new Person they would soon meet:

> "But when the Holy Spirit has come upon you, you will receive power and will tell people about me everywhere—in Jerusalem, throughout Judea, in Samaria, and to the ends of the earth." *Acts 1:8*

This was certainly not what they expected—yet the Holy Spirit was not entirely foreign, since Christ described Him earlier.

Consider this...

The Holy Spirit was someone they were familiar with, because He was God— the Spirit of God—a Person with distinct mind, will, and emotions. He was there at the beginning of Creation, "moving over the surface of the deep." [2]

∽ **The Holy Spirit is God, yet also a distinct Person of the Trinity.**

Yet, He was somewhat mysterious, a "Helper" Christ said, who would lead them daily. He would illuminate them and even indwell them and communicate with them:

> "But the Helper, the Holy Spirit, whom the Father will send in My name, He will teach you all things, and bring to your remembrance all that I said to you." *John 14:26* (NASB-U)

ANTICIPATION

They were to experience a profound encounter with the Holy Spirit—a permanent, unalterable fusion between the Spirit of God and the human spirit lasting into Eternity Future. It would be a life-altering Indwelling. Christ told the Disciples to get ready for their world to be changed:

> He told them, "Do not leave Jerusalem…in just a few days you will be baptized with the Holy Spirit." *Acts 1:4-5*

Then their world was shaken:

> He was taken up into the sky while they were watching, and he disappeared into a cloud. *Acts 1:9b*

They were left standing on top of the Mount of Olives, staring into a blank sky, left with this strange promise about the Holy Spirit, and otherwise empty hopes about the great Messianic Kingdom now snatched from their grasp.

∽ **They were expecting the Messianic Kingdom of the Old Covenant, but instead God introduced the Kingdom of the New Covenant.**

Slowly, they filtered back to Jerusalem and gathered together in a house near Herod's Temple. Other Believers came to ask what had happened, and soon there were about 120 of them wondering what to do. They prayed for answers for days, and they continued praying, not realizing that yet again their worlds would explode…

THE BIRTH OF AN ERA

It was the "Feast of First Fruits," because it was a celebration of the first harvest in early spring. It was an immensely popular festival that climaxed with the Day of Pentecost, and by this time huge numbers of Jewish pilgrims from across the Roman Empire were gathering in Jerusalem.

Christ's followers were still meeting in that house, ignoring the festival and praying for answers. Their quiet prayer meeting was forcefully disrupted:

> Suddenly, there was a sound from heaven like the roaring of a mighty windstorm in the skies above them, and it filled the house where they were meeting. Then, what looked like flames or tongues of fire appeared and settled on each of them. And everyone present was filled with the Holy Spirit… *Acts 2:2-4*

Consider this…

At last, after ages of alienation, God rushed into those Believers who were cleansed from sin. The Holy Spirit filled their hearts with a vigor that proclaimed a new beginning for humanity.

They were exhilarated! It fulfilled Christ's promise given a few days earlier:

> "When the Holy Spirit has come upon you, you will receive power and will tell people about me everywhere—in Jerusalem, throughout Judea, in Samaria, *and to the ends of the earth.*" *Acts 1:8* (emphasis added)

They were energized, they poured into the streets where the Feast of Pentecost was in full swing, and their impact on the crowd was dramatic:

> Godly Jews from many nations were living in Jerusalem at that time. When they heard this sound, they came running to see what it was all about, and they were bewildered to hear their own languages being spoken by the believers. They were beside themselves with wonder. "How can this be?" they exclaimed. "These people are all from Galilee, and yet we hear them speaking the languages of the lands where we were born!" *Acts 2:5-8*

Taking charge,

> Peter stepped forward with the eleven other apostles and shouted to the crowd, "Listen carefully, all of you, fellow Jews and residents of

Jerusalem! Make no mistake about this... What you see this morning was predicted centuries ago by the prophet Joel: 'In those days I will pour out my Spirit upon all my servants, men and women alike, and they will prophesy.'"

Then he announced the prophetic fulfillment of The Mystery:

> *"And anyone who calls on the name of the Lord will be saved."*
> *Acts 2:14-18 (emphasis added)*

People were arrested by that last sentence: "Anyone who calls on the name of the Lord will be saved." They listened in silence as Peter explained how Christ was crucified for Sin and resurrected from the dead as proof of their forgiveness.

✍ The Holy Spirit was the fulfillment of all the ancient prophecies about the reunion of God and man.

> "King David said this about Him... 'You have shown me the way of life, and you will give me wonderful joy in your presence.' And the Father, as he had promised, gave him the Holy Spirit to pour out upon us, just as you see and hear today." *Acts 2:28, 33b*

That day, about 3,000 people asked God to forgive their sins through Christ's death on the cross, and they too received the Holy Spirit, and they too experienced the same intimacy with God.

A MOVEMENT

A real movement was underway in Jerusalem; the Holy Spirit stirred the city like Christ did on Palm Sunday, irrevocably changing the lives of everyone He touched. Like Christ, He also left division and turmoil in His wake.

✍ People were so enthralled by the life-changing effect of the Holy Spirit, everything else paled in comparison.

Many of those caught up in the movement were foreign pilgrims normally concerned with returning to their homelands, but instead they delayed their departure and stayed with the Believers:

> They joined with the other believers and devoted themselves to the apostles' teaching and fellowship, sharing in the Lord's Supper and in prayer. A deep sense of awe came over them all, and the apostles performed many miraculous signs and wonders. *Acts 2:42-43*

Although the original Believers only numbered about 120, the task of hosting 3,000 new guests fell to them—causing no small hardship. Yet everyone was so excited, the hard-pressed hosts gladly sacrificed to accommodate these strangers:

And all the believers met together constantly and shared everything they had. They sold their possessions and shared the proceeds with those in need. *Acts 2:44-45*

Consider this...

This was no mere philosophical movement—there was something supernatural here as the Holy Spirit brought dynamic, internal upheaval that spilled into the streets. This is what it looks like when someone becomes indwelt by the Holy Spirit and the human spirit comes alive once again.

It took on the character of a celebration, with people not only selling their possessions and sharing resources, but also enjoying a newfound sense of community they never knew before:

They worshiped together at the Temple each day, met in homes for the Lord's Supper, and shared their meals with great joy and generosity—all the while praising God and enjoying the goodwill of all the people. And each day the Lord added to their group those who were being saved. *Acts 2:46-47*

This group was growing like wildfire! Peter healed a crippled man and caused a huge commotion as people flocked to see what had happened. He started teaching about Jesus Christ, and in one day another 5,000 people were added to their number. Within weeks they grew from 120 to almost 10,000, and still the movement showed no signs of slowing down.

The Jewish authorities were understandably shaken by the rapid growth of Christ's Disciples—they thought they were rid of him! They tried desperately to stop it by arresting Peter and John. They threatened and flogged them, ordering them to stop teaching about Jesus Christ, but it was no use. Nothing could possibly stop this movement because the Holy Spirit, not humans, engineered it.

THE BODY OF CHRIST

This was a movement unlike any other mass movement in history—political, military or religious. This was held together by the irresistible power of the Holy Spirit stretching two directions at once: vertically, by the intimate tie between the Creator and humans made in His image, and horizontally, as a unity between humans that was so strong, Believers gladly "shared everything they had." They began calling each other "brother" and "sister," and they all loved God as their Father.

✎ This movement clearly was not institutionally organized.

All this explosive growth was spontaneous. The Believers lacked any clear organization at first—nothing beyond a tacit respect for the original 12 Disciples. Groups 10,000-strong-and-growing could never boast such an informal structure; yet this passage says they were tightly bound together, meeting "constantly and sharing everything they had." They were organically bound like a family.

Yet "family" is an inadequate description: how many families share such strong enthusiasm and mutual charity? This was different. It was a community they never knew before Pentecost, and there could be no denying it afterwards. Without any formal structure, without laws or taxation, they shared a fire of love ignited and fanned by the presence of the Holy Spirit among them.

THE AWAKENED HEART
 ✍ **This was a mass movement of loving relationships.**

Consider this…
It is historically the first evidence of the Holy Spirit's presence in someone's life: the compassion, desire and ability for intimacy suddenly appear.

Each time someone receives the Holy Spirit, a new ability to relate beyond natural experience begins. Those from broken homes or bankrupt relationships—guarded, comfortably numb and defensive—even these report a strange warming of the heart:

> Now you can have sincere love for each other as brothers and sisters because you were cleansed from your sins when you accepted the truth of the Good News. *1 Peter 1:22*

All this is the mark of the Holy Spirit. He was the ancient Agent of relationship between the Creator and the created, between the Prophets and Yahweh, and now He does it with any Believer in Christ Jesus.

THE ORGANIC UNITY
 ✍ **This organic unity between Believers in Christ is called the Body of Christ.**

KOINONIA The Bible used the term Koinonia[3] to describe this phenomenon: It means "sharing," or "to have in common." Often the word is translated "Fellowship" to describe The Body meeting together.

At the heart of Koinonia is a genuine love for one another, just as Jesus commanded earlier: "By your love, all men will know you are my Disciples." *John 13:35.* It was so evident to onlookers that this Fellowship is a very different kind of meeting: "[They] shared their meals with great joy and generosity...enjoying the goodwill of all the people." *Acts 2:46-47*

This is a true fulfillment of God's original purpose when creating humanity—co-rulers with Him, building together The Kingdom. He commissioned this to Adam and Eve, but they rebelled. At last God calls us "fellow-heirs" with Jesus Christ, "partakers of the divine nature," "adopted," "His children," and of course, "His Body, the fullness of Him who fills all in all."[4]

Body of Christ—such an ingenious and profound phrase God chose to describe His community of Believers. Through the agency of the Holy Spirit, Jesus Christ establishes His personal presence and reign on Planet Earth as the Messiah King—and humans take part as mediators of His Kingdom through His Body.

Because Believers are tied together, there is a shared responsibility:

> But now there are many members, but one body. And the eye cannot say to the hand, "I have no need of you"; or again the head to the feet, "I have no need of you." *1 Corinthians 12:20-21* (NASB-U)

Consider this…

After the Holy Spirit enters, it is impossible to live in an isolated world. Even when a Believer in Jesus Christ sits at home, alone, he "cannot say… 'I have no need of you'" to the rest of the Body of Christ. Even when alone, Believers are not isolated.

A CONQUERING LOVE

This eternal truth about the Body of Christ—its interdependency—brings a far-reaching and exciting implication. The Believers in Jerusalem understood it: freedom from a suffocating devotion to self.

> **The Body of Christ repudiates the Principle of Sin.**

At the heart of the satanic rebellion against God is the aspiration that, "I will be like God," and it fuels the System teeming with selfish people driven by selfish goals. The only way to unite such people is with force—or personal profit—and still unity is tenuous:

> "Hell is other people." *Jean Paul Sartrev*

The System is so fragile and deeply flawed, an endless cycle of rising powers disintegrating into chaos, then destroyed by the next rising power.

God's plan to expand His Kingdom relies on a newfound ability to love people, an approach devoid of the System's overwhelming coercion. Such kind acceptance

STALIN VERSUS CHRIST Stalin, the ruthless communist dictator, was in seminary studying to be a priest when he read the words of Christ to "love your enemy" and "turn the other cheek".." In disgust he gave up on Christianity because these principles were so obviously absurd and naive.[6] The world suffered immeasurably for half a century because this man embraced a new profession: Communist politics. Ruthlessness made sense to Stalin, and using it he forged a great Soviet Empire.

Yet today we can see the wisdom behind Jesus Christ's Kingdom principles. Stalin is despised by all, and his great Soviet Empire disintegrated a few decades after his death. Yet the Kingdom of Jesus Christ continues to grow, sweeping across Stalin's old empire. The Backward Thinking of God and His Kingdom lasts into eternity, while the Counterfeit Kingdom fails.

would unravel it. Jesus Christ came to set people free from slavery:

> It was for freedom that Christ set us free. *Galatians 5:1a* (NASB-U)

Only God's Kingdom built on love has the power and legitimacy to last through Eternity Future. Jesus laid out the blueprint for building His Kingdom:

> "So now I am giving you a new commandment: Love each other. Just as I have loved you, you should love each other. Your love for one another will prove to the world that you are my disciples." *John 13:34-35*

The captives in the Kosmos are drawn by the unparalleled love of Christ driving The Kingdom. This is not reproducible inside The System because it requires the Holy Spirit who manifests God's unconditional and unlimited love. This love engendered euphoria in Jerusalem as the Body of Christ grew and grew:

> God's message was preached in ever-widening circles. The number of believers greatly increased in Jerusalem, and many of the Jewish priests were converted, too. *Acts 6:7*

UNWELCOME CHANGE

Some Disciples saw the far-reaching implications of The Kingdom. Stephen in particular realized that all the old symbols were now obsolete. This was radical and threatened the status quo. With such powerful economic and political systems already built, the religious elite thought the Mosaic Covenant was God's Eternal Plan, itself unalterable and sacred.

⤳ Old Covenant symbols were replaced by the New Covenant substance.

Most blasphemous of all was Stephen's contention that Herod's Temple in Jerusalem was now utterly useless—even an obstacle to the growth of The Kingdom. His insight was simple. The Temple was a part of a bygone era of symbols that led to Christ. Such things as the Holy of Hollies clearly pictured how nobody can enter God's presence while stained with sin, but now the thick veil of separation was torn from top to bottom, and God was free to enter the hearts of men.

Consider this...

This meant God's presence had moved from the Holy of Holies into the hearts of people. There was a new kind of Temple now called the Body of Christ:

> And now God is building you, as living stones, into his spiritual temple. *1 Peter 2:5a*

When Stephen began teaching that the Temple was no longer needed, it was an attack against national Israel and its institutions. Infuriated religious leaders seized and dragged him before the Sanhedrin, the high ruling council who sentenced Jesus to death:

> "This man is always speaking against the Temple and against the law of Moses. We have heard him say that this Jesus of Nazareth will destroy the Temple and change the customs Moses handed down to us." *Acts 6:13-14*

Stephen rose to his defense, and fed their accusations with substance:

> "The Most High doesn't live in temples made by human hands. As the prophet says, 'Heaven is my throne, and the earth is my footstool. Could you ever build me a temple as good as that?'" *Acts 7:48-50*

His logic was inescapable: how could a solitary Temple contain God? He must have forgotten, however, that Jesus was crucified for saying the same thing.[7]

⤳ Sacred Space is a foundational doctrine for the Cult of Man.

Consider this…
The Cult of Man historically replaces the real Creator God with god-in-a-box. Sometimes it is a statue, but more often a lavish building with manufactured, ethereal atmospheres of the divine soaked with liturgies and rich tradition.

Humans always attempt to define and limit God. More hideous, Sacred Space grants divine status for brutal, inhumane kingdoms. People will kill defending their Sacred Space, as the Sanhedrin had done with Jesus. Those sitting in judgment of Stephen could not refute his logic, yet they were deeply offended by it, threatened by it, and became an angry mob:

> Then they put their hands over their ears, and drowning out his voice with their shouts, they rushed at him. *Acts 7:57*

Suddenly the euphoric atmosphere of this early Christian movement was shattered by violence when Stephen was stoned to death. He became the first martyr of the new movement, and it was now evident the stakes were growing higher.

A BLOOD BATH

An overwhelming force of hatred and opposition was unleashed on this new movement, led by a rising star: the ingenious and energetic Saul of Tarsus. He was the primary instigator behind Stephen's trial and execution,[8] and the Believers quickly learned how skillful and zealous he was:

> A great wave of persecution began that day, sweeping over the church in Jerusalem, and all the believers except the apostles fled into Judea and Samaria… Saul was going everywhere to devastate the church. He went from house to house, dragging out both men and women to throw them into jail. *Acts 8:1-3*

Like a possessed man, Saul decimated the Body of Christ in Jerusalem and taking along a small army, gained authority to pursue them into remote regions.

The waves of persecution were so infectious even Herod Antipas, the Judean monarch normally apathetic about religious affairs, joined the fray by beheading James, one of the original 12 Disciples. The execution so pleased the religious elite, Herod the politician moved against Peter, the central figure of this movement, and seized him for execution.

Overnight, the celebration in Jerusalem was transformed into a blood bath. Whole families were imprisoned, people were executed, and Peter was about to die. A coordinated effort drove this conspiracy, finally hatched after long planning, from Satan's kingdom, at its apex of glory in the Roman Empire. Satan would not allow God's Kingdom to take over, unchallenged.

Consider this…

The most gruesome Christian persecutions begin with the Ruler of this World, who "was a murderer from the beginning and has always hated the truth."

Before His death, Jesus clearly warned the Disciples of this ferocious, satanic opposition:

> "Look, I am sending you out as sheep among wolves… you will be handed over to the courts and beaten in the synagogues. And you must stand trial before governors and kings because you are my followers…"
> *Matthew 10:16-18*

✑ The Body of Christ threatens the iron grip of the Cult of Man on the hearts and minds of people.

How could this Body of Christ possibly survive with all the resources and overwhelming armies of The System at Satan's disposal; with the new movement widely dispersed and hiding from Saul's zealous hatred, and its paltry leadership dwindled by execution, without swords, armies or defensive fortresses?

Saul of Tarsus soon discovered how surprisingly formidable this Body of Christ was. There was an invisible strength and resilience beneath the surface, unlike any other manmade organization—Someone called the Holy Spirit. Saul was about to confront Him firsthand.

AN INVISIBLE STRENGTH

Saul was enraged, "breathing threats and murder against the disciples," headed for a blood bath at Damascus when he met a terrifying person:

> As he was nearing Damascus on this mission, a brilliant light from heaven suddenly beamed down upon him! He fell to the ground and heard a

voice saying to him, "Saul! Saul! Why are you persecuting me?" "Who are you, sir?" Saul asked. And the voice replied, "I am Jesus, the one you are persecuting!" *Acts 9:3-5*

This was bad, very bad: it was the dreaded name "Jesus," and Saul was in trouble. The encounter left Saul blind, and his campaign screeched to a halt; in fact, it reversed direction. Saul was now convinced the Disciples were telling the truth, and Jesus was alive, resurrected, and clearly was the prophesied Messiah!

From this point forward, the considerable weight of Saul's zeal and genius was devoted to building the Body of Christ. It was a monumental coup d'état engineered by Christ! Ironically, Christ replaced the martyred Stephen with his accuser and executioner, and changed Saul's name to "Paul."[10]

The invisible strength struck next in Jerusalem, where Peter awaited execution:

The night before Peter was to be placed on trial, he was asleep, chained between two soldiers...Suddenly, there was a bright light in the cell, and an angel of the Lord stood before Peter. The angel tapped him on the side to awaken him and said, "Quick! Get up!" And the chains fell off his wrists. *Acts 12:6-7*

Stunned, Peter learned a timeless truth: God's Kingdom is never derailed.

THE INVISIBLE KINGDOM

The Kingdom was launched as an invisible power from the beginning. Jesus described this to the Disciples:

One day the Pharisees asked Jesus, "When will the Kingdom of God come?" Jesus replied, "The Kingdom of God isn't ushered in with visible signs. You won't be able to say, 'Here it is!' or 'It's over there!' For the Kingdom of God is among you." *Luke 17:20-21*

The Kingdom was something that occurred deep inside people's hearts, a new life sparked by the Holy Spirit:

...we are joined together in his body by his strong sinews, and we grow only as we get our nourishment and strength from God. *Colossians 2:19b*

❧ The Body of Christ is an invisible entity.

This is why the Body of Christ grew so rapidly despite the intense persecution and opposition of the first century. There were no buildings or headquarters, no "president" or mass assemblies or any other visible human organization to stamp out. They met in small groups, in homes. It was a dynamic force more resilient than the powerful armies of The System.

What clearly attracted people despite the threat of persecution and death, was the prospect of containing the Eternal Life of God. This strikes at the core problem on Planet Earth, spawned in the Garden of Eden.

Consider this...
The problem destroying people's lives is not good versus evil—it is eternal life versus eternal death.

As the movement spread, these believers became known as Christians, meaning "little Christ's." Originally a derogatory term, Christians readily accepted it because they were indeed propagating the spiritual life of Christ.

> **The function of the Body of Christ, therefore, is to offer life—God's Eternal Life—to every person.**

The role of the Body of Christ is to offer this Eternal Life, reaching deep into the darkness of Satan's Counterfeit Kingdom. That young Body of Christ gladly shouldered the dangers because of their genuine love.

INVISIBLE REWARD

Yet this Invisible Body of Christ concept brings significant drawbacks for those accustomed to the rewards of The System. With an invisible Kingdom, there are no financial rewards, since currency carries no weight with the Almighty God. No palaces, crowns, estates or inheritance can be hoarded in The Kingdom.

Consider this...
The reward of The Kingdom is the joy of sharing Eternal Life with ex-captives of the Kosmos. Motivated by love, this is reward enough for a Believer.

THE MISSIONARY JOURNEYS After Saul became the Apostle Paul, his life became a living example of this exciting and revolutionary new conquest. He set out on three short journeys, taking the good news to cities across the Roman Empire. These "missionary journeys" on foot lasted less than six years altogether. Yet, by the time he was finished, Christianity was a revolutionary fire sweeping the Roman Empire. The explosive news preceded Paul's arrival in new areas:

"'Paul and Silas have turned the rest of the world upside down, and now they are here disturbing our city,' they shouted." *Acts 17:6b*

The early church did just that, and multiplied rapidly throughout the Roman Empire and beyond. Within 60 years, the church numbered in the millions; and within 300 years it conquered the mighty Roman Empire.

The Kingdom of God grows exponentially when Believers simply share the gospel, and love those for whom Christ died. Within three decades, the church grew from 120 to 200,000 people, and then 500,000 by the end of the first century.[11] By the time of Nero's persecution in Rome in A.D. 64, Roman historian Tacitus said "a great multitude" of Christians proliferate the massive city, and thus became "martyred with cruel tortures."[12]

No movement throughout history has grown so fast, even with the modern advantage of guns and mass communications.[13] This was despite many ongoing local and empire-wide attempts to kill the movement through the most barbarous tortures and executions.[14]

Still, an Invisible Kingdom with invisible results can be discouraging. There was no institution, no empire-wide councils, census, membership pledges or fees. How could first century Believers possibly tally the results?

As he awaited execution in a cold prison cell at the end of his life, Paul was discouraged looking back at what seemed like pathetic pockets of struggling groups left in his wake. In his last letter, written to his closest friend Timothy, Paul was alone in a prison cell except for Dr. Luke: "Everyone has abandoned me," he writes.

Yet from a spiritual viewpoint, Paul knew he was wealthier than the Emperor of Rome:

> I have fought a good fight, I have finished the race, and I have remained faithful. And now the prize awaits me—the crown of righteousness that the Lord, the righteous Judge, will give me on that great day of his return. And the prize is not just for me but for all who eagerly look forward to his glorious return. *2 Timothy 4:7-8*

For Paul it was all about the reward of loving relationships: vertically between man and God, and horizontally between humans.

Consider this...

It may not glitter like gold or compare to the majesty of crowns, but true fulfillment comes from stepping into God's design for our humanity—becoming truly Relational Beings—with lasting, eternal reward.

MEMBERSHIP RULES How is it possible to ascertain membership in the Body of Christ? It surprises people to discover that no formal definition of membership exists in the Bible. No specific words can be said, no vow or pledge can be made to convince God—who, after all, "sees the thoughts and intentions of the heart." The closest definition of membership given by the Bible is found in Romans: "for whoever will call on the name of the Lord will be saved." *Romans 10:13* (NASB-U)

From a biblical perspective, only the person who received the Holy Spirit and the Holy Spirit Himself truly knows if that person is actually part of the Body. God's "Invisible Church" is beyond the reach of human control.

Things are different with an Institutional Church with membership rosters, where initiates undergo a process or sign a pledge.

These are two completely different approaches to membership: a spiritual criterion of the heart for the Body of Christ, and external, visible criteria for institutions. In this book, we attempt to avoid the confusing term "church" when referring to the Body of Christ, because it is so closely associated in people's minds with human institutions. The real need is for spiritual Koinonia between Christians—the institutional trappings may change—and real membership in The Kingdom means belonging to the invisible Body of Christ.

PERSECUTION

Not all was well with the Body of Christ. Significant problems arose that could only have a source in Satan, God's enemy.

Persecution was ineffective against the love of the Body—Believers forgave too easily, they reacted too lovingly. Their property was often seized, but their hearts were not deeply attached to the System and they weathered temporary loss, painful though it was.[15]

Even more amazing to the Romans, these people rarely renounced their faith even when faced with the arena and watching wild beasts tear apart their family members. By A.D. 64, the Roman historian Tacitus reports that Emperor Nero was killing Christians on a large scale:

> They died by methods of mockery; some were covered with the skins of wild beasts and then torn by dogs, some were crucified, some were burned as torches to give light at night. All of this aroused the mercy of the people. *Tacitus*[16]

Persecution often had the opposite intended effect, and the movement still continued growing in mass appeal across the Empire.[17] As Believers were thrown into the arena to face death, spectators marveled at how they died with such confidence and peace. Across the empire curiosity grew about this strange movement: Were the Resurrection claims true? The death of one Believer in the arena often brought scores of spectators to Christ.

INFILTRATION

A much more menacing threat loomed over the Body of Christ, however. Jesus warned the Disciples about it:

> "The Kingdom of Heaven is like a farmer who planted good seed in his field. But that night as everyone slept, his enemy came and planted weeds among the wheat…" *Matthew 13:24-25*

Jesus interpreted the Parable for them:

> "…The good seed represents the people of the Kingdom. The weeds are the people who belong to the evil one. The enemy who planted the weeds among the wheat is the Devil…" *Matthew 13:38-39*

Here was a hideous strategy foretold: rather than crush the Body of Christ, why not simply assimilate it into the Counterfeit Kingdom, like all the other kingdoms of man? Once incorporated, it becomes yet another powerful tool for Satan to continue his grip on humanity.

 Much of church history describes Satan's efforts to incorporate God's Kingdom into his own Counterfeit Kingdom.

Paul faced this very problem:

> No wonder, for even Satan disguises himself as an angel of light. Therefore it is not surprising if his servants also disguise themselves as servants of righteousness. *2 Corinthians 11:14-15a*

Paul was describing the efforts by some to mix Grace with the Religion of Merit—Christ's death on the cross covered some sins, but still every effort must be made to prove and earn acceptance with God. This mixture became known as Legalism.

✑ A Religion of Merit cannot mix with a Relationship of Faith.

Consider this…

This is one of God's most basic principles: Grace plus Law always equals Law. God does not tolerate the crucifixion of His Son to become confused with man's Religion of Merit.

The Bible is clear that Christ's death paid for all the sins of a Believer: past, present and future.

> For the death that He died, He died to sin once for all; *Romans 6:10a* (NASB-U)

> But He, having offered one sacrifice for sins for all time, sat down at the right hand of God…For by one offering He has perfected for all time those who are sanctified. *Hebrews 10:12,14* (NASB-U)

Anyone who teaches Christ only paid for some sins is teaching a Religion of Merit, not Christianity. Any religion teaching Good Works or rituals are still required for acceptance with God is not teaching Christianity:

THE SEEDS OF LEGALISM It began early, shortly after Paul returned from his First Missionary Journey. A raging controversy erupted over Grace:

"Even that question [of Grace] wouldn't have come up except for some so-called Christians there—false ones, really—who came to spy on us and see our freedom in Christ Jesus. They wanted to force us, like slaves, to follow their Jewish regulations." *Galatians 2:4*

These people claimed obedience to the Law of Moses was still required for God's acceptance, and it is called Legalism—the old Religion of Merit wrapped in Christian disguise. The attack against Grace was an attack against Christ's work on the cross, claiming his death only forgave sins committed before becoming a Christian. A true Christian makes every effort to follow the Law of Moses and earn acceptance before God, they taught. This included the necessity to become circumcised, as the Law of Moses prescribed, according to the Judaizers.

What the Judaizers tried to do seems so harmless. In effect, they only proposed adding a few rules to help Believers keep from sinning. Yet invariably, the rules are always the trite, external changes, like circumcision, that humans can keep, ignoring "the weightier portions of the Law," as Christ said to the Pharisees. *Matthew 23:23*

> Behold I, Paul, say to you that if you receive circumcision, Christ will be of no benefit to you. *Galatians 5:2* (NASB-U)

> You have been severed from Christ, you who are seeking to be justified by law; you have fallen from grace. *Galatians 5:4* (NASB-U)

Paul was horrified to see this Legalism infiltrating the groups he started, and launched into a vitriolic renunciation of any connection between Christianity and a Religion of Merit:

> But even if we or an angel from heaven should preach a gospel other than the one we preached to you, let him be eternally condemned! *Galatians 1:8* (NIV)

For the rest of Paul's life, he fought against the poisoning of God's Grace by Legalism, and it soon preoccupied the Early Church. Clearly Satan was on the attack to destroy The Kingdom.

FURTHER CONSIDERATION

THE NEW MAN

Not one kingdom or government on earth has ever been formed on the basis of "Love one another as I have loved you…" What makes this unparalleled approach possible with The Kingdom is the Inner Transformation:

> You were dead because of your sins and because your sinful nature was not yet cut away. Then God made you alive with Christ. He forgave all our sins. *Colossians 2:13*

Jesus Christ brought such radical changes: the Atonement, Redemption, Reconciliation with God…and finally, Inner Transformation. God altered our basic identity and began reversing the effects of The Fall.

INNER TRANSFORMATION

Adam and Eve died spiritually when they became engulfed by the Principle of Sin. A vital, central part of their humanity became useless and dead, leaving a gaping hole in their human natures. They were meant to contain God's Eternal Life like a glove; but they lost it, and life became empty and flat.

Through Reconciliation God now indwells Believers, who contain the very life of God. This brings more than a relationship with Him; it also means radical change. It is impossible to contain the life of Creator God without experiencing a revolutionary Inner Transformation.

God not only brings Atonement for sins, He removed Sin—the Human Nature that loves sinning. This opens a new world of possibilities:

> What this means is that those who become Christians become new persons. They are not the same anymore, for the old life is gone. A new life has begun! *2 Corinthians 5:17*

> He saved us, not because of the good things we did, but because of his mercy. He washed away our sins and gave us a new life through the Holy Spirit. *Titus 3:5*

THE HUMAN SPIRIT

At the core of our being, our most precious possession is a unique capacity to actually contain the very life of God. It is called the Human Spirit, containing the faculty to relate on a spiritual dimension, and share our feelings and thoughts with God. It is this faculty that is revived and made alive by the Holy Spirit:

> He has given us his very great and precious promises, so that through them you may participate in the divine nature. *2 Peter 1:4a* (NIV)

This brings us full-cycle back to the Garden, and to God's original purpose for mankind embodied within The Mystery: "I will dwell in them and walk among them." His gift of Sovereign Free Will became limited after The Fall as we entered slavery inside the Kosmos; but God is in the act of creating new possibilities and, new choices for us.

> Sin is no longer your master, for you are no longer subject to the law, which enslaves you to sin. Instead, you are free by God's grace. *Romans 6:14*

This triggers a whole new identity, called our Identity in Christ—and it brings real changes into the life of a Believer:

> We have Spiritual Life (1 John 5:11, 12), whereas before we were spiritually dead.

> We are in the Body of Christ (1 Corinthians 12:13), whereas before we were alone, trapped in the Kosmos.

> We are totally forgiven (Acts 10:34), whereas before we were objects of God's Wrath.

> We are totally righteous, wholly like God (2 Corinthians 5:21), whereas before we were dominated by Fallen Nature.

> We have God's unlimited Power within us through the Holy Spirit (Romans 6:4), whereas before we were governed by The Principle of Sin.

APPROPRIATING THE NEW LIFE

The Christian life is an exciting discovery of our great privileges and our riches in Christ. But how is it done?

Fortunately, God has outlined the most simple and easy-to-understand ways to allow the Holy Spirit to transform our lives. Sometimes called The Means of Growth, these channels of receiving the spiritual life of God are simple steps of faith anyone can take, anywhere at any time:

Through God's Word, our fallen way of thinking is transformed.

> And do not be conformed to this world, but be transformed by the

renewing of your mind, so that you may prove what the will of God is, that which is good and acceptable and perfect. *Romans 12:2* (NASB)

For the word of God is full of living power. It is sharper than the sharpest knife, cutting deep into our innermost thoughts and desires. It exposes us for what we really are. *Hebrews 4:12*

Through Prayer, we deepen our relationship with the Holy Spirit and receive illumination:

I pray that from his glorious, unlimited resources he will give you mighty inner strength through his Holy Spirit. *Ephesians 3:16*

Pray at all times and on every occasion in the power of the Holy Spirit. Stay alert and be persistent in your prayers for all Christians everywhere. *Ephesians 6:18*

Through Koinonia (sharing and spending time with the Body of Christ), our infant spiritual life matures as God works through the other members of the Body, and as God teaches us how to love sacrificially, the way Christ loved us.

Speaking the truth in love [to each other], we are to grow up in all aspects into Him who is the head, even Christ. *Ephesians 4:15* (NASB)

We know love by this, that He laid down His life for us; and we ought to lay down our lives for the brethren. *1 John 3:16* (NASB)

With Suffering, God can bring us victory by using it to remove our Sin Nature and the selfish world view dominating our lives—if we trust Him with it. In the hands of God, meaningless suffering can become meaningful discipline with a redemptive outcome.

And we know that God causes everything to work together for the good of those who love God and are called according to his purpose for them. *Romans 8:28*

For momentary, light affliction is producing for us an eternal weight of glory far beyond all comparison, while we look not at the things which are seen, but at the things which are not seen; for the things which are seen are temporal, but the things which are not seen are eternal. *2 Corinthians 4:17* (NASB)

Believers engaged in all of these will experience the incredible revolution of the New Man—part of The Mystery God planned long ago.

THE EXTRAORDINARY STRATEGY OF DISCIPLESHIP

Let a man regard us in this manner, as servants of Christ and stewards of the mysteries of God.

1 Corinthians 4:1

ALTERING HISTORY

Nothing disrupted the flow of human history like the appearance of Jesus Christ. His death and resurrection released humanity from a single destiny of slavery, trapped inside the Counterfeit Kingdom—a future utterly without hope—and exchanged it for our eternal inheritance as children of God's household, "co-heirs with Christ." He opened boundless new horizons for the future of the human race.

Yet, most important for our future, before His Crucifixion He mobilized a following to proclaim the freedom of the cross across the Roman Empire.

This movement was not any mob action, however. God unleashed a Kingdom through a strategic conquest so brilliant, no human mind could devise it. The strategy was unearthly, so foreign to the World System that even the ferocious and brilliant "Ruler of this World" could not outmaneuver it, no matter what resources, armies or persecutions he rallied against it.

✍ **Jesus Christ established the Kingdom of God in the most unlikely fashion by raising an army of only 12.**

He called them "Disciples." Unlike any other kingdom-builder before or after, Christ deliberately avoided the gathering crowds.[1] Instead, as His ministry progressed the Bible repeatedly says, "He took the 12 aside by themselves…"[2] He left very few followers in His wake, really only these 12 Disciples. What possible chance for success could this small group accomplish for the Kingdom of God?

A DECEPTIVE BRILLIANCE

Jesus trained the 12 in a strange practice called Discipleship, something very foreign and not at all reproducible by human kingdoms. As a strategy, Discipleship was so simple, easily performed by slaves or fishermen, and produced only modest consequences: individual results, one with another.

It was a time-consuming and highly constrictive focus, yet deceptively brilliant because underlying Discipleship was the principle of multiplication. One became two, two to four, four to eight and so on until the exponential growth spread its tentacles throughout the cities of the Roman Empire within a lifetime.

Unlike human kingdoms, God rejects conquest by brute force or mass appeal. Requiring no well-organized systems or great financial reserves, Discipleship spontaneously appears anywhere, unexpectedly, even in remote villages. Growth like this becomes impossible to stamp out, and persecution only scatters the flames of its growth.

Discipleship is the epitome of the Invisible Body of Christ.

It isn't an organization and it lacks the splendor of great human enterprises. Discipleship is a deeply relational process extending far beyond the transmission of slogans or zeal. It becomes a life-transforming process, a repetition of the personal relationship experienced by those original 12 Disciples who lived with Christ.

WITHOUT PRECEDENCE

There is no corollary to Discipleship found among kingdom-building strategies in the World System. It is principally a spiritual encounter, because at its core Discipleship transmits the spiritual life of Jesus Christ from one person to another.

It is a strategy practiced and founded squarely on love—the love of God that so deeply stirs and strangely warms the heart of someone who meets the Holy Spirit. This love spills into the lives of surrounding people through Discipleship. Mentoring is a bad synonym, because Discipleship extends beyond mere training.

Discipleship is no academic teacher-pupil relationship, even though instruction certainly transpires. Not seen in a classroom, Jesus discipled the 12 with great personal involvement and patience:

> …having loved His own who were in the world, He loved them to the end. *John 13:1* (NASB-U)

THE PRINCIPLE OF SACRIFICIAL LOVE

Jesus cited His own Discipling of the 12 as the epitome of deep, sacrificial love:

> So now I am giving you a new commandment: Love each other. Just as I have loved you, you should love each other. Your love for one another will prove to the world that you are my disciples." *John 13:34-35*

"As I have loved you" means that Discipleship is something more caught than taught:

> "Jesus lived his life before his followers, and they caught it: Jesus was contagious."

Love was to become the hallmark of Discipleship, such a love that outsiders watch with astonishment and envy, and so "prove to the world you are my disciples."

The Master-apprentice relationship employed by some religions is antithetical to Discipleship. Such a domineering relationship is utterly reprehensible in God's Kingdom. This is because the so-called Master is steeped in the aloofness and self-importance that characterizes the Principle of Sin—man's fallen, proud nature.

Instead, the Principle of Sacrificial Love defines the Discipleship relationship:

> "Do not be called leaders; for One is your Leader, that is, Christ. But the greatest among you shall be your servant." *Matthew 23:10-11* (NASB-U)

Jesus trained His 12 generals to become servants of others, a stark contrast to the Master Sergeant with new recruits. This Principle of Sacrifice was a warm, non-threatening and very attractive relationship, something few privates recall about their sergeants in boot camp:

> "I no longer call you servants, because a master doesn't confide in his servants. Now you are my friends, since I have told you everything the Father told me." *John 15:15*

Jesus proved He did not regard them as inferiors because He brought them into the very counsel-chamber of God as co-heirs: "Since I have told you everything the Father told me," He said. We now have access to the secrets of God, as Paul says:

> He made known to us the mystery of His will, according to His kind intention which He purposed in Him... *Ephesians 1:9a* (NASB-U)

✍ There would be no superior-inferior roles in Discipleship.

When Jesus revealed the thoughts and intentions of God's heart to the Disciples, He made himself completely vulnerable to them. Officers in human armies understand such fraternizing with new recruits degrades the discipline of the ranks. In God's new army, Jesus trained men who would make their lives deeply intermingled and vulnerable to new Disciples.

Consider this...

Their struggles and weaknesses were to be shared in Discipleship the way Jesus invited His Disciples into the Garden of Gethsemane, to share His nightmarish struggle the night before The Crucifixion.

✍ What a tragedy it is to confine Discipleship to a formal, weekly appointment.

The 12 were actively engaged in the life and ministries of Jesus, not only watching but participating and leading alongside Christ. They too, performed miracles, and at times unleashed the power of God's Kingdom. Discipleship is anything but a boring meeting:

> I have made mistakes in this regard. I have tried to train men by gathering them together in a quiet basement once a week to discuss the Christian life and then supplement this with occasional seminars or special meetings. It didn't work. But men who have ministered with me in the push and shove of life, out where we face victory and defeat daily, out in the world of real living, are today productive for Christ. I have watched them bear fruit that remains.[3]

Jesus summarized what it would take to make Discipleship work:

> "So no one can become my disciple without giving up everything for me." *Luke 14:33*

Consider this...

This is where the Bible calls for sacrifice: for the sake of Christ, the Kingdom and the people to be liberated from slavery. It is a war that requires sacrifice.

Christianity is not a Religion of Merit, it is not asceticism, but it does call for sacrifice—that is, Sacrificial Love, the true "goal of our instruction."[4] Discipleship is fueled by Sacrificial Love. And so, Jesus taught extensively one very basic principle, restated in various forms throughout His ministry:[5]

> "If anyone wishes to come after Me, he must deny himself, and take up his cross and follow Me. For whoever wishes to save his life will lose it, but whoever loses his life for My sake and the gospel's will save it." *Mark 8:34-35* (NASB)[6]

> "Truly, truly, I say to you, unless a grain of wheat falls into the earth and dies, it remains alone; but if it dies, it bears much fruit. He who loves his life loses it, and he who hates his life in this world will keep it to life eternal." *John 12:24-25* (NASB)

Thus Jesus defined the essential, driving motivation for change in the Christian life. It is a love-driven desire for change, not guilt-driven. It is Sacrificial Love, not sacrifice in order to be loved.

THE IMPOSSIBLE TASK

Jesus was acutely aware that with time, people would resort to shortcuts to grow The Kingdom. Discipleship might get entangled with monumental systems and complex organizations—systems within systems, man's historical effort to build something apart from God—or worse, loving Discipleship might be replaced by the more authoritarian relationships so foundational to the coercive Kosmos.

Christ was unambiguously dogmatic that Discipleship was to remain the singular strategy and growth of the new Kingdom of God. Solemnly He charged them with the Great Commission:

> "Therefore, go and make disciples of all the nations..." *Matthew 28:19a*

What an overwhelming task that surely challenged their minds: "All the nations..." Still not finished, He prescribed an impossibly rigorous course for each new Disciple:

> "Teach these new disciples to obey all the commands I have given you..." *Matthew 28:19b*

No teaching classroom could possibly accommodate this requirement to pass along "all the commands I have given you." The Disciple John understood it:

> And I suppose that if all the other things Jesus did were written down, the whole world could not contain the books. *John 21:25*

ᑐ **Such is the monumental task of Discipleship: transferring the very life of Christ from one to another.**

Consider this...

This is the enigma of God's strategy for kingdom-building: based on a model not found elsewhere, it encompasses the spiritual life of Christ and spreads across the face of the earth on an individual basis—beginning with only the 12!

This knowledge could only pass along slowly, through personal relationships— only the mind of God could contrive such an unexpected strategy.

THE SECRET OF DISCIPLESHIP

There lies the secret of Discipleship: it requires the very mind of God to accomplish the task. Jesus punctuates the Great Commission with that very point:

> "...And be sure of this: I am with you always, even to the end of the age." *Matthew 28:19*

ᑐ **Discipleship is a deeply spiritual activity, depending on the presence and activity of the Holy Spirit.**

DISCIPLESHIP AND THE MYSTERY

Going all the way back to the creation of man, we see that God's Mysterious Plan meant establishing a race of conquerors on Planet Earth in opposition to Satan's Kingdom. The Satanic Rebellion was confined to Planet Earth, living in exile, yet still dangerous and unresolved.

Until the creation of man, the Counterfeit Kingdom was never seriously threatened. When God inserted Adam and Eve into that disorder, Satan was clearly unimpressed by the new menace. He was certainly wiser, more gifted and experienced than these strange, spindly and naked creatures called humans. Satan did not recoil. He aggressively pounced on Adam and Eve, won, and dragged the captives into his domain along with their offspring as slaves.

What never entered into Satan's low estimation of man was God's ancient purpose to "dwell in them and walk among them." This Indwelling never occurred with the angels—humans were the first. It changed everything. The Indwelling turns humans into formidable and dangerous enemies. This is so evident in the lives of Christ's Disciples, and their Disciples:

> "Their ministry was set in the context of prisons, beatings, threatenings, earthquakes, shipwrecks, plots to murder, miracles, and many other events…The devil tried his best to stop them, but they got the job done. They stuck with it." *Leroy Eims*[7]

Consider this…

When God linked Discipleship with the Indwelling, He unleashed a movement of conquest that truly threatened the ancient strongholds and kingdoms of Satan for the first time.

Jesus said:

> "Upon this rock I will build my church, and all the powers of hell will not conquer it." *Matthew 16:18*

Little wonder Discipleship is such an impossible task! It requires dependence on the Holy Spirit and fulfills God's plan to "dwell in them." God established a race of dangerous enemies of the Counterfeit Kingdom through the power of the Holy Spirit. Like tumbling dominoes, Satan's strongholds have to release their captives:

> "If the love of Jesus Christ has found a home within our hearts, then we are the carriers of an awesome power that is simply waiting to be unleashed. From all eternity God has chosen to grow his kingdom through us. And it's unstoppable. It is stronger than the force of gravity." *George McDonald*

FULFILLED AS BUILDERS

God imparted to us His marvelous capacity to build, as we saw in Genesis 1. After The Fall, this drive to build became a perverted desire to build systems, treasures and kingdoms for ourselves. Yet God intended us to build something far more exciting: relationships that last into eternity! This goes to the center of our need as Eternal Beings.

Today there remains a magnificent sense in which we naturally experience this God-given drive: by building families. God intended us to "be fruitful...and subdue the earth." We are designed foremost as relationship builders and family builders. With successful families, humans are great society builders with the capacity to "subdue the earth."

Intuitively, we know family-building is deeply significant to our humanity. So many become disillusioned with dysfunctional family life, or depressed by its brevity as kids grow up. Family-building can leave us empty because our builder-desire is unfulfilled.

Yet the genius of God's Eternal Plan becomes evident in Discipleship, because it fulfills that deeply ingrained need to build something relational that lasts. This is the point Jesus made:

> "I chose you and appointed you to go and bear fruit—fruit that will last"
> *John 15:16* (NIV)

The Body of Christ is indeed the new Family of God, tied together by the love Discipleship engenders, the "fruit that will last" into Eternity Future. The Discipler spawns a vast family of Eternal Souls through multiplication.

Discipleship family-building is so completely unlike a guru with a devoted follower, as the Eastern religions practice. It is an active Koinonia, an ever-growing fellowship of lives, and it never festers in isolation:

> He did not prepare them to go out to a life of secluded fellowship with one another, so He did not prepare them in a secluded fellowship.[8]

∾ **Discipleship is the natural outgrowth of a healthy, excited Body of Christ that operates like a family as God intended.**

When people first receive the Holy Spirit, they enter the Body of Christ as spiritual newborns, truly infants. Within a healthy group, they are nurtured by a loving Discipler. A more spiritually mature person takes interest and disciples this newborn away from the worldly culture and toward Jesus Christ.

Consider this...

What a joy it is to bring a newborn into healthy adulthood! Unlike earthly families, which often disintegrate as time passes, the Family of God only grows closer together—even though Disciples reach maturity and move on to begin discipling others.

This is not institutional growth; it is a fulfillment of our design as relationship builders. With successful Discipleship we become great social builders resulting in a thriving, living Body of Christ like Jesus founded.

DYSFUNCTIONAL FAMILIES

Why then do so many Christian organizations fail to produce Disciples? Sometimes even a local Family of God becomes dysfunctional, cold and alienated like families in the Kosmos.

Successful family-building requires a fundamental change of relational habits. Typically in the Kosmos, people easily divide against each other. It is a competitive, harsh and critical atmosphere that breeds resentment and alienation.

∞ **We live in a world that exerts a tremendously alienating influence.**

Those judgmental attitudes will destroy a family because the young ones are so incredibly weak and have so far to grow; their immaturity leaves much to criticize, if we want. Parents who engage in this will never motivate growth.

In healthy families, the harshness of Satan's kingdom is replaced with a godly atmosphere of forgiveness, hope and excitement for the young ones. Mature parents will not withdraw or grow resentful when their kids fail. Like nobody else, parents see their child's abundant potential just waiting to be unleashed with nurturing care.

Consider this...

This "heart of hope" is equally necessary in the work of building the Family of God through Discipleship. It means that older Christians must leave behind the relational habits of criticism and harshness learned in the Kosmos.

The potential discipler must have a heart for people. He must see others in light of their potential for God ...Unless we see people in that light, we will tend to relegate them to some program that we hope will do the job for us...Without loving concern, our Discipling process will be cold and mechanical.[9]

∞ **Some groups become "cold and mechanical" by focusing on behavior instead of practicing Discipleship.**

Older Christians sometimes demand change without instruction and patience. The focus centers on moral failures. Orders are given, judgment is passed, and a harsh atmosphere develops. Thus, the Family of God degrades into dysfunctional hypocrisy, because even the older ones lack the maturity to Disciple. But, they do learn the secrets of camouflaging problems.

Equally dysfunctional, some groups replace Discipleship with polite alienation, maintaining a safe distance in order to avoid the deep immaturities that plague their organization.

With these dysfunctional syndromes, the attraction of the Body of Christ fades away, and the Christian organization becomes passé:

"Your love for one another will prove to the world that you are my disciples." John 13:35

THE SECOND INGREDIENT

Discipleship is so different from comradeship or simple friendship, even though it clearly necessitates a close, personal attachment. There is abundant fun and joy to be found in Discipleship, but the impact is not so trite.

∞ **Discipleship necessitates instruction in the Word of God.**

Nurturing newborns with God's view of creation and purpose, Revelation ignites a spiritual upheaval unequalled by friendly advice:

> Like newborn babies, long for the pure milk of the word, so that by it you may grow in respect to salvation. *1 Peter 2:2 (NASB-U)*

Consider this…

Discipleship should never be confused with camaraderie or simple companionship, because God's truth and instruction is so dominant. The Discipleship relationship revolves around opening the Bible and studying it together.

STEWARDS OF THE MYSTERIES

Discipleship is a miraculous process that changes those formerly alienated from God into "Stewards of the Mysteries of God" as Paul says:

> Let a man regard us in this manner, as servants of Christ and stewards of the mysteries of God. *1 Corinthians 4:1 (NASB-U)*

It is difficult to describe the impact of studying "the Mysteries of God" with someone filled with the authority of the Holy Spirit. The Disciples experienced this with Jesus:

> They said to each other, "Didn't our hearts feel strangely warm as he talked with us on the road and explained the Scriptures to us?" *Luke 24:32*

"Hearts feel strangely warm" when the Scriptures are opened by this kind of Discipler. Their studies with Jesus rose above mere fascination. His instruction was strategic—He equipped them. These 12 required equipping because they were soon headed for stressful times:

> He would send them forth to preach to the high council of the Jews, to the philosophers of Athens, to the worshippers of idols, to the wicked barbarians, to Roman soldiers—to any and everyone who would listen. He knew His training had to be in depth because these men would face formidable opposition…Shallow training and lighthearted commitment would not stand the test. They were saved to save others, but it would be a rough and rocky road most of the way.[10]

When The Body stops producing "Stewards of the Mysteries of God," the chain-reaction of Discipleship fizzles, newborns never mature, and precious few discover any significant role in The Kingdom.

Consider this...
Without significant roles, people grow restless and discontent within the Body. Soon the Counterfeit Kingdom attracts believers with empty promises of fulfillment and significance.

∽ **Discipleship without equipping produces perpetually dependent and immature babies.**

Without many Stewards, paid professionals necessarily take center-stage, and the living Body of Christ morphs into a human organization fed by money and orchestrated by professionals while potential Stewards become observers.

This combination of contagious love and compelling truth is inseparable for igniting the true spiritual growth of the Body of Christ:

> "But speaking the truth in love, we are to grow up in all aspects into Him who is the head, even Christ." *Ephesians 4:15* (NASB-U)

"Truth in love" is passed through multiplying generations of Christians by Discipleship: close, vulnerable relationships where the needs are evident and biblical answers are specific.

THE PRINCIPLE OF SELECTION
Discipleship is persuasion, the very heart of Christian ministry, and requires a certain degree of competency in handling the Mysteries of God:

> Therefore, knowing the fear of the Lord, we persuade men...
> *2 Corinthians 5:11* (NASB)

∽ **Discipleship is persuasion, but not coercion, and occurs only within the realm of two-way love relationships.**

Jesus called on His Disciples to "pick up the cross and follow me," and those willing to do so He called "Disciples." He was very selective: "Follow Me!" he said only to certain ones willing.[11]

Paul, too, described Discipleship as a two-way relationship:

> The things which you have heard from me in the presence of many witnesses, entrust these to faithful men who will be able to teach others also.
> *2 Timothy 2:2* (NASB)

Those "able to teach" are the "faithful men" who themselves are responding to "pick up your cross."

THE GLORY OF GOD REVEALED

From the viewpoint of the Kosmos, Discipleship is a mundane and trite feat compared to the monumental projects of the World System. It is barely noticed, even if deeply appreciated by a few transformed lives.

Yet within the obscurity of Discipleship we find the fulfillment of God's Eternal Plan for the creation of humanity, to "dwell within them, and walk among them."[12] This purpose is called Human Agency. Although God could easily transform lives without human intervention, because He elected us as co-workers and "Stewards of the Mysteries of God,"[13]

He seeks those willing to undertake an exalted position as His viceroys:

> We are Christ's ambassadors, and God is using us to speak to you. We urge you, as though Christ himself were here pleading with you, "Be reconciled to God!" *2 Corinthians 5:20*

Sometimes this Ambassadorship is called evangelism, but the Bible actually calls it Discipleship, expressing the more life-changing work God intends for Human Agency. Discipleship starts with evangelism, but goes far beyond the initial introduction into God's Kingdom. It elevates newborn Christians into "Stewards of the Mysteries of God," who Disciple others into the Kingdom. Evangelism by multiplication ultimately brings more people into the Kingdom than evangelism alone.

Billy Graham is famous for his evangelism, yet even he realized his large crusades pale in significance compared to Discipleship:

> Mass crusades in which I believe and to which I have committed my life will never finish the Great Commission; but a one by one ministry will.[14]

SURPRISED BY GOD
∞ **God will some day surprise everyone with His view of history.**

We will discover history was actually commissioned by God to obscure Disciplers who played the most pivotal roles in God's Kingdom Plan, perhaps not the great names recognized by historians. People like Henrietta C. Mears become spiritual giants in God's Kingdom. She discipled and raised up Bill Bright, the founder of Campus Crusade for Christ, who in turn triggered a vast network of Discipleship ministries spread throughout the world.

Consider this...

Eloquent public speakers and popular leaders will never enjoy the impact of the obscure yet effective Discipler in God's Kingdom.

Preachers, leaders and organizers play a role in God's Kingdom, but they cannot match the Discipler's role. While preachers lecture, Disciplers actually carry out God's "truth-in-love" principle of Kingdom growth:

> Speaking the truth in love, we are to grow up in all aspects into Him who is the head, even Christ. *Ephesians 4:15* (NASB-U)

POISONED BY MAN

Church history seems so depressing on the surface. Certainly by the time Emperor Constantine absorbed the Great Church into the Roman Empire, the Visible Church[A] imported many unsavory traits from the Counterfeit Kingdom. Too often the organization grew by cruelty and oppression, armies and despots just like all the other human kingdoms.

Yet somewhere inside the Visible Church, although quite often outside it, God continued to build the true Body of Christ, the invisible Kingdom multiplied by Discipleship. Numerous gross errors developed, theologically and in practice, that plagued the Visible Church. Yet through Discipleship, God continued to work whenever individual Christians responded to the indwelling of the Holy Spirit.

The Franciscan, Jesuit and Benedictine movements perhaps erred by absorbing beliefs never taught by Christ. Yet, they also contained the currents of Discipleship used by God to grow the invisible Body of Christ. Later, the Protestant Reformation spawned an explosion of Discipleship movements like the Waldensians, Anabaptists, Huguenots, Moravians, Wesleyans and more. Sometimes these new movements picked up strange, new beliefs not found in the Bible. Yet, wherever people "called out in the name of the Lord," the indwelling Holy Spirit stirred Discipleship in the hearts of believers.

Consider this...
Today the Holy Spirit is seeking individuals willing to make a loving commitment to reach the lost and become Disciplers. This is the essence of the Great Commission and the most fulfilling kind of ministry any Christian can engage in.

Discipleship becomes repressed, however, whenever the Body of Christ becomes heavily entangled with those "traditions of men" Christ fought against. It also becomes repressed when the Body is absorbed by Human Kingdoms, where the real presence and life of the Holy Spirit is excluded. At times like these, Discipleship slows to a trickle.

THE MODERN SHORT CUT

In what Francis Schaeffer calls the "Post-Christian Era" of the modern West, Discipleship is again slowing to a trickle. The new phenomena of large, ponderous

(A) We use the term Visible Church referring to where the Body of Christ operates within human institutions – the Institutional Church.

churches still offer people a chance to meet the Holy Spirit. Yet, the emphasis is drifting away from what Leroy Eims appropriately calls "The Lost Art of Discipleship."

For more than half a century, the Western church has been in decline. In England, less than ten percent of the population bothers attending, and America is quickly following suit. After decades of decline, still eight out of 10 churches continued to decline in America from 1994 to 2004, and church growth experts predict the same trend for the next decade.[15]

Costly programs are replacing personal Discipleship. According to one study:

> It still takes one hundred church attendees, a pastor and $100,000 a year to win a convert. Among evangelicals it is a bit better—1.7 conversions per year per 100 people in worship attendance. *Bill Hulls*[16]

Clearly the first-century Body of Christ commanded no such budgets, nor did it grow so slowly! Those Christians relied on Discipleship, not expensive programs. As Eims puts it:

> What then is the problem today? Why don't we see more of this going on? Why are fruitful, dedicated, mature disciples so rare? The biggest reason is that all too often we have relied on programs or materials or some other thing to do the job. The ministry is to be carried on by people, not programs. It is to be carried out by someone and not by some thing.

> Disciples cannot be mass produced. We cannot drop people into a "program" and see disciples emerge at the end of the production line. It takes time to make disciples. It takes individual, personal attention. It takes hours of prayer for them. It takes patience and understanding to teach

KEY CONSIDERATIONS Here are a few of the key points that make Discipleship such an ingenious plan inaugurated by Christ:

Renouncing the Kosmos—those who practice Christian Discipleship are renouncing the Principle of Sin governing the Kosmos.

Living the Abundant Life—Christian Discipleship fulfills our design for significance and rulership.

Sacrificial Love—Discipleship requires a genuine decision to "pick up the cross" by upsetting our protected worlds as we invite less mature, problematic people inside.

Deepening the Knowledge of God—Discipleship is a Word-oriented ministry guaranteed to deepen knowledge of "the Mysteries of God" for all involved.

Deepening Dependence on God—true Discipleship is so impossible and supernatural, it requires a closer walk with God.

A Stewardship—Discipleship is commanded by Christ for all to practice.

True Growth—Discipleship is the key growth of The Kingdom, both numerically and quantitatively: "Speaking the truth in love, we are to grow up in all aspects..." *Ephesians 4:15a* (NASB-U)

them how to get into the Word of God for themselves, how to feed and nourish their souls, and by the power of the Holy Spirit how to apply the word to their lives. And it takes being an example to them of all of the above. *Leroy Eims* [17]

REPEATING THE TRAGEDIES OF HISTORY
∽ Humans are typically unimpressed by the genius and kindness of God.

Consider the problems God has encountered with the heart of humanity:

When God presented His King Messiah riding triumphant on the back of a small donkey, what a disappointing picture He made.

When God sent the Christ with an offer of amnesty rather than judgment, and they crucified Him for it.

When God offers acceptance by Grace, it has been met with such indifference or even rejection. Grace is an affront to proud human nature. It feels like a guilty dog groveling, and the Religion of Merit continues to grow strong.

God shared The Mystery through Revelation. What a chance to understand how it all fits together! Yet, few Christians know or understand the Bible today, even though study tools and translations make it more accessible than ever before.[18] Revelation is a rude interruption to human will power.

∽ In each case, the tragic mistake is repeated: human pride offended by the kindness and genius of God.

History is repeated for God's blueprint of Kingdom growth: Discipleship. What is more thrilling than building a Family of God extending into the centuries? What is more exciting than The Kingdom growing with Eternal Beings ever-increasing in love? Still Discipleship dwindles in Western Christianity.

The reason is simple. God's blueprint is not glamorous, so Discipleship is minimized and forgotten easily. People are enthralled with the proud splendor of the Counterfeit Kingdom and build the luxurious buildings, massive organizations and impressive programs fed by a massive influx of money. When that happens, money inevitably dominates the conversation and focus of the Visible Church.

NUNC ET NUN
"Here and now" was Nietzsche's criticism of Christianity. Christians are unfairly criticized for being so "heavenly-minded they're no earthly good," as people say.

This is untrue. When people devote their lives to the stimulation of the Counterfeit Kingdom, they quickly discover after a few short years that nothing remains, no matter how good the warranty.

In the "here and now" of Discipleship, the fulfillment is overwhelming through the love relationships that are formed. Relationships with Eternal Beings will continue to yield returns that never end. Twenty years or 20 million years later, that Disciple is still around, and the relationship is still precious and deeply fulfilling.

ᔆ **No building program in the Kosmos delivers true satisfaction in the here-and-now like Discipleship.**

What seems so trite is actually a feat of glory. When the dust settles, only God's building is left standing, and He is building but one thing: The Body made of living stones, and Discipleship is God's mortar that binds the stones into place.

THE TRIUMPHAL ENTRY

Nowhere do you see the "Great Discipler" riding like Caesar, clothed in purple robes on the back of a white stallion, surrounded by the cheers and praise of an empire. Yet, Caesar's glory is deceptive. All the glory of Julius Caesar's empire lies in ruins in Rome, a mere trace of its former glory.

There will also be a Triumphal Procession for God's Stewards, but not in this life while everyone is too steeped in pride, and God will never feed the Principle of Sin. When death finally brings release from the grip of Fallen Nature, there will be an amazing moment, walking into the presence of God…

Someone will be there who recognizes the Faithful Steward, and he will turn and shout out to the others, "Here he is! This is the one—our great, great, great, great grandfather!" The word will spread, and others, spiritual offspring numbering in the thousands, gather to call out greetings. What gratitude and thankfulness and praise will be heaped on the Faithful Steward who discipled and ignited a chain reaction.

ᔆ **What thunderous applause will fill the heavenlies!**

Then, rising above the rest, there will be a deep, thunderous and joyful sound: "Well done, good and faithful servant! Enter into the joy of your master! You did well! You were a great Steward!"[19] It is the voice of King Messiah sitting on His throne of Glory and authority. It will surely be at that time we realize how true His promise is for each individual believer engaged in Discipleship:

> And be sure of this: I am with you always, even to the end of the age.
> *Matthew 28:18-19*

EPILOGUE
THE ULTIMATE SYSTEM

THE ASCENT OF HUMANITY

Jesus Christ proclaimed a dismal future for The System. As centuries pass, time and again it erupts in violence:

> You will be hearing of wars and rumors of wars. See that you are not frightened, for those things must take place, but that is not yet the end. *Matthew 24:6* (NASB-U)

Kingdoms arise and splinter through betrayal, intrigue, conquest and the "foolish wisdom of the world,"[1] as God calls it. So much perpetual bloodshed, wasteful and useless—if only it were possible to unite the splintered kingdoms! Yet questions bar the way: United under whose authority? Who to trust? Who will yield?

As centuries pass, various "enlightened" despots try to recapture Nimrod's vision of the Ultimate System—the unification of humanity. Each desperate attempt nearly grasps the prize, and then spirals into chaos and destruction. The only legacy is the river of blood:

> The cannon thunders ... limbs fly in all directions ... one can hear the groans of victims and the howling of those performing the sacrifice...it's Humanity in search of happiness. *Charles Baudelaire, French Poet* [2]

PROGRESS

The kingdom-building efforts are not entirely in vain, however. The Bible foresaw that over time human kingdoms become more refined. Lessons are learned, new experiments emerge, and slowly the Ultimate System appears within reach.

As these kingdoms gain sophistication, the Counterfeit Kingdom wraps around a new ethos. Finances and wealth—not relationships—pervade the ethics and pursuits of society. Simultaneously and unsurprisingly, the ability to build families deteriorates, the Bible says:

> But realize this, that in the last days difficult times will come. For men
> will be lovers of self, lovers of money, boastful, arrogant, revilers, disobe-
> dient to parents, ungrateful, unholy... *2 Timothy 3:1-2* (NASB-U)

Wealth is within the reach of commoners, not just the elite, and people become
"lovers of money." The System generates monoliths of success, but at such horrific price! People become cynical about love: "arrogant, revilers" as "lovers of self,
lovers of money" predominate. Jesus also predicted it:

> Because lawlessness is increased, most people's love will grow cold.
> *Matthew 24:12* (NASB-U)

✐ The glorious kingdoms of humanity offer success at the expense of what God values most.

With wealth, interest in the Kingdom fades, and the desperate need for God dis-
appears. For the first time in human history, the allure of wealth is a viable goal for
the majority of people. All this materializes because humanity discovers great new
and attractive systems. Democracy and Capitalism open new doors for wealth,
while technology and mass production raises the standard of living. The struggle
for mere sustenance is replaced by a struggle to "get ahead." Obesity—not starvation—becomes the greater affliction, and the Counterfeit Kingdom offers a tangible
illusion of security.

CHURCH, INC.

Coincidentally, the Body of Christ becomes institutionalized and wealthy. The
simple, joyous Koinonia of the First Century evolved into the lumbering, monolithic Great Church of the fourth century which Constantine incorporated into the
Roman Empire. Suddenly, a flood of ancient, pagan Roman traditions dominated
the church, shepherded along by hoards of pagan Roman priests and officials.
Many of these seized high positions of authority and solidified their powers with a
centralized church government.

Church leadership became a coveted and wealthy position, dominated by monar-
chies, and forming the powerful Institutional Church[A]—absorbed by the Kosmos,
it was another branch of government and a useful instrument of conquest and paci-
fication.[3] The wisdom of Jesus Christ to "turn the other cheek" was replaced by
something more useful to the Kosmos:

> "All national institutions of churches...appear to me no other than
> human inventions, set up to terrify and enslave mankind, and monopo-
> lize power and profit." *Thomas Paine, Political Theorist* [4]

(A) We use the term Institutional Church to mean institutionalism—emphasizing manmade institutions above
the biblical and spiritual character of the Body of Christ. Institutionalism occurs anywhere people begin wor-
shipping the institution of the church. We do not mean to infer that all church institutions are unbiblical.

A RELIGION OF MERIT

At the heart of Institutional Church lies the Religion of Merit. First Century attempts to dilute the meaning of the crucifixion and Grace failed, but with singular determination Satan continued sowing the weeds of Legalism. By the sixth century, Christianity developed into a harsh Religion of Merit woven by complex and esoteric theologies. The leadership was aloof and wealthy. The Institutional Church became the domain of esoteric and ascetic holy men, too complex and irrelevant for the commoner. Legalism lacks spiritual authenticity, as Paul described it:

> They will act as if they are religious, but they will reject the power that could make them godly. You must stay away from people like that. *2 Timothy 3:5*

By the seventh century, it was a simple matter for the armies of Islam to sweep across the former Christian strongholds of Antioch, Carthage and Alexandria. It was not political or military weakness, but rather the weakness of the new religion of the Institutional Church that gave way to Islam in the Middle East. Quite simply, Islam was a better Religion of Merit.[5]

Paul warned how this cancer of weakness would grow in Christianity:

> Learn from us the meaning of the saying, "Do not go beyond what is written." Then you will not take pride in one man over against another. *1 Corinthians 4:6*

None of these developments would occur except that God's Revelation was slowly disregarded and replaced with human wisdom and tradition. Examples abound. Beginning in the second century, a host of new literatures appeared with legalistic and esoteric doctrines.[6] New traditions appeared; Communion became a superstitious and magical rite which strayed far from the simple "Do this in remembrance of me" intention of Jesus.[7]

The Institutional Church was replaying Israel's old problem with God: diluting His Revelation with the traditions of men, as Christ pointed out:

> "Neglecting the commandment of God, you hold to the tradition of men." *Mark 7:8*

Satan has no quarrel with false religion which helps him to accomplish his highest goal: worship of himself in the place of God.[8]

∽ **Satan can seduce Christians into the World System whenever the Traditions of Men overshadow the Word of God.**

Consider this…

Learning, studying and understanding the Bible must always play a central role in Christian fellowship. Otherwise Christians become unstable and easily confused about truth, as Paul warns:

> [The leader's] responsibility is to equip God's people… Then we will no longer be like children, forever changing our minds about what we believe because someone has told us something different or because someone has cleverly lied to us and made the lie sound like the truth. *Ephesians 4:12a, 14a*

When the Religion of Merit grows and the Body of Christ takes on the character of an Institutional Church, the true joy and excitement of Christianity is pushed aside: the life of the Holy Spirit. With that, the excitement of Regeneration passes away, people no longer experience real change, and Christianity becomes a bore:

> Such regulations indeed have an appearance of wisdom, with their self-imposed worship, their false humility and their harsh treatment of the body, but they lack any value in restraining sensual indulgence. *Colossians 2:23*

A DIFFERENT MESSIAH

In the place of God's Spiritual Life, biblical prophecy says a new kind of "religion" will arise on a global scale. It will be a religion of tolerance, palatable to all, and counterfeiting the true "peace among men" available through Jesus Christ.[9]

The mind behind the New Spirituality is actually satanic, according to the Bible. At the heart of Satan's rebellion is the thirst for worship as God, and the time comes when—for a brief moment of history—he gets his worship.

Satan works through the agency of a man he raises up to ultimate power and position as the great savior of the world, one called Antichrist in the Bible.[10] The title does not mean this person is against Christ, but rather he is a counterfeit of Christ, and he comes to anoint the epitome of the Counterfeit Kingdom.

> He will exalt himself and defy every god there is and tear down every object of adoration and worship. He will position himself in the temple of God, claiming that he himself is God. *2 Thessalonians 2:4*

A DIFFERENT SALVATION
∽ Satan also offers 'salvation'—a counterfeit of God's Salvation— promising satisfaction within the Counterfeit Kingdom.

In the same way Jesus came as Savior of the world, and in the same way Jesus proposes to reign at His Second Advent, Antichrist also offers salvation to the world—but a different kind of salvation. He will promise peace and affluence within the Counterfeit Kingdom of this world, while God offers it only within His Kingdom. As the Bible describes it:

> While they are saying, "Peace and safety!" then destruction will come upon them suddenly like labor pains upon a woman with child, and they will not escape. *1 Thessalonians. 5:3* (NASB-U)

This person is also called by another term which describes him from God's perspective:

> There is a great rebellion against God and the man of lawlessness is revealed—the one who brings destruction. *2 Thessalonians 2:3b*

This Man of Lawlessness is also unflatteringly called The Beast. For the first time in history, he captures the loyalty of nations across the globe without firing a shot. The source of his charisma and power is the devil, also called The Dragon in the book of Revelation:

> The whole earth was amazed and followed after the beast; they worshiped the dragon because he gave his authority to the beast; and they worshiped the beast, saying, "Who is like the beast, and who is able to wage war with him?" *Revelation 13:3b-4* (NASB-U)

"The whole earth" is involved; it is not an obscure movement. On the surface, the new religion appears to revolve around Antichrist; but truthfully, it is the authority and power of the devil at the center.[11]

GOD'S RESPONSE

As humanity becomes more spiritually darkened and withdraws from the true Creator God, He responds by giving them their way:

> And just as they did not see fit to acknowledge God any longer, God gave them over to a depraved mind, to do those things which are not proper. *Romans 1:28* (NASB-U)

∾ **God will not always struggle against a heart of rebellion.**

There will come a time when even the Holy Spirit will be withdrawn from His role as a restrainer against the full effects of rebellion. Currently the Holy Spirit is holding back the forces of evil that crave the opportunity to seize all power:

THE NEW SPIRITUALITY The peaceful unification of humanity under the umbrella of a common religion is—for the first time in human history—entirely feasible today. Always, sectarianism and religious fervor has divided cultures. Today, a new religious atmosphere sweeps the globe:

"The god's name is tolerance. Officially sin does not exist in our society, but if there were one sin left it would be a belief in objective truth." *Erwin Lutzer* [12]

Lutzer goes on to describe the rise of Postmodernism that dominates today:

"We have moved from the conviction that everyone has a right to his own opinions to the notion that every opinion is equally right! We have moved from genuine pluralism...to syncretism, the idea that the beliefs of various religious can be mindlessly combined."[13]

> For the mystery of lawlessness is already at work; only he who now restrains will do so until he is taken out of the way.
> *2 Thessalonians 2:7* (NASB-U)

NIMROD'S DREAM

What a sad moment for humanity, because it means that God no longer strives to offer an alternative to Satan's Counterfeit Kingdom. Instead, Satan will be given freedom to establish his Kingdom in all its fullness and to bring in the Ultimate System apart from God—a disastrous condition that God has fiercely resisted for tens of thousands of years, beginning with Nimrod's ancient attempt with the Tower of Babel. At that time, God foresaw the dangerous strength of a humanity united apart from Him:

> The Lord said, "Behold, they are one people, and they all have the same language. And this is what they began to do, and now nothing which they purpose to do will be impossible for them. *Genesis 11:6* (NASB-U)

The Ultimate System will come about, just as Nimrod once dreamed, and erupt into the most violent and catastrophic time known on the face of the earth. Although God steps aside and allows the satanic rebellion free reign, it only survives for a mere seven years before it finally disintegrates into the chaos, destruction and death God always warned would bring about the end of humanity:

> And another angel, a second one, followed, saying, "Fallen, fallen is Babylon the great, she who has made all the nations drink of the wine of the passion of her immorality." *Revelation 14:8* (NASB-U)

✍ **Any kingdom established apart from God will fail.**

Consider this...
This is the eternal truth which at last becomes evident to all creation: any system elevated against the knowledge of God and His Eternal Kingdom will eventually implode by the chaos of rebellion. Only God is trustworthy enough to rule.

THE HOPE

This is when Jesus Christ must return with all the power and authority of a conquering king, and terminate human rule on earth. It comes at an urgent time, He says, because:

> "Unless those days had been cut short, no life would have been saved; but for the sake of the elect those days will be cut short."
> *Matthew 24:22* (NASB-U)

This period is known as the Tribulation Period, but it is not altogether tragic. Israel finds her long-awaited Messiah, Jesus Christ, at this time. Just when Satan's Ultimate System takes shape, Israel becomes increasingly the focus of worldwide conflict. The violence in the Middle East—revolving around Israel herself—draws the entire world into horrific conflict:

> "I will make Jerusalem and Judah like an intoxicating drink to all the nearby nations…On that day I will make Jerusalem a heavy stone, a burden for the world." *Zechariah 12:2-3*

Yahweh will never forget Israel, even though today we live in a period when His protection is partially removed from her. The centuries of inhumane suffering by Jews worldwide was never inaugurated by God, and He is deeply distressed by the suffering of His Chosen People, which the prophets described long ago.

> My grief is beyond healing; my heart is broken. Listen to the weeping of my people; it can be heard all across the land. *Jeremiah 8:18-19a*

The final, dramatic unfolding of God's Mysterious Plan will occur once Israel regains possession of Jerusalem again, and after thousands of years of exile from The Promised Land. God re-gathers the nation and incites the events and conditions which eventually bring about her revolutionary turnaround and embrace of Jesus Christ as King Messiah. Hardened hearts will melt, as the Bible prophesies:

> "My servant David will be their king, and they will have only one shepherd…They will live in the land of Israel where their ancestors lived, the land I gave my servant Jacob…And I will make a covenant of peace with them, an everlasting covenant…I will make my home among them. I will be their God, and they will be my people." *Ezekiel 37:24-28*

Because God has such a great love for His Chosen People, He is determined to return them into His Kingdom Plan. Speaking about Israel, the Bible promises this:

> For the gifts and the calling of God are irrevocable. *Romans 11:29* (NASB)

Israel was once the Chosen People of God—they continue to be His Chosen People, and He will continue to work with them as His Chosen Race.

ᴗ **God's dealings with Israel will demonstrate that He is a God of enduring Grace.**

NEW PROPHETS

God at this time raises prophets in the midst of Israel, following in the pattern of the great Old Testament men of God.[14] These prophets solemnly proclaim Israel must listen and turn to Jesus Christ as their King Messiah. They back up these bold proclamations with miraculous demonstrations of power—just as when God called Israel to repent in the Old Testament.

The combination of world-wide hostilities descending on Israel and the supernatural power of these prophets will stir Israel and cause a massive revival, a spiritual awakening throughout the nation:

> "I will pour out on the house of David and on the inhabitants of Jerusalem, the Spirit of grace and of supplication…"
> *Zechariah 12:10a* (NASB)

This amazing prophecy describes how Israel at that time will recognize the crucified Jesus as their Messiah:

> "…so that they will look on Me whom they have pierced; and they will mourn for Him, as one mourns for an only son, and they will weep bitterly over Him like the bitter weeping over a firstborn."
> *Zechariah 12:10* (NASB)

THE COLLAPSE OF THE COUNTERFEIT

Satan's Counterfeit Kingdom collapses into chaos, as Christ describes it:

> "For those days will be a time of tribulation such as has not occurred since the beginning of the creation which God created until now, and never will." *Mark 13:19* (NASB-U)

This word "tribulation" means literally "horror" because:

> "Nation will rise up against nation, and kingdom against kingdom"
> *Mark 13:8* (NASB-U)

THE TERROR OF WAR

The unity of mankind is not long-lasting, the peace breaks down, and again humanity plunges into wars. However this is the most horrific kind of war because it will be nuclear war. In yet another amazing prophecy describing the end of human government on earth, the Bible says:

MODERN NAIVETÉ It is a naïve and utopian hope that American-style democracy and freedoms will save the world. According to the Bible, humanity will get close to grasping this elusive dream. But then:

"While they are saying, 'Peace and safety!' then destruction will come upon them suddenly…"
1 Thessalonians 5:3 (NASB)

The problem with the human condition is not our style of government or economic standing. Changing the environment or increasing in knowledge will not change the sickness that God says eats away within the human heart: the hatred and overwhelming selfishness that governs our decisions. Humans love to divide against each other—but foremost against God.

Now this will be the plague with which the Lord will strike all the peoples who have gone to war against Jerusalem; their flesh will rot while they stand on their feet, and their eyes will rot in their sockets, and their tongue will rot in their mouth. *Zechariah 14:12* (NASB-U)

All this occurs while they are still "standing on their feet." Never before has it been possible for people to die and disintegrate while still standing on their feet—until we saw the horror of atomic warfare in the cities of Hiroshima and Nagasaki. Isaiah the prophet also describes the horror people experienced in those cities:

They will be terrified, Pains and anguish will take hold of them; They will writhe like a woman in labor, They will look at one another in astonishment, Their faces aflame. *Isaiah 13:8* (NASB-U)

Finally the human race has done it: brought about its own destruction. All the pride and rivalry and hatred that flows from the Principle of Sin will finally come to full harvest. The entire universe will shudder at the enormously self-destructive power of rebellion.

THE RETURN OF THE KING

God will allow free will, even if it results in rebellion; but He will not allow free will to destroy the earth. It is at this moment that Jesus Christ returns in all the Glory and Power of the Messiah King:

"And behold, with the clouds of heaven One like a Son of Man was coming, and He came up to the Ancient of Days and was presented before Him. And to Him was given dominion, Glory and a kingdom, that all the peoples, nations and men of every language might serve Him. His dominion is an everlasting dominion which will not pass away; and His kingdom is one Which will not be destroyed." *Daniel 7:13-14* (NASB-U)

There comes a time when God says, "Enough! No more will man rule this earth!" Authority and power will be taken away from the offspring of Adam and Eve. The Counterfeit Kingdom will end.

The advent of God's Kingdom is pronounced by the rule of a great and loving King Messiah:

And they will hammer their swords into plowshares and their spears into pruning hooks. Nation will not lift up sword against nation, And never again will they learn war. *Isaiah 2:4* (NASB-U)

THE MILLENNIAL KINGDOM

When King Messiah returns to earth to rule, the Bible says Satan is kept from meddling with Planet Earth for 1,000 years, a period known as the Millennial Kingdom of Christ. Mortal humans will populate this earth during His reign: survivors and believers spared from the destruction of the Great Tribulation.

The Millennial Kingdom of Christ will be a time of phenomenal advances as humanity leaves behind the destruction of war and bloodshed. The awesome capacity for accomplishment that lies latent within a united humanity will finally be unleashed, as God proclaimed was possible at the dawn of human history:

> The Lord said, "Behold, they are one people…and now nothing which they purpose to do will be impossible for them." *Genesis 11:6* (NASB-U)

> ∽ **Under Nimrod's rule, unified humanity was a threat; under Christ's rule, it will unleash boundless potential.**

It is impossible to imagine the exponential growth of our technologies and creativity under such a paradigm of consolidation and harmony by Christ's rule. Even the most imaginative science fiction falls short of what Christ will accomplish as the Eternal Plan of God is finally fulfilled:

> I heard a loud shout from the throne, saying, "Look, the home of God is now among his people! He will live with them, and they will be his people. God himself will be with them. *Revelation 21:3*

FINAL REBELLION AND JUDGMENT

The Millennial Kingdom of Christ will draw to a close when Satan is finally released, and he makes one last, desperate bid to seize power from Jesus Christ. Some of those living in the Millennial Kingdom of Christ will be caught up in his rebellion again—the offspring of the original inhabitants of the kingdom.

This final rebellion proves the heart of rebellion is not tied to environmental disadvantages. All those caught up in the last rebellion will have lived in the most pristine environment imaginable. Rather, rebellion emanates from a cold-hearted decision to turn away from the rule of God.

At this time God enters into the final judgment, known as the Great White Throne Judgment. The opportunity for amnesty is gone: here people approach God based on their deeds. All approaching the Great White Throne are those who rejected His Grace.

The deeds of unbelievers may be good or bad, but they are still from the Tree of the Knowledge of Good and Evil, which means Spiritual Death. No deeds are good enough for God to accept, just as no deeds are evil enough that Christ's death is inadequate payment for them. The issue has always been eternal life or eternal death, not good deeds or bad deeds.

THE NEW HEAVENS AND THE NEW EARTH

Jesus will vanquish every enemy, and the purpose of the millennial kingdom will then be fulfilled, since all of history ends at the feet of Jesus:

After that the end will come, when he will turn the Kingdom over to God the Father, having put down all enemies of every kind. *1 Corinthians 15:24*

At this time His authority will be established by virtue of the wisdom of His Eternal Plan:

So that at the name of Jesus every knee will bow, in heaven and on earth and under the earth, and every tongue will confess that Jesus Christ is Lord, to the glory of God the Father. *Philippians 2:10-11*

This marks the beginnings of everything new; and God literally erases the old way:

But the day of the Lord will come as unexpectedly as a thief. Then the heavens will pass away with a terrible noise, and everything in them will disappear in fire… *2 Peter 3:1*

God's Incredible Plan has come full circle—Eternity Future has begun. In Eternity Past, God's will was challenged by Satan as he rebelled against God. God solved the problem of the Rebellion with His Redemptive Plan.

OUR HEAVENLY HOME

"And I saw a new heaven and a new earth…and He who sits on the throne said, I am making all things new!" *Revelation 21:1a, 5a*

DESCRIBING HEAVEN Revelation 21 and 22 glowingly describe the vast riches of our future inheritance. In a vision from God, the apostle John saw the amazing splendor of our eternal home. It will be far more than anyone can experience here; more than we can presently comprehend.

Paul affirmed this when he "was caught up to the third heaven" and heard "inexpressible things, things that man is not permitted to tell." *2 Corinthians 12:2-4.* It was more glorious than he was able to express. He assures us "no eye has seen, no ear has heard, no mind has conceived what God has prepared for those who love Him." 1 Corinthians 2:9

What makes our future life in the New Heaven and New Earth so glorious is the reality of enjoying forever the personal presence of our Lord and Savior. As He promised His disciples, "I go to prepare a place for you … I will receive you unto Myself; that where I am there you will be also." *John 14:3*

Many of the welcome changes in our new home involve our personhood: there will be no pain, no sadness, no death, no hunger, or thirst. These negatives describe the sad aspects of life here on this rebellious planet. In contrast, our every hope and expectation will be fulfilled in the New Heaven and Earth to a greater extent than we have the capacity to understand. Our transformed body and personality will reflect God's creation of us in His image, as we will grow increasingly like Him throughout eternity.

In heaven, we will be able to express our creativity and productivity using our God-given abilities fully and unhindered. Our capacity for knowledge will be expanded and each person will fulfill the inheritance God has given us. This new life includes the privilege of reigning with Christ (Revelation 22:5) as we execute His decrees, participating with Him, always as His servants.

It will be fundamentally different from our present, space-time environment.

There will be no Tabernacle or special place to worship God:

> No temple could be seen in the city, for the Lord God Almighty and the Lamb are its temple. *Revelation 21:22*

The personal presence of God among us will fulfill His eternal plan and fulfill our desire for a close personal relationship with Him.

There is a beautiful river of life flowing from the throne of God and on either side the Tree of Life bearing fruit. This is reminiscent of the Tree of Life in the Garden of Eden, representing eternal life, which God did not allow Adam and Eve to eat after they sinned by disobeying Him:

> And the angel showed me a pure river with the water of life, clear as crystal, flowing from the throne of God and of the Lamb, coursing down the center of the main street. On each side of the river grew a tree of life...The leaves were used for medicine to heal the nations. *Revelation 22:1-2*

Heaven will be filled with the worship of God as we spontaneously join the angels around His throne to Praise Him for Who He is and what He has done for us:

> No longer will anything be cursed. For the throne of God and of the Lamb will be there, and his servants will worship him. *Revelation 22:3*

GOD'S ETERNAL KINGDOM

In Eternity Future, we will be God's family, the fulfillment of God's purpose—a picture of His great workmanship. As believers, we have a future that is real. New Earth is an objective place created of real matter. We will have an eternal resurrection body, not an ethereal ghost-like spirit. Our bodies will be perfect like Jesus' resurrection body, and we will be distinct individuals, actively involved in God's Kingdom.

God's Incredible Plan has come full circle. Will Earth change? Yes. Will the heavens change? Yes. Will the present Jerusalem change? Yes. Will we change? Yes, in the twinkling of an eye. God will dwell corporately, and we will function as one with Him. We will live on Earth forever in the perfect will of our Heavenly Father who has loved us from the beginning:

> The Spirit and the bride say, "Come." Let each one who hears them say, "Come." Let the thirsty ones come—anyone who wants to. Let them come and drink the water of life without charge. *Revelation 22:17*

TWO WAYS TO GOD

The two ways to God have sometimes been called "Plan A and Plan B." Plan A is our way of approaching God. Plan B is Grace: God's gracious provision for our sinful condition.

PLAN A

To make it clear what God expected of us in order to come into His presence, He gave us The Law. It was given in three basic forms:

- The Law of Moral Consciousness (Romans 1:19);
- The Law of Moses—God's value system entrusted to the nations of Israel (Exodus 20);
- The Law of Christ. This is where Christ interprets the Law of Moses from God's view: the motives and attitudes of our heart (Matthew 5-7).

Typically, we have one of the following responses to these revelations of God's Law:

OPEN MORAL REBELLION

This is a response of unbelief, not an intellectual problem with the existence of God. If a person admits God is there and the Bible is His Revelation to us, then that person's life is affected in substantial ways. Such a person can no longer live as he pleases and be his own god. Instead, he lives in rebellion against God, a vain attempt to deny His existence.

HUMAN RIGHTEOUSNESS

In this response, a person concentrates on being "better" than other people. Instead of focusing vertically on God and His perfect standards of Righteousness, this person compares himself with others on a horizontal plane (usually with those more sinful). This person feels he is just being "human." He incorrectly assumes he is "doing the best he can," and God will accept him on that basis.

LEGALISM: A RELIGION OF MERIT

Another response is found among those who believe they can keep God's Law. They base their approach to God on a Religion of Merit. They select the "keep-able" laws, and then build traditions and doctrines on those laws they have chosen to keep. For instance, the Jews of Jesus' day chose to keep the Sabbath holy; to which they added more than 600 rules on how to keep the Sabbath holy. The usual pattern is for people to become exclusive and self-righteous.

REPENTANCE

This is the response God desires from each one of us: He wants us to turn to Him and accept His gift of forgiveness and eternal life. To repent is to:

- acknowledge our inability to keep God's perfect law;
- drop our rebellion against God;
- admit the delusion of the Religion of Merit we have devised;
- recognize our own sin;
- trust God to do what we cannot do for ourselves.

Now we are candidates for Plan B, an approach to God on the basis of God's Grace.

PLAN B

Plan B is simple compared to Plan A. We must trust God and depend on His Grace. Grace is God's unconditional, unlimited Love poured out on those who do not deserve it and cannot earn it. We experience God's Grace by faith, a believing attitude of our will:

> God saved you by His special favor (Grace) when you believed. And, you can't take credit for this, it is a gift from God. *Ephesians. 2:8* (NLT)

God's character makes it necessary for us to approach Him under Plan B rather than Plan A. God is perfect, or righteous, and only those who are perfect can be in God's Presence. Therefore, God's wonderful provision for our sinful condition was to place all our sins on Christ—the perfect substitute—He took the judgment we deserved and became our Savior.

Under Plan B, our acceptance into God's presence is based on what Christ did on the Cross:

> For God made Christ, who never sinned, to be the offering for our sin, so that we could be made right with God through Christ.
> *2 Corinthians. 5:21* (NLT)

Our acceptance by God and eternal life are gifts of God's Grace, which we receive by believing in Jesus Christ:

> But to all who believed in Christ and accepted Him, he gave the right to become children of God. *John 1:12* (NLT)

To receive Eternal Life by Grace through faith in Christ is wonderful. It is the greatest discovery we can make, to understand the Creator God has an Incredible Plan for the universe, and He invites us to be active participants in it.

But our greatest joy comes when we discover this same Creator God has a purpose and plan for each of our individual lives, and we experience His love daily in a personal relationship with Him.

From the very beginning God loved us and desired that we respond to His seeking love and fellowship with Him. This is His Eternal Purpose, which is stated all through the Bible:

> I will live in them and walk among them. I will be their God and they will be my people. *2 Corinthians 6:16*

We as believers become the fulfillment of God's purpose: We are God's family. We will inherit the New Earth in Eternity Future, living forever in perfect accord with God's will.

ENDNOTES

CHAPTER 1

1 D. H. Lawrence (1885-1930), British author. "Introduction to The Dragon of the Apocalypse by Frederick Carter," in London Mercury (July 1930, repr. in Phoenix: The Posthumous Papers of D. H. Lawrence, pt. 4, ed. by E. McDonald, 1936) in *Columbia Dict. of Quotations.*

2 See Matthew 10:30: "...but the very hairs of your head are all numbered..."

3 "The most significant biblical evidence for the uniqueness of life on the earth is the incarnation and Second Coming of Jesus Christ." Donald B. DeYoung and John C. Whitcomb, *The Origin of the Universe,* p. 159. Additionally, Revelation 21:3 clearly states that God's throne is established among humanity.

4 See 1 John 4:8.

5 In Matthew 22:30, we find that angels do not marry, and have no children. The number of angels was fixed when God first created them. Also, in Job 38:4-7 angels were all created before the material universe. They witnessed God creating the material universe and "shouted for joy" and "sang together" watching the spectacle.

6 In Ephesians 6:12, it describes how angelic beings are well-organized, led by a hierarchy of "rulers," "world-rulers", and "princes."

7 Psalm 103:20 describes angels as "mighty creatures who carry out His plans..."

8 See Ephesians 1:21 where Paul describes both visible and invisible dominions.

9 See Revelation 5:11; ìôñéÜò is properly translated "myriad," which means "a countless or extremely great number." (OED).

10 In many recorded instances found in the Bible, angels have a most powerful impact on someone who meets it: "When he came I was frightened and fell on my face..." Daniel 8:17b (NASB).

11 Hebrews 2:7 says that man is made, for now, "lower than the angels." Whenever one of these creatures makes an appearance in history, observers are struck by their brilliance and beauty.

12 el Shaddai is a common title for God, used 48 times in the Old Testament, and translated "God Almighty." It means He is sovereign, all-powerful and self-sufficient qualities found in nobody else in the universe. Yet He grants this ability to others, "to make meaningful decisions, especially concerning their relationship to God. Because humanity was created in the image of God, freedom is an inherent part of human nature (Genesis 1:26)... Salvation and obedience are left to mankind's free will (Romans 10:12-13)." From Human Free Will in. See also "Further Consideration: God's Sovereignty and Human Choice" in Chapter 2.

13 Angels are called "sons of God" in Genesis 6:2, 4; Job 1:6; 2:1; 38:7. In the New Testament "sons of God" is used exclusively for humans in anticipation of God's intention for humanity: Matthew 5:9; 20:36; Romans 8:14, 19; Galatians 3:26.

14 Modern Pantheism is found in movements such as New Age, Post-New Age, and modern esotericism. These share "a religious perspective that is based on the acquisition of mystical knowledge." See New Age movement in *Britannica, Encyclopedia Britannica.*

15 Intuition in its philosophical denotation was coined by the Spanish mystic Benedict Spinoza, "in which it refers to supposedly concrete knowledge of the world as an interconnected whole, as contrasted with the piece-

meal, 'abstract' knowledge obtained by science and observation." See Intuition in ibid. This is essentially "20th century mysticism ('the treasure hidden in the centres of our souls')." See Mysticism in ibid.

16 From Hinduism in ibid.. "Indian philosophers do not seek to justify religious faith…theory itself, as theory, is regarded as being supremely worthy and efficacious." It is a "significant fact that Indian philosophers have not developed formal logic." (ibid.) Antinomies are common, as per Adolf Lasson: "Rationalism cannot conduct us to the essence of things; we therefore need intellectual vision." (Emphasis added) (ibid).

17 Tertulian quoted in Clark Pinnock, *Faith and Reason*, p. 303.

18 In contrast to the Bible's forensic evidential approach, the Islamic Qur'an offers an arcane substantiation very difficult to quantify, standing on the words and style of the Qur'an, which contain an "internal self-evidencing power" that "itself is a miracle and cannot be imitated by man." See Scripture in *Britannica*.

19 ibid., p. iii.

20 ibid., p.35.

21 Michael P. Green, *The Empty Cross of Jesus*, p.97 "The appearances of the (resurrected) Jesus are as well authenticated as anything in antiquity." (ibid.) "Taking all the evidence together, it is not too much to say that there is no (ancient) historic incident better or more variously reported than the resurrection of Christ. Nothing but the…assumption that it must be false could…suggest the idea of deficiency in the proof of it." Paul Little, *Know Why You Believe*, p. 30. We offer extensive evidence for the resurrection of Christ in chapter 16 which substantiate such views.

22 Gleason L. Archer, Jr., *Old Testament History and Recent Archeology*, p.5.

23 "In the case of Nostradamus, it is intimated that he purposely obscured the revelations for obvious reasons." Arnold D. Ehlert, *Book Review: The Complete Prophecies of Nostradamus*, p.503. Nostradamus was avoiding the Catholic Inquisitors with his obscurity, and it is surprising, that modern interpreters writing almost 500 years later are unfettered by Nostradamus' obscurity. Among other modern phenomena, "We find Mussolini (pp. 13, 33), Roosevelt (p. 42), Hitler (p. 41), and even Gen. Mark Clark depicted with clarity." (ibid.)

24 J. Barton Payne, *Encyclopedia of Biblical Prophecy*, p. 680-1.

25 Dennis McCallum, *Christianity: The Faith That Makes Sense*, p.107.

26 ibid., p.108.

27 Ravi Zacharius, *Jesus Among Other Gods*, p. 4.

28 Sir Frederic Kenyon, p.288. He adds: "The interval then between the dates of original composition and the earliest extant evidence becomes so small as to be in fact negligible."

29 Norman Geizler and Nix, *From God to Man*, p.139.

30 William Sanford LaSor, *Expositor's*.

31 Howard F. Voss, *Unger's*.

32 Kenyon, p.288.

33 See especially McDowell, or Geizler and Nix.

CHAPTER 2

1 Isaiah 14:12-14 calls him the "Son of the Dawn."

2 Lucifer is called the "anointed cherub who covers" the throne of God (Ezekiel 29:11-17), meaning he "covered" or "protected" the throne of God. He stood next to God Himself, at the center of the universe.

3 See 2 Corinthians 11:14, where Paul warns "For even Satan disguises himself as an angel of light."

4 "There are myriad approaches to both prayer and meditation. No way is the right way . . . The real thing is the actual experience of God." John Bradshaw, *Bradshaw On: The Family*, p. 234, 235.

5 Donald Grey Barnhouse, p. 41.

6 See Genesis 3 where Satan tells Eve "You surely shall not die!" Clearly, his tactic rests on calling God a liar. In the same way, God calls Satan "a liar and the father of lies" in John 8:44.

7 In Revelation 12:3, 4 and 7, the "dragon" identified as "that serpent of old, the devil" sweeps up "a third of the stars." The "stars" refers angels (Isaiah 24:21).

8 See Matthew 8:31; 10:1; Revelation12:7.

9 Neale Donald Walsh, *Conversations With God.*

10 Donald Grey Barnhouse, *The Invisible War,* p. 64.

11 See Revelation 12:9.

12 R.T Forster and V.P. Marston, *God's Strategy in Human History,* p. 8.

13 Donald Grey Barnhouse, *The Invisible War,* p. 51.

14 See 1 Peter 1:20.

15 R.T Forster and V.P. Marston, *God's Strategy in Human History,* p. 80.

16 "If a man does not keep pace with his companions, perhaps it is because he hears a different drummer. Let him step to the music which he hears, however measured or far away." Henry David Thoreau, *Walden* (1854) *Columbia Dictionary of Quotations.*

CHAPTER 3

1 See Ephesians 1.

2 Excerpted from *American Heritage Dictionary.*

3 See 1 Peter 1:12b where Peter is discussing God's interaction with humanity: "…It is all so wonderful that even the angels are eagerly watching these things happen."

4 Among the more erroneous interpretations of Genesis 1 is the so-called "Young Earth" theory discussed in Further Consideration.

5 "Dr. J. E. Orr, who has earned degrees in both science and theology, indicates that 'the conflict appears to be between debatable theories of some scientists and doubtful interpretations of some expositors rather than a conflict between the facts of science and the text of scriptures, between which there appears to be a very remarkable harmony.'" L. Duane Thurman, *How to Think about Evolution,* p. 37.

6 A "Religion" is "the belief in and worship of a superhuman controlling power" (OED) and Naturalism certainly extols natural processes beyond scientifically-verifiable limits. For example, "Statistically, Murray Eden of MIT has insisted that it is impossible that the universe and its complexity were produced by pure chance out of chaos in any amount of time that has so far been suggested." For a thorough treatment of these statistical problems, see James F. Coppedge, *Evolution.*

7 Francis A. Schaeffer, *No Final Conflict,* p. 35.

8 "or, a waste and emptiness." See Genesis 1:2 margin in *NASB Study Bible.*

9 For example, "The probability of a protein molecule resulting from a chance arrangement of amino acids is 1 in 10287…and the probability that one protein might occur by random action during the entire history of the earth is less than 1 in 10252…For a minimum set of the required 239 protein molecules for the smallest theoretical life, the probability is 1 in 10119879." James F. Coppedge, *Evolution,* p.114. Dr. Coppedge reprinted his book in 1993.

10 ibid., p. 95.

11 See side margin notes for Genesis 1:2 in *NASB Study Bible.*

12 See Donald B. DeYoung and John C. Whitcomb, *The Origin of the Universe* p. 149-62. They argue from the

Scriptures that the earth is indeed the centerpiece of God's focus.

13 See Genesis 1:4, 10, 12, 18, 21, 25 and 31.

14 See the marginal notes for Genesis 2:7 in NASB Study Bible where it notes that the Hebrew word "nephesh" is literally soul.

15 Lord Byron (1788–1824), English poet. Letter, 11 April 1817, to the poet Thomas Moore (published in Byron's Letters and Journals, vol. 5, ed. by Leslie A. Marchand, 1973–81) in *Columbia Dictionary of Quotations*.

16 "For when the dead rise, they won't be married. They will be like the angels in heaven." (Mark 12:25) The celibacy of angels is repeated in Matthew 22:30 and Luke 20:35.

17 See Genesis 2:9-10 (NLT).

18 See Genesis 2:22 (NLT).

19 "Her name is 'woman' because she was taken out of a man" because "the Hebrew for woman sounds like the Hebrew for man." (See Genesis 2:23 side margin in NASB Study Bible.)

20 See Genesis 3:8 (NASB).

21 Donald Grey Barnhouse, *Invisible War,* p. 41.

22 ibid., p.29.

23 ibid., p.41.

24 D. H. Lawrence (1885–1930), British author. Letter, 4 Sept. 1913 (published in *The Letters of D. H. Lawrence,* vol. 2, ed. by George J. Zytaruk and James T. Boulton, 1981) in *Columbia Dictionary of Quotations.* He goes on to say about marriage, "I wish to add that my state of bliss is by no means perfect."

25 See 1 Corinthians 1:27.

26 C. S. Lewis, *Weight of Glory,* p.13.

27 See Psalm 8:5-6.

28 "In the 1960s the Creation Research Society promoted the theory of young-earth creationism, relying on catastrophism, the doctrine that large-scale changes in the earth's crust are explained by violent, unrepeatable geologic events, such as the biblical flood. The theory eventually became called scientific creationism or creation science." See Creation Research Society in Microsoft, Encarta.

29 See Usher in ibid.

30 Francis A. Schaeffer, *No Final Conflict,* p. 40, 23.

31 ibid., p. 34.

32 Michael J. Behe, *Darwin's Black Box,* p. x (Preface).

33 Francis Crick, *Life Itself.* Crick later hypothesized that life through DNA was only possible if perhaps it was planted here by extraterrestrial travelers.

34 L. Duane Thurman, *How to Think about Evolution,* p. 76.

35 After demonstrating the statistical impossibility of the spontaneous assembly of proteins (see above), Dr. Coppedge quotes Joseph Louis Comte Lagrange: "If the probability of an event is infinitely slight, it is equivalent to the practical impossibility of happening within certain time limits." James F. Coppedge, *Evolution.*

36 Paleontologist G. G. Simpson, cited in L. Duane Thurman, *How to Think about Evolution,* p. 103. The absence of a fossil record supporting the smooth evolutionary transitions erroneously depicted in textbooks has led Simpson among other scientists to postulate a theory called "Punctuated Equilibrium" in which millions of years of stasis is followed by episodes of rapid evolution. This well-known aspect of the fossil record coincides well with the Genesis 1 account.

CHAPTER 4

1 T. Austin-Sparks, *What is Man?*, p. 87.

2 See 1 Timothy 3:6, 7.

3 Erica Jong (b. 1942), U.S. author. *How to Save Your Own Life* (1977) in *Columbia Dictionary of Quotations*.

4 R.T Forster and V.P. Marston, *God's Strategy in Human History*, p. 46.

5 The most common and general Greek word used for sin is hamartia, which means "to miss the mark," and commonly carries the idea of making a mistake or failing to meet a goal. The Hebrew Old Testament used almost 40 different words translated "sin," but they all share the concept of "deviation from the right way." See hamartia in *Dictionary of New Testament Theology.*

6 It is alarming to see how divergent our view of death is from God's. In our parlance, somebody is "living it up," while God sees living death. For example, "But she who gives herself to wanton pleasure is dead even while she lives." 1 Timothy 5:6 (NASB-U).

7 Susan Sontag (b. 1933), U.S. essayist. Illness As Metaphor, ch. 7 (1978) in *Columbia Dictionary of Quotations*

8 See Hebrews 2:14 (NASB).

9 F. Scott Fitzgerald (1896–1940), U.S. author. John, in *The Diamond as Big as the Ritz,* ch. 11 (1922), uttered before falling asleep, in ibid.

10 See Colossians 1:21 (NIV) and Ephesians 2:1.

11 In Matthew 6:7, Jesus describes the meaninglessness of chants: "When you pray, don't babble on and on as people of other religions do. They think their prayers are answered only by repeating their words again and again."

12 See See 2 Corinthians 11:14-15 (NASB).

13 Sartre, *Last Interview with Jean Paul Sartre,* page 39. Sarte admits this sense of a creator is entirely inconsistent with his atheistic world view: "Naturally this is not a clear, exact idea that I set in motion every time I think of myself. It contradicts many of my other ideas; but it is there, floating vaguely."

14 "Therefore we do not lose heart, but though our outer man is decaying, yet our inner man is being renewed day by day." (2 Corinthians 4:16 NASB-U).

15 See Jessie Penn Lewis, *Soul and Spirit,* p. 4.

16 See Genesis 2:7 and 2 Corinthians 4:7. "'Earthen' or 'clay' jars, as opposed to bronze ones, were readily discarded; because clay was always available, such containers were cheap and disposable if they were broken or incurred ceremonial impurity—an odd container for a rich treasure." See 2 Corinthians 4:7 in "The New Testament World: A Chronology" in *Bible Background Commentary: New Testament.*

17 The indwelling presence of God is only promised to humans, never to the angels: "Now the dwelling of God is with men, and he will live with them." (Revelation 21:3 NIV) Angels are God's messengers, helpers, workers and they sing His praises; but they are not His co-rulers: "and if children, heirs also, heirs of God and fellow heirs with Christ." (Romans 8:17a NASB-U).

18 "The man without the Spirit does not accept the things that come from the Spirit of God, for they are foolishness to him, and he cannot understand them, because they are spiritually discerned." (1 Corinthians 2:14 NIV).

19 Blum, *BibSac* Jan-Mar 1981, p. 57.

20 See Psalm 8:4-6.

CHAPTER 5

1 George Bernard Shaw (1856–1950), Anglo-Irish playwright, critic. Letter, 19 Aug. 1909 to dramatist and patron Lady Gregory (published in Collected Letters, vol. 2, 1972) in *Columbia Dictionary of Quotations*.

2 Albert Camus (1913–60), French-Algerian philosopher, author. *Notebooks*, vol. 3 (1966), entry for 7 Sept. 1939. in ibid.

3 See Genesis 4:9.

4 God punished Cain by forcing him into a nomadic lifestyle, and Cain complains to God, "Behold, You have driven me this day from the face of the ground; and from Your face I will be hidden, and I will be a vagrant and a wanderer on the earth, and whoever finds me will kill me." Genesis 4:14 (NASB-U). Clearly God was protecting the rest of Adam's household by driving Cain away, and this posed a very real threat to his life should he run across any of his relatives. Cain chose to interpret God's wise move as a personal rejection, something God never said and clearly never intended because God responds by offering Cain protection in verse 15. Truthfully, Cain not only walked away from Adam's household that day, he also walked away from God.

5 See Lamech in *Holman*.

6 See kosmos in *Dictionary of New Testament Theology*.

7 "Heart of Darkness" (1902) by Joseph Conrad. "His book conjured up an atmosphere of foreboding, treachery, greed, and exploitation" where "Conrad's narrator, Marlow, again leads his listeners into the shadowy recesses of the human heart, with its forever unresolved and unpredictable capacities for good and evil." See Tragedy- Neoclassical in *Encyclopedia Britannica*.

8 See Seth in *Holman Bible Dictionary*.

9 See Genesis 5:22, which only briefly describes Enoch as one who "lived…in close fellowship with the Lord." We know so little of this amazing character, but his life was so intimately tied with God, that he "was taken up to heaven without dying—'suddenly he disappeared because God took him.' But before he was taken up, he was approved as pleasing to God." (Hebrews 11:5).

10 Bertrand Russell [Earl] (1872–1970), British philosopher, mathematician. Power, ch. 1, "The Impulse to Power" (1938) in *Columbia Dictionary of Quotations*.

11 The record of Seth and his line is deeply significant to the central theme of the Bible. "In such narratives as these, the author clearly betrays his interest in the "seed" (Genesis 3:15) of the woman. Chapter 5 shows just how seriously the author takes the promise in 3:15. The focus is on the 'seed' and the one who will crush the head of the snake. A pattern is established in chapter 4 that will remain the thematic center of the book." See Genesis 4:25 in *Expositor's*.

12 See Genesis 7:16, which delivers an ominous note of surrounding the Ark. When Noah and his family "entered as God had commanded him; and the Lord closed it behind him." (NASB-U) The end of all opportunity was suddenly gone, the door was sealed shut, and the opportunity for free choice was finished. Christ describes this in Luke 17:27, warning that opportunity to decide is not exhaustive: no decision is a decision.

13 The rainbow in Genesis 9:13 was part of a promise God gave not to destroy mankind this way again. It was not necessarily the first rainbow ever seen by man, but rather a symbol God used to make His point: "the rainbow would serve as a continuing pledge that the earth would not be flooded again." See Genesis 9:13 in Walter C. Kaiser and Peter H. Davids, et al., *Hard Sayings of the Bible*.

14 See Luke 17:22-27, where Christ describes how people vested heavily in the Kosmos will be living in ignorant bliss, just like Noah's day, "before the flood, the people enjoyed banquets and parties and weddings right up to the time Noah entered his boat and the flood came to destroy them all." (Luke 17:27).

15 See Genesis 10:11. Archeology substantiates this passage by showing that Nineveh was first colonized by Babylonians as the Bible claims. See "Assyria" in *Unger's*.

16 See Daniel 4:30; Revelation 14:8; 16:19; 17:5; 18:2, 21. Babel means "gate of the god," and Genesis 11

makes an obvious play on words: "What they designed as "a gate of god" (ba„bel)12(12) was from God's perspective "confusion" (ba„lal)" Curtis, "Interpreting Jacob's Encounter At Peniel," JETS June 1987, p. 129-37.

17 "A recently discovered Sumerian tablet also tells for the first time from an extrabiblical perspective the story of a time when all languages were one on the earth." See Genesis 11:9 in Walter C. Kaiser and Peter H. Davids, et al., *Hard Sayings of the Bible.*

18 Some archeologists think Nimrod's tower most likely functioned as an astrological observatory: "The typical Mesopotamian temple-tower, known as a ziggurat, was square at the base and had sloping, stepped sides that led upward to a small shrine at the top." See Genesis 11:4 in *NASB Study Bible.*

19 A Contribution to the Critique of Hegel's Philosophy of Right, Preface (1844) in *Columbia Dictionary of Quotations.*

20 "The tower of Babel was most likely a ziggurat, a common structure in Babylonia at this time. Most often built as temples, ziggurats looked like pyramids with steps or ramps leading up the sides. Ziggurats stood as high as 300 feet and were often just as wide; thus they were the focal point of the city. The people in this story built their tower as a monument to their own greatness, something for the whole world to see." See Genesis 11:3 in LAN.

21 ibid., Prolog:XIV.

22 Francis A. Schaeffer, *No Final Conflict,* p. 23.

23 ibid., p. 45.

24 Archer points out that even the imminent liberal scholar Hans Albright concluded the Flood was "so widespread as to be found all over the world, even in pre-Columbian South America." Although Albright still viewed the biblical account with suspicion, he concluded such a global knowledge of the flood "finds a most reasonable explanation in some catastrophic event which took place at the close of the Glacial Period in Pleistocene times." Archer, Jr, "Old Testament History and Recent Archeology," *BibSac* Jan-Mar 1970, p. 13.

25 See Genesis 6 in Walter C. Kaiser and Peter H. Davids, et al., *Hard Sayings of the Bible.*

CHAPTER 6

1 Ur is a historic city situated just south of ancient Babel that has been extensively excavated since 1852, so that "As a result of archaeological excavation, the city of Ur is now one of the best-known sites of southern Babylonia." See Ur in *Unger's.*

2 See Joshua 24:2, where "…Terah, the father of Abraham…served other gods." (NASB-U) Interestingly, "Terah's name may be derived from a Hebrew word meaning 'moon.' The moon was the patron deity of Ur." See Joshua 24:2 in *Expositor's.* "…the prevailing religion was utterly polytheistic." ibid.

3 ibid.

4 See labe in Eugene H. Merrill, TWOT.

5 Merrill, "Ebla and Biblical Historical Inerrancy," *BibSac* Oct 83, p. 306.

6 In Genesis 12:6 Abram first sacrificed at "the great tree of Moreh at Shechem." (NIV). The tree is mentioned because "a large tree was often a conspicuous feature at such holy places. But Abram worshiped the Lord there, not the local deity." See Genesis 12:6 in *NASB Study Bible.*

7 See 2 Corinthians 6:16.

8 See James 2:23.

9 See Genesis 21:18.

10 See Hebrews 11:19: "Abraham assumed that if Isaac died, God was able to bring him back to life again. And in a sense, Abraham did receive his son back from the dead."

11 Mount Moriah is, "The rocky outcropping in Jerusalem located just north of the ancient city of David." See Mount Moriah in *Holman*.

12 For an excellent summary of liberal views, see Witmer, "Periodical Reviews: Wellhausenism Evaluated after a Century of Influence," BibSac Oct–Dec 1979, p. 78–95.

13 Ebla consists of over 15,000 clay tablets, many of which are still not translated, mostly documents of trade and commerce for the area. Harrison, "Ebla" in *The New Unger's Bible Dictionary*.

14 Merrill, "Ebla and Biblical Historical Inerrancy," *BibSac* Oct 83, p. 310. Merrill adds: "Just before this startling revelation had been publicized John Van Seters and Thomas L. Thompson had independently published their position in regard to Genesis 14. They maintained that the chapter was totally untrustworthy as history and in fact was written 1,000 years after Moses."

15 Quite often these supposed historical inaccuracies are identified only because there are no external corroborative evidences: "The assumption is that unless a person, place, or event in early Israel's history can be validated by extrabiblical documentation it must be unhistorical. The fallacy in such method ought to be obvious for if this principle were applied to all of ancient (and even modern) history virtually nothing could be recovered from the past in the name of history." ibid., p. 311.

16 Nelson Glueck, *Rivers in the Desert*, p. 31.

17 See Genesis 25:26 and Jacob in ibid.

18 "Both by temperament and no doubt by training as well Jacob seems to have been an independent and self-sufficient individual. He clearly was not unaware of God and of his need for God's help, but he basically lived by the principle that God helps those who help themselves." Curtis, "Interpreting Jacob's Encounter At Peniel," JETS June 1987, p. 129-37.

19 The story of Jacob wrestling with the angel in Genesis 32:26 is certainly "one of the most enigmatic incidents in all of Scripture...The struggle between the two men continued, and when the man saw that he could not prevail against Jacob he caused Jacob's thigh to be thrown out of socket. It seems probable that this was the point at which Jacob realized that his adversary was more than an ordinary 'man.' One wonders if Jacob's determination in the struggle did not take a different direction at this point as he realized that his adversary was in fact God himself." ibid., p. 130.

20 See Israel in *Unger's*.

21 Curtis, "Interpreting Jacob's Encounter At Peniel," JETS June 1987, p. 131.

22 ibid., p. 135.

23 See Romans 3:1, 2.

24 See Luke 24:44.

25 See Genesis 3:15.

26 See Genesis 12:3.

27 "The scepter will not depart from Judah...until the coming of the one to whom it belongs, the one whom all nations will obey." (Genesis 49:10) Also, to King David God says, "Your dynasty and your kingdom will continue for all time before me, and your throne will be secure forever." (2 Samuel 7:16) This Davidic Covenant is restated often (see Psalm 89:3-4, 34-47; Isaiah 9:7 and 16:5; Jeremiah 23:5; 30:8-9; 33:14-17, 20-22, 25-26; Ezekiel 37:24-25; Hosea 3:4-5; Amos 9:11; Luke 1:33—and more). It is impossible to read the Old Testament without receiving a clear picture that God intends to rule through mankind, specifically through Judah and David's lineage, in the person of King Messiah.

28 "God chose him for this purpose long before the world began, but now in these final days, he was sent to the earth for all to see. And he did this for you...and gave him great glory, [so] your faith and hope can be placed confidently in God." (1 Peter 1:20-21).

29 "For at the right time Christ will be revealed from heaven by the blessed and only almighty God, the King of kings and Lord of lords." (1 Timothy 6:15).

30 See Revelation 12:1-6, where Satan is relentlessly hounding Israel: "the context seems to refer to the emerging nation of Israel in its suffering prior to the second coming of Christ. This is further supported by the verses which follow." See Revelations 12:1-2 in John F. Walvoord, *BKC-New Testament.*

CHAPTER 7

1 "It was not long after the expulsion of the Hyksos that a general antiforeign feeling developed against the inoffensive Hebrews." Archer, Jr, "Old Testament History and Recent Archeology," *BibSac* Jan-Mar 1970, p. 25.

2 Ibid, p.24. See also Exodus 12:37, where the men are numbered at "about 600,000," but the Exodus includes "many people who were not Israelites" but were believers who "may have been Egyptians and others who were drawn to the Hebrews by God's mighty works and who decided to leave Egypt with them." See Exodus12:37 in *NASB Study Bible.*

3 "God formed his chosen nation in the midst of the separatist Egyptians because, unlike Abraham and Isaac, the sons of Jacob were beginning to form unholy alliances with the syncretistic Canaanites." Waltke, "Book Reviews: Genesis, The Anchor Bible," BibSac, p. 80-81... God's attitude towards the Canaanites was exceptionally harsh because they were an exceptionally barbarous and violent culture, even by ancient standards, with rampant human sacrifice: "the picture of Canaanite religion in Moses' day was also 'singularly repulsive.' Albright describes it thus: "Among the Canaanites extremely depraved practices were inextricably bound up with religion. Ritual prostitution of both sexes was rampant.... Homosexuals formed a recognized guild in Canaanite temples.... Snake worship and human sacrifice were rife." Free, "Archeology and Biblical Criticism," BibSac Oct-Dec 1956, p. 322. Even if the Israelites had not been assimilated, they likely would have been raided, plundered and destroyed by warring bands of Canaanites, whose power grew increasingly potent over the next 400 years.

4 The term "Hebrew" is quite possibly derived from the "Hebiru People," a people mentioned in ancient texts from this area from 2000 to 1200 B.C. The word apparently means "outcast" or "renegade." See Hebrew in *Holman.*

5 At the time of Moses, Egypt was at its height of glory, led by the "Napoleon of Egypt" Thutmose III. Rea, "The Time of the Oppression and the Exodus," *Grace Theological Journal,* p. 5-14.

6 See Exodus 7:22; 8:15, 19, 31.

7 See Exodus 12:29, 30 in *NASB Study Bible.*

8 See Exodus 12:23. The Destroyer "was not clearly distinguished from Yahweh himself" and so may not be the "Angel of Death" popularized by Cecil B. DeMille in his landmark film, "The Ten Commandments." See The Destroyer in *ISBE.*

9 "The Lord caused the Egyptians to look favorably on the Israelites, and they gave the Israelites whatever they asked for. So, like a victorious army, they plundered the Egyptians!" (Exodus 12:36).

10 R.T Forster and V.P. Marston, *God's Strategy in Human History,* p. 72-75.

11 For some other instances of Israel's rebellion in the wilderness, see Numbers 11:1ff; 14:2ff; 16:8ff; Deuteronomy. 9:23ff.

12 For the sake of brevity, the remainder of Exodus 34:7 was omitted. It continues: "...yet He will by no means leave the guilty unpunished, visiting the iniquity of fathers on the children and on the grandchildren to the third and fourth generations." (NASB-U) Superficially it seems that verse 7(a) ("who forgives iniquity, transgression and sin") contradicts verse 7(b) ("yet...by no means leave the guilty unpunished"). Yet "the guilty" in 7(b) are those who reject God's kind offer of forgiveness in 7(a). The stakes are high with God: either we approach him on the basis of His forgiveness in 7(a), or else we approach on the basis of justice and pay for our guilt as 7(b) describes.

13 David Jenkins (b. 1925), British theologian, bishop of Durham. Quoted in: Guardian (London, 24 Dec. 1984) in *Columbia Dictionary of Quotations.*

14 "The Egyptian letter on Papyrus Anastasi I (thirteenth century B.C.) describes fierce warriors in Canaan that are seven to nine feet tall. Two female skeletons about seven feet tall from the twelfth century have been found at Tell es-Sa'ideyeh in Transjordan." See Numbers 13:22 in Craig S. Keener, *BBC: New Testament.*

15 "If there is anyone who curses his father or his mother, he shall surely be put to death." Leviticus 20:9 (NASB-U).

16 "Whether Moses or any of the Israelites knew the depth of the health protection God was giving is not the point. The point is that God knew, and 20th-century science now is able to identify specific benefits." Fawver and Overstreet, "Moses and Preventive Medicine," BibSac Jul-Sep 1990, p. 270-85. Doctor Fawver offers numerous examples where "provisions were also given by God to Abraham and Moses in the interest of preventive medicine."

17 The temporal nature of the Mosaic Code is addressed extensively in Galatians 3, for example. See Chapter 15, Further Consideration: A Change in Covenants.

CHAPTER 8

1 Joshua was a true seeker who "wanted to be where God manifested Himself. He would have been present on many occasions when the Lord spoke to Moses face to face; thus the enjoyed an intimacy with God excelled only by Moses…he ascended higher on the glory-covered mountain than any of his contemporaries. The lesson for us does not need to be spelled out." J. Oswald Sanders, *Enjoying Intimacy with God,* p. 14.

2 See Matthew 1:5, where Rahab is one of only two women named in the lineage of Jesus Christ. The point is clear that God is not aloof from the human condition, and offers grace and honor to anyone with a willing heart, like Rahab.

3 Jericho is "modern Tell es-Sultan, site of more than two dozen ancient cities, built and destroyed, one above the other. Many had powerful, double walls…" See Joshua 6:1 in *NASB Study Bible.*

4 Numerous excavations at Jericho have produced fascinating and consistent evidence for Joshua's conquest, including "the abundance of grain within the city at the time of its fall, destruction by fire, and even ruins of toppled walls produced what is being called impressive evidence that the fortified city was destroyed about 1400 B.C." Waltke, "The Date of the Conquest," *Westminster Theological Journal,* Fall 1990, p. 192.

5 "It was providential that the nation Israel, with its testimony to the knowledge of the one true God and with its obligation to make known that fact, should inherit a country that formed a geographical bridge between the ancient centers of pagan civilization." See Canaan in *Unger's.*

6 The Phoenicians were "the most sophisticated and urbane of the ancient peoples of the land of Canaan. The Phoenicians, who lived in the area of modern Lebanon (or what is left of that land), were a warring, seafaring people." Allen, Ronald B. "Psalm 87, a Song Rarely Sung." Bibliotheca Sacra 153, no. 610 (1996): p. 139.

7 Unger, "Archeology and the Israelite-Aramaean Wars Pt. 1," BibSac Apr-Jun 1949: p.178-79.

8 See 1 Samuel 10:10; "Possibly Samuel was the first who founded such a school of prophets. For in or near the city of Ramah we first find nayoth, or colonies of such disciples (1 Samuel 18:19ff)" See Prophets in *ISBE.*

9 See 2 Samuel 12:7; 1 Kings 14:7; 1 Kings 16:2.

10 "To Solomon, David's son, God promised that his throne and kingdom would continue forever… All conservative scholars are agreed that Christ fulfills the anticipation of these prophecies, and even unbelieving Jews anticipate that the coming Messiah will fulfill these prophecies." Walvoord, "The Incarnation of the Son of God," *BibSac,* p. 41-2.

11 "New Testament scholarship has long recognized the threefold character of the messianic office and ministry—prophet, priest, and king—and has seen in Jesus Christ the full embodiment of these roles." Unger, "Royal Priesthood: An Old Testament Messianic Motif," BibSac, p. 50. See also Deuteronomy. 18:15 and Acts 7:51-53.

12 In 1 Samuel 28 where the *KJV* titles it "The Witch of Endor" should more properly be titled "The

Necromancer," because Saul is not actually seeing a witch in the modern sense of the word—as someone casting spells—but rather "a woman who is the mistress of a ghost." See Witchcraft in *ISBE*. Since God is unambiguous in the Bible that He does not sanction spiritual activity through magic, there can be only one other source for such activity: namely, the demonic realm, where spirits are in rebellion against God's authority. See Exodus 22:18; Deuteronomy 18:10.

13 See 1 Samuel 16:12.

14 See Philistines in *Unger's*.

15 See Goliath in ibid.

16 David decisively defeated the Philistines (2 Samuel 5:17-25; 1 Chronicles 18:1; 2 Samuel 21:15-22) as well as the Moabites, Aramaeans, Ammonites, Edomites, and Amalekites (2 Samuel 8:10; 12:26-31). See David in ibid.

17 "In a few years the whole territory from the Euphrates to the river of Egypt, and from Gaza on the west to Thapsacus on the east, was under his sway (2 Samuel 8:3-13; 10)." See David in *Easton's*.

18 See 2 Samuel 11:2-27.

19 See 2 Samuel 23:39.

20 "Chronicles identifies this hill with Mount Moriah, where Abraham had been willing to offer Isaac (2 Chronicles 3:1; Genesis 22:1-14). So the Temple mount today in Jerusalem is called Mount Moriah." See Temple in *Holman*.

21 Ross, *BibSac* Jul-Sep: p.234.

22 ibid., p.234. "Numerous debasing practices, including sacred prostitution, homosexuality, and various orgiastic rites, were prevalent."

23 Gleason L. Archer, Jr, *A Survey of Old Testament*, p. 280. Archer describes the archeological support for infant sacrifice.

24 See Molech in *Holman*.

25 Youth for Christ/USA. *Life Application Study Bible*. Wheaton, IL: Tyndale House Publishers, 1996. See Leviticus 20:1-3 in *NASB Study Bible*.

CHAPTER 9

1 *International Standard Bible Encyclopedia:* iExalt, 1998: Idolatry, in loc.

2 See Pentecost, "Daniel-Introduction" in *Bible Knowledge Commentary-Old Testament*.

3 For the "sin of Jeroboam," see 1 Kings 15:26; 15:34; 16:19; 16:31.

4 "The first effect of her influence was the immediate establishment of the Phoenician worship on a grand scale at the court of Ahab. At her table were supported no less than 450 prophets of Baal and 400 of Astarte (1 Kings 16:31-32; 18:19), whereas the prophets of Jehovah were slain by her orders (1 Kings 18:13; 2 Kings 9:7)." See Jezebel in *Unger's*.

5 The battle of Qarqar (or KarKar) in 853 B.C. was a "pivotal battle, which decided the fate of all Southern Syria and Palestine. It is well known, however, in history from the description of it in the famous Monolith Inscription of Shalmaneser, now one of the treasures of the British Museum. Ahab is mentioned prominently as a member of the coalition." Unger, "Archeology and the Israelite-Aramaean Wars Pt. 1," BibSac Apr-Jun 1949, p. 178-79. It is noteworthy the Bible never mentions this battle, primarily because Ahab relied on his pagan alliances rather than God, and the Bible never attempts to follow the general history of the region.

6 See 1 Kings 16:33.

7 See 1 Kings 22, which records the entire story of Ahab's pathetic attempts to avoid his death as prophesied by

God through disguising himself and asking the king of Judah to wear his clothes. The king of Judah survived, but Ahab was killed by a random arrow.

8 "For example, King Omri in I Kings 16 is dismissed as an evil man, without drawing attention to facts known by us from non-Biblical sources—Omri's great power, administrative genius and international reputation." Carson, "Three Books On The Bible: A Critical Review," JETS September 1983, p. 356.

9 Omri's life is condensed to a mere dozen verses in 1 Kings 16:16-28, and summarized in verse 25: "But Omri did what was evil in the Lord's sight, even more than any of the kings before him."

10 See 1 Kings 22:26. It is clear Ahab remained an unbeliever until the end.

11 T. S. Eliot (1888–1965), Anglo-American poet, critic. The Love Song of J. Alfred Prufrock. From Columbia Dictionary of Quotations.

12 See Genesis 10:11. For a full discussion about Nimrod, see chapter five.

13 From an inscription of Tiglath-Pileser I in Charles, "Plundering the Lion's Den," Grace Theological Journal Fall 1989, p.183.

14 Northern Israel was initially conquered by Assyria under Tiglath-pileser III in 745 B.C., but only paid tribute. Later she rebelled against the Assyrians, and Sargon II finished the job of destroying Israel in 721 B.C. The rise of Assyrian empire was gradual but ominous, beginning with Ashurnasirpal II (883-859), "who made his land a formidable fighting machine and who swept everything before his ruthless cruelty." Over such a long period, God sent numerous prophets to warn Israel. Written at this time were the books of Ezekiel, Amos, Joel, Isaiah, Jonah, Hosea, Micah, Nahum, Jeremiah and Zephaniah. From Assyria in *Unger's*.

15 Sennacherib's invasion of Judea is quite significant because it is firmly anchored in extra-biblical historical sources—in this case, Sennacherib's inscriptions. Interestingly, the biblical accounts square up against multiple extra-biblical chronologies. See McFall, "A Translation Guide to the Chronological Data in Kings and Chronicles," *BibSac* Jan-Mar 1991.

16 "Their bodies were impaled on the walls...a barbarous custom widely practiced by the Assyrians, as is shown by reliefs on the palace gate of Shalmaneser III..." Benton, "The Philistines and the Early Kingdom of Israel," Grace Theological Journal Winter 1967, p. 29.

17 See Assyria in ISBE.

18 "In Fear and Trembling (1846) Kierkegaard proposed that individuals make a 'leap of faith' into a religious life, which is inherently paradoxical, mysterious, and full of risk." From "Kierkegaard," in Encarta.

19 See Jeremiah. 7:9-10, 14; Micah 3:11.

20 Dennis McCallum, *The Summons*, p. 112, citing anthropologist Anthony Wallis.

21 In the Hinnom Valley human sacrifice accompanied the worship of Baal and Molech. See 2 Kings 23:10 and 2 ChronIcles. 28:3 (where king Ahaz sacrificed his sons) and 2 ChronIcles. 33:6 (where king Manasseh sacrificed several of his sons). They also built idols inside Solomon's Temple (2 ChronIcles. 33:7).

22 For the persecution of the prophets: see 2 ChronIcles. 36:16; Jeremiah. 2:30; 26:20ff; and Hebrews. 11:37.

23 Assyria's enemies included the Scythians and the Medes, who were too willing to join Babylonia in the war. Nahum's prophecy is dated no later than 654 B.C. Nineveh fell in 612 B.C., so it was prophesied at least 40 years before the event occurred. See Johnson, "Nahum-Introduction" in *Bible Knowledge Commentary-Old Testament*.

24 "Some scholars feel that Assyria was God's instrument of deliverance since Damascus was surrounded and tribute exacted. Although Jehoahaz had to pay tribute as a diplomatic gift to Assyria, the land had rest from Syrian terror." Nichols, JETS Fall 1975, p. 250

25 The entire books of Nahum and Jonah along with large passages of scripture are addressed specifically to the Assyrians. Others warning the Assyrians of impending destruction include Micah, Nahum, Zephaniah, Isaiah, and Jeremiah.

26 Archer, Jr, "Old Testament History and Recent Archeology," *BibSac* Jan-Mar 1970

27 McFall, "A Translation Guide to the Chronological Data in Kings and Chronicles," *BibSac* Jan-Mar 1991, p.4

28 ibid., p.43.

CHAPTER 10

1 Since 959 B.C. when it was built by Solomon, the nearest anyone came to plundering the temple was during Sennacherib's 701 B.C. invasion. However, Sennacherib's army was destroyed, and because Hezekiah's faith in God stirred so much fear in the surrounding nations, much treasure made its way back into the temple.

2 Jehoiakim was a monster who violently plundered his own people and oppressed the poor (Jeremiah 22:13-23), energetically pushing idolatry onto the rest of Israel (Jeremiah 25:1-7) and killed Uriah the prophet (Jeremiah 20-23). This is especially tragic since his father, King Josiah, was such a godly man.

3 Known as the Battle of Carchemish in 605 B.C., Pharaoh Neco along with the remnants of Assyria's armies were driven by Nebuchadnezzar from Syria, leaving Palestine an open road for Babylonian armies. Nebuchadnezzar "attacked Jerusalem in September 605 B.C. It was on this occasion that Daniel and his companions were taken to Babylon as captives." These hostages were part of the tribute paid by Jehoiakim. Pentecost, "Daniel-Introduction" in Bible Knowledge Commentary-Old Testament.

4 See Jeremiah 22:18-19; 36:30. Apparently Jehoiakim was initially taken to Babylon (2 Chronicles. 36:6-7), then escaped and was later killed as Jeremiah prophesied, according to Josephus (Ant., X, vi, 3). See Genung, "Jehoiakim" in *International Standard Bible Encyclopedia.*

5 Temple treasures had been depleted before, but Jerusalem was never overrun and sacked like this. Judah's kings were always able to select which treasures were offered as tribute, and consequently Nebuchadnezzar discovered artifacts dating back to Solomon's time and before (2 Kings 24:13).

6 There were actually three incursions into Palestine by the Babylonians with increasing severity: in 605 B.C., 597 B.C. and 586 B.C. In-between, roving armies continually swept through a Palestine stripped of its military strength.

7 "From the viewpoint of a human observer, it seemed that the religion of the Hebrews had been completely discredited. Their God, Yahweh, had apparently shown Himself inferior in power to the mighty gods of Assyria and Babylon… monotheism was exposed to universal scorn as an empty fraud." Zondervan, "Daniel-Introduction" in *Expositor's Bible Commentary.*

8 See NASB margin translation notes in Daniel 2:2, or NIV where "Chaldeans" is translated "astrologers."

9 Zuck, "The Practice of Witchcraft in the Scriptures," *BibSac.*

10 Assyria's destruction prophesied: Isaiah 10:12-19; 14:24-25; 30:31-33; 31:8-9; Zech. 10:11. The entire book of Nahum prophesies the destruction – see Nahum 1:8-10; 1:14; 2:6; 2:8-10; 2:13; 3:3; 3:11-15; 3:17. Babylon's destruction prophesied: Isaiah 13:1-22; 14:4-22; 21:1-10; 47:1-15; Jeremiah 25:12; 50:1-51:64, among others.

11 See Daniel 7:19,23.

12 [Martin, 1985 #240]

13 Nostradamus was an occultic astrologer whose incomprehensible writings are often touted as clear prophecies, such as this one supposedly foretelling the death of President Roosevelt:

"For a long while shall be seen in the air a gray bird,
Near Dola and the Tuscan land,
Holding in his beak a green bough,
Then a great one shall die and the war be finished." Ehlert, "Book Review: The Complete Prophecies of Nostradamus," *BibSac* Oct-Dec 47, p.503.

14 The Talmud is a vast collection of rabbinic teachings: "It comprises the work of some 400 to 500 rabbis over a period of more than 800 years, some say 1,000 years, from 400 B.C. to 600 A.D." Feinberg, "The Old Testament in Jewish Thought and Life Pt.1," *BibSac* Jan-Mar 1954, p.30.

15 Although Jewish literature was produced during the "Silent Years," it was never at the hands of a Prophet. God stopped sending them after Malachi, as the Jews themselves recognized in the 1st Century A.D.: "From Artexerxes to our own time, the complete history has been written but has not been deemed worthy of equal credit with the earlier records because of the failure of the exact succession of the prophets." (Flavius Josephus, Against Apion 1:8)

16 "Alexander apparently went to Jerusalem, offered sacrifices to God in the temple under the direction of the High Priest Jaddua, and was shown from the Book of Daniel that he was predicted to destroy the Persian Empire (cf. Daniel 8:5-7, 20, 21). He accepted this interpretation, granted the Jews' request that Jews in Palestine, Babylonia, and Media be allowed to live according to their ancestral laws and be exempt from tribute every sabbatical year." Hoehner, "Between the Testaments" in *Expositor's Bible Commentary: Introductory Articles,* p.180.

17 See Daniel 8:22ff and chapter 11.

18 See Daniel 7:19,23.

19 J. Barton Payne, *Encyclopedia of Biblical Prophecy.*

CHAPTER 11

1 See also John 1:3; Hebrews 1:2.

2 Nazareth was located next to cosmopolitan Sepphoris, which was a Roman military colony and one of Herod's capital cities, so that "Nazareth had a bad name among their neighbors for irreligion or some laxity of morals." See Nazareth in *Unger's.*

3 John 1:46.

4 "In looking to some of the other chronological notations in the gospels, the evidence led to the conclusion that Christ was born in the winter of 5/4 B.C. Although the exact date of Christ's birth cannot be known, either December, 5 B.C. or January, 4 B.C. is most reasonable." Hoehner, "Chronological Aspects of the Life of Christ Part I: The Date of Christ's Birth," *BibSac* Oct 1973, p. 351. We are using the 4 B.C. date, which is most commonly held.

5 See Luke 2:1-2; 3:1.

6 Prophecies concerning the Messiah descending in the "Kingly Line" of David: Isaiah. 9:1-7; 11:1-5; Jeremiah. 30:4-11; Ezekiel. 34:23-24; 37:24-25; Amos 9:11-15. For the amazing fulfillment of Jeremiah's 22:30 prophecy, "This prophecy also helps explain the genealogies of Christ in Matthew 1 and Luke 3. Matthew presented the legal line of Christ through his stepfather, Joseph… who was a son of Jehoiachin…Had Christ been a physical descendant of Joseph and not virgin-born, He would have been disqualified as Israel's King. Luke presented the physical line of Christ through Mary, who was descended from David through the line of his son Nathan…In that way Christ was not under the 'curse' of Jehoiachin." See Jeremiah 25:12-14 in *BKC-Old Testament.*

7 Poverty: "He will eat curds and honey at the time He knows enough to refuse evil and choose good." (Isaiah 7:15 NASB-U) These are the foods typical of someone living in poverty. Martin, "Isaiah" in ibid. Isaiah 7:15, in loc. Galilean birth: "…on the other side of Jordan, Galilee of the Gentiles. The people who walk in darkness will see a great light; those who live in a dark land, the light will shine on them." (Isaiah 9:1-2 NASB-U) Certainly, "it is striking that Jesus' upbringing and early ministry was mostly in that very area near the Sea of Galilee. His presence certainly 'honored' that area." See Isaiah 9:1 in ibid.

8 Yamauchi, JETS Winter 1971, p.36.

9 ibid., p.37, quoting again from the famous *Gospel of Thomas.*

10 See Trinity in *Unger's.*

CHAPTER 12

1 Interestingly, Jesus made about 300 gallons of wine, according to John 2:6. That it was wine—not grape juice —is certain, because the Greek word "oinos" is used here, which can only mean wine. The wine steward also declared it "the best wine" which could never be said of grape juice.

2 See Mark 1:15 and Matthew 4:23.

3 See Mark 4:37-41.

4 See John 6 and Matthew 14 for the size of these crowds. However, the size of the crowd did not include women and children in the count, so there were likely twice or three times the numbers given. John F. Walvoord, *BKC-New Testament,* John 6, in loc.

5 See Mark 3:8 and Luke 6:17.

6 Søren Kierkegaard (1813–55), Danish philosopher. Either/Or, vol. 2, "Balance between Esthetic and Ethical" (1843; tr. 1987). From *Columbia Dictionary of Quotations.*

7 (OED).

8 See Exodus 29:45; Leviticus 26:12; Jeremiah 31:1; Ezekiel 37:27.

9 Edersheim, Life and Times of Jesus the Messiah, p.1606.

10 ibid., p.1579.

11 ibid., p.1612.

12 ibid., p.1598.

13 See Mark 7:4. Called ablution, ceremonial cleansing was practiced constantly, and thus the large, 30-gallon ceremonial cleansing pots in John 2.

CHAPTER 13

1 Perhaps Cain was unaware of the importance of blood sacrifice, and his grain offering was an innocent error. Yet after the sacrifice there was no doubt that only a blood sacrifice was acceptable. At this point, Cain could easily concede and offer the blood sacrifice.

2 See Sacrifice in *Holman.*

3 Although this passage in Leviticus 1:4 was not given until the time of Moses, certainly the blood sacrifice was known in early human history at the time of Abel, because Abel knew the correct approach from the outset. Additionally, in Job 1:5 and 42:8—the earliest book of the Old Testament, by all accounts—it is clear, blood sacrifice was known as an act of Substitution.

4 See Romans 4:16.

5 In Exodus 6:6, Redeem is the Hebrew word ga'al, used for example in the freeing of an Israelite slave who sold himself in time of poverty (Leviticus 25:48ff).

6 See The Passover and Feast of Unleavened Bread in *Unger's.* He notes: "The deliverance of Israel from Egypt was accompanied by their adoption as the nation of Jehovah." This same principle occurs to those Redeemed by Christ's blood, who become redeemed from slavery and also receive their "adoption as sons" (Romans 8:15).

7 Oscar Wilde (1854–1900), Anglo-Irish playwright, author. "The Soul of Man under Socialism," in *Fortnightly Review* (London, Feb. 1890) in *Columbia Dictionary of Quotations.*

8 Joseph Conrad (1857–1924), Polish-born English novelist. Razumov, in Under Western Eyes, pt. 4, ch. 2 (1911) in ibid.

9 Jean-Jacques Rousseau (1712–78), Swiss-born French philosopher, political theorist. Opening sentence of "The Social Contract," ch. 1 (1762). More than a hundred years earlier, John Milton had written in his pamphlet *The Tenure of Kings and Magistrates* (1649): "No man who knows aught, can be so stupid to deny that all men naturally were born free."

10 Boris Yeltsin (1931), Russian politician, president. Remark during a visit to the U.S. Quoted in: *Independent* (London, 13 Sept. 1989) in ibid.

11 C. S. Lewis (1898–1963), British author. *A Grief Observed,* pt. 1 (1961) in ibid.

CHAPTER 14

1 Anderson, "Christianity and the World Religions" in *Expositor's Bible Commentary: Introductory Articles.*

2 ibid.

3 ibid.

4 Feinberg, "The Old Testament in Jewish Thought and Life Pt.1," BibSac Jan-Mar 1954, p. 29.

5 More precisely, the halakah was under development during Christ's time, which formed the basis for the Talmud: "The Talmud represents a continuation of the application of the oral law (halakah) to every sphere of Jewish life. This process probably began with the early Jewish sect known as the Pharisees....Some of the halakah embodied in the Talmud is attributed to early rabbis and may reflect Jewish practice in the time of the writers of the New Testament or of Jesus." Humphries-Brooks, "Talmud" in *Holman Bible Dictionary.*

6 See Exodus 19:6; Leviticus 11:44; Leviticus 20:7; 20:26; Ephesians. 1:4; 1 Peter 1:16.

7 See Ethics: the origin of Ethics in *Encyclopedia Britannica* and Ethics in *Encarta.* These studies prove humans are innately moral agents.

8 Immanuel Kant (1724–1804), German philosopher. "Metaphysics of Ethics" (1797), quoted by James Stalker, "Conscience" in *Dictionary of New Testament Theology.*

9 This "foremost" command is repeated throughout the Law: Deuteronomy. 6:5; 7:9; 10:12; 11:1, 13, 22; 13:3; 19:9; 30:6,16, 20.

10 See Psalm 36:6.

11 (OED).

12 See Exodus 16:32-33.

13 See Numbers 17:1-11 and Hebrews 9:4.

14 See Deuteronomy 9:10 and 10:5.

15 Descriptions of the Mercy Seat, Shekinah Glory the angels are in Exodus 25:18-22; Lev. 16:2; 15.

16 Atonement: in Hebrew, kaphar, to "cover, cancel"; the Greek equivalent is katallage, meaning "exchange, reconciliation." See Atonement in *Unger's.*

17 See Leviticus 16:21-22.

18 At the coming of Christ, the sacrificial system was removed as a requirement for approaching God, yet the Bible also tells us that there will come another time in the future when He will institute the sacrificial system as a memorial to the act of Christ's death on the cross. This is why we see such prophesies as Malachi 3:3, where the Levites—now purified by Christ Himself, no longer by ritual cleansing—are presenting sacrifices once again.

19 See Psalm 2 and 22, for example.

20 Hebrews 9:22.

CHAPTER 15

1 For a more detailed analysis of the Daniel 9 prophecy—including issues surrounding dates and interpretation – see The Time of Christ's Coming Predicted in Dennis McCallum, *Christianity: The Faith That Makes Sense.* Also Josh McDowell, *The New Evidence That Demands a Verdict.*

2 See John 6:15.

3 See Sidebar, *The Significance of Daniel* in Chapter 10.

4 Edersheim, *Life and Times of Jesus the Messiah,* p. 1239.

5 See Jerusalem in *ISBE.*

6 See Mark 13:1 in Grassmick, "Mark" in B*ible Knowledge Commentary-New Testament.*

7 ibid.

8 See Exodus 21:32.

9 Edersheim, *Life and Times of Jesus the Messiah,* p.1317.

10 See Mark 9:34; 10:37f; Luke 9:46. Here in Luke 22:24 the Greek word öëëüíâéëïò.is used for "dispute" and it means "fond of strife"— characterizing the Disciples at this time. See Luke 22:24 in Foundation, *NAS Hebrew-Aramaic* and *Greek Dictionaries.*

11 Although the gospel accounts do not directly state Judas sat next to Christ, Edersheim points out several inferences made. Judas was close enough to dip out of the same bowl as Christ (Matthew 26:23), and when Jesus told Judas he knew about the betrayal, nobody else except John heard it because Judas sat next to Christ. Edersheim further points out that Judas as seated in the place of honor—traditionally at the left hand. Edersheim, *Life and Times of Jesus the Messiah,* p.1331.

12 See Flavius Josephus, Against Apion 1:8.

13 Ronald Reagan (1911-2004), U.S. Republican politician, president. Speech, 20 March 1981, to Conservative Political Action Conference, Washington, D.C. (published in Speaking My Mind, 1990) in *Columbia Dictionary of Quotations.*

14 The Seder is the Passover meal at which, "The Hallel (praise) Psalm were sung or chanted antiphonally in connection with the Passover—the first two (Psalm 113-114) before the meal, the remaining four (Psalms 115-118) after it to conclude the evening observance. Such verses as Psalm 118:6-7, 17-18, 22-24 gain added significance on Jesus' lips just before His suffering and death." See Mark 14:26 in John F. Walvoord, *BKC-New Testament.*

15 See John 13:2.

16 See Isaiah 53:7; Matthew 26:63; Matthew 27:12-14; Mark 14:61; Mark 15:5; Luke 23:9; John 19:9.

17 See Jeremiah 51:7; also parallel ideas exist in Genesis 15:16.

18 See Jeremiah Job 21:20; Psalm 75:8; Isaiah 51:17; 51:22; Jeremiah 25:15; 51:7.

19 Although Luke 22:44 could mean that Christ's blood flowed profusely like a gaping wound, it is interesting that Luke was a doctor and also the only account of this "sweating blood," which is "possibly hematidrosis, the actual mingling of blood and sweat as in cases of extreme anguish, strain or sensitivity." See Luke 22:44 in *NASB Study Bible.*

20 See John 10:30 (NASB-U), esp. NASB margin notes.

21 For Jesus' intention to die, see Matthew 16:21; 17:23; 20:19; Mark 8:31; 9:31; 10:34; Luke 9:22; 18:31-33, among others.

22 J. Dwight Pentecost, *Thy Kingdom Come,* p. 172.

23 ibid., p.176.

24 The consecration of Israel: See Exodus 6:7; 16:12; 23:25; Leviticus 11:44.

25 The superiority of the Abrahamic Covenant over the Mosaic Covenant is discussed at length in Galatians 3.

26 Let secular government govern: See Matthew 22:21; Mark 12:17; Luke 20:25; John 18:36.

27 "Governing the church" includes a vast array of instructions throughout the entire New Testament. Christ first introduced these new "rules" in Matthew 18:15-17.

28 There are so many examples of the arbitrary replacement of the Mosaic Covenant within the Christian community; it could fill a book. One example is infant baptism. Baptism is clearly commanded for adults in the New Testament (Matthew 28:18ff), which causes problems for infant baptism. Yet this practice continues because it is based on the strict injunctions for infant circumcision found in the Mosaic Covenant. See Infant Baptism in *Holman*.

29 See 1 Corinthians 9:21; Galatians 6:2; 5:14; James 1:25; 2:8.

CHAPTER 16

1 Taken with liberty from the book, *The Death of Truth,* edited by McCallum, et.al.

2 For example, "Brandon thinks that the characterization of Pilate in the gospels as being a weak, abject figure as opposed to that given in Josephus and Philo is ludicrous." Hoehner, "Chronological Aspects of the Life of Christ Part IV: The Year of Christ's Crucifixion," *BibSac* Oct-Dec 1974.

3 ibid., p. 345-6.

4 See sidebar, "Daniel 9" in chapter 15. Because the Passover fell on a Friday, only two dates are possible for the crucifixion: A.D. 30 and 33. The Sejanus plot was not uncovered until A.D. 31. Pilate would have been in the prime of his authority at that time, and very unwilling to allow the Jews he despised so much push him around.

5 Ôéôëïò (titlos)—titulus in Latin—in John 19:19 is translated "a title, an inscription," and was a legal document "on which was inscribed the charge on which He had been condemned…it was customary to carry this board before the prisoner." Edersheim, *Life and Times of Jesus the Messiah,* p. 1398.

6 ibid., p.1340.

7 Donald Grey Barnhouse, *Invisible War,* p. 222.

8 See Cross in *ISBE.*

9 Green, "The Meaning of Cross-Bearing," *BibSac* Apr-June 1983, p.124, 126. After the massive blood loss and all-night torture, Jesus faltered, unable to carry the cross alone any further, and Simon the Cyrene helped –apparently becoming a believer in the process. See Mark 15:21, which bears a historical note for his readers that "Simon is the father of Alexander and Rufus." These two were apparently known to those in the Jerusalem church, and therefore most likely were Christians themselves. See also Romans 16:13.

10 John F. Walvoord, *BKC-New Testament,* Mark 15:23-24, in loc.

11 See Crucifixion in *Unger's.* Also, Edwards, MD and Gabel, MDIV, et al., "On the Physical Death of Jesus Christ," *JAMA* March 21, 1986.

12 See Cross in *ISBE.* "The suffering of death by crucifixion was intense, especially in hot climates. Severe local inflammation, coupled with an insignificant bleeding of the jagged wounds, produced traumatic fever, which was aggravated by the exposure to the heat of the sun, the strain of the body and insufferable thirst. The skin swelled about the rough nails and the torn lacerated tendons and nerves caused excruciating agony. The arteries of the head and stomach were surcharged with blood and a terrific throbbing headache ensued."

13 Edwards, MD, et al., "On the Physical Death of Jesus Christ," *JAMA* March 21, 1986.

14 "Lifting of the body would also painfully scrape the scourged back against the rough wooden stipes. (2, 7)

Muscle cramps and paresthesias of the outstretched and uplifted arms would add to the discomfort. (7) As a result, each respiratory effort would become agonizing and tiring and lead eventually to asphyxia." ibid.

15 See John 19:31; "In the only known archeological find of a crucifixion, which came to light in 1968, the skeletal remains revealed that the lower legs had been shattered by a single blow." See John 19:31 in John F. Walvoord, *BKC-New Testament.*

16 (OED).

17 "Using the Jewish method of counting hours from sunrise (and sunset) Mark alone recorded that Jesus' crucifixion took place at the third hour, that is, 9 a.m. This seems to conflict with the time reference 'the sixth hour' in John 19:14. But John probably used the Roman (modern) method of counting hours from midnight (and noon); thus he put Jesus' trial before Pilate at 'about the sixth hour,' that is, approximately 6 a.m." Grassmick, "Mark" in *Bible Knowledge Commentary—New Testament,* Mark 15:34, In loc.

18 "At the ninth hour (3:00 p.m.) with only three hours remaining on the Day of Preparation, Jesus cried out. This was the time for the Passover lamb to be slain at the Temple (1 Corintians 5:7)" Farner, "The Lord's Supper until He Comes," *Grace Theological Journal,* Fall '85, p. 393.

19 See Mark 15:38 in Craig S. Keener, *BBCB.C.: New Testament.*

20 "The Veils before the Most Holy Place were 40 cubits (60 feet) long, and 20 (30 feet) wide, of the thickness of the palm of the hand, and wrought in 72 squares, which were joined together; and these Veils were so heavy, that, in the exaggerated language of the time, it needed 3000 priests to manipulate each." Edersheim, *Life and Times of Jesus the Messiah,* p. 1413.

21 "According to (probably) first-century Jewish tradition, the priests were supposed to pierce Passover lambs with a wood pole from their mouth to their buttocks...A foot soldier was armed with a short sword and a pilum, or lance... Such a lance could easily penetrate the pericardial sac which surrounds and protects the heart and contains watery fluid." See John 19:34 in Craig S. Keener, *BBCB.C.: New Testament.*

22 Elisabeth Kübler-Ross is one such notoriety. See "The Experience of Death" in *The Vestibule,* ed. Jess Weiss (New York: Pocket Books, 1972), pp. 57–64; cf. "Life after Death?" *Newsweek,* July 12, 1976, p. 41.

23 "Some near-death experiences have been reported during the absence of brain waves. Eminent cardiologist Schoonmaker announced the results of his 18-year study of 1,400 near-death experiences, including those of about 55 persons whose experiences took place while flat EEG readings were recorded" and his study presented "strong evidence that consciousness may exist after death." Habermas, "Paradigm Shift," *BibSac* Oct. 89, p. 445.

24 Susan Sontag (b. 1933), U.S. essayist. "Illness As Metaphor," ch. 7 (1978) in *Columbia Dictionary of Quotations.*

25 Michael P. Green, *The Empty Cross of Jesus,* p. 97.

26 "Taking all the evidence together, it is not too much to say that there is no ancient historic incident better or more variously reported than the resurrection of Christ." Paul Little, *Know Why You Believe,* p. 30.

27 Lee Strobel, *The Case for Christ,* p. 99, quoting a prominent scholar and archeologist.

28 Even liberal scholars consider the Jesus Seminar, "the views of a tiny minority of mostly second-rate scholars working at mostly second-rate schools," and are an embarrassment because their work "explains why so much of contemporary New Testament scholarship is viewed with derision by mainstream historians...The scholarship that under girds the Jesus Seminar and similar enterprises is based on wild speculation and minuscule evidence." Hutchinson, *Jesus Seminar Unmasked.* See Timothy Luke Johnson, The Real Jesus.

29 Walvoord, "Christ in His Resurrection," *BibSac* July-63, p.195.

30 "Liberals and neo-orthodox scholars have summarily rejected the facts of the Scriptural records, often with hardly any supporting argument. Common among such scholars is the view that Christ arose only in a spiritual sense-continued existence after His death, but not a bodily resurrection... that what actually happened is that Christ appeared to the disciples in visions or dreams. With no documentary proof whatever, they consider the accounts of the appearances of Christ on the resurrection day and immediately subsequent to it as later fabrications." (italics ours) ibid., p.195.

31 See Luke 24:27; 45-48; Acts 1:3.

32 All the Disciples—except for possibly John—were variously executed throughout the course of the first century. A conspiracy of this caliber, involving so many names, would surely fall apart in the face of such a high cost.

33 Books claiming first-hand knowledge of the Resurrection include: Matthew, Mark, Luke, John, Acts, 1 Corinthians, and 1 John. There are hundreds of witnesses, Paul writes in 1 Corinthians 15:4-9, most of whom were still living and available for questioning at the time he wrote the letter.

34 Other Old Testament prophecies include Isaiah 53:10b and Psalm 22.

35 See Glory in *Unger's*.

36 ibid.

CHAPTER 17

1 See 1 Corinthians 15:3-8, which provides a long list of names who saw the risen Christ.

2 See Genesis 1:2.

3 See Acts 2:42 quoted earlier. In verse 44 the Koinonia is used a bit differently: "And all those who had believed…had all things in common."

4 See Romans 8:17; 2 Peter 1:4; Ephesians 1:23.

5 Jean-Paul Sartre (1905–1980), French philosopher, author. Garcin, in No Exit, sc. 5 in *Columbia Dictionary of Quotations.*

6 "Davrishevi remembered [Stalin's] grandmother reading the New Testament to them—the story of Judas's kiss of betrayal. 'But why didn't Jesus draw his saber?' little Soso asked indignantly. 'He couldn't do that,' Grandma answered. 'He had to sacrifice himself for our salvation.' That was something little Soso was incapable of understanding. All through his childhood he had been taught to answer blow with blow." Edvard Radzinksky, *Stalin*, p. 26.

7 See Mark 14:58, where the paramount reason for the crucifixion of Jesus given at his trial was speaking against the Temple.

8 In Acts 7:58 the executioners "laid aside their robes at the feet of a young man named Saul," which was the Apostle Paul's earlier name, and this signified that he was playing a primary role in Stephen's death. This is underscored in Acts 8:1 where "Saul was in hearty agreement with putting him to death."

9 See John 8:44.

10 This was an appropriate name change. "Saul" means "demanded," and Saul was a dangerous, dogmatic zealot; but "Paul" means "little," because Paul was humbled by Christ's power: "If I must boast, I would rather boast about the things that show how weak I am." (2 Corinthians. 11:30 NLT)

11 Robert Coleman, *Master Plan of Discipleship*, p.39. Coleman notes the 500,000 figure is considered high by some, but not the 200,000 figure for the end of the first century.

12 Tacitus, Annales, xv, 44.

13 Communism grew at an alarmingly fast rate in the 20th century, but the number of dedicated communists actually numbered very few, compared to the populations conquered in the name of Communism.

14 Some historians attempt to downplay Early Church persecution, but these revisionist histories fail to explain why all the apostles and church leaders were martyred. To be sure, there were brief periods of inactivity, but certainly not during the early growth of the church: "For 200 years, to become a Christian meant the great renunciation, the joining a despised and persecuted sect, the swimming against the tide of popular prejudice, the coming under the ban of the Empire, the possibility at any moment of imprisonment and death under its most fear-

ful forms." See Persecution in *ISBE*. There were ten major eras of persecution interspersed by almost uninterrupted local outbreaks, documented in chapters 5-10 in Justo L. Gonzalez, *The Story of Christianity.*

15 See Hebrews 10:34 where some were imprisoned, others lost all their property, yet they "accepted it with joy."

16 Tacitus, Annales, *Annals* 15.44.

17 "In A.D. 111 or 112, [Pliny] writes to the emperor Trajan a letter in which he describes the growth of the Christian faith. He goes on to say that 'many of all ages and of all ranks and even of both sexes are being called into danger, and will continue to be so. In fact the contagion of this superstition is not confined to the cities only, but has spread to the villages and country districts.'" See Persecution in *ISBE*.

CHAPTER 18

1 He occasionally taught large crowds, yet He deliberately thinned the numbers, alienating much of his potential following. See for example John 6:66; also in Luke 9:57-62 Christ turns away so many who wish to follow him by raising almost impossible standards. With the crowds he was vague and elusive, but spent long hours instructing the 12 about "the mysteries of the kingdom of heaven." See Matthew 13:11.

2 See Matthew 20:17, no. 278, p. 17, Bill Hull, *Jesus Christ, Disciple-Maker* (Grand Rapids, MI: ??? House).

3 Hull, p.36.

4 "But the goal of our instruction is love from a pure heart and a good conscience and a sincere faith."
1 Timothy 1:5 (NASB).

5 For Christ's teachings on the denial of self, see also Matthew 10:38; 16:24; Mark 8:34-9:1; Luke 9:23; 14:27; John 12:24.

6 "One must deny himself decisively ('deny' is an aorist imperative) saying no to selfish interests and earthly securities. Self-denial is not to deny one's personality, to die as a martyr, or to deny 'things' (as in asceticism). Rather it is the denial of 'self,' turning away from the idolatry of self-centeredness and every attempt to orient one's life by the dictates of self-interest." See Mark 8:34 in [Grassmick, 1985 #262]

7 Leroy Eims, p. 47, *The Lost Art of Disciplemaking,* (Zondervan Navpress, 1978).

8 Leroy Eims, p. 36.

9 Leroy Eims, p. 86.

10 Leroy Eims, p. 34.

11 For Christ's principles of selectivity, see Matthew 9:9; Mark 2:14; Luke 9:59-60; John 1:43; 21:19.

12 See 2 Corinthians 6:16.

13 See 1 Corinthians 4:1.

14 Billy Graham, 1978, p. 147, *The Holy Spirit* (Word Books).

15 "Although the present number of Protestant churches—324,000—will swell to about 375,000 in the nineties, both church attendance and church membership will decline" [Barna, 1990 #283], p.129. Also, p.12.

16 Hull, p. 12. Statistics are from a study bv Bob Gilliam with the Church Development Survey in five hundred churches in Evangelical denominations over a 10-year period.

17 Leroy Eims, p. 45.

18 In 1963, two out of three people believed that the Bible was the actual word of God...By 1999, the numbers had reversed. See Gallup, 1999.

19 See Matthew 25:31.

EPILOGUE

1 See 1 Corinthians 1:20 where it says, "Has not God made foolish the wisdom of the world?"

2 Charles Baudelaire (1821–67), French poet. Appendix to Prose Poems,"Plans and Notes: For Civil War" (published in Complete Works, vol. 1, "Shorter Prose Poems," ed. by Yves-Gérard le Dantec; Revelation by Claude Pichois, 1953) from *Columbia Dictionary of Quotations.*

3 See Justo L. Gonzalez, *The Story of Christianity.*

4 Thomas Paine (1737-1809), Anglo-American political theorist, writer. The Age of Reason, pt. 1, "The Author's Profession of Faith" (1794) in *Columbia Dictionary of Quotations.*

5 Although the Muslim conquerors of these areas did persecute the church, it was relatively minor until the 11th Century—certainly never on the scale of Rome's persecutions which the Early Church survived. The Institutional Church of the seventh century died in Muslim-controlled areas simply because Islam was a superior Religion of Merit and more readily grasped by the average man.

6 Examples include the Didache (the "teachings"), the Shepherd of Hermas, the letters of Clement and Ignatius. These writings were not attempts to introduce new Scriptures, per se, but they contained injunctions and thoughts which became doctrinaire. For example, the letters of Ignatius and Cyprian established the authority of the bishop as supreme, undercutting the Bible's emphasis on plurality of eldership in Titus 1:5 and 1 Peter 5:1. ("Where the bishop is, there is the church," Cyprian concludes—Stiansen, "Church Reform," *BibSac* Apr-Jun 1948, p.214). Such autonomous and absolute authority granted to any single human is an obvious breeding-ground for corruption and ignores the biblical doctrine of man's inherent falleness and untrustworthiness. ("But Jesus didn't trust them, because he knew what people were really like." John 2:24.)

7 See Luke 22:19. A mystical view of communion was clearly developing by the time of Ignatius in the early second century: The bread and cup are "the medicine of immortality, an antidote that we may not die." Dollar, "The Lord's Supper in the Early Church, Part I," *BibSac* Apr-Jun 1960, p. 149.

8 See 2 Thessalonians 2:11; 2 Timothy 3:2-5.

9 "Glory to God in the highest, and on earth peace among men, with whom He is pleased." Luke 2:14 (NASB-U). This was heralded by the angels at the birth of Christ, peace is God's intention for mankind through Jesus Christ.

10 "The Gk. preposition anti in composition sometimes denotes substitution, taking the place of another; hence, 'false Christ'...In the OT he is prefigured under the 'king of Babylon' (Isaiah 14:4); the little 'horn' (Daniel 7:8; Daniel 8:9); the king 'insolent and skilled in intrigue' (Daniel 8:23); 'the prince who is to come' (Daniel 9:26); the willful king (Daniel 11:36). In the NT he is called 'the man of lawlessness,' 'the son of destruction' (2 Thes. 2:3-8); 'antichrist' (1 John 2:18); and 'the beast' (Revelation 13:1-10)." See Antichrist in *Unger's.*

11 "The dragon" is clearly identified a few verses earlier as Satan in Revelation 12:9. "The great dragon was hurled down—that ancient serpent called the devil, or Satan, who leads the whole world astray." (NIV).

12 Erwin Lutzer, *Christ Among Other Gods,* p. 28.

13 ibid., p. 30.

14 See Revelation 11:3-6.

REFERENCES

CHAPTER 1

The Columbia Dictionary of Quotations (Columbia University Press, 1998).

The New Oxford Dictionary of English, Second Edition (Oxford: Oxford University Press, 1998).

Archer, G. L., Jr. *Old Testament History and Recent Archeology from Abraham to Moses,* (1970).

Britannica Encyclopedia Britannica, from *Encyclopedia Britannica Ultimate Reference Suite* 2004 DVD (Reference-Software:, 2003).

DeYoung, D. B. and Whitcomb, J. C. *The Origin of the Universe,* (1980).

Ehlert, A. D. Book Review: *The Complete Prophecies of Nostradamus* (1947).

Geizler, N. and Nix *From God to Man* (Chicago, IL: Moody Press, 1974).

Green, M. P. *The Empty Cross of Jesus* (Downers Grove, IL: Intervarsity Press, 1984).

Kenyon, S. F. *The Bible and Archaeology* (New York, NY: Harper and Row, 1940).

LaSor, W. S. *The Dead Sea Scrolls* (Grand Rapids, MI: Zondervan, 1979).

Little, P. *Know Why You Believe* (Downers Grove, IL: Intervarsity Press, 1971).

McCallum, D. *Christianity: the Faith that Makes Sense* (Wheaton, IL: Tyndale House Publishers, 1992).

McDowell, J. *The New Evidence That Demands a Verdict* (Nashville, TN: Thomas Nelson Publishers, 1999).

Payne, J. B. *Encyclopedia of Biblical Prophecy,* 1st Edition (New York, NY: Harper and Row, 1973).

Voss, H. F. *The Dead Sea Scrolls* (Chicago, IL: Moody Press, 1988).

Zacharius, R. *Jesus Among Other Gods* (Nashville, TN: Thomas Nelson Publishers, 2002).

CHAPTER 8

Easton's Bible Dictionary (Nashville, TN: Thomas Nelson Publishers, 1897).

Holman Bible Dictionary. (Broadman & Holman Publishers, 1991).

International Standard Bible Encyclopedia. (iExalt, 1913).

The New Unger's Bible Dictionary. (Moody Press, 1988).

Zondervan NASB Study Bible (Grand Rapids, MI: Zondervan, 1999).

Archer, Gleason L., Jr, *A Survey Of Old Testament Introduction* (Chicago, IL: Moody Bible Institute, 1974).

Ross, A. P., "Studies in the Book of Genesis Part 1:The Curse of Canaan." *Biblioteca Sacra* 1980, vol.137 no. 547.

Sanders, J. Oswald, *Enjoying Intimacy with God* (Chicago, IL: Moody Bible Institute, 1980).

Unger, M. F., "Archeology and the Israelite-Aramaean Wars Part 1." *Biblioteca Sacra* 1949, vol.106 no. 422.

Unger, M. F., "Royal Priesthood: An Old Testament Messianic Motif." *Biblioteca Sacra* 1993, vol.150 no. 594.

Waltke, B. K., "The Date of the Conquest." *Westminster Theological Journal* 1990, vol.52 no. 2.

Walvoord, J. F., "The Incarnation of the Son of God." *Biblioteca Sacra* 1948, vol.105 no. 417.

CHAPTER 10

Ehlert, A. D., "Book Review: The Complete Prophecies of Nostradamus." *Biblioteca Sacra* 1947, vol.104 no. 416.

Feinberg, C. L., "The Old Testament in Jewish Thought and Life Part I." *Biblioteca Sacra* 1954, vol.111 no. 441.

Genung, J. F., "Jehoiakim" in *International Standard Bible Encyclopedia* (iExalt, 1913).

Hoehner, H. W., "Between the Testaments" in *Expositor's Bible Commentary:* Introductory Articles (Grand Rapids, MI: Zondervan, 1979).

Payne, J. Barton, *Encyclopedia of Biblical Prophecy,* 1st ed. (New York, NY: Harper and Row, 1973).

Pentecost, J. D., "Daniel-Introduction" in Bible Knowledge Commentary-Old Testament (Scripture Press, 1985).

Zondervan, "Daniel-Introduction" in *Expositor's Bible Commentary* (Grand Rapids, MI: Zondervan, 1976).

Zuck, R. B., "The Practice of Witchcraft in the Scriptures." Biblioteca Sacra 1971, vol.128 no. 512.

CHAPTER 12

*The Columbia Dictionary of Quotations. (*Columbia University Press, 1998).

The New Oxford Dictionary of English, 2nd ed. (Oxford: Oxford University Press, 1998).

Edersheim, *The Life and Times of Jesus the Messiah* (1953).

Walvoord, John F., *Bible Knowledge Commentary-New Testament Scripture Press* (1985).

CHAPTER 15

Holman Bible Dictionary. (Broadman & Holman Publishers, 1991).

International Standard Bible Encyclopedia. (iExalt, 1913).

*The Columbia Dictionary of Quotations. (*Columbia University Press, 1998).

Zondervan NASB Study Bible (Grand Rapids, MI: Zondervan, 1999).

Edersheim, *The Life and Times of Jesus the Messiah* (1953).

Foundation, *NAS Hebrew-Aramaic and Greek Dictionaries. (*WordSearch, 1998).

Grassmick, J. D., "Mark" in *Bible Knowledge Commentary-New Testament* (Scripture Press, 1985).

McCallum, Dennis, *Christianity: the Faith that Makes Sense* (Wheaton, IL: Tyndale House Publishers, 1992).

McDowell, Josh, *The New Evidence That Demands a Verdict* (Nashville, TN: Thomas Nelson Publishers, 1999).

Pentecost, J. Dwight, *Thy Kingdom Come: Tracing God's Kingdom Program and Covenant Promises Throughout History* (Grand Rapids, MI: Kregel Publications, 1995).

Walvoord, John F., *Bible Knowledge Commentary-New Testament* (Scripture Press, 1985).

EPILOGUE

The Columbia Dictionary of Quotations. (Columbia University Press, 1998).

The New Unger's Bible Dictionary. (Moody Press, 1988).

Dollar, "The Lord's Supper in the Early Church, Part I: The Lord's Supper in the Second Century." *Biblioteca Sacra* 1960, vol.117 no. 466.

Gonzalez, Justo L., *The Story of Christianity* (New York, NY: Harper and Row, 1984).

Lutzer, Erwin, *Christ Among Other Gods* (Chicago, IL: Moody Press, 1994).

Stiansen, P., "Church Reform in the Late Middle Ages." *Biblioteca Sacra* 1948, vol.105 no. 418.

BIBLIOGRAPHY

BOOKS

Zondervan *NASB Study Bible*. Edited by Kenneth Barker, Zondervan Software. Grand Rapids, MI: Zondervan, 1999.

The New Oxford Dictionary of English. Edited by Oxford University Press. 2nd ed. Oxford: Oxford University Press, 1998.

Easton's Bible Dictionary, 1897.

The American Heritage Dictionary of the English Language. 3rd ed: Houghton Mifflin Company, 1992.

Expositor's Bible Commentary: Introductory Articles. Edited by Frank E. Gaebelein. 1 Vol., Zondervan Software. Grand Rapids, MI: Zondervan, 1979.

Gleason L. Archer, Jr. *Encyclopedia of Bible Difficulties*. Grand Rapids, MI: Zondervan, 1982.

Gleason L. Archer, Jr. *A Survey of Old Testament Introduction*. Chicago, IL: Moody Bible Institute, 1974.

T. Austin-Sparks. *What Is Man?* Indianapolis, IN: Premium Literature Company.

George Barna. *The Barna Report 1992-1993: America Renews Its Search for God*. Venture, CA: Regal Books, 1992.

George Barna. *The Frog in the Kettle*. Venture, CA: Regal Books, 1990.

Donald Grey Barnhouse. *The Invisible War*. Grand Rapids, MI: Zondervan, 1967.

Michael J. Behe. *Darwin's Black Box: The Biochemical Challenge to Evolution*. New York, NY: Simon & Schuster, 1996.

John Bradshaw. *Bradshaw On: The Family*. Deerfield Beach, FL: Health Communications, 1988.

Chapman. *The Case for Christianity*. Eerdmans Publishing Co., 1981.

Robert Coleman. *The Master Plan of Discipleship*. Old Tappan, NJ: Fleming H. Revell, 1987.

Robert Coleman. *The Master Plan of Evangelism*. Fleming H. Revell, 1963.

Charles Coleson. *Being the Body*. Nashville, TN: Thomas Nelson, Inc., 2003.

James F. Coppedge. *Evolution: Possible Or Impossible?* Grand Rapids, MI: Zondervan, 1973.

Francis Crick. *Life Itself*.

Leroy Eims. *The Lost Art of Disciple-Making*. Colorado Springs, CO: NavPress, 1978.

R. T Forster and V. P. Marston. *God's Strategy in Human History: A Challenging New Look at God's Sovereignty and Man's Responsibility*. Minneapolis, MN: Bethany House, 1984.

Joseph P. Free. *Archaeology and Bible History*. Wheaton, IL: Scripture Press Publication, Inc., 1973.

George Gallup and D. Lindsay. *Surveying the American Religious Landscape: Trends in U.S. Beliefs*. Morehouse Publishing, 1999.

Norman Geisler and Nix. *From God to Man*. Chicago, IL: Moody Press, 1974.

Nelson Glueck. *Rivers in the Desert.* Philadelphia, PA: Jewish Publication Society, 1969.

Justo L. Gonzalez. *The Story of Christianity.* 2 vols. Vol. 1. New York, NY: Harper and Row, 1984.

Billy Graham. *The Holy Spirit.* Word Books, 1978.

Michael P. Green. *The Empty Cross of Jesus.* Downers Grove, IL: Intervarsity Press, 1984.

R. L. Harris. *Inspiration and Canonicity.* Grand Rapids, MI: Zondervan, 1969.

Bill Hull. *Jesus Christ, Disciple-Maker.* Grand Rapids, MI: Baker Book House, 2004.

Timothy Luke Johnson. *The Real Jesus: The Mistaken Quest for the Historical Jesus and the Truth of the Traditional Gospels.* San Francisco, CA: Harper, 1999.

Walter C. Kaiser, Peter H. Davids, F. F. Bruce and Manfred T. Brauch. *Hard Sayings of the Bible.* WordSearch. Downers Grove, IL: InterVarsity Press, 1996.

Craig S. Keener. *IVP Bible Background Commentary: New Testament.,* Wordsearch. Downers Grove, IL: InterVarsity Press, 1993.

K. A. Kitchen. *Ancient Orient and the Old Testament,* Carol Stream, IL: Tyndale Publishers, 1966.

C. S. Lewis. *A Weight of Glory and Other Addresses.* New York, NY: Macmillan Publishing Company, 1962. Reprint, 1979.

C. S. Lewis. *Mere Christianity.* New York, NY: Macmillan Publishing Company, 1952.

Jessie Penn Lewis. *The Soul and Spirit.* Fort Washington, PA: Christian Literature Crusade, 1980.

Paul Little. *Know Why You Believe.* Downers Grove, IL: Intervarsity Press, 1971.

Erwin Lutzer. *Christ Among Other Gods.* Chicago, IL: Moody Press, 1994.

Dennis McCallum. *Christianity: The Faith That Makes Sense.* Wheaton, IL: Tyndale House Publishers, 1992.

Dennis McCallum. *The Summons.* Colorado Springs, CO: NavPress, 1993.

Josh McDowell. *Evidence That Demands a Verdict: Historical Evidences for the Christian Faith.* Arrowhead Springs, CA: Campus Crusade for Christ, 1972.

Josh McDowell. *The New Evidence That Demands a Verdict.* Nashville, TN: Thomas Nelson Publishers, 1999.

Eugene H. Merrill. *The Theological Wordbook of the Old Testament.* Edited by Gleason L. Archer, Jr, R. L. Harris and Bruce K. Waltke, Wordsearch. Chicago, IL: Moody Bible Institute, 1980.

Roger E. Olson. *The Story of Christian Theology.* Downers Grove, IL: InterVarsity Press, 1999.

J. Barton Payne. *Encyclopedia of Biblical Prophecy.* 1st ed. New York, NY: Harper and Row, 1973.

J. Dwight Pentecost. *Thy Kingdom Come: Tracing God's Kingdom Program and Covenant Promises Throughout History.* Grand Rapids, MI: Kregel Publications, 1995.

Edvard Radzinsky. *Stalin.* Translated by H. T. Willetts. 1st ed. New York, NY: Doubleday, 1996.

Fritz Rodenour. *So What's the Difference?* Ventura, CA: Regal Books, 1980.

J. Oswald Sanders. *Enjoying Intimacy With God.* Chicago, IL: Moody Bible Institute, 1980.

Edith Schaeffer. *Christianity Is Jewish.* Wheaton, IL: Tyndale House Publishers, 1977.

Francis A. Schaeffer. *No Final Conflict: The Bible Without Error in All That It Affirms.* Downers Grove, IL: Intervarsity Press, 1975.

R. C. Sproul. *Knowing Scripture,* Downers Grove, IL: InterVarsity Press, 1977.

Lee Strobel. *The Case for Christ: A Journalist's Personal Investigation of the Evidence for Jesus,* 2001.

L. Duane Thurman. *How to Think About Evolution and Other Bible-Science Controversies.* 2nd ed. Downers Grove, IL: InterVarsity Press, 1978.

Neale Donald Walsh. *Conversations With God.* East Rutherford, NJ: G. P. Putnam's Sons, 1996.

John H. Walton and Victor H. Matthews. *Bible Background Commentary: Genesis-Deuteronomy,* Wordsearch. Downers Grove, IL: InterVarsity Press, 1997.

John F. Walvoord. *Bible Knowledge Commentary-New Testament.* Edited by John F. Walvoord, Roy B. Zuck, Kenneth Barker and Eugene H. Merrill, WordSearch. Scripture Press, Colorado Springs, CO, 1985.

John F. Walvoord. *Bible Knowledge Commentary-Old Testament.* Edited by John F. Walvoord, Roy B. Zuck, Kenneth Barker and Eugene H. Merrill, WordSearch. Scripture Press, Colorado Springs, CO, 1985.

JOURNALS

Allen, Ronald B. "Psalm 87, a Song Rarely Sung." *Biblioteca Sacra* 153, no. 610 (1996): 139.

Archer, Gleason L., Jr. "Old Testament History and Recent Archeology From Abraham to Moses." *Biblioteca Sacra* 127, no. 505 (1970): 3.

Baker, Bruce A. "Romans 1:18-21 and Presuppositional Apologetics." *Biblioteca Sacra* 155, no. 619 (1998): 280.

Bennetch, John Henry. "Genesis: An Apologetic." *Biblioteca Sacra* 103, no. 409 (1946): 110-11.

Bennetch, John Henry. "Scripture Cannot Be Broken." *Biblioteca Sacra* 102, no. 407 (1945): 312.

Benton, Robert W. "The Philistines and the Early Kingdom of Israel." *Grace Theological Journal* 8, no. 1 (1967): 29.

Blum, Edwin A. "Augustine: The Bishop and Theologian." *Biblioteca Sacra* 138, no. 549 (1981): 57.

Brindle, Wayne A. "The Origin and History of the Samaritans." *Grace Theological Journal* 5, no. 1 (1984): 57.

Carson, D. A. "Three Books on the Bible: A Critical Review." *Journal of the Evangelical Theological Society* 26, no. 4 (1983): 356.

Charles, J. Daryl. "Plundering the Lion's Den: A Portrait of Divine Fury (Nahum 2:3-11)." *Grace Theological Journal* 10, no. 2 (1989): 183.

Chisholm, Robert B., Jr. "Structure, Style, and the Prophetic Message: An Analysis of Isaiah 5:8-30." *Biblioteca Sacra* 143, no. 569 (1986): 56.

Curtis, Edward M. "Structure, Style and Context As a Key to Interpreting Jacob's Encounter at Peniel." *Journal of the Evangelical Theological Society* 30, no. 2 (1987): 129-37.

DeYoung, Donald B. and John C. Whitcomb. "The Origin of the Universe." *Journal of the Evangelical Theological Society* 1, no. 2 (1980): 149-62.

Dollar, George W. "The Lord's Supper in the Early Church, Part I: The Lord's Supper in the Second Century." *Biblioteca Sacra* 117, no. 466 (1960).

Edwards, William D., MD, Wesley J. Gabel, MDIV and Floyd E. Hosmer, MS, AMI. "On the Physical Death of Jesus Christ." *Journal of the American Medical Association* 256 (1986).

Ehlert, Arnold D. "Book Review: The Complete Prophecies of Nostradamus." Review of The Complete Prophecies of Nostradamus Translated, edited and interpreted by Henry C. Roberts. Crown. *Biblioteca Sacra* 104, no. 416 (1947): 501-05.

Farner, Donald. "The Lord's Supper Until He Comes." *Grace Theological Journal* 6, no. 2.

Fawver, Larry J and R. Larry Overstreet. "Moses and Preventive Medicine." *Biblioteca Sacra* 147, no. 548 (1990): 270-85.

Feinberg, Charles Lee. "The Old Testament in Jewish Thought and Life, Part I." *Biblioteca Sacra* 111, no. 441 (1954): 27-38.

Free, Joseph P. "Archeology and Biblical Criticism, Part 3: Archeology and Liberalism." *Biblioteca Sacra* 113, no. 452 (1956): 322.

Gangel, Kenneth O. "Evangelical Education for the 21st Century." *Biblioteca Sacra* 149, no. 596 (1992).

Green, Michael P. "The Meaning of Cross-Bearing." *Biblioteca Sacra* 140, no. 558 (1983).

Habermas, Gary R. "Paradigm Shift: A Challenge to Naturalism." *Biblioteca Sacra* 146, no. 584 (1989).

Hoehner, Harold W. "Chronological Aspects of the Life of Christ, Part 1: The Date of Christ's Birth." *Biblioteca Sacra* 130, no. 520 (1973).

Hoehner, Harold W. "Chronological Aspects of the Life of Christ, Part 4: The Year of Christ's Crucifixion." *Biblioteca Sacra* 131, no. 524 (1974).

Kantzer, Kenneth S. "Revelation and Inspiration in Neo-Orthodoxy, Part 2: Method of Revelation." *Biblioteca Sacra* 115, no. 459 (1958): 222.

McFall, Leslie. "A Translation Guide to the Chronological Data in Kings and Chronicles." *Biblioteca Sacra* 148, no. 589 (1991).

Mcgrath, Alister E. "The Challenge of Pluralism for the Contemporary Christian Church." *Journal of the Evangelical Theological Society* 35, no. 3 (1992).

Merrill, Eugene H. "Ebla and Biblical Historical Inerrancy." *Biblioteca Sacra* 140, no. 560 (1983).

Merrill, Eugene H. "Fixed Dates in Patriachal Chronology." *Biblioteca Sacra* 137, no. 547 (1980): 241-51.

Nichols, David. "The Ancient Near East 853-745 B.C." *Journal of the Evangelical Theological Society* 18, no. 4 (1975).

Phillips, W. Gary. "Evangelical Pluralism: A Singular Problem." *Biblioteca Sacra* 151, no. 602 (1994): 141.

Pinnock, Clark. "Faith and Reason." *Biblioteca Sacra* 131, no. 524 (1974): 523.

Rea, John. "The Time of the Oppression and the Exodus." *Grace Theological Journal* 2, no. 1 (1961): 5-14.

Ross, Allen P. "Studies in the Book of Genesis Part 1: the Curse of Canaan." *Biblioteca Sacra* 137, no. 547 (1980).

Stiansen, Peder. "Church Reform in the Late Middle Ages." *Biblioteca Sacra* 105, no. 418 (1948).

Unger, Merrill F. "Royal Priesthood: An Old Testament Messianic Motif." *Biblioteca Sacra* 150, no. 594 (1993): 50.

Unger, Merrill F. "Archeology and the Israelite-Aramaean Wars, Part 1." *Biblioteca Sacra* 106, no. 422 (1949): 178-79.

Unger, Merrill F. "Ezekiel's Vision of Israel's Restoration, Part 3." *Biblioteca Sacra* 107, no. 425 (1950).

Unger, Merrill F. "The Need of Expository Preaching in the Twentieth Century." *Biblioteca Sacra* 111, no. 443 (1954): 232.

Waltke, Bruce K. "Book Reviews: Genesis, the Anchor Bible." Review of Genesis, The Anchor Bible. *Biblioteca Sacra* 123, no. 489 (1966): 80-81.

Waltke, Bruce K. "The Date of the Conquest." *Westminster Theological Journal* 52, no. 2 (1990).

Walton, John H. "The Four Kingdoms of Daniel." Review of The Complete Prophecies of Nostradamus Translated, edited and interpreted by Henry C. Roberts. Crown. *Journal of the Evangelical Theological Society* 29, no. 1 (1986): 25-36.

Walvoord, John F. "The Person and Work of Christ, Part 15: Christ in His Resurrection." *Biblioteca Sacra* 120, no. 479 (1963).

Walvoord, John F. "The Incarnation of the Son of God." *Biblioteca Sacra* 105, no. 417 (1948): 41.

Witmer, John A. "Periodical Reviews: Wellhausenism Evaluated After a Century of Influence." Review of "Wellhausenism Evaluated after a Century of Influence," Raymond F. Surburg. *Biblioteca Sacra* 135, no. 544 (1979): 356-57.

Yamauchi, Edwin. "The Gnostics and History." *Journal of the Evangelical Theological Society* 14, no. 1 (1971).

Zuck, Roy B. "The Practice of Witchcraft in the Scriptures." *Biblioteca Sacra* 128, no. 512 (1971).

MAGAZINES

Hutchinson, Robert L. "Jesus Seminar Unmasked: Bible Scholar Luke Timothy Johnson Takes on the Radical Revisionists." Review of The Real Jesus: The Mistaken Quest for the Historical Jesus and the Truth of the Traditional Gospels. *Christianity Today,* April, 1996, 28-30.

MARTHA McCALLUM

Martha McCallum is an experienced discipler, Bible teacher and Christian leader. She grew up in Kenya, Africa, where her parents were long-term missionaries. She graduated with a Science degree from Wheaton College in 1944, and worked as a microbiologist at the Michigan Department of Health. She then married John McCallum, a physical chemist and had four sons.

As a stay-at-home mom, Martha, was invited into many church and home Bible studies to teach the original version of *The Scarlet Thread,* then called *God's Incredible Plan.*

Martha has served for 25 years in Xenos Christian Fellowship, a non-denominational church started by two of her sons in 1970 on The Ohio State University campus.

KEITH McCALLUM

Keith McCallum is an accomplished Bible teacher and Christian leader. He graduated from The Ohio State University with a degree in journalism. He did graduate work in theology at Ashland Seminary in Ashland. Ohio.

Keith works as a software developer and serves as the lead pastor of Xenos Christian Fellowship in Cleveland, Ohio. He lives there with his wife Darlene and their three sons.